Teaching Reading
Pre-K – Grade 3

Laurie Elish-Piper
Northern Illinois University

Jerry L. Johns
Emeritus, Northern Illinois University

Susan Davis Lenski
Portland State University

KENDALL/HUNT PUBLISHING COMPANY
4050 Westmark Drive   Dubuque, Iowa 52002
www.kendallhunt.com/readingresources.html

Book Team

Chairman and Chief Executive Officer: Mark C. Falb
Senior Vice President, College Division: Thomas W. Gantz
Director of National Book Program: Paul B. Carty
Editorial Development Manager: Georgia Botsford
Vice President, Production and Manufacturing:
　Alfred C. Grisanti
Assistant Vice President, Production Services:
　Christine E. O'Brien
Prepress Project Coordinator: Carrie Maro
Cover Designer: Suzanne Millius

Books by Jerry L. Johns and Susan Davis Lenski

Improving Reading: Strategies and Resources (four editions)
Reading & Learning Strategies for Middle & High School Students
(with Mary Ann Wham and Micki M. Caskey) (three editions)
Improving Writing: Resources, Strategies, and Assessments
Celebrating Literacy! The Joy of Reading and Writing (with
June E. Barnhart, James H. Moss, and Thomas E. Wheat)
Language Arts for Gifted Middle School Students

Ordering Information

Address: Kendall/Hunt Publishing Company
　　　　　 4050 Westmark Drive
　　　　　 Dubuque, IA 52004
Telephone: 800-247-3458, ext. 4
Web site: www.kendallhunt.com

Books by Jerry L. Johns

Basic Reading Inventory (nine editions)
Spanish Reading Inventory
Secondary & College Reading Inventory (two editions)
Literacy for Diverse Learners (edited)
Handbook for Remediation of Reading Difficulties
Informal Reading Inventories: An Annotated Reference Guide
(compiled)
Literacy: Celebration and Challenge (edited)

Books by Jerry L. Johns and Laurie Elish-Piper

Balanced Reading Instruction: Teacher's Visions and Voices
(edited)

Books by Jerry L. Johns and Roberta L. Berglund

Fluency: Strategies & Assessments (three editions)
Strategies for Content Area Learning (two editions)
Comprehension and Vocabulary Strategies for the Elementary
Grades (two editions)

Author Addresses for Correspondence and Workshops
Laurie Elish-Piper
E-mail: laurieep@niu.edu

Jerry L. Johns, Consultant in Reading
E-mail: jjohns@niu.edu

Susan Davis Lenski
sjlenski@comcast.net

Previously entitled: Teaching Beginning Readers

Cover photos © 2006 by Rubberball and PhotoDisc.

Copyright © 1999, 2002, 2006 by Kendall/Hunt Publishing Company

ISBN 13: 978-0-7575-3876-6
ISBN 10: 0-7575-3876-2

Printed in the United States of America
10 9 8 7 6 5 4 3 2

Brief Contents

Contents

Preface

Goal of This Book

When we began researching the need for a third edition of *Teaching Reading Pre-K–Grade 3* we determined the scope of the book needed to be broadened to focus on children from Pre-K to third grade. We met this goal by adding teaching and assessment strategies to address the wide range of abilities of children in these grades. As writing progressed, we reaffirmed our goal of providing teachers with research-based, practical teaching and assessment strategies to support the reading development of all children in their classrooms.

New to This Edition

- To match developments in reading research, new sections and teaching strategies were added concerning vocabulary, informational text, and strategic reading.
- A new chapter, Differentiating Reading Instruction, by Paula H. Helberg helps teachers understand how to implement ideas from this book into their daily classroom instruction.
- Teaching strategies in every chapter are expanded to provide suggestions for teaching each core area of reading.
- The Home-School Connections are updated to reflect our belief that family involvement and support are critical components in the reading and literacy development of children.
- The family letters from the Home-School Connections are provided in both English and Spanish.
- A bonus chapter on teaching writing and spelling is provided on the CD-ROM included with each book.

Question and Answer Approach

Chapters 1 through 7 begin with a series of questions that an inservice or preservice teacher might ask. These questions are answered with research and expert opinion to help establish the importance of the major areas presented in the chapters.

Strategies, Activities, and Assessments

Following the questions and answers, a series of teaching strategies and activities are provided for each of the major areas. If we have identified an appropriate assessment strategy, it is provided at the end of that chapter, thus linking assessment and teaching strategies.

Tips for English Language Learners

We have noted a growing diversity in many schools, and we planned this revision to aid teachers who need extra assistance in working with young learners whose first language is not English. Each English Language Learners box throughout the chapters contains tips for instruction.

Home-School Connections

Many ideas and activities are presented in the form of Home-School Connections. These reproducible letters are placed appropriately in the chapters for you to duplicate and send home. Each Home-School Connection contains several ideas for how families can help their children improve their early literacy skills. English and Spanish copies of the letters are available on the CD-ROM.

Reproducible Record Sheets

There are blackline masters for the assessment record sheets in the book, and copies are also provided on the CD-ROM. You may duplicate these record sheets and use them as you record children's responses to the assessments that you have selected.

Appendices

The Appendices list Professional Organizations and Agencies (Appendix A) and Word Families (Appendix B). The Appendices can be found on the CD-ROM.

How to Use This Book

Take a look at the table of contents to become familiar with the major areas included in each chapter. For example, if you look in Chapter 3, Phonemic Awareness and Phonics, you will find the subject phonemic awareness (Section 3.2). You can see there are seven step-by-step teaching strategies followed by an extensive list of activities, tips, and center ideas. You will also find ideas for Home-School Connections.

Chapters 1 through 7 are arranged in the same format:

Overview, including Questions & Answers

Numbered Section Headings

Student Learning Goals with Related Assessments

Background Information

Numbered Teaching Strategies

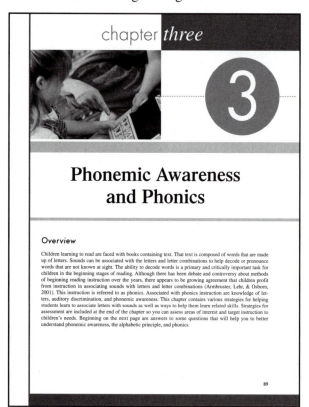

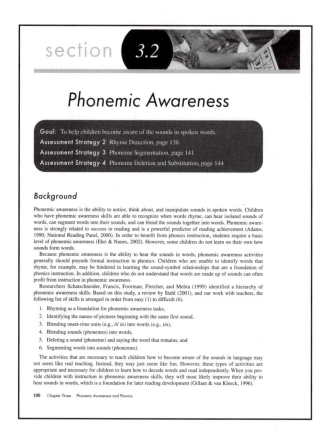

The last section of each chapter contains assessments related to topics presented in the chapter. Assessment Strategies 2, 3, 4, and 5 all relate to phonemic awareness. There are two forms for each of these assessments as well as reproducible Record Sheets that provide an easy way to note the student's performance.

CD-ROM (included with each book)

Each book is packaged with a dual platform CD-ROM that contains **all** the pages that can be reproduced for noncommercial educational purposes by teachers for use in their classrooms. Included on the CD-ROM are the following:

- Home-School Connections—twenty resources to send home that help link and reinforce important skills and strategies you taught at school. Each family letter is provided in English and Spanish.
- Assessment Record Sheets—contains **all** the Record Sheets you need to note children's responses or summarize results from the assessments you select.
- Bonus Chapter—Writing and Spelling
- "Animals" picture story book
- Listing of professional organizations
- Resources for teaching word families

Note from the Authors

We continue to be grateful to teachers for their support of our work. Teaching is a challenging profession. We are pleased that so many teachers and prospective teachers have found our books helpful in providing high-quality instruction that can help more children become thoughtful readers.

Laurie, Jerry, and Sue

Acknowledgments

We wish to thank all those teachers and reading specialists who offered ideas and suggestions for the third edition. Appreciation is expressed to the following professionals who provided systematic and helpful feedback to strengthen the book:

Ricardo De Los Monteros Espinosa
Garfield Elementary School
Elgin, IL

Lana Haddy
Grand Prairie Elementary School
Joliet, IL

Paula A. Helberg
Steeple Run Elementary School
Naperville, IL

Suzi Hinrichs
Winfield Primary and Winfield Central Schools
Winfield, IL

Erin Magoon
Northern Illinois University Reading Clinic
DeKalb, IL

Dora Reyes
Verda Dierzen Early Learning Center
Woodstock, IL

Molly Williams
Jeffrey C. Still Middle School
Aurora, IL

Special thanks is extended to Paula A. Helberg for sharing her experience and expertise on differentiating reading instruction by writing chapter 8 of this book.

We also wish to thank Ricardo Espinosa who translated the Home-School Connections Letters into Spanish. His attention to detail is greatly appreciated.

About the Authors

Laurie Elish-Piper is an Associate Professor of Reading in the Department of Literacy Education at Northern Illinois University. She directs the Reading Clinic and teaches reading courses for undergraduate, graduate, and doctoral students, including practicums in reading assessment and instruction. Prior to her current position, Dr. Elish-Piper worked as an elementary and middle school teacher and an educational therapist in a clinical setting. She has also developed, implemented, and evaluated family literacy programs for inner-city families and their young children.

Dr. Elish-Piper is active in many professional organizations. She serves on the Board of Directors of the College Reading Association, as the Chair of the Parents and Reading Committee of the Illinois Reading Council, and as a member of the Family Literacy Committee of the International Reading Association. She is co-editor of *Exploring Adult Literacy* and serves on the Editorial Board of *The Reading Teacher* and several other publications.

Dr. Elish-Piper consults with schools and family literacy programs across the Midwest. She also regularly presents at international, national, state, and local professional conferences. Her research, publications, and presentations focus on family literacy, parent involvement, reading strategy instruction, and literacy teacher education. She has authored or co-authored more than 40 publications including books, chapters, articles, videos, and instructional materials.

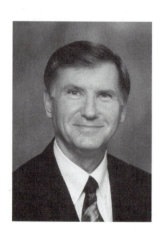

Jerry L. Johns has been recognized as a distinguished professor, writer, and outstanding teacher educator. His career was spent at Northern Illinois University along with visiting professorships at the University of Victoria in British Columbia and Western Washington University. He has taught students from kindergarten through college. Dr. Johns now serves as a consultant and speaker to schools and professional organizations.

Dr. Johns is a past president of the International Reading Association, Illinois Reading Council, College Reading Association, and Northern Illinois Reading Council. He has received recognition for outstanding service to each of these professional organizations and is a member of the Illinois Reading Council Hall of Fame. Dr. Johns has served on numerous committees of the International Reading Association (IRA) and was a member of the Board of Directors. He has also received the Outstanding Teacher Educator in Reading Award from the International Reading Association.

Dr. Johns has been invited to consult, conduct workshops, and make presentations for teachers and professional groups throughout the United States and in seven countries. He has also prepared nearly 300 publications that have been useful to a diverse group of educators. His *Basic Reading Inventory,* now in its ninth edition, is widely used in undergraduate and graduate classes, as well as by practicing teachers. Dr. Johns recently coauthored the fourth edition of *Improving Reading: Strategies and Resources,* the second edition of *Improving Writing, Visualization: Using Mental Images to Strengthen Comprehension,* and the third edition of *Fluency: Strategies & Assessments.*

Susan Davis Lenski is a Professor at Portland State University (PSU) in Oregon. Before joining the faculty at PSU, Dr. Lenski taught in public schools for 20 years and at Illinois State University for 11 years. Her teaching experiences include working with children from kindergarten through high school. Dr. Lenski currently teaches graduate reading and language arts courses.

Dr. Lenski has been recognized by several organizations for her commitment to education. Among her numerous awards, Dr. Lenski was presented with the Nila Banton Smith Award from the International Reading Association; she was instrumental in her school receiving an Exemplary Reading Program Award from the International Reading Association; and she was inducted into the Illinois Reading Hall of Fame. She is currently on the International Reading Association's Board of Directors.

Dr. Lenski's research interests focus on strategic reading and writing and adolescent literacy. She also conducts research on preparing teacher candidates. Dr. Lenski has conducted numerous inservice presentations in the United States, Canada, Guatemala, the Philippines, and Panama and has presented at many state and national conferences. Dr. Lenski has published more than 60 articles and twelve books.

Introduction

Continuum of Children's Development in Early Reading and Writing

The International Reading Association (IRA) and the National Association for the Education of Young Children (NAEYC) have collaborated to produce a continuum that illustrates children's literacy development in the early years. This continuum is grounded in a view of literacy that is developmentally appropriate. IRA and NAEYC define developmentally appropriate as "challenging but achievable with sufficient adult support" (1999, p. 15). In other words, while children tend to progress along a continuum of literacy skills, they must be supported, instructed, and guided to make maximum progress.

The purpose of the continuum is to help educators understand the goals of literacy instruction and to determine if children are making appropriate progress in literacy growth. It is important to note, however, that the continuum is not a rigid sequence of steps that all children must follow. Reading and writing are complex processes that are influenced by individual differences; therefore, it is expected that children will move through the phases of the continuum at their own rates. In addition, children may overlap phases, meaning that they may exhibit characteristics in more than one phase at the same time.

The continuum and this book are based on the belief that teachers must be knowledgeable about a variety of strategies to assess and foster individual children's literacy development. Effective teachers "make instructional decisions based on their knowledge of reading and writing, current research, appropriate expectations, and their knowledge of individual children's strengths and needs" (International Reading Association & the National Association for the Education of Young Children, 1998, p. 15). This continuum is useful for helping teachers set appropriate goals for literacy instruction and assess individual children's progress toward those goals. The continuum is divided into five phases.

Five Phases

Continuum of Children's Development in Early Reading and Writing

---

Awareness and Exploration
(Preschool)

Experimental Reading and Writing
(Kindergarten)

Early Reading and Writing
(First Grade)

Transitional Reading and Writing
(Second Grade)

Independent and Productive Reading and Writing
(Third Grade)

Illustrative examples are provided for each phase in terms of what children can do, what teachers do, and what parents and family members do to support children's continued literacy development. We offer this continuum to help you consider the most important aspects of literacy development, instruction, and assessment of the children you teach.

CONTINUUM OF CHILDREN'S DEVELOPMENT
IN EARLY READING AND WRITING

Note: This list is intended to be illustrative, not exhaustive. Children at any grade level will function at a variety of phases along the reading/writing continuum.

Phase 1: Awareness and exploration (goals for preschool)

Children explore their environment and build the foundations for learning to read and write.

Children can:
- enjoy listening to and discussing storybooks
- understand that print carries a message
- engage in reading and writing attempts
- identify labels and signs in their environment
- participate in rhyming games
- identify some letters and make some letter-sound matches
- use known letters or approximations of letters to represent written language (especially meaningful words like their name, and phrases such as "I love you")

What teachers do:
- share books with children, including Big Books, and model reading behaviors
- talk about letters by name and sounds
- establish a literacy-rich environment
- reread favorite stories
- engage children in language games
- promote literacy-related play activities
- encourage children to experiment with writing

What parents and family members can do:
- talk with children, engage them in conversation, give names of things, show interest in what a child says
- read and reread stories with predictable texts to children
- encourage children to recount experiences and describe ideas and events that are important to them
- visit the library regularly
- provide opportunities for children to draw and print using markers, crayons, and pencils

Phase 2: Experimental reading and writing (goals for kindergarten)

Children develop basic concepts of print and begin to engage in and experiment with reading and writing.

Kindergartners can:
- enjoy being read to and themselves retell simple narrative stories or informational texts
- use descriptive language to explain and explore
- recognize letters and letter-sound matches
- show familiarity with rhyming and beginning sounds
- understand left-to-right and top-to-bottom orientation and familiar concepts of print
- match spoken words with written ones
- begin to write letters of the alphabet and some high-frequency words

What teachers do:
- encourage children to talk about reading and writing experiences
- provide many opportunities for children to explore and identify sound-symbol relationships in meaningful contexts
- help children to segment spoken words into individual sounds and blend the sounds into

(continues)

From Learning to read and write: Developmentally appropriate practices for young children, *The Reading Teacher, 52,* 193–216. Copyright © 1998 International Reading Association. Reprinted with permission. This is a joint position statement of the International Reading Association and the National Association for the Education of Young Children.

whole words (for example, by slowly writing a word and saying its sound)

- frequently read interesting and conceptually rich stories to children
- provide daily opportunities for children to write
- help children build a sight vocabulary
- create a literacy-rich environment for children to engage independently in reading and writing

What parents and family members can do:
- daily read and reread narrative and informational stories to children
- encourage children's attempts at reading and writing
- allow children to participate in activities that involve writing and reading (for example, cooking, making grocery lists)
- play games that involve specific directions (such as "Simon Says")
- have conversations with children during mealtimes and throughout the day

Phase 3: Early reading and writing (goals for first grade)

Children begin to read simple stories and can write about a topic that is meaningful to them.

First graders can:
- read and retell familiar stories
- use strategies (rereading, predicting, questioning, contextualizing) when comprehension breaks down
- use reading and writing for various purposes on their own initiative
- orally read with reasonable fluency
- use letter-sound associations, word parts, and context to identify new words
- identify an increasing number of words by sight
- sound out and represent all substantial sounds in spelling a word
- write about topics that are personally meaningful
- attempt to use some punctuation and capitalization

What teachers do:
- support the development of vocabulary by reading daily to the children, transcribing their language, and selecting materials that expand children's knowledge and language development
- model strategies and provide practice for identifying unknown words
- give children opportunities for independent reading and writing practice
- read, write, and discuss a range of different text types (poems, informational books)
- introduce new words and teach strategies for learning to spell new words
- demonstrate and model strategies to use when comprehension breaks down
- help children build lists of commonly used words from their writing

What parents and family members can do:
- talk about favorite storybooks
- read to children and encourage them to read to you
- suggest that children write to friends and relatives
- bring to a parent-teacher conference evidence of what your child can do in writing and reading
- encourage children to share what they have learned about their writing and reading

Phase 4: Transitional reading and writing (goals for second grade)

Children begin to read more fluently and write various text forms using simple and more complex sentences.

Second graders can:
- read with greater fluency
- use strategies more efficiently (rereading, questioning, and so on) when comprehension breaks down
- use word identification strategies with greater facility to unlock unknown words
- identify an increasing number of words by sight

(continues)

- write about a range of topics to suit different audiences
- use common letter patterns and critical features to spell words
- punctuate simple sentences correctly and proofread their own work
- spend time reading daily and use reading to research topics

What teachers do:
- create a climate that fosters analytic, evaluative, and reflective thinking
- teach children to write in multiple forms (stories, information, poems)
- ensure that children read a range of texts for a variety of purposes
- teach revising, editing, and proofreading skills
- teach strategies for spelling new and difficult words
- model enjoyment of reading

What parents and family members can do:
- continue to read to children and encourage them to read to you
- engage children in activities that require reading and writing
- become involved in school activities
- show children your interest in their learning by displaying their written work
- visit the library regularly
- support your child's specific hobby or interest with reading materials and references

Phase 5: Independent and productive reading and writing (goals for third grade)

Children continue to extend and refine their reading and writing to suit varying purposes and audiences.

Third graders can:
- read fluently and enjoy reading
- use a range of strategies when drawing meaning from the text
- use word identification strategies appropriately and automatically when encountering unknown words

- recognize and discuss elements of different text structures
- make critical connections between texts
- write expressively in many different forms (stories, poems, reports)
- use a rich variety of vocabulary and sentences appropriate to text forms
- revise and edit their own writing during and after composing
- spell words correctly in final writing drafts

What teachers do:
- provide opportunities daily for children to read, examine, and critically evaluate narrative and expository texts
- continue to create a climate that fosters critical reading and personal response
- teach children to examine ideas in texts
- encourage children to use writing as a tool for thinking and learning
- extend children's knowledge of the correct use of writing conventions
- emphasize the importance of correct spelling in finished written products
- create a climate that engages all children as a community of literacy learners

What parents and family members can do:
- continue to support children's learning and interest by visiting the library and bookstores with them
- find ways to highlight children's progress in reading and writing
- stay in regular contact with your child's teachers about activities and progress in reading and writing
- encourage children to use and enjoy print for many purposes (such as recipes, directions, games, and sports)
- build a love of language in all its forms and engage children in conversation

chapter one

Attitudes, Interests, and Background Knowledge

Overview

Children learn a great deal before they arrive in preschool or kindergarten (Neuman & Dickinson, 2001). They learn how to walk and talk as well as how literacy is used in their homes. They build a rich store of background knowledge about the world from the daily events they experience such as going to the grocery store, riding the bus, and playing in the park. This view of learning aligns with the emergent literacy perspective that suggests that literacy development is a complex process that begins at birth. Furthermore, literacy learning is a social process wherein a child experiences language used for real life processes by other members of the family and community (McGee & Richgels, 2003).

Children bring their attitudes, interests, background knowledge, and oral language foundations to the emergent literacy process. You can enhance children's emergent literacy development by linking your teaching to children's interests and nurturing positive attitudes toward reading and writing. In addition, by helping children build and activate their background knowledge about the world and their experiences, you can assist children with making connections with texts they read and write. By supporting children's oral language development, you increase the likelihood that they will have the necessary foundations to draw from as they learn to read and write (Watson, 2001). Effective teachers of young children know the importance of building on what the child brings to the learning context as well as providing the child with new experiences and opportunities. The following questions address some issues commonly raised by teachers about the roles of attitudes, interests, and background knowledge in literacy development.

Questions/Answers

Why are attitude and interest so important for emergent literacy development?

If a child doesn't have a positive attitude about learning and an interest in the topic being studied, it is difficult for that child to get excited and motivated about learning. Certainly all children do not come to school with positive attitudes and interests that parallel the curriculum; however, this does not mean that the situation is impossible. Teachers can do much to help develop positive attitudes by creating nurturing classroom communities, providing scaffolding to help children succeed, and supporting children's self-concepts as learners. In addition, teachers can build children's interests by sharing their own enthusiasm, by making topics personally meaningful, and by providing firsthand or vicarious experiences. For example, if you are planning to teach a unit on farm animals to a group of kindergarten children in an urban setting, you might arrange for a field trip to a farm or zoo so children can see the animals firsthand. If such trips are not possible, you might bring in videos or DVDs of farm animals so the children can "see them in action." Such experiences, whether firsthand or vicarious, will increase the likelihood that children will be interested in learning more about the topic, in this case, farm animals.

If a child lacks background knowledge, can I really do anything to make a difference?

Some children come to school with a rich store of background knowledge gained through their experiences: books they have heard, outings they have taken to places like zoos and museums, and activities in which they have participated. Unfortunately, some children come to school with fewer experiences, and, as a result, they may be unfamiliar with some concepts that are taught in school. If a child has limited background knowledge, a teacher can provide firsthand experiences, vicarious experiences through books, videos, or DVDs, and concrete objects for the child to explore. Specific strategies for building and activating background knowledge are provided in Section 1.2.

section **1.1**

Desire to Read

> **Goal:** To help children develop positive attitudes, interests, and motivation toward reading.
>
> **Assessment Strategy 1** Interviews about Reading, page 24
> **Assessment Strategy 2** News about Me, page 29
> **Assessment Strategy 3** Elementary Reading Attitude Survey, page 32

Background

Children are born with a desire to learn. They are interested in the people, things, and events around them. Two of the things most children want to learn when they come to school are to read and write (Cochrane, Cochrane, Scalena, & Buchanan, 1988).

The desire to read and write is an important foundation for all literacy learning. Children who view reading and writing as interesting, exciting, and meaningful will be more likely to engage in reading and writing. As with any skill, additional practice and engagement with reading and writing leads to improved competence (Guthrie & Wigfield, 2000).

You can capitalize on young children's natural interest and curiosity by providing a classroom environment that invites children into literacy. Classroom environments that contain many types of print, offer easy access to reading and writing materials, provide for choice, and immerse children in literacy activities motivate and support children's literacy development (Sulzby & Teale, 1991).

There are simple strategies and activities you can use in your classroom to arouse and build on children's natural curiosity and interest in literacy. The teaching strategies and activities that follow provide suggestions to assist you with creating a classroom environment and literacy program that will help children develop positive attitudes, interests, and motivation toward reading.

Section 1.1   *TEACHING STRATEGY*

MORNING MESSAGE

The Morning Message is a daily routine that provides a meaningful context for reading and writing. The teacher writes a Morning Message to children to share important information about the upcoming day and concludes by asking children a related personal question. Children may try to read the message on their own, and then the teacher engages in shared reading to guide the children through the reading. Finally, children discuss, draw, or write a response to the personal question.

 **DIRECTIONS**

1. Write a short message on the chalkboard or on chart paper. The message should include important information about the upcoming day. The message then concludes by asking the children a related personal response question. A sample message is shown below.

> Dear Boys and Girls,
>
> Today is art day. We will be painting pictures. We will use blue, green, red, and yellow paint. I like to use many colors in my paintings. What colors will you use when you paint today?
>
> Your friend,
> Mrs. Shaffer

2. Post the message prior to the children's arrival in the classroom. Provide ample time for the children to look at the message and informally discuss it among themselves.

3. Gather the children around the message. Read the message aloud to the children. Use your hand or a pointer to highlight the text as it is read.

4. Reread the message. Encourage the children to join in with the reading.

5. Discuss the ideas in the message. Discuss the question in the message. Provide time for students to informally discuss their responses to the question.

6. Ask children to record their responses to the question by either drawing or writing responses in their journals.

7. Provide time for children to share their responses. Sharing can be done in small groups or with the entire group.

Aa Bb Cc Tips for English Language Learners

- Add pictures to the morning message to help English Language Learners understand the context of the message.
- Encourage English Language Learners to partner with other children to explore the morning message before you discuss it as a group.
- If you know any words in the child's home language, consider using both the English language and the child's language for those words in the morning message. This action will support English Language Learners as well as encourage the other children to learn words in another language.

SHARED READING

Shared Reading replicates the bedtime story sharing situation with an individual, a small group, or a classroom of children. This strategy allows children to participate in and enjoy books they cannot read on their own (Mooney, 1990). The emphasis of this strategy is on enjoyment of the story as a whole. Teachers can introduce a wide range of exciting books to children through Shared Reading.

✍ DIRECTIONS

1. Select a children's book with predictable text and engaging illustrations. If you are reading with a large group of children, a Big Book will work well.

2. Have children sit so they all can hear the story and see the illustrations. A story rug is a helpful addition to the classroom.

3. Show the children the cover of the book and read the title. Ask them to make predictions about the contents of the book. Invite selected children to respond to some of the ideas that are shared.

4. Read the story aloud, inviting children to read along if they would like to do so.

5. Provide time for the children to share their personal responses and favorite parts of the book.

6. Reread the book, inviting the children to read along if they would like to do so.

7. Place the book in the classroom library so the children can read it during their free time.

Aa Bb Cc   Tips for English Language Learners

- Select predictable books with clear illustrations to provide clues for English Language Learners during shared reading. An extensive listing of predictable books can be found in Johns and Lenski (2005).

- Provide time for English Language Learners to engage in a picture walk to see the story before starting the shared reading. The picture walk allows children to look at the pictures and think about what the story line might be before hearing the actual story. To do a picture walk, have the children look at the cover and discuss what they see. Progress through the book, directing the children's attention to pictures that convey important information about the story. Direct helpful questions to the children. After viewing and discussing the pictures, begin reading the story with the children.

FAVORITE BOOK SHOW AND TELL

Since literacy is a social process, children benefit from meaningful opportunities to share and discuss books with their peers. The Favorite Book Show and Tell strategy allows children to share their favorite books as well as to learn about books their classmates enjoy. This strategy also supports the children's listening and speaking skills.

DIRECTIONS

1. Inform children that you will be having Favorite Book Show and Tell time each day. Explain to the children that each of them will have a chance to share a favorite book with the class. Clarify that the books can come from the children's homes, the public library, the school library, or the classroom library. Explain that the books can be new to the class or ones that have been read and shared together. Allow children to repeat a book if it is a favorite for more than one child in the classroom. Also, explain that children can select books that have been read to them or books they have read on their own.

2. Model the Favorite Book Show and Tell process using a book the children know from the classroom. Show the book to the children and say something such as, "The book *Lily's Purple Plastic Purse* is written by Kevin Henkes (1996). It is one of my favorites because it is funny, and Lily is an interesting character. I also like the pictures because they have some funny surprises hidden in them. The book has a happy ending, and it teaches a lesson too. I would recommend this book to anyone who likes funny books and stories about school."

Favorite Book Show and *Tell*

Your Name _____

Book Title _____

_____

Author _____

Illustrator _____

I like this book because _____

_____

_____

Draw something you liked from the book.

┌───┐
│   │
│   │
│   │
│   │
│   │
│   │
│   │
└───┘

POEMS, SONGS, AND RHYMES

A very natural and engaging way to help young children develop a favorable attitude toward reading is to capitalize on a wide variety of poems, songs, and nursery rhymes. It is possible to use these literary pieces to help develop sound awareness, speech-to-print matching, language flow, concepts for letters and words, and an understanding of print conventions (e.g., print goes from left to right and top to bottom in English). Some of the popular types of rhymes include lullabies ("Rock-a-bye Baby"), singing game rhymes ("Ring-a-Round O'Roses"), counting-out rhymes ("One, Two, Buckle My Shoe"), tongue twisters ("Peter Piper"), nonsense rhymes ("If All the World Were Paper"), and verse stories ("The Queen of Hearts"). They often appeal to children because of their sounds, rhymes, and strong rhythms.

DIRECTIONS

1. Consider the maturity and interest of children when selecting a poem, song, or rhyme. It should be fun for the children and have the potential to help achieve a a variety of teaching goals. For example, reciting "Jack and Jill" might be used to help children develop an understanding of rhyming.

2. Begin by sharing the selected material aloud. The children should listen. Read the material again and invite the children to join in as they are able. Read the material a third time in an echo reading fashion: read a line and have children echo it back to you. Then talk about the selection and invite children to share their ideas or reactions.

3. Present the material on a piece of chart paper or an overhead transparency. Read it while pointing to the words. Help the children understand that you are reading the words. Point out how the print flows and how the words rhyme. Carefully select the one or two aspects of language you wish to emphasize. Keep the sharing active and lively, stressing the joy and fun of the material.

4. Select additional material to share each day. Move gradually from oral sharing to reading the printed word. Some of the rhymes can be acted out ("One, Two, Buckle My Shoe") so take every opportunity to actively engage children.

5. As children begin memorizing the material, take opportunities to have them say the rhyme from memory at various times during the day. These words in memory can be used in later lessons to develop speech-to-print match and other print concepts. Songs may be particularly enjoyable to the children and help them make connections to print as they demonstrate their interest. Children can also be shown how to keep time with the rhyme by clapping their hands or rocking back and forth.

6. Write the various poems, songs, and rhymes on chart paper and post them around the room. Invite the children to read the materials independently, with partners, or in small groups.

7. One variation is to use dramatization with nursery rhymes (Roush, 2005). For "Little Boy Blue," get pictures, objects, or a video of the following: horn, sheep, meadow, corn, and haystack. Children can dramatize the rhyme by doing the following:

Pretend to blow a horn.

"Baa" like a sheep.

Eat corn like a cow.

Put hands up as if questioning where Little Boy Blue is.

Pretend to be asleep.

Activities, tips, & Center Ideas

1. Provide daily class time for self-selected reading. Consider using a fun acronym as a name for this activity (e.g., DIRT: Daily Independent Reading Time or DEAR: Drop Everything And Read). Provide access to a wide variety of reading materials and allow children to find a comfortable place to read in the classroom. You can also provide a short sharing time after children have completed their reading.

2. Model your enthusiasm and love for reading. Bring in your favorite books and share them with the children. Discuss how and why reading is important to you. Provide a special display of your favorite books in the classroom. Update the display on a regular basis.

3. Create a print-rich classroom environment that includes access to and displays of various types of print. Possible types of print are listed below.

   - labels for important classroom locations and materials
   - lists of children's names (e.g., who lost a tooth, birthdays)
   - sign-in sheet
   - message board
   - posters with captions
   - displays of the children's work and writing
   - announcements
   - classroom rules and procedures
   - chart and language experience stories
   - children's books and magazines

4. Read aloud to the children at least once a day, more often if possible. Focus on the children's enjoyment of and personal reactions to the story. Consider using different voices and sound effects to make read-aloud experiences motivating for the children. Provide time for children to ask questions and discuss their responses to the story.

5. Schedule time for children to share with their classmates the books they are reading and stories they are writing. Learning what their peers are reading and writing often serves as a motivator for children to pursue similar reading and writing tasks. Consider using a special chair such as a rocking chair to make the sharing experience more special. Provide options so children can share with a small group of children or the entire class.

6. Implement a home-school reading program through the use of reading backpacks. Fill several small backpacks or book bags with children's books on specific topics or by particular authors. Include construction paper, markers, crayons, pencils, and a small notebook in the backpack. Attach a short note explaining that parents and children are invited to share the books and write or draw about their favorite parts. When children return the backpack to school, provide time for them to share their responses. Post their responses on a bulletin board or in the classroom library. Change the contents of the backpacks frequently and rotate them around the classroom so all children can take home a reading backpack on a regular basis.

7. Arrange the classroom so children have easy access to literacy materials. For example, consider establishing a writing center that contains different types of paper, markers, pencils, pens, a computer, a children's typewriter, letter stamps, picture dictionaries, scissors, glue, tape, letter tiles, magnetic

letters, and other writing supplies. Label storage areas for materials in the center so children can find and put away materials themselves.

8. Create literacy play centers so children can explore literacy through meaningful play situations. A list of literacy play centers and suggested materials is provided in the box below.

LITERACY PLAY CENTERS

Post Office Center

mailboxes
envelopes
paper
stationery
stickers or stamp pads
address labels
boxes
packages
cash register
play money

Restaurant Center

menus
order pad and pencil
tablecloth
dishes
glasses
silverware
napkins
list of daily specials
cash register
play money

Office Center

phone
computer or typewriter
message pad
pens and pencils
paper
calculator
note pads
file folders
rubber stamps and stamp pad

Grocery Store Center

grocery cart
food packages
price stickers
advertisements
coupons
cash register
play money
shopping lists
grocery bags

---

9. Implement a message board in the classroom. Consider using a bulletin board with a pocket or envelope for each child. To introduce the message board, write a personalized message to each student in the classroom. Provide daily time for children to write messages to their classmates. To keep the message board going, you may want to write messages to several children each day.

10. Invite children to engage in artistic responses to literature. Provide opportunities for children to explore creative dramatics, art, music, dance, and movement activities after reading a book. These types of responses actively involve children in learning and literature.

11. Introduce children to various genres of literature by doing brief book talks. During book talks, focus on enticing children to want to read the books without giving away the stories. After conducting book talks, make the books available in the classroom library.

12. Develop a cross-age reading buddy program. This type of program pairs a younger child and an older child so they can read together. The focus of this type of activity is on enjoying the stories and making reading fun.

13. Develop a classroom listening center so children can follow along as they listen to a tape-recorded version of a book. Rotate the books and tapes in the listening center on a regular basis.

14. Implement a guest reader program to invite various adults from the school and community to share their favorite books with children. Designate a special place in the classroom to display books shared by guest readers.

15. Establish a well-stocked classroom library and provide daily time for children to browse through the library and select materials. Suggestions for creating a classroom library are detailed in the following list.

CREATING A CLASSROOM LIBRARY

Specific, named location	The classroom library is in a highly visible area, and it has a specific name.
Partitioned and private	The classroom library is separated from other areas in the classroom by book shelves, book carts, or other partitions.
Comfortable	The library contains comfortable seating such as bean bag chairs, carpet squares, or pillows.
Number of books	Provide a minimum of five to eight books per child.
Assortment of books	Provide books from varied genres and reading levels. Be sure to include other reading materials such as magazines, pamphlets, materials written by the children, and class books.
Organization	Organize books and provide labels to show the organization (e.g., genres, themes, topics, authors, or reading levels).
Shelving	Include some open shelving so students can see book covers. Shelve other books with the spines facing out to provide room for more books in the available space.
Literature Displays	Include displays with posters, felt boards, stuffed animals, and puppets that are related to children's books.

READING AT HOME

Dear Families,

Here are some ideas to get your child interested in reading.

- Take your child to the library regularly to check out books on topics of interest. Ask the children's librarian for suggestions. Also, find out about special library events for children. Most public libraries offer summer reading programs, story times, and other programs free of charge.

- Give your child books as gifts to show the importance and value of books and reading.

- Set aside time to read to your child every night. Right before bedtime works well for many families. Make this a special quiet time that you and your child look forward to at the end of the day.

- Write notes to your child and encourage your child to write notes back to you. You can tuck notes in a lunch box or backpack, or you can post them on the refrigerator or bathroom mirror. If your child cannot read independently yet, use a combination of drawings with words such as

I ♥ You!

I hope you enjoy these ideas.

Sincerely,

Background Knowledge

Goal: To help children expand their experiences and build background knowledge.

Background

Classroom environments should support and encourage children to make personal connections with a wide range of printed materials (Gambrell & Dromsky, 2000). Children can learn more effectively when they can relate new learning to something they already know. This type of previous knowledge is often referred to as background knowledge or schema (Anderson, 1994), and it is an important foundation for constructing meaning in reading and writing. Some children come to school with experiences that help them connect school learning to their life experiences. Other children come to school with limited experiences and exposure to events, objects, and books (Salinger, 1999).

The concept of building background knowledge focuses on providing new experiences to children. Building background knowledge is greatly supported by providing children with concrete experiences and opportunities to use their senses to examine materials and objects. Because young children learn by doing, playing, being actively involved, and having hands-on experiences are essential for building background knowledge.

Activating background knowledge refers to the process of helping children remember what they already know about a topic. You can help children activate their background knowledge by making connections between what they already know and what they will learn. Simple techniques such as making predictions, discussing or drawing what is already known about a topic, or brainstorming how two topics are alike are examples of strategies you can use to help activate children's background knowledge.

By planning simple experiences related to a topic of study or book, you can build and activate children's background knowledge, thus increasing the likelihood that they will understand and learn the new concepts. Specific suggestions for building and activating children's background knowledge are provided below.

Section 1.2 *TEACHING STRATEGY*

OBJECT EXPLORATION

The Object Exploration strategy provides children with concrete experiences related to an upcoming unit of study. Young children learn through active involvement and hands-on experiences, and this strategy provides them with opportunities to personally explore and examine materials before they begin a new unit of study. In addition, vocabulary and concepts are introduced in relation to the concrete objects, thereby providing a useful framework for children to understand and learn the new words and ideas related to the topic of study.

✒ DIRECTIONS

1. Identify an upcoming unit of study and gather concrete objects related to the unit. For example, if you are studying eggs, gather raw eggs, cracked eggs, hard-boiled eggs, brown eggs, duck eggs, and magnifying glasses.

2. Tell the children you will be starting a new unit. Inform them of the topic for the new unit. Show them the concrete objects you have gathered and tell them they will be examining these materials to prepare for the unit.

3. Provide exploration time for the children to use their senses to explore and examine the objects. Share magnifying glasses so the children get a closer look at the objects.

4. Ask the children to brainstorm words that describe the objects they have explored. Write the words on the chalkboard, a piece of chart paper, or an overhead transparency. Make a separate list for each object. For example, if children explored eggs as described in step 1, make lists of the describing words on chart paper labeled *raw egg, cracked egg,* and *hard-boiled egg.*

5. Discuss the words on the lists and what the children learned about the objects. Inform the children that they will be learning many things about the topic in the new unit.

6. Display the brainstorming lists in the classroom. Add new words to the lists as children participate in additional activities related to the unit.

Section 1.2   *TEACHING STRATEGY*

BOOK BOXES

Book Boxes are collections of artifacts related to a story, poem, or informational book. A Book Box is decorated according to the focus of the book, and it contains at least three important objects related to the book. Teachers can use Book Boxes to introduce a book to children by sharing the objects, discussing why the objects are included, and inviting the children to make predictions about the book.

✒ DIRECTIONS

1. Identify a story, poem, or informational book that you will be sharing with children.

2. Read the book to identify at least three important objects that are mentioned in the book.

3. Gather these objects or pictures of the objects and place them in a box.

4. Decorate the box according to the focus of the book, and write the title and author of the book on the box.

5. Prior to reading the book with the children, show them the Book Box. Discuss the decorations on the box and the title and author of the book.

6. Remove one object from the box. After the object is identified, discuss what it is and why it is included in the Book Box. Invite children to make predictions about what other objects might be in the Book Box and why.

7. Share the other objects in the Book Box. Invite the children to make predictions about what the book will be about based on the objects in the Book Box.

8. Introduce the book to the children and read it with them as a teacher read-aloud, shared reading activity, or guided reading activity.

9. After reading, have children make connections with each object and the context of the book.

- Add labels to the objects in the Book Box to support the vocabulary acquisition of English Language Learners. As you discuss each object, point to the label and use the label consistently. By using the same term consistently, English Language Learners will be more likely to acquire and remember the new words.

Section 1.2 **TEACHING STRATEGY**

3

KNOWLEDGE CHART

A Knowledge Chart focuses on children's prior knowledge about a topic and their new knowledge about a topic after reading (Macon & Macon, 1991). This strategy invites children to share their knowledge about the topic of a book they will be reading by brainstorming words and ideas related to the topic. After the book is read, children then focus on the new knowledge they learned about the topic, thus connecting their background knowledge with new learning.

DIRECTIONS

1. Select an informational book the children will be reading or that you will be reading to them. Identify the topic of the book.

2. Create a Knowledge Chart on the chalkboard, a piece of chart paper, or an overhead transparency. A sample Knowledge Chart is shown below.

KNOWLEDGE CHART	
Prior knowledge about _____	**New knowledge about** _____

3. Tell the children the book is about a specific topic. Show them the Knowledge Chart, identify the topic, and ask them to brainstorm what they already know about the topic. Write their ideas on the Knowledge Chart.

4. Explain to the children that they should think about the ideas on the Knowledge Chart as they read or listen to the book. Tell them that you will be asking them to share their new knowledge about the topic after they have read or listened to the book.

5. Read the book with the children as a teacher read-aloud, shared reading activity, or guided reading activity. Discuss the book with the children.

6. Ask the children to share the new knowledge they learned about the topic. Add this information to the Knowledge Chart.

7. Engage the children in a discussion about how their prior knowledge compared to their new knowledge. It may also be necessary to identify prior knowledge statements that are not consistent with the text. Remind them that thinking about what they already know about a book or topic is an important strategy that good readers use to prepare for reading.

BRAINSTORMING

Brainstorming allows children to share what they already know about a topic. This strategy is completed in a group setting; therefore, children who have little or no background knowledge about the topic can benefit from hearing what other children share. During this process, an idea shared by one child will often trigger a related idea for other children. By building and activating their background knowledge, children will be more prepared to understand and remember what they read or what is read to them.

⟡ DIRECTIONS

1. Once you have selected a topic for study, present the key word to children by writing it on a piece of chart paper. For example, if you are going to begin a unit on the ocean, write the word *ocean* on chart paper. Draw a circle around the word and be sure to leave space around it to record the children's ideas.

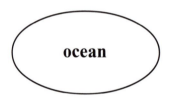

2. Tell children that you want them to share all of the things that come to mind when they hear the word *ocean*. Explain that this process is called brainstorming and that you welcome all responses.

3. Provide time for the children to share their responses as you write them on chart paper.

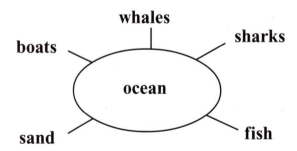

4. After children have had a chance to share their ideas, explain that brainstorming is a great way to prepare for reading.

5. Tell the children that they will be reading books and doing activities related to the ocean. Explain that some of their brainstormed ideas may be covered in the unit and that they will also learn new information on oceans. You may want to revisit the brainstormed ideas during the course of the unit to confirm existing ideas and to add new ideas.

Aa Bb Cc | Tips for English Language Learners

- Provide concrete materials related to the topic for brainstorming so English Language Learners can use the objects as a springboard for ideas. For example, when brainstorming about oceans, provide a shell, sand, and toy fish. Pictures can be used if concrete objects are not available.

- Provide thinking time before asking children to share their responses. Give English Language Learners several minutes to think about the topic or to discuss it with a peer, and they will be more likely to have related ideas and the words to share them.

Section 1.2 **TEACHING STRATEGY**

PREDICTING WITH PICTURES

Predicting before reading or listening to text serves several purposes. First, it activates background knowledge. In addition, it sets a purpose for reading and piques children's curiosity and interest in the text.

DIRECTIONS

1. Select a book to share with children that has an interesting title and cover art. For example, you may choose to share *Me on the Map* by Joan Sweeney (1996).

2. Explain to children that you are going to show them the cover and title of a book and then ask them to predict what they think the book will be about and why. Discuss their predictions. Record their predictions on the chalkboard or a piece of chart paper. For example, children may share the following predictions.

   It's about the world because I see water and land.

   I think it's about a girl who is going on a trip because she's in the picture with a map.

3. Have children read the story (or listen to you read it aloud). They should pay careful attention to identify which of their predictions are accurate as well as those that are not.

4. Stop the reading at several logical points and ask the children if their predictions were accurate or not. Encourage discussion as appropriate.

5. At the end of the story, discuss how pictures and predictions will help children get ready to read and improve their understanding of the story. Use actual statements made by the children to make helpful and meaningful connections. Be sure to help children realize that not all predictions will be correct.

K-W-L

K-W-L (Ogle, 1986) is intended to help students activate background knowledge prior to reading an informational selection or beginning a unit of study. The *K* invites students to share or list what they *know* about a topic before they read or begin a unit of study. The *W* identifies *what* students want to find out, and the *L* indicates what students *learned* from the reading material or unit of study. A chart (see below) is typically used with the strategy.

⟆ DIRECTIONS

1. Present children with a K-W-L chart on the chalkboard or provide an individual copy of the chart for each student. Young children can participate orally while the teacher writes ideas. Older children can write their own ideas individually or in small groups. The teacher should then develop a master chart.

K—What We Know	**W**—What We Want to Find Out	**L**—What We Learned and Still Need to Learn

Categories of Information:

2. Explain the chart to children. For the first few times the strategy is used, children may profit from participating as a whole group with the teacher recording their ideas. The goal of the *K* is to invite children to brainstorm what they think they know about the topic. Incorrect statements should also be listed; they will be evaluated in light of the reading selection or unit of study. It is also possible for children to suggest categories of information they hope to find out during the reading or unit of study. For example, if the topic is whales, some possible categories are types and sizes, where they live, and what they eat. Model as needed and guide children in developing appropriate categories. You might ask children about enemies of whales if they do not suggest that category.

3. Have children then suggest some questions that they want to have answered. Write these questions in the *W* column. Capitalize on children's interests and any uncertainties that may be evident from the initial brainstorming. The goal should be to move students to the point that they generate their own questions; however, do not expect this outcome in the initial use of K-W-L.

4. After children have read the selection, they should write down what they have learned, what they still want to find out, and any initial information that was revealed to be incorrect as a result of the reading. Further reading and research may help children find answers to those questions that were unanswered.

5. Variations of K-W-L can include mapping ideas from what was learned (e.g., different types of whales; what whales eat) and preparing a written summary of their learning.

Activities, tips, & Center Ideas

1. Take frequent field trips to locations in the community such as the library, grocery store, dairy, fire station, farm, post office, veterinarian's office, hospital, and restaurant. Exposure to these locations will help to build children's background knowledge about important locations, people, jobs, and things in their communities.

2. Invite guest speakers into the classroom to share information and artifacts related to their jobs, hobbies, or travels. Provide time for children to examine the artifacts and ask questions. Consider speakers with interesting jobs or hobbies and be sure to contact children's parents, community members, and school personnel when looking for guest speakers. Consider the concrete artifacts that a guest speaker will be able to bring to share with children during a presentation. A list of possible guest speakers is provided in the box.

GUEST SPEAKER IDEAS

Banker	Farmer	Photographer
Musician	Cook	Artist
Receptionist	Nurse	Painter
Dentist	Veterinarian	Gardener
Weather forecaster	Store clerk	Doctor
Traveler	Florist	Secretary
Bus driver	Dog trainer	Astronomer
Mechanic	Computer professional	Construction worker
Hobbyist	Collector	Sports enthusiast

---

3. Help children visualize a place, event, or person by sharing photos or videos with children prior to reading about the new topic of study. This technique works well when you cannot bring real objects or speakers into the classroom.

4. Create jackdaws to introduce a new topic of study. A jackdaw is a collection of artifacts related to a topic or book. Jackdaws may contain concrete objects, photographs, a list of related words, a time line of events, clothing or personal items related to a character, and various other materials. A jackdaw is displayed like a mini-museum in the classroom, and it serves as an excellent introduction to a new area of study (Rasinski & Padak, 2004). You and the children can also add materials to the jackdaw throughout the unit.

5. Invite children to bring in interesting artifacts and collections to share during Show and Tell time. Encourage other children to ask questions about the Show and Tell objects. Provide time for several children to Show and Tell each day. Create a classroom area to display Show and Tell materials for the students to explore during their free time.

6. Read to children on a daily basis to expose them to new ideas, experiences, and information. Vary the types of books you read to include poetry, fiction, nonfiction, fairytales, folk tales, and other genres. Provide time to discuss the books after reading them. After sharing the books, place them in the classroom library so the children can explore or reread them during their free time.

7. Provide access to appropriate reference materials so children can look up information on topics about which they want to learn more. For example, create a classroom research center that contains children's dictionaries, children's encyclopedias, easy-to-read nonfiction books, computer resources, children's magazines, and informational posters.

8. Invite children to complete a Quickdraw or Quickwrite about a new topic of study. In a Quickdraw or Quickwrite, children are told about a new topic they will be studying. Children then draw or write what they already know about that topic. After two or three minutes of drawing or writing time, provide an opportunity for children to share their ideas. Discuss their knowledge about the topic as an introduction to the new topic of study.

9. Supply interesting hands-on materials and place them in the classroom discovery center so children can explore them during their free time. Change the materials in the discovery center on a regular basis. Suggestions for the discovery center are in the following list.

SUGGESTED MATERIALS FOR CLASSROOM DISCOVERY CENTERS

Science Materials

Rocks
Shells
Plants
Magnifying glasses
Magnets
Scales
Leaves
Pinecones
Fossils
Children's microscopes
Nonfiction books on science topics

Art Materials

Paints
Brushes
Assorted papers
Markers
Glue
Scissors
Crayons
Hole punch
Ribbons
Cloth scraps
Posters showing various styles of art

Music Materials

Rhythm sticks
Drums
Materials to make simple instruments
Triangles
Recorders
Tape recorders
Tapes or CDs of various types of music
Song books
Charts with song lyrics
Conductor's baton

Math Materials

Counters
Graph paper
Number lines
Calculators
Adding machines
Number blocks
Math manipulatives
Abacus
Pencils
Paper

EXTENDING BACKGROUND

Dear Families,

Here are some ideas to get your child excited about learning.

- Take your child on frequent outings to the park, zoo, museums, and other interesting places. Talk about what you see and do at these places. Take photographs or buy postcards to put in a scrapbook or box. Look at the scrapbook or in the box regularly and discuss your memories of the special outings. You may also wish to write the date and a short caption for each photograph or postcard to help you and your child remember the outing.

- Watch educational programs with your child. Discuss the programs to share interesting new things you both learned from the programs. Many excellent informational programs on animals and nature can be found on public broadcasting stations. In addition, many cable channels offer educational programming.

- Check out informational books from the library. Read and discuss these books with your child. Some popular topics for children include animals, weather, food, crafts, how-to books, holidays, travel, history, and famous people.

I hope you have fun trying these ideas.

Sincerely,

Assessments of Interests and Attitudes Toward Reading

Goal: To assess a child's interests and attitudes toward reading.

Background

Responsive teachers know the children in their classrooms well and incorporate this information into lesson planning, materials selection, and approaches to teaching. Teachers can get to know children through conversations and daily activities. In addition, interviews, surveys, and questionnaires are helpful tools for learning more about the children you teach. Observations are also very useful as you seek to learn about children's attitudes toward reading.

A S S E S S M E N T   C H A P T E R   1

INTERVIEWS ABOUT READING

OVERVIEW	Interviews about Reading are designed to determine the child's understanding of the nature of reading, the purposes for reading, and the child's attitude toward reading.
MATERIALS NEEDED	1. Record Sheets on pages 25–28 2. Tape recorder (if desired)
PROCEDURES	1. Duplicate the appropriate Record Sheet on pages 25–28. If the child does not yet read, choose the Emergent Reader Interview. If the child is beginning to read, use the Early Reading Interview. 2. You may decide to tape-record the interview rather than write the child's responses on the page in the Record Sheet during the interview. If you tape-record the interview, set up the tape recorder and test it to make sure it is working properly. 3. With the child, say, "Today we're going to talk about reading and your ideas about reading. There are no right or wrong answers. I'm going to ask you some questions. To answer the questions, just tell me what you are thinking." 4. If you are tape-recording the interview, say, "I'm going to turn on the tape recorder so that I can remember what you say. Do you mind?" (Teacher: Be sure to test the tape recorder.) 5. If you are writing the child's responses, say, "I will be writing down what you say so that I can remember your comments. Is that all right with you?" 6. Begin asking the interview questions in the order they are written. If the child does not answer, prompt with easy questions such as "Do you have any brothers or sisters?" and "What animals do you like?" Once the child feels comfortable answering the questions, proceed with the interview.
SCORING AND INTERPRETATION	Record the child's responses as accurately as possible. Then read the responses looking for overall patterns. Informally determine whether the child views himself or herself as learning to read and whether the child has a positive or negative attitude toward reading. Record your qualitative judgment of the child's attitude and understanding about reading with an X on the continuum provided on the separate record sheets on page 26 and page 28.

Interviews about Reading
(Emergent Reader: PreK-K)

Name _____ Date _____

1. Do you like to have someone read to you?   ____ Yes   ____ No

   Who do you like to read to you? _____

2. What kinds of stories do you like? _____

3. Tell me the name of a favorite story. _____

4. Do you have any books at home?   ____ Yes   ____ No

   About how many books do you have at home? _____

   Where do you keep the books? _____

5. Who do you know that likes to read? _____

6. Are you learning to read?   ____ Yes   ____ No

   Tell me what you have learned so far. _____

7. Do you want to learn how to read better?   ____ Yes   ____ No

   Tell me more about that. _____

8. Do you think you will be a good reader?   ____ Yes   ____ No

   What makes you say that? _____

9. What makes a person a good reader? _____

   _____

10. What is reading? _____

   _____

Qualitative Judgments of Interviews about Reading (Emergent Reader: PreK–K)

Name _____ Date _____

	Not Evident Low Seldom Weak Poor	Some	Evident High Always Strong Excellent
Overall interest in reading			
Familiarity with specific stories			
Availability of books			
Knowledge of reading role models			
Confidence in learning to read			
Motivation to learn to read			
Knowledge of purpose for reading			

Observations, Comments, Notes, and Insights

Interviews about Reading
(Early Reader: Grades 1–3)

Name _____ Date _____

1. Do you like to have someone read to you?   ____ Yes   ____ No

   Who do you like to read to you? _____

2. What kinds of stories do you like? _____

   _____

3. Tell me the name of a favorite story. _____

4. Do you have many books at home?   ____ Yes   ____ No

   How many books do you think you have? _____

5. Who do you know that likes to read? _____

   _____

6. Do you think you are a good reader?   ____ Yes   ____ No

   Why or why not? _____

7. What makes a person a good reader? _____

   _____

8. When you are reading and come to a word you don't know, what do you do?

   _____

9. What do you do when you don't understand what you are reading?

   _____

10. What is reading?

   _____

Qualitative Judgments of Interviews about Reading (Early Reader: Grades 1–3)

Name _____ Date _____

	Not Evident Low Seldom Weak Poor		Some		Evident High Always Strong Excellent
Overall interest in reading	├	┼	┼	┼	┤
Familiarity with specific stories	├	┼	┼	┼	┤
Availability of books	├	┼	┼	┼	┤
Knowledge of reading role models	├	┼	┼	┼	┤
Confidence in learning to read	├	┼	┼	┼	┤
Motivation to learn to read	├	┼	┼	┼	┤
Knowledge of word identification strategies	├———————————————————————┤				
Knowledge of comprehension strategies	├	┼	┼	┼	┤
Knowledge of purpose for reading	├	┼	┼	┼	┤

Observations, Comments, Notes, and Insights

NEWS ABOUT ME

OVERVIEW	News about Me provides information about the child's background, interests, and life, It can be completed as an interview, or older children can respond in writing. Teachers can use the information to recommend books, adjust the curriculum, or make connections between the classroom and the child's life.
MATERIALS NEEDED	1. News about Me Record Sheet on pages 30–31. 2. Tape recorder (if desired)
PROCEDURES	1. Duplicate the News about Me Record Sheet (pp. 30–31). 2. Explain to the child that you want to learn more about him or her by using the News about Me Record Sheet to help gather information. 3. If you plan to give the assessment as an interview, you may wish to tape-record the child's responses. 4. If the child will be responding in writing, explain that he or she should seek assistance if any of the questions are unclear. Also explain that in some sections students may not answer all the questions (for example, no pets).
SCORING AND INTERPRETATION	Review the child's responses, noting any information that may help you suggest appropriate books for the child. Note any connections you can make to the curriculum.

RECORD SHEET

News about Me

A News Story about _____ **Date** _____

(write your name here)

News about My Family

I have _____ brothers and sisters.

They are _____ years old.

I like to play with _____ .

My mother and I like to _____ .

My father and I like to _____ .

I (like/do not like) to play alone.

I help at home by _____ .

The thing I like to do at home is _____

_____ .

News about My Pets

I have a pet _____ .

I (do/do not) take care of my pet _____ .

I do not have a pet because _____

_____ .

I would like to have a pet _____ .

News about My Books and My Reading

I like to read about _____

_____ .

The best book I ever read was _____

_____ .

I (do get/do not get) books from the library.

I have _____ books of my own at home.

I read aloud to _____ .

_____ reads to me.

News about My Friends

My best friend is _____ .

I like (him/her) because _____

_____ .

We play _____ .

I would rather play (at my house/at my friend's house) because _____

_____ .

News about Things I Like and Dislike

I do not like _____ .

I like _____ .

I am afraid of _____ .

I am not afraid of _____ .

News about my Wishes

When I grow up, I want to be _____

_____

_____

If I could have three wishes I would wish

(1) _____

_____ .

(2) _____

_____

(3) _____

_____

_____ .

page 1

News about My Travels and Adventures

I have traveled by:

_____ bus	_____ car
_____ airplane	_____ truck
_____ boat	_____ train
_____ bicycle	_____ van

I have visited these places:

_____ circus	_____ zoo
_____ farm	_____ park
_____ hotel	_____ museum
_____ bakery	_____ library
_____ airport	_____ fire station

_____ factory, and _____ .

The best adventure I ever had was _____

_____

_____

_____

_____

_____ .

News about My Hobbies and Collections

One of my best hobbies is _____

_____ .

I collect _____ .

I want to collect _____ .

My other hobbies are _____

_____ .

Movie, Radio, and Television Favorites

I see _____ movies each week.

I like to listen to _____ on the radio.

I see _____ television programs a day.

My favorite programs are _____

_____ .

News about My School Subjects

My favorite subject is _____ .

The subject I dislike most is _____ .

I am best at _____ .

I wish I was better in _____ .

Write any other news about yourself below.

_____

_____

_____

_____

_____

_____

page 2

ELEMENTARY READING ATTITUDE SURVEY

OVERVIEW	The Elementary Reading Attitude Survey provides insight into children's attitudes toward recreational and school reading. In addition, a total score can be calculated to get an overall idea of a child's attitude toward reading. The assessment can be administered individually or to a group of children.
MATERIALS NEEDED	1. One copy of the Elementary Reading Attitude Survey (pages 34–38) for each child and one copy for teacher 2. Scoring Sheet on page 39 3. Percentile Ranks on page 40
PROCEDURES	1. Explain to the children that you are going to give them a survey to find out how they feel about reading. 2. Tell them there are no right or wrong answers and urge them to be honest in their responses. 3. Display the Garfield responses on the overhead projector and explain what each of the Garfields means: happiest, slightly smiling, mildly upset, and very upset. Discuss examples of when the children feel each of these emotions. 4. Distribute the Elementary Reading Attitude Survey. Instruct the children to circle the Garfield that matches their feelings for each question. 5. Read each question aloud, providing wait time for the children to respond.
SCORING AND INTERPRETATION	1. To score the survey, count four points for each leftmost (happiest) Garfield circled, three for each slightly smiling Garfield, two for each mildly upset Garfield, and one point for each very upset (rightmost) Garfield. Three scores for each student can be obtained: the total for the first 10 items, the total for the second 10, and a composite total. The first half of the survey relates to attitude toward recreational reading; the second half relates to attitude toward academic aspects of reading. 2. You can interpret scores in two ways. One is to note informally where the score falls in regard to the four points on the scale. A total score of 50, for example, would fall about midway on the scale, between the slightly happy and slightly upset figures, therefore indicating a relatively indifferent overall attitude toward reading. The other approach is more formal. It involves converting the raw scores into percentile ranks by means of Table 1 on page 40. Be sure to use the norms for the right

grade level and to note the column headings (Rec = recreational reading, Aca = academic reading, Tot = total score). If you wish to determine the average percentile rank for your class, average the raw scores first; then use the table to locate the percentile rank corresponding to the raw score mean. Percentile ranks cannot be averaged directly.

NORMS FOR THE ELEMENTARY READING ATTITUDE SURVEY

To create norms for the interpretation of the Elementary Reading Attitude Survey scores, a large-scale study was conducted late in January 1989, at which time the survey was administered to 18,138 students in Grades 1–6. Several steps were taken to achieve a sample that was sufficiently stratified (that is, reflective of the American population) to allow confident generalizations. Children were drawn from 95 school districts in 38 states. The number of girls and boys was almost equivalent. Ethnic distribution of the sample was also close to that of the U.S. population in 1989. The proportion of African-Americans (9.5%) was within 3% of the national proportion, whereas the proportion of Hispanics (6.2%) was within 2%.

Percentile ranks at each grade for both subscales and the full scale are presented in Table 1 on page 40. These data can be used to compare individual students' scores with the national sample and they can be interpreted like achievement-test percentile ranks.

McKenna, M. C., & Kear, D. J. (1990). Measuring attitude toward reading: A new tool for teachers. *The Reading Teacher, 43,* 626–639. Reprinted with permission of Michael C. McKenna and the International Reading Association.

Elementary Reading Attitude Survey

Name _____ Date _____

School _____ Grade _____

GARFIELD © 1978 United Feature Syndicate, Inc.

1. How do you feel when you read a book on a rainy Saturday?

2. How do you feel when you read a book in a school during free time?

3. How do you feel about reading for fun at home?

4. How do you feel about getting a book for a present?

5. How do you feel about spending free time reading?

GARFIELD © 1978 United Feature Syndicate, Inc.

6. How do you feel about starting a new book?

7. How do you feel about reading during summer?

8. How do you feel about reading instead of playing?

3

9. How do you feel about going to a bookstore?

10. How do you feel about reading different kinds of books?

11. How do you feel when the teacher asks you questions about what you read?

12. How do you feel about doing reading workbook pages and worksheets?

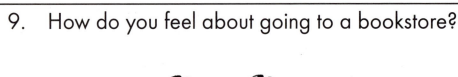

4

13. How do you feel about reading in school?

14. How do you feel about reading your school books?

15. How do you feel about learning from a book?

16. How do you feel when it's time for reading in class?

© Paws, Inc. The Garfield character is incorporated in this test with the permission of Paws, Incorporated, and may be reproduced only in connection with the reproduction of the test in its entirety for classroom use until further notice by Paws, Inc., and any other reproduction or use without the express prior written consent of Paws is prohibited.

Chapter One   Attitudes, Interests, and Background Knowledge   **37**

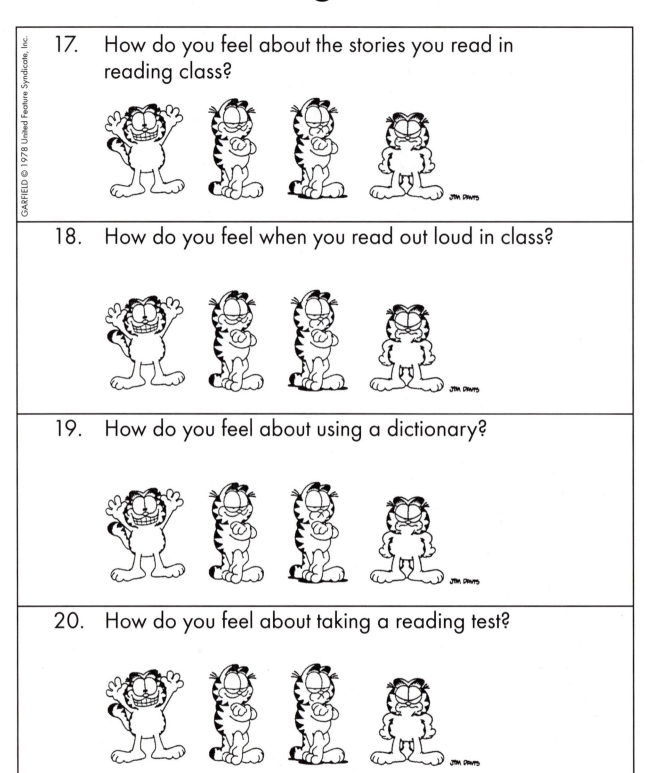

17. How do you feel about the stories you read in reading class?

18. How do you feel when you read out loud in class?

19. How do you feel about using a dictionary?

20. How do you feel about taking a reading test?

Elementary Reading Attitude Survey
Scoring Sheet

Student Name _____

Teacher _____

Grade _____ Administration Date _____

Scoring Guide

4 points	Happiest Garfield
3 points	Slightly smiling Garfield
2 points	Mildly upset Garfield
1 point	Very upset Garfield

Recreational reading

1. _____
2. _____
3. _____
4. _____
5. _____
6. _____
7. _____
8. _____
9. _____
10. _____

Raw score: _____

Academic Reading

11. _____
12. _____
13. _____
14. _____
15. _____
16. _____
17. _____
18. _____
19. _____
20. _____

Raw score: _____

Total raw score (Recreational + Academic): _____

Percentile Ranks

Recreational	
Academic	
Full scale	

Table 1   Mid-Year Percentile Ranks by Grade and Scale

RAW SCORE	Grade 1			Grade 2			Grade 3			Grade 4			Grade 5			Grade 6		
	REC	ACA	TOT	REC	ACA	TOT	REC	ACA	TOT	REC	ACA	TOT	REC	ACA	TOT	REC	ACA	TOT
80			99			99			99			99			99			99
79			95			96			98			99			99			99
78			93			95			97			98			99			99
77			92			94			97			98			99			99
76			90			93			96			97			98			99
75			88			92			95			96			98			99
74			86			90			94			95			97			99
73			84			88			92			94			97			98
72			82			86			91			93			96			98
71			80			84			89			91			95			97
70			78			82			86			89			94			96
69			75			79			84			88			92			95
68			72			77			81			86			91			93
67			69			74			79			83			89			92
66			66			71			76			50			87			90
65			62			69			73			78			84			88
64			59			66			70			75			82			86
63			55			63			67			72			79			84
62			52			60			64			69			76			82
61			49			57			61			66			73			79
60			46			54			58			62			70			76
59			43			51			55			59			67			73
58			40			47			51			56			64			69
57			37			45			48			53			61			68
56			34			41			44			48			57			62
55			31			38			41			45			53			58
54			28			35			38			41			50			55
53			25			32			34			38			46			52
52			22			29			31			35			42			48
51			20			26			28			32			39			44
50			18			23			25			28			36			40
49			15			20			23			26			33			37
48			13			18			20			23			29			33
47			12			15			17			20			26			30
46			10			13			15			18			23			27
45			8			11			13			16			20			25
44			7			9			11			13			17			22
43			6			8			9			12			15			20
42			5			7			9			10			13			17
41			5			6			7			9			12			15
40	99	99	4	99	99	5	99	99	6	99	99	7	99	99	10	99	99	13
39	92	91	3	94	94	4	96	97	5	97	98	6	98	99	9	99	99	12
38	89	88	3	92	92	2	94	95	4	95	97	5	96	98	8	97	99	10
37	86	85	2	88	89	2	90	93	3	92	95	4	94	98	7	95	99	8
36	81	79	2	84	85	2	87	91	2	88	93	3	91	96	6	92	98	7
35	77	75	1	79	81	1	81	88	2	84	90	3	87	95	4	88	97	6
34	72	69	1	74	78	1	75	83	2	78	87	2	82	93	4	83	95	5
33	65	63	1	68	73	1	69	79	1	72	83	2	77	90	3	79	93	4
32	58	58	1	62	67	1	63	74	1	66	79	1	71	86	3	74	91	3
31	52	53	1	56	62	1	57	69	0	60	75	1	65	82	2	69	87	2
30	44	49	1	50	57	0	51	63	0	54	70	1	59	77	1	63	82	2
29	38	44	0	44	51	0	45	58	0	47	64	1	53	71	1	58	78	1
28	32	39	0	37	46	0	38	52	0	41	58	1	48	66	1	51	73	1
27	26	34	0	31	41	0	33	47	0	35	52	1	42	60	1	46	67	1
26	21	30	0	25	37	0	26	41	0	29	46	0	36	54	0	39	60	1
25	17	25	0	20	32	0	21	36	0	23	40	0	30	49	0	34	54	0
24	12	21	0	15	27	0	17	31	0	19	35	0	25	42	0	29	49	0
23	9	18	0	11	23	0	13	26	0	14	29	0	20	37	0	24	42	0
22	7	14	0	8	18	0	9	22	0	11	25	0	16	31	0	19	36	0
21	5	11	0	6	15	0	6	18	0	9	20	0	13	26	0	15	30	0
20	4	9	0	4	11	0	5	14	0	6	16	0	10	21	0	12	24	0
19	2	7		2	8		3	11		5	13		7	17		10	20	
18	2	5		2	6		2	8		3	9		6	13		8	15	
17	1	4		1	5		1	5		2	7		4	9		6	11	
16	1	3		1	3		1	4		2	5		3	6		4	8	
15	0	2		0	2		0	3		1	3		2	4		3	6	
14	0	2		0	1		0	1		1	2		1	2		1	3	
13	0	1		0	1		0	1		0	1		1	2		1	2	
12	0	1		0	0		0	0		0	1		0	1		0	1	
11	0	0		0	0		0	0		0	0		0	0		0	0	
10	0	0		0	0		0	0		0	0		0	0		0	0	

chapter *two*

Oral Language and Literacy Knowledge

Overview

Oral language is the basis for learning to read (Roskos, Tabors, & Lenhart, 2004). As children hear language, they begin to form generalizations about words and meanings. Children learn that talk carries meaning and that the words they use can cause reactions in others. As children experiment with oral language, they increase the number of words they know and become facile with grammatical structures. They also begin to develop literacy knowledge as they learn that oral language can be written and read.

Children begin to develop literacy knowledge through exposure to print in their environment. Environmental print is the words and phrases that children see in their neighborhoods and as they travel to other areas (Prior & Gerard, 2004). Some places are filled with environmental print, such as signs, message boards, logos, and billboards. Other places, such as rural areas and inner-city neighborhoods, may have little environmental print (Orellana & Hernandez, 2003). Because the print that children see on a day-to-day basis helps them understand the purposes of print, teachers often fill their classrooms with print.

Young children learn about print through experiences with stories; they don't innately know how print works. Children need to learn that letters arranged in certain ways form words, that words are separated by spaces, that words form sentences, that print is read from left to right, and that meaning can be constructed from the words. These and other print concepts are developed as children have experiences listening to stories, seeing print, and watching others read.

As children hear stories read to them, they develop a sense of story. They begin to know that stories have a beginning, a middle, and an end. Through multiple exposures to stories, children also learn that stories have a plot, setting, characters, and theme. As they become familiar with stories, children are able to predict events and discern what is missing from the stories that they hear.

Questions/Answers

Language develops naturally in children. Do they learn print concepts the same way?

Yes and no. Children learn language through listening to others speak, but they also have an inherent knowledge of grammatical structures (Chomsky, 1968). Children can learn print in the same way—through experiences. There are, however, some important differences. If children are not exposed to print in their surroundings, they do not automatically develop an understanding of print concepts. Therefore, young children need guided experiences in order to learn print concepts, such as parents reading to their children. Experts suggest that young children should be introduced to at least 100 books every year (Neuman, Celano, Greco, & Shue, 2001).

Many of the children in my classroom have not experienced story reading with their parents. What should I do?

When children have had few experiences with stories at home, they need extra story reading in school through a literature-based instructional program (Morrow & Gambrell, 2001). Reading books aloud and showing children that pages turn from right to left, that you read from top to bottom, and that sentences are read from left to right are essential understandings to develop. Provide many experiences during the school day for children to learn these concepts. Frequently read Big Books to children, showing them how to turn pages, sweeping your hand under the print, and illustrating the directionality of the print. Have other adults and older children read to your class as well. In addition, provide children with opportunities to read (look through) picture books, remind them to practice reading every day, and provide a print-rich environment in the classroom.

We spend most of our time in preschool teaching the letters of the alphabet, but I know the children in my classroom are weak on print concepts. Will my focus on letters eventually help students learn about print?

Children need to understand how print works before they can benefit from instruction on letters and sounds (Au, 1998), but that doesn't mean you should only concentrate on print concepts. If children have had few experiences with books and have little knowledge of print concepts, you should spend much of your time with these foundational skills. However, you can still teach letters and the sounds associated with letters during shared reading. An emphasis on stories, rather than individual letters, will help children develop concepts about print more rapidly (International Reading Association, 2005).

Will children develop a sense of stories through reading, or do I need to teach it?

Most children develop a sense of story as they listen to stories being read (Stein & Glenn, 1979), but this story sense can be refined through instruction. For example, many children in the primary grades understand that a story needs to have a setting and main characters, but they may not understand that the plot of a story will have a "problem" that needs to be resolved. Teaching children how stories work helps them improve their comprehension of text, and it also facilitates their writing of stories (Pressley, Allington, Wharton-McDonald, Block, & Morrow, 2001).

What is the role of oral language instruction in the typical preschool, kindergarten, or primary classroom? With all of the emphasis on skills and testing, do I need to address oral language as well?

Oral language is the foundation for reading and writing (Watson, 2001). In *Standards for the English Language Arts* (1996), the National Council of Teachers of English and the International Reading Association address oral language in several of the standards. Teachers can nurture oral language development in a number of ways including Show and Tell, creative dramatics, peer-led discussions, and storytelling. Oral language is typically woven into various activities throughout the day rather than taught as a separate subject. As teachers plan their lessons, they are encouraged to consider how listening and speaking experiences will complement and enhance their lessons. The unprecedented attention that is now focused on early literacy instruction in preschool and kindergarten underscores the critical need for children's solid foundation in oral language (McGee & Richgels, 2003).

Are preschool children too young to learn about print concepts?

No! Children as young as 2-years old can develop emerging understandings about books and print (Strickland & Schickedanz, 2004). Children this young may not be able to explain how books work, but they can begin to make generalizations that books open on the right side and the pages are turned from right to left. All preschool children should be given opportunities to learn about words, print, and books.

Do children who speak a dialect of English need differentiated instruction?

Yes, they do. Experts in African-American dialects, for example, believe that many children who hear and speak a dialect of English that is not like "school language," are at a disadvantage when they begin learning to read (Harris-Wright, 2005). Teachers should spend additional time talking with dialect speakers so that the children learn how school language is different from their home language. As they learn how to use school language, the children can become proficient in speaking both their dialect and school English.

section 2.1

Oral Language

> **Goal:** To help children expand and enhance their oral language development.

Background

Oral language provides the foundation for reading and writing (Clay, 1998). Research summarized by Tabors and Snow (2001) indicates that young children who are exposed to a second language in a setting outside the home, such as a preschool, move through four phases of language use. First, children continue to use their home language, often unaware that the language they are hearing is different from the one they use and hear at home. Second, children stop using their home language with those who do not understand it. They make nonverbal requests and point and mime. They also develop receptive use of the language during this phase. Third, children progress to using telegraphic and formulaic language. They name people and objects, count, and use catch phrases (OK, yes, mine, lookit) for getting into and out of social situations. Finally, children move to a productive use of the new language making many mistakes as they figure out how English works.

  Children draw on their listening and speaking vocabularies as they read and write. In addition, as children develop their oral language, they become more aware of shades of meaning and different ways of expressing thoughts. Some children come to school with well-developed oral language skills in English. Other children may need more support to develop their oral language. All young children can benefit from engaging in activities and strategies that foster oral language development.

Section 2.1 *TEACHING STRATEGY* **1**

SHOW AND TELL QUESTION CONNECTION

The classic activity of Show and Tell is an excellent way to promote children's oral language development. Including a question-answer time as part of Show and Tell will further enhance the language development opportunities offered by this strategy. In addition, because children are sharing a favorite object, they are highly motivated to convey their ideas and information to others.

DIRECTIONS

1. Explain to the children that you will be doing an activity called Show and Tell Question Connection and each of them will have a chance to bring in a favorite object to share with the class.

2. Demonstrate the process by sharing one of your favorite objects. For example, you might bring in a large pinecone you collected from a recent camping trip.

3. Explain to the children that first you will Show and Tell about the pinecone. For example, you might say, "I got this big pinecone when I went camping in Indiana last fall. I like this pinecone because it is long and sturdy. It smells like the forest, and it makes me think of all of the fun I had on this camping trip."

4. Next, tell the children that you will move into the Question phase of the activity. Invite children to ask you questions about the pinecone or anything you shared. If a child's question is unclear, help him or her rephrase it. Respond to each question.

5. Tell the children that you are now going to move on to the Connection part of the activity. Explain that any of the children who would like to share a personal connection with the object or ideas shared are invited to do so. For example, one child might say that there is a pine tree in the park.

6. Develop a schedule so each child has a chance to bring in an object to share.

7. You might want to develop a chart with the key words for this strategy (Show, Tell, Questions, Connections).

Aa Bb Cc Tips for English Language Learners

- Meet with English Language Learners before they share in the Show and Tell Question Connection activity. Discuss the object they have selected, offering English words as necessary. This preparation should result in increased confidence and clarity when English Language Learners do their sharing.

Section 2.1 *TEACHING STRATEGY*

EXPAND-A-SENTENCE

This strategy encourages children to add descriptive words and phrases to a simple sentence to enhance and extend the meaning of the sentence. By doing so, children can begin to understand the importance of using descriptive words and explaining things clearly and completely.

DIRECTIONS

1. Select a simple sentence. Write the sentence on the chalkboard. For example, you may select the following sentence: The boy ran.

2. Ask children to expand the sentence by adding one or more words to make the sentence more interesting and informative. Children may offer words to expand the sentence as in the following examples.

   The little boy ran.

   The little boy ran home in the rain.

   The little boy ran home quickly in the rain.

3. Once the sentence has been expanded several times, write the new expanded sentence on the chalkboard below the original sentence. Discuss the differences between the two sentences. Ask the children which sentence is more interesting or informative.

4. Continue the strategy using several other sentences. Invite students to suggest simple sentences.

5. One variation of this strategy is to have partners expand a simple sentence orally. This variation promotes greater engagement and use of language.

Aa Bb Cc — Tips for English Language Learners

- Provide word cards for English Language Learners to use to expand sentences. By providing several possible choices, you can help English Language Learners focus on what makes sense in the sentence rather than on trying to generate new ideas.

Section 2.1   **TEACHING STRATEGY**   **3**

PROGRESSIVE STORYTELLING

Children love to tell stories, especially those with wild, imaginative events and characters. The Progressive Storytelling strategy invites children to add to an evolving story. Children must listen closely to make sure their additions make sense.

DIRECTIONS

1. Gather a group of six to eight children together in a circle on the carpet or around a large table. Explain to the children that they are going to work together as a group to tell a story.

2. Remind children that stories are more fun when interesting words are used and exciting events and characters are involved.

3. Tell the children that you will begin the story and then move around the circle or table in order so each child can add to the story. Explain that children can say "Pass" if they cannot think of something to add at that time.

4. Begin the story by sharing an opening sentence such as, "Once upon a time in a land far, far away, there lived a little boy who had a very special talent."

5. Rotate around the circle so each child can add to the story.

6. When the story reaches you again, provide closure to the story.

Aa Bb Cc — Tips for English Language Learners

- Invite English Language Learners to share their additions near the beginning of the story to decrease the likelihood that another child will already have shared similar ideas.

- Provide several props related to the story opening. Invite English Language Learners to select a prop to help them make additions to the story.

PICTURE TALK

Picture Talk is especially useful for children who are learning English or who need to expand their vocabulary. This strategy provides a supportive environment to develop concepts, build background, and expand vocabulary.

DIRECTIONS

1. Gather a wide range of pictures that are of potential interest to young children. The pictures can be of various objects, or they can depict various social situations. There are also commercial files of pictures that can be purchased.

2. Have a small group of children who need language development opportunities sit so they can easily see the picture. Provide time for the children to study the picture.

3. Invite children to tell you about the picture. Use guiding questions as needed. For example, if the picture is of a child with a toothbrush in the bathroom, ask questions like the following:

   - Is the child a boy or a girl?
   - What is the child doing?
   - What is this called (pointing to toothbrush)?
   - What will be done with the toothbrush?
   - What might the child do next?

4. As children respond to the questions, repeat and elaborate as needed. The goal should be to help the children express themselves. Provide plenty of positive reinforcement.

5. Use concrete objects to supplement the pictures. For example, a toothbrush could be described (color, shape) and the bristles could be felt. If necessary provide words to describe the bristles: "The bristles are short and soft."

6. Make a genuine effort to use pictures that connect with children's lives. Everyday events, objects, and animals are useful beginnings.

Activities, tips, & Center Ideas

1. Display an interesting picture or object. Invite children to orally describe what they see.

2. Invite children to tell a story from a wordless picture book. For a list of wordless picture books, see Johns and Lenski (2005).

3. Provide props, puppets, or felt board shapes in a learning center to encourage children to tell stories based on the objects.

4. Institute a "Turn to Your Neighbor" policy in your classroom so all children have a chance to share, even when time is short. Tell children to "turn to your neighbor," share an idea, and then switch roles.

5. Play the game of telephone to promote careful listening and speaking. Have the children sit in a large circle. Begin the game by whispering a message in one child's ear. Have that child whisper the message in the next child's ear, and so on. Continue until the message travels through the entire group. Share the final message. Discuss any differences between the original message and the final message. Emphasize the importance of listening and speaking carefully in order to understand and be understood.

6. Ask open-ended questions to encourage children to share longer, more complex responses. For example, you might ask children, "What would you do and why?" and "What was your favorite part and why?"

7. Provide thinking time before calling on children to share their ideas. Tell children you want them to think five seconds before raising their hands.

8. Brainstorm lists of interesting words to replace overused words such as *good, said,* and *happy.* Display these words in the classroom. Use them in your conversations with children and invite them to use the more descriptive words in their speech.

9. Provide time for role-playing and creative dramatics so children can explore and apply language in interesting contexts. Puppets may be especially helpful.

10. Read aloud to children from a wide variety of books and genres to model interesting, effective, engaging language. Discuss examples of particularly interesting or engaging words, phrases, or sentences from the books.

11. Provide children's songs and rhymes on audio tapes or CDs. Encourage children to sing along or say the rhyme.

12. Puppets, puppet theaters, and puppet-making kits can help engage children in stories and oral language activities.

LANGUAGE ACTIVITIES

Dear Families,

To help your child build language skills, try these activities at home.

- Talk to your child about the day, asking open-ended questions such as, "What is something interesting that happened to you today?" and "What made you happy today?" By providing many opportunities for conversation, your child will get valuable practice in explaining things clearly.

- Label objects, ask questions, and invite your child's observations as you do daily activities such as grocery shopping, cooking, playing in the park, or walking through your neighborhood.

- Read to your child. Describe and discuss the pictures. Share favorite parts. Later, work together to tell the story to another family member.

- Have conversations during family meals. Talking about daily events is a great way to help your child develop and expand language skills.

Sincerely,

section 2.2

Print Concepts

Goal: To help children learn concepts about print in books.
Assessment Strategy 1 Print Concepts, page 72

Background

As children grow, they learn about the world around them and gradually develop literacy skills. Knowledge about reading and writing begins early in children's lives (Teale & Sulzby, 1989). Very young children begin to notice that reading and writing are part of their world. For example, young children learn that their environment is full of print. They see print material such as newspapers and magazines in their homes, they see print on television, and they recognize signs and logos on products and in stores. As children begin to notice print, they are progressing toward literacy (Clay, 1985). Regardless of their backgrounds, all children are learning about their world and how literacy fits into their lives (Taylor, 1983).

Even though all children have important background experiences, they have had various degrees of exposure to books. Some children have participated in thousands of hours of shared reading with caring adults. Other children have had very little experience with books. The amount of experience children have had with books is important in their acquisition of literacy. Most children who have been read to have learned some of the basics of literacy knowledge. They may know that books are for reading, that books open from right to left, where the pictures in books are, what print is used for, and so on. Children need to understand the purpose of books and concepts about print in order for reading instruction to be effective.

Many young children have learned that print carries meaning, and they know how to open a book and turn the pages. However, many children still do not know the terminology of reading—the concept of a letter, a word, a sentence, or sounds (Johns, 1980). As children begin to learn to read, they need to learn how language operates, that a written word matches a spoken word, that spaces are used between words, and that sentences are set off with punctuation. This literacy knowledge is an important precursor to independent reading.

When children do not know concepts about print, they need instruction in those concepts. Children need a solid base of literacy knowledge in order to firmly grasp other aspects of the reading process. The following teaching strategies provide suggestions that promote children's literacy knowledge.

Section 2.2 **TEACHING STRATEGY**

SHARED READING

One of the purposes for shared reading is to introduce children to concepts about print. Many children are unfamiliar with book parts, how books are read, and the relationship between words and speech. Providing children with explicit instruction about the parts of books can help them increase their literacy knowledge.

DIRECTIONS

1. Choose a Big Book to read to children. (A Big Book is an oversized book that is often used in shared reading.) Before reading the book, identify concepts about print that you want to introduce. Some of the concepts that children need to learn are listed below.

   - books are for reading
   - the front and back of a book
   - the top and bottom of a book
   - pages turn from right to left
   - the difference between print and pictures
   - print carries meaning
   - pictures on a page are related to what the print says
   - print is read from left to right
   - print is read from top to bottom
   - the page that begins the story
   - what a title of a book is
   - what an author is
   - what an illustrator is

2. Introduce the concepts you want to teach as you read to students as in the example below.

   Teacher: Today we're going to read *Little Cloud* by Eric Carle (1996). What do you see on the cover of this book?

   Students: Clouds!

   Teacher: Yes, you see a picture of clouds. The front of the book is called the cover, and on the cover we usually find a picture and the name of the author. What's an author?

   Students: The person who wrote the book.

   Teacher: Right, and the author of *Little Cloud* is Eric Carle.

   I'm going to open the cover. Now what do you see?

   Students: The same picture of clouds.

   Teacher: Yes, this page is the title page and it has a picture and the name of the author again. Now, I'm going to begin reading with my hand sweeping under the words. Notice how my hand moves from left to right as I read to show you how I am saying the words.

3. After children have participated in shared reading, reinforce the concepts you have introduced by asking children to point to the cover of the book, the illustrations, and the name of the author, and by having them sweep their hands under the words to show the direction to read.

4. Give all children their own books to read. Reinforce the concepts you introduced by having students point to the cover of their individual books, the illustrations, and the name of the author. Then have children move their hands under the print of the books, reading if they can.

5. Spend several sessions each week introducing concepts about print. During each session, review the previous lesson that you taught. Some children require many exposures to print before they increase their understanding of print concepts.

Tips for English Language Learners

- Children whose home language does not follow the same conventions of print as English may have difficulty learning English print concepts. Identify the home languages of the children in your class and find out the differences between those languages and English. Point out the differences to children as in the following example.

  "I know when your parents and grandparents read Chinese at home you read from right to left. That's how you read Chinese, but in English you read a different way. When you read English, you start reading at the top of the page and read from left to right. Different languages have different ways of reading books, and you can learn more than one way to read."

Section 2.2   *TEACHING STRATEGY*   **2**

LANGUAGE EXPERIENCE APPROACH (LEA)

The Language Experience Approach (LEA) helps children make connections between spoken and written language (Stauffer, 1970). Children's dictation serves as the foundation for the LEA. The main premises of the undergirding LEA are that children can talk about what they have experienced, their words can be written down, and they can read what they say. The Language Experience Approach begins with the children's experiences and own language; therefore, it provides a personalized connection between learning about spoken and written language.

DIRECTIONS

1. Provide a hands-on experience for children such as a field trip to an apple orchard or a zoo.

2. Invite children to tell about their experiences with the hands-on activity by dictating a story. This can be done with individual children, small groups, or a class of children.

3. Inform children that you will record their ideas in writing.

4. Write children's dictations on chart paper. Be sure to write exactly what the children say. Do not make corrections for grammar or usage unless you have been teaching a specific writing convention, such as the use of *I* in *Cheryl and I*. An example of a dictated experience follows.

   Yesterday we went to the zoo, and we saw lots of animals. We saw a bear and he was eating lunch but we don't know what it was he was eating. We saw a momma giraffe with her baby. She was way tall! We saw lots of other animals too.

5. When the children have completed the story, read it aloud to them, identifying print concepts that you want to emphasize as in the following example.

   Teacher: I'm going to read this story back to you. Where should I start reading? Show me where to begin. (Child points to the first word.) Yes, I need to start reading at the top of the page at the first word I see.

   (Teacher reads first line.)

   Yesterday we went to the zoo, and we saw lots of animals.

Teacher: How many words do I have in the first sentence? Remember, a sentence starts with a capital letter and ends with a period. Which word has a capital letter? (Yesterday) Where is the period? (After animals) How do I tell where the words begin and end? (Spaces between words) Count the number of words with me.

6. Reread the story, inviting children to participate in the reading if they would like to do so. Reread the story several times. Discuss ideas contributed by specific children.

7. Guide children to understand that the story's content came from their words and ideas. Discuss how their words can be spoken, written, and then read.

8. Have the children illustrate the story and bind it into a Big Book. Place the Big Book in the classroom library so the children can read and reread it during their free time.

Aa Bb Cc Tips for English Language Learners

- English uses the Roman alphabet, but not all languages do. Some of the English Language Learners in your classroom may use an alphabet that looks very different from English. Children who are not familiar with the Roman alphabet may have difficulty distinguishing capital letters from lowercase letters, ending marks, and even spaces between words. English Language Learners unfamiliar with the Roman alphabet will need extra assistance learning print concepts.

Section 2.2   *TEACHING STRATEGY*   **3**

LEARNING ABOUT PRINT THROUGH WRITING

One of the challenges children encounter when learning print concepts is that children cannot distinguish which direction to read when a book is facing them. When teachers read Big Books with children, they generally face them so they can show the books' illustrations. Children looking on may be confused about which direction to read print, especially since young children rarely have a good understanding about which direction is "left" and which is "right." When children write their own stories, however, they can learn these print concepts quickly.

DIRECTIONS

1. Tell children that you would like them to write a story. Give children unlined paper or lined paper with space for a picture.

2. Begin by having children write about their family as in the following example.

   Today, I'd like you to write a story for me about your family. When we write stories, we can write words first or we can draw pictures first. You can decide which you want to do. To start your story, tell me a little bit about each of the people in your family.

   I'll show you what I mean. I'd like to write about my family. I have a husband named Larry, so I'll start with a few sentences about my husband.

My husband's name is Larry. He is the band director at the high school. He also plays a trumpet in the community band.

I also have twin girls who are in third grade. I'll write about them next.

Larry and I have twin girls named Adele and Anne. They are eight years old and look exactly alike except for one thing: Adele has short curly hair and Anne has long, wavy hair. Larry and I have lots of fun with our girls.

Now write about your family.

3. As children write, help them write from left to right, from top to bottom, and with spaces between words. Encourage children to write several lines of print, spelling words with developmental spelling. (See the CD-ROM for ideas about developmental spelling.)

4. Have children read their stories to you or to their peers in groups. Compile the stories into a book and place the book where children can read it. Encourage children to read the book, reminding them to use what they know about print concepts when they read.

Aa Bb Cc Tips for English Language Learners

- Learn simple words from the languages that are represented in your classroom. When writing simple stories, substitute words from the home language of one of the children in your classroom. The English-speaking children will enjoy learning words from a new language, and the ELLs will be able to connect their language background to the story you are writing. In addition, the ELLs will be able to learn that the concept of a word applies to their home language as well as English.

Section 2.2 *TEACHING STRATEGY* 4

WHAT CAN YOU SHOW US?

What Can You Show Us? (Richgels, Poremba, & McGee, 1996) is a strategy that uses story reading with children's exploration of text to help them increase their literacy knowledge. When children use meaningful text to discover concepts about print, they are apt to be engaged in personal learning. What Can You Show Us? allows teachers to reinforce children's discoveries and guide them into learning about books, words, and print.

▶ DIRECTIONS

1. Select a Big Book to read to the children or write a dictated story on the chalkboard or on chart paper. Preview the story by telling the children that there is a new story on the chalkboard or on the easel. Tell them to look at the story during the day.

2. After children have had time to look at the story, direct their attention to the text by asking them to talk with each other about what they see. Then point out the title of the story, the author's name, and the cover illustration.

3. Before reading the story, ask the children, "What Can You Show Us?" Invite a child to come to the front and show the class something about the text. After the first child has identified something about the story, have other children repeat the process. Children may identify letters, words, or pictures, or they may tell the other children something about the book. Encourage all responses.

4. Read the story to the children. Then reinforce what the children noticed by repeating things they have said. For example, if a child points to the title of the story *Where the Wild Things Are* (Sendak, 1963), point to the title and repeat it. If a child has pointed to a letter, have the children identify that letter in other words or on other pages of the story. If there is a concept that you want the children to notice, an exclamation point, for example, tell children that you also have noticed something. Show children the element you want to introduce.

5. Tell children that there are many things about stories that they can notice on their own. Have the story available so that children can look at it after you have finished the lesson. Repeat this strategy often until children become familiar with concepts related to books.

Section 2.2   *TEACHING STRATEGY*

FINGERPOINT READING

When children understand the concept of words, they should begin to practice this skill by engaging in fingerpoint reading. Fingerpoint reading can help children learn directionality, track print, and understand where words begin and end. McGee and Richgels (2003) recommend that teachers use words in pocket charts rather than Big Books so that children can easily see the spaces between words.

DIRECTIONS

1. Select a story or poem that is familiar to children. Short poems work well for many preschool children although some children are able to follow longer pieces.

2. Read the story or poem with the children using the shared reading format. Read the piece several times, encouraging children to read aloud with you.

3. Select a 10–15-word portion of the text to use for fingerpoint reading. You might use the first few lines of a Big Book story, a short poem, or a summary of a story.

4. Write the words on heavy paper or sentence strips and place them in a pocket chart.

5. Read the text from the pocket chart aloud, pointing to each word as you read it. Refer to the original story or poem so that children understand that the words in the pocket chart are the same as the words in the story or poem.

6. Provide children with a short pointer made from a straw, an unsharpened pencil, or a ruler.

7. Invite one or two children to come to the pocket chart and read the words with you, pointing to each word. Guide children's hands if necessary so that they point to one word at a time.

8. Provide children with longer texts as they become familiar with fingerpoint reading and as they begin to understand print concepts.

Activities, tips, & Center Ideas

1. Sit with a small group of children. Hand little books to each of the children. Explain that the spines of books are on the left and that books open from the right. Have children identify their left hand. You might do this by showing them that the thumb and index finger on their left hand form an L shape. Have them place the spine of the book in the curve of their left thumb and index finger. Then have them open the book.

2. Explain that when you read a book you turn pages from right to left. After children have placed a book with the spine to the left, have them practice turning pages of the book. Encourage them to turn one page at a time. Show children that each page is different and that they will need to look at each page when reading.

3. Give children books to read. Tell them that most books begin with a word. Have them identify the first word in the book. Then explain that books have an ending word. Have children identify the last word in the book.

4. Help children identify the top and bottom of books by giving them picture books. Arrange several picture books on a table. Ask children to pick up a book and open it to a picture. Tell them that they should be able to identify the subject of the picture. Have them tell you what the picture shows. Explain that when a book is held correctly, they will be able to tell what the picture is about.

5. Gather together paper, pencils, and crayons. Staple the paper so that it is in book form. Sit with a small group of children. Explain that you will be showing the children how to write a book. Have one child dictate a title. Show children where to place the title on the cover of the book. Then open the book to the first page and have another child dictate a sentence. Write the sentence on the first page. Show children where the sentence belongs and discuss where they could draw a picture. Continue writing several sentences. Show children how to turn the pages and to write the book from beginning to end. Then have children illustrate the pages. When the book is complete, read it to the children.

6. Print children's names on index cards and show one of them to the children. Point to a child's first name, say it, and then point to the child's last name and say it. Show the children the space that separates the first and last names by pointing to them. Tell the children that there are two words on the card. Frame each word with your hands. Have children frame their first name and then their last name on their index cards. Give each child the index card with his or her name on it.

7. Have children dictate a story or use a sentence from a Big Book. Write the sentence on heavy paper or tagboard. Read the sentence aloud. Then cut the sentence apart at each word. Have children put the words together and place them in a pocket chart to make up the sentence. Read the sentence together, noting how the words make up a sentence.

8. Write a sentence on the chalkboard or on chart paper. Make word cards that match the words in the sentence. Give the word cards to several children. Ask children to find the word in the sentence that matches their word card. Tell children that they have a word and that the words together make up a sentence. Point to the beginning capital letter and the ending punctuation mark. Then have children read the entire sentence.

9. Read books to children several times each day. With each reading, remind children of one of the concepts about print.

10. Read a story to the children. Write all of the words from a sentence in the story on sentence strips. Then cut them apart so that each word and punctuation mark is separate. Have each child hold one of the words or punctuation cards. Have children rearrange themselves to make the sentence.

11. Explain that after each word there should be a space to show where the word stops and the next word begins. Use a book to show children how spaces are used between words in stories. Explain that spaces between words should be the same size. Have children write their own stories. Their writing will probably use developmental spelling. After children write, have them place their index finger or a pencil after each word to determine whether they have included spaces in their writing.

12. Practice counting words (Cunningham, 2000). Give children 10 counters (plastic disks, paper squares, raisins, or anything similar) in a paper cup. Start by counting some familiar objects in the room such as bulletin boards, doors, or plants. Have children place one of their counters on their desks as you point to each object. Be sure children return their counters to their cups at the end of each count. Then tell children that you can also count words by putting down a counter for each word as it is said. Model the process with the sentence "Today is Tuesday." First, say the sentence naturally. Then say the sentence slowly, pausing after each word, so children can put down a counter for each word. Ask children how many words you said. Proceed to other sentences, capitalizing on children's interests. As children begin to understand that words can be counted, invite them to offer their own sentences. They should say the sentence twice, once in the normal way and then one word at a time.

13. When reading from a Big Book or from sentences on the chalkboard, move your hand from left to right underneath the print. Explain that when reading you need to read the words at the left first, then read to the right one word at a time. Show children how to move to the next line of print. Slowly show children how to track print. After you have modeled the left to right progression of print, help children track their own reading from left to right by guiding their hands as they read. Encourage young children to read with a moving hand until they no longer need to physically track words.

14. Have children collect pictures from magazines of things they like. Paste the pictures on a poster board and label each picture. Emphasize the concept of a word by reading the labels one at a time.

15. Label items in your classroom and read the words aloud with the children. Remind the children that each item is described by a "word." You may also want to use phrases (e.g., the brown door).

EXPERIENCES WITH PRINT

Dear Families,

Children learn about reading by having many experiences with print. Here are some easy ways to get your children involved with print.

- Reading with your children provides them with experiences to learn how print works. Read one or more books with your children every day—bedtime is a favorite time for many children and parents. When you read, move your hand under the print to show your child which direction to read. Discuss what you read using questions such the ones that follow.

    What would you do if you were the main character?
    What was your favorite part of the story?
    Which picture is your favorite?

- Write Language Experience Stories with your child. Have your child tell you a story. Write the story down as closely as you can to the child's original words. As you write, show your child which direction to write and how to make spaces between words. Have the child illustrate the story. Read the story together frequently.

- Have paper, crayons, markers, and pencils available to your child at all times. Encourage your child to write notes, lists, and stories, knowing that these experiences will build knowledge about print concepts. Praise your child for all attempts to write.

Sincerely,

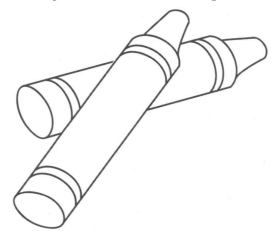

From Laurie Elish-Piper, Jerry L. Johns, and Susan Davis Lenski, *Teaching Reading Pre-K–Grade 3* (3rd ed.). Copyright © 2006 by Kendall/Hunt Publishing Company (1-800-247-3458, ext. 4). May be reproduced for noncommercial educational purposes.

section 2.3

Sense of Story

Goal: To help children develop a sense of story.

Background

Young children need to develop background knowledge about how stories are structured and what characteristics and components stories possess. This knowledge is important to emergent readers because it allows them to anticipate and understand stories and how they work. A sense of story provides children with a framework for understanding the stories that are read to them and the stories they read to themselves (Lukens, 1995).

Children who come to school with many home reading experiences typically possess a good sense of story because of the many stories that have been read to them by their families or caregivers. Children who have not been read to on a regular basis prior to coming to school will need to be immersed in stories and reading experiences so they too can develop a sense of story (Edwards, 1986).

Story selections for emergent readers should focus on simple stories with related illustrations and large, clear print. Story sharing should be an interactive process with many opportunities for children to discuss, ask questions, and note observations about the stories (Salinger, 1999). If you share stories with children on a daily basis in the classroom, you will notice that children will develop an understanding of the characteristics and components of stories as well as an interest in reading.

Section 2.3   **TEACHING STRATEGY**
1

SIMPLE STORY ELEMENTS

The Simple Story Elements strategy helps children verbalize what they know about how stories are structured. This strategy focuses on the places, people and animals, and things that happen in a story (Johns & Lenski, 2005). This strategy will help children develop a foundation about the components all stories possess. After children understand this strategy, story mapping and other story element activities can be introduced.

DIRECTIONS

1. Select a familiar children's book with a clear, simple story line. A familiar story such as a fairy tale works well when introducing this strategy. If possible, select a story that all or at least most of the children already know.

2. Ask the children to tell you what they know or remember about the story. List these ideas on the chalkboard.

3. After the children have had a chance to share their ideas, group their responses into the following three columns on the chalkboard: places, people and animals, and things that happen. For example, if you were using *The Three Little Pigs,* the children might list the following ideas.

Places	People and Animals	Things That Happen
in the woods	three little pigs	Wolf blows down houses.
pigs' houses	Big Bad Wolf	

4. Explain to the children that all stories include information on the places, people and animals, and things that happen in the story. Go on to discuss that a story must have all of these parts.

5. Read the familiar story to the children. Ask them to listen carefully to see if the ideas listed on the chalkboard are correct or if changes need to be made. For example, if you were using *The Three Little Pigs,* the revised list might contain the ideas listed below.

Places	People and Animals	Things that Happen
in the woods	three little pigs	Wolf blows down straw house.
straw house	Big Bad Wolf	Wolf blows down wood house.
wood house		Wolf can't blow down brick house.
brick house		

6. Ask children to suggest ideas that need to be added, removed, or changed. Be sure to ask children to support and explain their responses.

7. Repeat this strategy with other stories, including stories that are new to children.

Section 2.3 *TEACHING STRATEGY*

2

PLOT RELATIONSHIPS CHART

The Plot Relationships Chart helps children understand and identify the major plot elements in fictional stories. This strategy uses the clue words *Somebody, Wanted, But,* and *So* to help children develop an understanding of how the main character, goal, problem, and solution of a story fit together (Schmidt & Buckley, 1991).

DIRECTIONS

1. Select a children's book that has clear plot elements: main character, goal, problem, and solution.

2. Read the story aloud to the children. Provide time for the children to discuss the story.

3. Place a blank copy of the Plot Relationships Chart on the chalkboard, an overhead transparency, or a piece of chart paper. A sample chart is provided below.

PLOT RELATIONSHIPS CHART

SOMEBODY	WANTED	BUT	SO

4. Tell the children they will be using the chart to learn about the important parts of stories and how they fit together.

5. Guide the children through identifying the main character of the story by asking them, "Who is the important *Somebody* that the story is about?" Discuss the children's responses and, when agreement is reached, write the main character's name in the *Somebody* column on the chart.

6. Use this pattern to guide the children through identifying and discussing the other plot elements.

7. Explain to children that all stories have these important parts. Provide additional opportunities to work with the Plot Relationships Chart and other stories. A modification of the Plot Relationships Chart is the Plot Relationships Frame. A sample frame is provided below. A reproducible of the Plot Relationships Frame can be found on page 62.

_____ wanted _____
              Somebody

but _____ so _____ .

Title ———————————————

Plot Relationships Chart

SOMEBODY	WANTED	BUT	SO

STORY STAR

The Story Star is a variation of a story map. Story maps provide visual representations of the major elements in a story. Story maps help children see and understand how the elements of a story fit together so they can understand what they are reading. There are many variations of story maps that can be used to help children develop an understanding of story elements, but those that have a simple format and focus on a limited number of elements are most appropriate for emergent and beginning readers. The Story Star is a very basic type of story map that is appropriate for use with young children.

DIRECTIONS

1. Select a children's book with a simple story line and clear story elements: main character, setting, events, problem, and solution.

2. Introduce the book to the children and invite them to make predictions about the book based on its title and cover illustration.

3. Read the book aloud to the children. Provide time for them to discuss the story and their personal reactions to it.

4. Display a blank Story Star on the chalkboard, an overhead transparency, or a piece of chart paper. Explain to the children that you will use the Story Star to identify the important parts of the story. A sample Story Star is provided below.

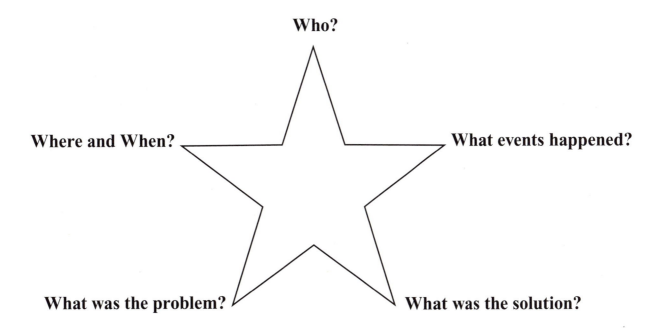

5. Begin with the main character from the story and ask the children, "Who was the story about?" Discuss their responses and explanations. Write the main character's name on the Story Star. If desired, a picture of the main character can also be added to this part of the Story Star.

Name _____ Date _____

Title _____

Story Star

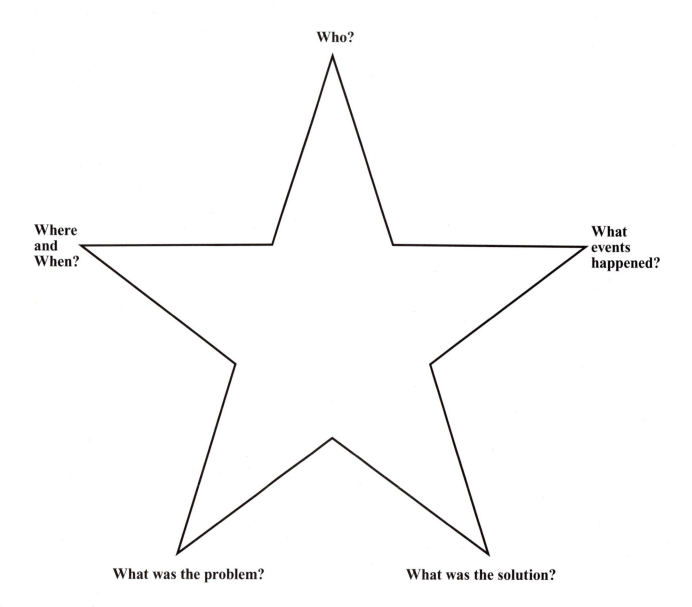

Who?

Where
and
When?

What
events
happened?

What was the problem?

What was the solution?

STORY FACES

Story Faces (Staal, 2000) are adaptations of story mapping that incorporate visual cues to help children remember the elements of story structure. Story Faces organize story elements with a graphic using two eyes, a nose, and a mouth. This graphic prompts children to remember each of the components of a story.

DIRECTIONS

1. Use one of the two Story Faces, the happy Story Face or the unhappy Story Face, or draw your own based on the examples that follow. The eyes should be circles with the terms *setting* and *characters* printed in them. The nose represents the *problem,* and the mouth represents the *events.*

2. Read a story to the children that has a clear setting, plot, and characters. Write the words *setting, plot, and characters* on an overhead transparency or on the chalkboard. Explain that the setting is the time and place of the story, the plot consists of a problem and events in sequence, and the main characters are who the story is about. Remind children that characters can be animals or people.

3. Tell children to listen for the setting, plot, and main characters as you read the story to them.

4. Duplicate one of the Story Faces that follow and distribute it to children. Choose the happy face if the story is a cheerful one or the unhappy face if the story is sad.

5. An example from *Lost in the Museum* (1979) by Miriam Cohen follows.

   What is the word in the left eye on this face? (Setting) Do you remember what the setting is? (Time or place of the story) What is the setting of the story *Lost in the Museum?* Write it in the circle for the left eye. Let's add some more details for eyelashes.

   Write the names of the main characters from the story in the right eye. Add some details for eyelashes.

   What problem did the main characters have? Write it in the place for the nose.

   What happened in the story? Let's write the events in the circles that make up the mouth.

   How did the story end? That idea should be in the last circle for the mouth where it says *Solution.*

Aa Bb Cc   Tips for English Language Learners

- Story structures are culturally developed and defined, so children from some cultures will not be familiar with stories as we know them. If children from other cultures have a difficult time understanding the structure of stories, provide lots of practice using Teaching Strategy 1 (Simple Story Elements) and Teaching Strategy 3 (Story Star). Allow children who have difficulty developing a sense of story to work in collaborative groups until they feel confident enough to work independently.

Happy Story Face

Name _____ Date _____

Book Title: _____

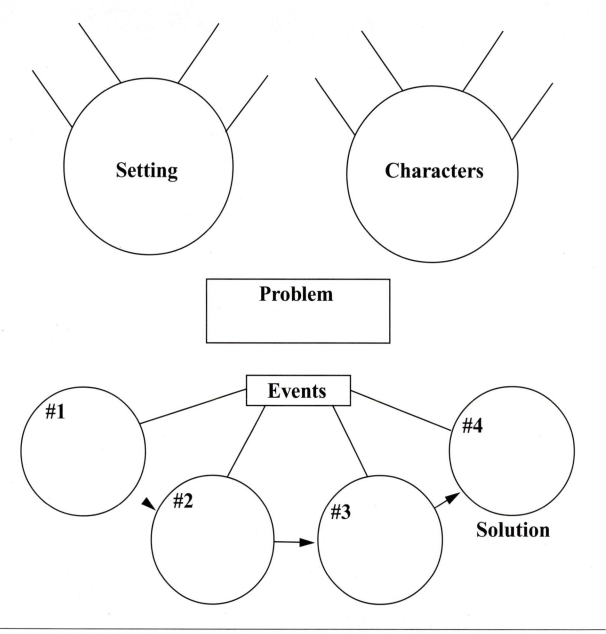

Setting

Characters

Problem

Events

#1

#2

#3

#4

Solution

Unhappy Story Face

Name _____ Date _____

Book Title: _____

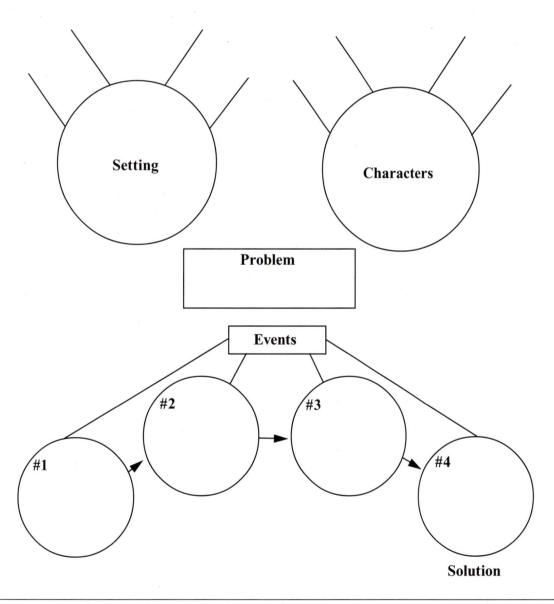

Setting

Characters

Problem

Events

#1   #2   #3   #4

Solution

INDEPENDENT READING

Children of all ages can learn about stories when they engage in independent reading (Strickland & Schickedanz, 2004). When children read books by themselves, even if they are only looking at the pictures, they learn that stories have a beginning, a middle, and an end. Children can also learn that stories follow a sequence of events as they read books on their own.

DIRECTIONS

1. Select a group of leveled books or picture books that are appropriate for independent reading for your children. Children do not have to be able to read every word on the page for them to benefit from the books, so include some books at higher reading levels as well as books that they can read.

2. Have children move to a comfortable place to read. Tell children that they can read at their desks or tables, on the floor, on the carpet, or in another comfortable location.

3. Place a timer in the front of the room. Tell children that they will be reading "on their own" for five to ten minutes. Explain to children that they will not be able to move from their location for those five to ten minutes.

4. Place a STOP sign or another signal in a visible place in the room cueing children that they will need to stay in their places as they read. Remind children not to talk with you during this time.

5. Allow children to select two to three books to read in their places. If children have difficulty selecting their own books, you may need to give books to them.

6. Tell children that they will be reading their books by themselves. Remind children to read quietly but do not discourage them from quietly saying words.

7. Review book handling skills with children if necessary. Show children how to open the books and how to turn the pages. If children do not need to be shown how to use books, continue to the next step.

8. Encourage children to fingerpoint as they read. Fingerpointing can help children follow the words throughout the book.

9. Tell children that they will be reading independently. Explain that the word "independent" means by themselves. Tell children that most adults read by themselves. You might want to give examples of situations when children have seen older children or adults reading independently.

10. Give children the time allowed to read independently.

11. After the time is up, have children talk about the stories that they have read. The discussion can be done in partners or as a whole group. Encourage children to retell their stories using their sense of stories by prompting them to provide a beginning, a middle, and an end.

12. Schedule independent reading daily and increase the time children read independently as they become familiar with the activity.

Activities, tips, & Center Ideas

1. Read to children on a daily basis. Expose them to a variety of good stories. During and after reading stories, provide time for children to ask questions, note observations, and discuss the stories. Place books you have read to the children in the classroom library so they can read and look at the books during their free time.

2. Use storytelling to expose children to stories and to develop a sense of story through oral language. Select a simple story and collect several props to help you tell the story. Provide time for discussion after telling the story. Encourage the children to retell the story to a classmate.

3. After reading a story with the children, invite small groups of children to retell the story using simple props, puppets, or a felt board. Place these materials in a classroom literacy center so children can engage in retelling activities during center time or their free time.

4. Have children complete simple story boards for the important elements of stories. For example, divide a piece of construction paper into four equal sections. Label the sections *Who, When, Where,* and *What.* Ask the children to draw and label *Who* the story was about, *When* the story took place, *Where* the story happened, and *What* the important events in the story were. Provide time for children to share and discuss their story boards. A sample story board format is provided below.

Who?	When?
Where?	What?

5. Invite children to use creative dramatics to act out favorite stories. If possible, supply simple props and costumes for children to use in their story dramas. Provide time for children to share their story dramas with other children.

6. Have children illustrate major events from a story. These illustrations can then be sequenced to match the events in the story. Stories such as Eric Carle's *The Very Hungry Caterpillar* (1969) work well for this type of story sequencing activity.

7. Provide access to a well-stocked classroom library so children can look at and read books on a daily basis. Schedule a daily time for children to read and discuss self-selected books.

8. Use wordless picture books to engage children in talking about the story and discussing the important components of the story. For a list of wordless picture books with clear, simple story lines, consult Johns and Lenski (2005).

9. Encourage parents to read stories to and with their children on a daily basis. Provide access to appropriate books by sharing books from the classroom and school libraries.

SHARING STORIES

Dear Families,

Sharing stories with your children will support their reading development. Here are some tips for sharing stories.

• When your children are watching television, ask them what the setting is for the story or who the main characters are. Remind children that television shows have some of the same elements that stories have.

• Encourage your children to tell stories to their siblings. Remind children to organize their stories in a sequence of events.

• Read to your children every day. When you read with your children, try these suggestions.

> Sit close and get comfortable. Make reading an enjoyable experience.
>
> Let your children choose the books you read so they will be interested in reading.
>
> Talk about the books you are reading with your children. Ask "thinking" questions such as:
>> "What is your favorite part and why?"
>> "What would you do in that situation and why?"
>> "What do you think will happen next and why?"

I hope you and your children enjoy sharing stories at home.

Sincerely,

---

section 2.4

Assessments of Literacy Knowledge

Goal: To assess the child's literacy knowledge.

Background

You can assess children's literacy knowledge through ongoing, informal observations during day-to-day classroom activities. However, sometimes in classroom situations you can't be sure how well certain children understand how print works. You may want to assess these children individually through an Assessment of Print Concepts, story retelling, or informational retelling. Harp (2000) suggests that you can use this type of assessment to verify your observations in the classroom. After you have reached conclusions about the child's literacy knowledge, you can tailor your instructional emphasis to meet the child's needs.

1

PRINT CONCEPTS

OVERVIEW	The Print Concepts assessment measures how well a child knows the components of a book. Children need to have adequate book handling skills before they will be able to read independently. For example, if a child doesn't understand that print is read from left to right, reading will be impossible. You, will find two types of Assessment of Print Concepts: one that includes a short text and one you can use with your choice of books. Both methods measure how well a child understands how books are read.
MATERIALS NEEDED	1. The book *Friends* (page 75) or *Animals* (on CD-ROM) 2. A pencil 3. A copy of the Print Concepts Record Sheet from page 87 that corresponds to the form selected for use
PROCEDURES	1. Tear out the short book, *Friends,* that follows, or use the book *Animals* found on the CD-ROM. Use a simple binding for the book. 2. Decide which book you want to use. Some teachers like to use Form 1 (*Friends*) at the beginning of the year and Form 2 (*Animals*) later in the year. 3. Show the book to the child. Say, "I'd like you to show me some of the things you know about reading. You won't have to read." Query the child with the statements on Form 1 (page 87) or Form 2 (on CD-ROM) as you read the book to the child. 4. Circle a plus (+) if the child gives the correct response and a minus (–) if the child gives an incorrect response. Total correct responses.
SCORING AND INTERPRETATION	Score the Print Concepts assessment by totaling the number of correct responses on the Record Sheet and by determining which types of questions were correct or incorrect. In additions, use the Qualitative Judgments of Print Concepts Record Sheet (p. 88) to interpret the assessment. First, determine the child's engagement-with the task. Decide how engaged the child was and place an X on the continuum from low engagement to high engagement. If the child scored low in this area, see Chapter 1 for ideas on ways to increase the child's motivation to read. Then use the child's scores on the assessment to decide how well the child understands print directionality, punctuation, uppercase and lowercase letters, knowledge of letters, knowledge of words, and ability to frame a sentence. There is no magic number that will tell you whether the child is secure in these areas or insecure. However, if a child misses even one of the questions, you should continue instruction in that area.

Additional Ways of Assessing Print Concepts

1. You can informally assess print concepts by watching children "read" during independent reading time. Notice whether the child holds the book rightside-up, whether pages are turned from right to left, and whether the child turns each page. If a child does not handle books with understanding, continue instruction in print concepts.

2. You can also assess print concepts in a one-on-one situation using a child's choice of books. To assess print concepts, use the following prompts.

   - Show me how to hold this book so I can read it.
   - Show me the front cover.
   - Show me the back cover.
   - Where would I begin reading this book?
   - Where are the words?
   - Where are the pictures?
   - Show me one word.
   - Show me the end of the book.

Note:

Remove and bind the following *Friends* booklet for use with Form 1 of the Print Concepts Assessment (Section 2.4).

Friends

by Dorie Cannon & Cheryl Mangione

It is Saturday.

Dog and Cat have

been waiting all

week for this day.

1

First they go running.

It makes them

feel good.

2

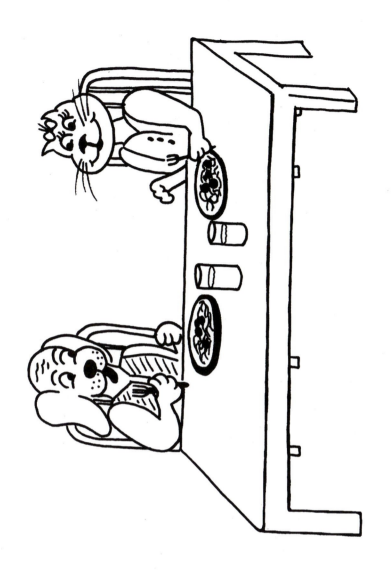

Wow, are they hungry now!

3

Dog and Cat go

to the park.

They like riding

their bikes.

They play ball.

This is fun!

Cat says, "Where can
we read? Let me see.

How about under
that tree?"

"Great idea," says Dog.

Cat and Dog sing.

They laugh.

Being friends is

a lot of fun.

It is time to go

home now.

8

It has been

a long day.

Dog and Cat are

very tired.

They are so happy!

The two friends

dream about what

will happen

tomorrow.

2.4 Print Concepts—"Friends"

Name _____ Date _____

Page

	+	–	1.	Hand the book to the child and say, "Show me the front of this book."
1	+	–	2.	Say, "Point to where I should start reading." *Read page 1.*
2	+	–	3.	Ask, "Which way should I go?" Check for knowledge of left to right. *Read first line of page 2.*
2/3	+	–	4.	Ask, "Where should I go after that?" Check for knowledge of a return sweep to the left. *Read rest of page 2 and page 3.*
3	+	–	5.	On page 3, point to the comma and ask, "What's this or what's this for?"
4	+	–	6.	*Read text on page 4.* Point to a period and ask, "What's this or what's this for?"
5	+	–	7.	*Read text on page 5.* Point to the exclamation mark and ask, "What's this or what's this for?"
6	+	–	8.	*Read text on page 6.* Point to the question mark and ask, "What's this or what's this for?"
6	+	–	9.	Point to a lowercase letter *(w, g, c)* and say, "Find a capital letter like this, find an uppercase letter like this, or find the big one like this."
7	+	–	10.	*Read text on page 7.* Say, "Show me one letter." (Two 3″ × 5″ cards may be useful for items 10–19.)
	+	–	11.	Say, "Show me two letters."
	+	–	12.	Say, "Show me only one word."
	+	–	13.	Say, "Show me two words."
	+	–	14.	Say, "Show me the first letter of a word."
	+	–	15.	Say, "Show me the last letter of a word."
	+	–	16.	Say, "Show me a long word."
	+	–	17.	Say, "Show me a short word."
	+	–	18.	Say, "Show me a sentence."
8/9	+	–	19.	*Read text on pages 8 and 9.* Point to a capital letter *(I, D, T)* and say, "Find a small letter like this or find a lowercase letter like this."
10	+	–	20.	*Read text on page 10.* Close the book and hand it to the child with the back cover showing and say, "Show me the title or show me the name of the book."

☐ Total Correct

Qualitative Judgments of Print Concepts

Name _____ Date _____

	Not Evident Low Seldom Weak Poor	Some	Evident High Always Strong Excellent
Overall engagement			
Understanding of print directionality			
Knowledge of punctuation			
Correspondence of uppercase and lowercase letters			
Knowledge of letter and letters			
Knowledge of word and words			
Ability to frame a sentence			

Observations, Comments, Notes, and Insights

chapter three

Phonemic Awareness and Phonics

Overview

Children learning to read are faced with books containing text. That text is composed of words that are made up of letters. Sounds can be associated with the letters and letter combinations to help decode or pronounce words that are not known at sight. The ability to decode words is a primary and critically important task for children in the beginning stages of reading. Although there has been debate and controversy about methods of beginning reading instruction over the years, there appears to be growing agreement that children profit from instruction in associating sounds with letters and letter combinations (Armbruster, Lehr, & Osborn, 2001). This instruction is referred to as phonics. Associated with phonics instruction are knowledge of letters, auditory discrimination, and phonemic awareness. This chapter contains various strategies for helping students learn to associate letters with sounds as well as ways to help them learn related skills. Strategies for assessment are included at the end of the chapter so you can assess areas of interest and target instruction to children's needs. Beginning on the next page are answers to some questions that will help you to better understand phonemic awareness, the alphabetic principle, and phonics.

Questions/Answers

Is learning the alphabet important for reading?

In a word, yes. Children "need to recognize letters and their distinguishing features in order to work effectively with print; learning the names of the letters is also very useful" (Graves, Juel, & Graves, 2001, p. 99). Over the years, reading professionals have generally accepted that children's knowledge of letters of the alphabet is an early predictor of later reading success (Adams, 1990). It has also been recognized that alphabet knowledge is generally a result of a literacy-rich environment where children have played with alphabet blocks and/or magnetic letters within a broader context of being read to and engaging in many natural and meaningful activities related to print. The fact that these experiences generally occur in the preschool years stresses the important role that parents play in their children's acquisition of literacy.

What is meant by the alphabetic principle?

Simply stated, children learning to read must develop an understanding of how sounds are represented by the letters of the alphabet. The alphabetic principle is "the understanding that there are systematic and predictable relationships between written letters and spoken sounds" (Armbruster, Lehr, & Osborn, 2001, p. 12). Stanovich (2000) notes that "this principle may be induced; it may be acquired through direct instruction; it may be acquired along with or after the buildup of a visually based sight vocabulary—but it must be acquired if a child is to progress successfully in reading" (p. 162). When phonics is taught, the alphabetic principle is developed.

I've been hearing a lot about phonemic awareness. What is it?

Phonemic awareness (PA) refers to the child's ability to focus on and manipulate phonemes in spoken words. Phonemes are the smallest units of spoken language that make a difference in the meaning of words, so phonemic awareness is the ability to manipulate these small units of sound. There are over 40 phonemes in English. Phonemic awareness tasks include phoneme identity (What sound is the same in *baby, bus,* and *ball?*), phoneme isolation (Tell me the first sound in *make*), phoneme blending (What word is /k/ /i/ /t/?), phoneme categorization (Which word does not belong? *cat, cup, rug*), phoneme segmentation (What are the sounds in dog? /d/ /o/ /g/), phonemic addition (What word do you have if you add /s/ to the beginning of top?), phoneme substitution (The word is cat. change the /t/ to /n/.) and phoneme deletion (What is *fill* without the /f/?). "The theoretical and practical importance of phonological [or phonemic] awareness for the beginning reader relies not only on logic but also on the results of several decades of empirical research" (Snow, Burns, & Griffin, 1998, p. 54). In a review of the research related to PA and reading achievement, the analysis revealed that PA training produced positive effects on both word reading and comprehension (National Reading Panel, 2000).

Phonics instruction seems to come and go. What's the latest on phonics?

As you probably know, phonics is a way of teaching beginning reading that stresses grapheme-phoneme relationships. Graphemes are letters and phonemes are sounds, so phonics is associating letters and sounds to help pronounce words. Effective reading programs have always had a phonics component. In more recent years, it has become clear that systematic phonics instruction "makes a bigger contribution to children's growth in reading than alternative programs providing unsystematic or no phonics instruction" (National Reading Panel, 2000, p. 2–92). There is not one right way that systematic phonics is taught; however, common characteristics include explicit instruction and a planned sequence of introducing the grapheme-phoneme relationships.

Why is phonics important in reading?

When most children come to school, they have a speaking vocabulary that numbers in the thousands of words. They can use and understand many different words, but these same children are typically able to recognize at sight only a small fraction of words in print. If children are taught to associate the sounds with the letters, they have a way to decode or pronounce words. Many of the words used in beginning reading instruction are probably familiar to children (because they have used them in daily conversations), and phonics provides a way for children to unlock or decode the words in print. When this process occurs, the child is likely to be able to relate the written word to a word already spoken or heard and construct a meaning from the text. As you can see, using sound-symbol relationships is one of the important cueing systems in reading.

Alphabet Knowledge

Goal: To help children learn the names of the letters of the alphabet.

Assessment Strategy 1 Alphabet Knowledge, page 132

Background

Children learn much about reading through oral language activities. They learn the sounds of the language and how words form sentences. Children can even read some familiar words before learning the individual letters of the alphabet. As children learn about written language, they learn that language is made up of sounds, words, and sentences. Consider the young child who can identify a stop sign without knowing the names of the individual letters. Environmental print such as a stop sign is familiar to children. When children see words repeatedly, they can learn the words, even though they don't know the names of the letters in the words.

As children learn about the nature of language, however, they need to be directed to learn the names of the letters of the alphabet and to distinguish one letter from another. Learning the names of the letters of the alphabet is a developmental process. Letter names have little meaning to children before they possess some knowledge about language (Morrow, 2001). Adams (1990) concluded that "the best predictor of beginning reading achievement is a child's knowledge of letter names (p. 61.)

Children need to know the letters of the alphabet to become independent readers (Ehri, 1987). As children progress beyond becoming aware of the sounds of language, such as rhyming words, they need to be able to distinguish among the letters so that they can learn how to read unknown words. It is unrealistic to think that a young reader could learn enough sight words to be able to read a new story. Therefore, children need to learn that words are made up of letters, and they need to learn the names of the letters of the alphabet.

There are many approaches to teaching the alphabet. Some teachers introduce a letter a week throughout the school year. Others teach letters in the context of words and stories. There is not one right way to teach the alphabet, although some experts believe that teaching the letters of the alphabet in context is more meaningful for children (Morrow, 2001). The following teaching strategies, activities, and ideas will assist you with teaching the letters of the alphabet.

ALPHABET SONG

The Alphabet Song has been used in many homes and classrooms for years. It is a song known by many children and is a very natural and meaningful way to help children learn the alphabet.

DIRECTIONS

1. Secure a recording of the Alphabet Song. It is typically sung to the tune of *Twinkle, Twinkle, Little Star.* Tell children that you will help them learn the Alphabet Song. A number of children may say that they already know it, so encourage them to sing along.

2. Sing the Alphabet Song and encourage children who know the song to teach it to other children. Children can be asked to stand when the letter that begins their first (or last) name is sung.

3. Because the Alphabet Song is learned by repeated singing, make the connection to the printed letters above the chalkboard or on a wall chart. Point to the letters as the song is sung and then invite a child to point to the letters with you.

4. Make individual letter cards and randomly pass them out to children. Sing the Alphabet Song slowly and have a child stand as that letter is sung.

5. Distribute a letter card to each child and have the children line up as the Alphabet Song is sung slowly.

6. Have children sing the Alphabet Song in those few moments while waiting for the bell to excuse the class or at other times where there is a minute available before an activity begins.

7. Share the book *Letters and Sounds* by R. Wells (2001). Included with the book is an audiotape containing the Alphabet Song and other activities.

USING ALPHABET BOOKS

Alphabet books are books that have letters arranged in sequential order from A through Z. There are many attractive alphabet books available on a large number of topics (see Johns & Lenski, 2005). Reading alphabet books to children helps them become familiar with the names of the letters in alphabetical order. Alphabet books also provide a wide range of words that start with each letter in the alphabet, which helps children learn how to associate a letter with a number of words.

DIRECTIONS

1. Choose an alphabet book to read to children. Most libraries have a large collection of alphabet books. For a listing of over 100 alphabet books, refer to Johns and Lenski (2005).

2. Show the children the cover of the book and read the title to them. Tell them that this book will have the letters of the alphabet and that it will be about a specific topic. Tell them what the topic of the book is. For example, *Alphabears* (Hague, 1984) is a book that shows different bears with names that begin with the letters of the alphabet in alphabetical order.

3. Before reading, invite children to recite the letters of the alphabet with you.

4. Read the alphabet book, making note of any special features. Point out that each page has a letter of the alphabet in alphabetical order.

5. After reading the book, have children recite the letters of the alphabet in order. Provide assistance as needed.

6. After reading the book several times, have children read along with you.

7. Tape-record the book and place the book and the tape in a listening center for children to listen to during free time.

Aa Bb Cc | Tips for English Language Learners

- Help children learn to recognize the letters in their names. Relate these letters to the alphabet in your classroom.

- As you sing the Alphabet Song, pair a child learning English with another child who already knows the song.

- Send home a recording of the Alphabet Song and an easy-to-use tape player. Encourage the child and his or her parents to sing along.

- Obtain simple alphabet books containing familiar illustrations that the child is likely to recognize. Invite the child to take the book home and share it. Simple and clear illustrations can also help the child learn words.

Section 3.1   *TEACHING STRATEGY*   **3**

LETTER ACTIONS

Young children tend to be very active, so the strategy Letter Actions (Cunningham, 2005) has great appeal for most children. The strategy Letter Actions entails identifying an action word that begins with a specific letter and associating that letter with the action. When children are able to associate an action with the name of a letter, they more readily learn the letters of the alphabet.

DIRECTIONS

1. Identify the name of a letter that you want to teach. Write the name of a letter on one side of a large index card.

2. For each letter, think of an action that children could perform in your classroom or outside. List the action on the reverse side of the index card. For example, if you wanted to teach the letter *n,* you could write *nod* on the reverse side of the card.

3. Show the children the side of the card that has the name of the letter written on it. Say the name of the letter. Have the children repeat the letter name.

4. Tell the children that they will be performing an action that begins with that letter. Show them the side of the card with the action written on it. Read the action.

5. Have the children perform the action while saying the name of the letter. Reinforce the association by repeating the same action card more than once.

6. After the children have learned several letters and actions, have a child choose a card and lead the class in performing the action.

7. The following is a sample list of actions that can be used in conjunction with Letter Actions.

argue	fall	kick	paint	unbend
bounce	gallop	laugh	quack	vacuum
catch	hop	march	run	walk
dance	itch	nod	sit	xylophone (play)
eat	jump	open	talk	yawn
				zip

Section 3.1 **TEACHING STRATEGY**

IDENTIFYING LETTERS

Children need to learn the letters of the alphabet in proper order, and they also need to learn how to identify letters in the context of words. Some children will have difficulty making the link from saying the letters of the alphabet to identifying letters in combination with other letters to form words. To help them learn letters in the context of words, point out letters in Big Books, the Morning Message, or their names. Guiding children to identify letters in print will help them learn how to read.

DIRECTIONS

1. Choose a story, Morning Message, or one of the children's names to teach children how to identify letters. The story can be one that you read to the children, a dictated story, or a Big Book with which the children are familiar. Be sure the material is large enough for all children to see.

2. Read the story, message, or name aloud to the children. Then have the children read it with you.

3. Place several letter cards on the table in front of you. Have a child choose a letter from the stack.

4. Have the child identify the letter. If the letter is a *d,* for example, the child should say *d.*

5. Ask the children to locate any letter in the story that matches the letter chosen by the child. In this case, children should look for the letter *d.* Have one child at a time come up to point out examples of the letter in the story. If the story does not have that particular letter, the child should replace the letter in the stack and choose another letter.

6. Repeat until all of the letters in the stack have been chosen.

7. Do this activity regularly so children are able to identify the letters easily.

Section 3.1 **TEACHING STRATEGY**

ALPHABET SCRAPBOOKS

Children learn about letters as they have repeated opportunities to identify, discuss, read, and write them (Bear, Invernizzi, Templeton, & Johnston, 2004). An ongoing activity that helps children learn letters and connect them to words is making alphabet scrapbooks. In this activity, children create a page for each letter of the alphabet by writing the letter, drawing pictures, and cutting and pasting photos of things that begin with the letter. For children who are more advanced in letter knowledge (or as the school year progresses), they can also write high-frequency words that begin with the target letter. The alphabet scrapbook can also be used as a resource—a type of picture dictionary—as children read and write.

✎ DIRECTIONS

1. Prepare a blank scrapbook for each child by stapling or comb-binding together 14 sheets of heavy construction paper or card stock. This scrapbook will allow one page for each letter as well as a front and back cover.

2. As you teach and review specific letters, have children complete the corresponding page in their alphabet scrapbook.

3. For the first alphabet scrapbook page, model the process for children. For example, for the letter *m* you might say the following.

   > I am going to make the *m* page for my alphabet scrapbook. First, I'm going to write a capital *M* and a lower case *m* at the top of the page. Next, I'm going to think of things I can draw that start with the letter m. Let's see, I can draw a monkey and a man. In this magazine, I see a picture of a muffin so I'll cut that out and use my glue stick to add it to the page. I wonder if I know any words that I can write that begin with the letter m. Oh yes, I know how to write *my* and *mom*. I'll add those to my alphabet scrapbook page.

4. Provide children with markers, magazines, scissors, and glue sticks to complete their scrapbook page.

5. As children complete a page in their alphabet scrapbook, provide time for them to share and discuss the letter and the pictures and words they included on their page.

6. Provide time for children to review pages they previously completed in their alphabet scrapbooks as a way of reinforcing their alphabet knowledge.

Activities, tips, & Center Ideas

1. Create an alphabet center in your classroom. Stock the center with plastic letters for word building, letters to trace, alphabet puzzles and games, alphabet books, alphabet stamps, and alphabet flash cards. Allow children time to use the materials in the center on a regular basis.

2. Place a layer of sand or salt in a small container. Have children trace the letters of the alphabet in the sand or salt.

3. Play Letter Bingo. Give each child a card filled with letters of the alphabet and markers to cover the letters. Call a letter and hold up a card with the letter on it. Have children find the letter on their Bingo cards. The first child to cover a row gets Bingo.

4. Create an alphabet path on the floor of your room. Write each letter of the alphabet on a large piece of construction paper. Laminate the pieces of paper, randomly arrange them around your room, and tape them to the floor. Have students walk on the alphabet path saying the letters of the alphabet as they walk.

5. Distribute letter cards to each child. Give each child one card. Call out a letter. Ask the child holding that letter to stand and repeat the name of the letter. Then ask children to say a word that begins with that letter.

6. Provide the children with letter snacks. As you introduce a letter, give children a snack whose name begins with that letter. For example, when you teach the letter *a*, provide each child with a piece of apple.

7. Place a handful of alphabet cereal on a napkin on each child's desk. Have the children sort the cereal letters in alphabetical order. Give children plain round or square cereal to mark the place of letters that are not in the cereal pile. Tell children that if they have more than one of the same letter, they should place the duplicate letters in a row.

8. Write a letter on the chalkboard with a wet sponge or paintbrush. Have children call out the name of the letter before the water evaporates and the letter disappears. Children can also practice writing particular letters with a wet sponge or paintbrush on the chalkboard or on small slates.

9. Distribute copies of newspapers or pages from magazines to each child. Identify a letter and have children circle the letter or use a highlighter marker to show where they find it on a page.

10. Spell out a child's name with letter cards or plastic letters. Use all uppercase letters. Have the child use lowercase letters to match the uppercase letters. Scramble the top row and have the child unscramble the letters to form the correct spelling of the name.

11. Create letter posters by brainstorming words that start with a specific letter. After introducing a letter, have children think of words that start with that letter. If children are unable to correctly identify words beginning with that letter, provide several words for them. Write the words with different color markers or crayons. Display the posters in the classroom or bind them into a class alphabet book.

12. Place a set of five to seven pairs of letter cards face down on a table. You should have two cards for each letter. Have children turn over two cards at a time saying the names of the letters. If the cards match, children keep them. If the cards do not match, have children replace the cards. The object is to match pairs of alphabet cards.

ALPHABET BOOKS

Dear Families,

Learning the alphabet is an important step in becoming a reader. Alphabet books are a great way to help your children learn their ABCs.

Here is a list of alphabet books you and your children may enjoy reading together. As you share alphabet books with your children, be sure to talk about the letters, words, and pictures. You can also find other alphabet books at the library or in bookstores.

- *Alphabet Adventure* (2001) by Audrey Wood
- *Alphabet Under Construction* (2002) by Denise Fleming
- *Arf! Beg! Catch! Dogs from A to Z* (1999) by Henry Horenstein
- *Kipper's A to Z* (2001) by Mick Inkpen
- *Maisy 's ABC* (1995) by Lucy Cousins
- *My Pop-up Surprise ABC* (1996) by Robert Crowther

Your children may also enjoy making an alphabet book with you. To make an alphabet book, you can take a stack of 13 pieces of paper. You can staple or use a hole punch and yarn or string to fasten the book together.

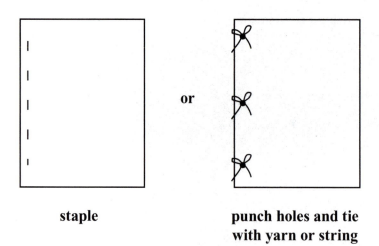

staple

or

punch holes and tie
with yarn or string

page 1

On each page write a capital and lower case letter.

Use pictures from magazines or draw pictures for each letter of the alphabet. It may take you and your children a week or more to make the alphabet book. Read the alphabet book with your children often to practice their "ABCs."

I hope you and your children enjoy these alphabet book activities.

Sincerely,

page 2

section 3.2

Phonemic Awareness

> **Goal:** To help children become aware of the sounds in spoken words.
>
> **Assessment Strategy 2** Rhyme Detection, page 138
>
> **Assessment Strategy 3** Phoneme Segmentation, page 141
>
> **Assessment Strategy 4** Phoneme Deletion and Substitution, page 144

Background

Phonemic awareness is the ability to notice, think about, and manipulate sounds in spoken words. Children who have phonemic awareness skills are able to recognize when words rhyme, can hear isolated sounds of words, can segment words into their sounds, and can blend the sounds together into words. Phonemic awareness is strongly related to success in reading and is a powerful predictor of reading achievement (Adams, 1990; National Reading Panel, 2000). In order to benefit from phonics instruction, students require a basic level of phonemic awareness (Ehri & Nunes, 2002). However, some children do not learn on their own how sounds form words.

Because phonemic awareness is the ability to hear the sounds in words, phonemic awareness activities generally should precede formal instruction in phonics. Children who are unable to identify words that rhyme, for example, may be hindered in learning the sound-symbol relationships that are a foundation of phonics instruction. In addition, children who do not understand that words are made up of sounds can often profit from instruction in phonemic awareness.

Researchers Schatschneider, Francis, Foorman, Fletcher, and Mehta (1999) identified a hierarchy of phonemic awareness skills. Based on this study, a review by Stahl (2001), and our work with teachers, the following list of skills is arranged in order from easy (1) to difficult (6).

1. Rhyming as a foundation for phonemic awareness tasks,
2. Identifying the names of pictures beginning with the same first sound,
3. Blending onset-rime units (e.g., /t/ in) into words (e.g., tin),
4. Blending sounds (phonemes) into words,
5. Deleting a sound (phoneme) and saying the word that remains, and
6. Segmenting words into sounds (phonemes).

The activities that are necessary to teach children how to become aware of the sounds in language may not seem like real teaching. Instead, they may just seem like fun. However, these types of activities are appropriate and necessary for children to learn how to decode words and read independently. When you provide children with instruction in phonemic awareness skills, they will most likely improve their ability to hear sounds in words, which is a foundation for later reading development (Gillam & van Kleeck, 1996).

The teaching strategies, activities, and ideas that follow emphasize oral language activities that support phonemic awareness. As you teach children how to hear the sounds in our language, you should be aware of children's progress. Through informal assessment, you can judge whether children are able to hear sounds and rhymes. As you notice children's proficiency in hearing rhymes, sounds in isolation, and blended sounds, you can teach transition strategies that emphasize sounds but begin to introduce letters. Be sure that your phonemic awareness instruction is appropriate to the children's level of literacy development. After you introduce letters with phonemic awareness activities, you can start the teaching of phonics so that children will begin to associate letters with sounds.

Section 3.2   *TEACHING STRATEGY*

I SPY RHYMES

One of the foundational skills for establishing how language works is the ability to identify rhyming words. Being able to hear word rhymes helps children develop an understanding that word families can represent the same sound in different words. The strategy I Spy Rhymes helps children listen for and identify rhyming words.

DIRECTIONS

1. Read a book or poem aloud that contains several rhyming words. Tell children that they should be listening for words that rhyme. Remind children that rhyming words will sound alike. Say a rhyming word pair such as *bike* and *like*. Tell children that *bike* and *like* rhyme because they have the same ending sound.

2. Reread the story or poem. Draw children's attention to the words that rhyme.

3. Read a second story or poem. Tell children that when they hear a rhyming word pair, they should stand and say, "I spy _____ and _____ ." The children should say the rhyming word pair as in "I spy *bike* and *like*."

4. Most stories or poems that you read will have several different rhyming words. Allow children to say all of the rhymes. If they miss some, reread the story or poem emphasizing the rhymes that were not heard.

5. Repeat the activity several times each week until the children are able to identify rhyming words easily.

Section 3.2   *TEACHING STRATEGY*   2

FIRST SOUNDS

The First Sounds strategy helps children identify pictures that begin with the same sounds. This is a type of phoneme isolation task that helps children recognize the beginning sounds in words. It also helps children develop phoneme identity (recognizing same sound in different words) and phoneme categorization (recognizing a word in a group that begins with a different sound). It is one of the easier phoneme awareness tasks, and children find it fun. First Sounds will help children understand that words have sounds as well as meanings (National Reading Panel, 2000). Using pictures also makes the task more concrete for beginning readers.

✎ DIRECTIONS

1. Obtain three objects. The names of two of the objects should begin with the same sound. For example, you may select a bag, a bat that is used to play ball, and a toy car.

2. Tell children that you want them to use their eyes and ears for this activity. Have them look at the bag and tell you what it is. Ask children to listen to the first sound in the word *bag*. Stress the beginning sound as you say *bbbag*. Be sure children understand the task. You could also have children note how they form their lips to say the word.

3. Hold up the toy car and have children name it. Then ask them to listen to the first sound as you say the word emphasizing the first sound. Repeat the instruction in step 2.

4. Hold up the two objects and have the children name each object. Then ask, "Do the words begin with the same first sound?" Say the words slowly, stressing the first sound in each word. Then say something like, "You must have listened carefully. The two words do not begin with the same sound." If necessary, have the children note how they formed their mouths to say each word.

5. Hold up the bat and ask children to name it. Have them listen to the first sound as you slowly say *bbbat*. Then invite children to close their eyes and listen carefully as you say two words (e.g., bat and bag). Ask, "Do *bat* and *bag* begin with the same first sound? Raise your hand if they do." Reinforce correct responses and then hold up both objects, name them, and say that they begin with the same first sound.

6. Then select the toy car and ask the children to name it. Compare it to the first sound of bag and help children realize that the two words begin with different first sounds. Repeat this process with the car and the bat.

7. Place the three objects on a table. Review first sounds in the words. Have the children decide which objects begin with the same first sound. The remaining object (car) is "out" because it does not begin with the same first sound as the other two words.

8. Extend the lesson by using other objects or pictures in the classroom (e.g., book, desk, boy) to help solidify the concept of first sounds in words.

9. To provide additional teaching or practice opportunities, enlarge the pictures that follow. In each row of pictures, two of them begin with the same sound.

Aa Bb Cc — Tips for English Language Learners

- When selecting pictures to use for instruction, try to find those that will be common to the experiences of English Language Learners. You could also ask the child to name the picture in his or her language and then compare it to the English word to determine if the words begin with the same first sound.

- Some English Language Learners may find it difficult to make or hear some of the sounds in English. For example, native speakers of Spanish may have problems with the sounds for *b, d, h, j, m, n, r, t, th, v, w,* and *y.* Speakers of Cantonese may have difficulty with the sounds associated with *th, s, n,* and *r* (Johns & Lenski, 2005). Be patient and supportive as children learn some of the unique sounds in English.

Section 3.2 **TEACHING STRATEGY** 3

SOUND BOXES

Sound Boxes help children segment the sounds in a word. Sound Boxes were originally developed by Elkonin (1973) and can be used to help young children develop phonemic awareness. When children use Sound Boxes, they learn that words are made up of phonemes, or sounds, and that most words contain more than one sound.

DIRECTIONS

1. Select words that are familiar to the children. Prepare cards with simple illustrations along with a matrix that contains a box for each sound in the word. Note that the boxes represent each sound, not necessarily each letter. Secure sufficient counters (plastic chips, pennies, or beans) for each child. An example of a picture with sound boxes follows.

2. Slowly say the word represented by the picture and push the counters one sound at a time into the boxes. Model the process a second time. Invite the children to say the word as you move the counters. For example, if you are using the sound box for the word duck, say the word and then the sounds as in this example: "Duck. /d/ /u/ /k/." As you say the first sound, /d/, move a counter into the first box. Then say /u/ and move a second counter into the second box. Finally, say the sound /k/ and move the counter into the third box. Remember to say the sounds, not the letters, of the word.

3. Provide another example and begin to transfer the responsibility of identifying the sounds to the children. Encourage children to identify the picture and to pronounce the word carefully and deliberately. The goal is to emphasize each sound without distorting the word and to put a counter in each box while saying each sound.

4. After children have learned how to use sound boxes, eliminate the boxes below the pictures and have children move the sound counters to the bottom of the picture.

5. Pictures with sound boxes are provided on pages 108–109 for additional teaching examples or practice activities.

Section 3.2 *TEACHING STRATEGY*

PUT IT TOGETHER

Children who are able to sound out words successfully are usually able to blend the sounds associated with the letters into a word. Blending sounds is one of the components of phonemic awareness and is an important skill for beginning readers (Ericson & Juliebo, 1998). The strategy Put It Together helps children learn how to blend sounds into words.

DIRECTIONS

1. Explain that you will be saying a word by its sounds. If you have a puppet available, say that the puppet only likes to say whole words. Tell children that you will be saying the sounds of the word and that the puppet will say the whole word.

2. Tell children to listen carefully as you say the sounds of the word. Then say the sounds of a word such as /l/ /u/ /n/ /ch/ for the word *lunch*. Have the children put the word together by blending the sounds into a whole word. If the children say the word correctly, have the puppet repeat the word.

3. After children are able to blend sounds, try the strategy with other words.

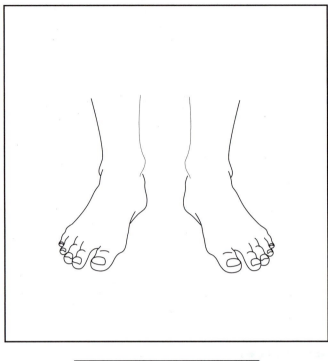

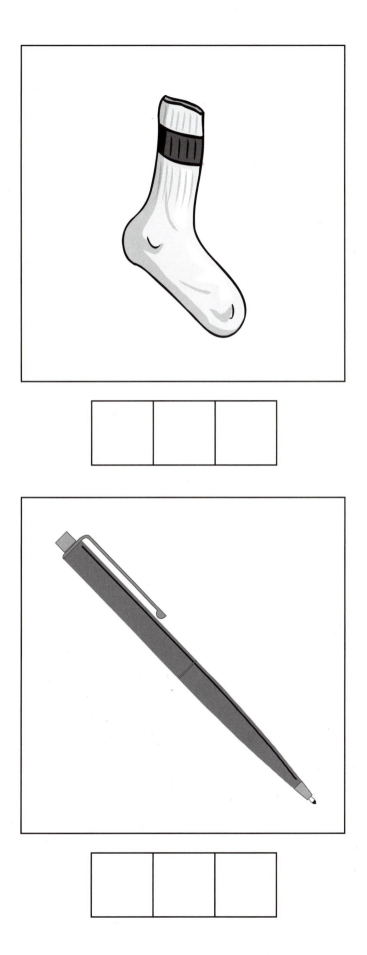

5

ADD A SOUND

Phoneme addition is the ability to make a new word by adding a phoneme to a word (Armbruster, Lehr, & Osborn, 2001). This task requires children to focus closely on spoken words and to blend a phoneme with an existing word. While this task is one of the more difficult phonemic awareness skills, it can be taught to children by using oral games and activities such as the Add a Sound Strategy (Adams, Foorman, Lundberg, & Beeler, 1998).

DIRECTIONS

1. Ask the children to sit on the floor in front of you. Explain to them that sometimes a new word can be made by adding a sound to a word. As an example, you might say the following.

   I have the word *at* and I want to add the sound /p/. *p-p-p . . . at, p-p-p . . . at. PAT.* The new word is *pat.* We put a new sound on the beginning of at and made the new word *pat.*

2. Continue this process asking the children to say the new sound and word parts with you in unison to provide ample practice. For example, you might say the following.

   I have the word *ox.* Say the word *ox* with me. Ox. I want to add the beginning sound /b/ to *ox.* Say the sounds with me, *b-b-b- . . . ox, b-b-b- . . . ox.* What's the new word? *Box!* Now suppose I want to add the beginning sound /f/ to *ox.* What's the new word? Let's say the sounds: *f-f-f- . . . ox, f-f-f- . . . ox.* The new word is *fox.*

3. Repeat the strategy with other words focused on beginning phoneme addition until the children are able to complete the task easily.

4. When children are able to consistently add beginning sounds, move to doing the activity with ending sound additions such as *hat* + /s/ = *hats, ban* + /d/ = *band, bee* + /t/ = *beet, he* + /t/ = *heat, so* + /p/ = *soap,* and *car* /t/ = *cart.*

SOUND BITES

The ability to recognize the word that remains when a phoneme is removed is called phoneme deletion (Armbruster, Lehr, & Osborn, 2001). This type of phoneme manipulation is one of the more difficult phonemic awareness tasks, but it can be taught to children using simple activities and game such as the Sound Bites strategy (Lane & Pullen, 2004) described below.

DIRECTIONS

1. Select a puppet and give it an alliterative name such as Tom Tiger.

2. Explain to the children that the puppet will take sound bites out of words to match the beginning sound of its name.

3. Demonstrate by saying the following.

   This puppet is named Tom Tiger. He loves to bite the /t/ out of words. I have a word *tan,* but Tom bit out the /t/. What word do I have left? The word I have left is *an.*

4. Continue with other words such as *trip* (rip), *trot* (rot), and *table* (able).

5. Repeat the Sound Bites activity with other puppets to focus on target letters such as Leo Lion who bites out the /l/ in words or Marty Monkey who bites out the /m/ in words.

6. As children are able to complete this task easily with beginning sound deletions, move to deleting ending sounds which is more difficult.

7. If you wish to focus on all beginning sounds rather than targeting a single sound for deletion, you may select a puppet such as Beginning Bunny who takes a sound bite off the beginning of each word such as *slip* (lip), *cat* (at), and *bring* (ring). For ending sounds you could use a puppet called Ending Eagle who takes a sound bite off the ending sound of each word such as *cart* (car), *stars* (star), and *teacher* (teach).

Section 3.2 *TEACHING STRATEGY*

BREAK AND MAKE

Another phonemic awareness component is the ability to manipulate sounds by substituting one sound for another in a word. The strategy Break and Make gives children practice making new words from an initial word and hearing the difference between the words. Children are asked to break up a word and make a new word. As children break and make words, they hear the sounds in word families. You can use letter tiles with the Break and Make strategy if the children are ready to begin the transition from hearing sounds in words to understanding that the sounds they hear are associated with letters. In this activity, however, emphasize sound substitution, not the letter-sound correspondence.

DIRECTIONS

1. Select a word from a word family that has easily identifiable sounds. (You can find word families in Appendix B on the CD-ROM.) Write the word on the chalkboard, a piece of chart paper, or an overhead transparency. Then form the word with manipulatives such as letter cards or tiles. Display the word for the children.

2. Read the word aloud. Say the word slowly and deliberately. Then have the children say the word with you. Repeat the word several times.

3. Tell children that you will make a new word from the first word by changing one letter. Break the word apart by moving the letter cards or tiles. Replace a letter from the word. For example, if your first word was *book* and you changed the first letter to *l,* you would have the word *look.* To explain the process to the children, you might say, "The word is *book.* If I change /b/ to /l/ the new word is *look.* If the first word was *can* and you changed the last letter to *t,* the new word would be *cat.*" Say the words as you change them. Have the children say the new words with you. Explain that some words are different only in one sound and that children need to listen to words carefully to distinguish between the sounds in words.

4. Invite children to participate in the Break and Make strategy using various word families.

Activities, tips, & Center Ideas to Develop Rhyme

1. Read rhyming books or nursery rhymes to children every day. Reread many of the children's favorites several times. As children become familiar with specific rhymes, have them say the rhymes along with you as you read. From time to time, stop reading before the last word in a rhyming line and have children supply the rhyming word.

2. Call on children whose names have many rhyming words such as *Mike* and *Pam.* Say a word that rhymes with one of the names. Have children repeat the word along with the name that rhymes with it as in *Mike* and *spike* and *Pam* and *ram.*

3. Tell children that you are going to say three rhyming words. Say three words that rhyme such as *run, fun,* and *bun.* Tell children that you want them to listen carefully to the words and then think of more words that rhyme with the words that you said. For example, children could say the words *sun* and *spun.* If children make up a word, tell them that they need to think of words that everyone knows. Repeat this activity several times each week with different rhyming words.

4. Help children hear the difference between words that rhyme and words that do not rhyme. Say three words, two of which rhyme. For example, say *sail, mail,* and *made.* Have children say the three words with you. Then ask children which two words rhyme.

5. Sing or chant songs that contain rhyming words. Some songs that work well are *Five Little Monkeys, The Wheels on The Bus, The Name Game, A Hunting We Will Go, This Old Man,* and *The Ants Go Marching.* Sing or chant songs several times a day. After singing, point out some of the rhyming words.

6. Have a group of children act out their favorite nursery rhyme. Have the other children guess the name of the rhyme. Then have all of the children say the rhyme aloud.

7. Say a word that has many rhyming words such as *day.* Have children brainstorm words that rhyme with the original word such as *may, say, ray,* and *pay.* When possible, have children draw pictures of several of the words that rhyme with the original word.

8. Have children create silly rhyming names for characters in their favorite books or for their pets. For example, Clifford the Big Red Dog could be named Bifford. Encourage children to have fun with rhymes.

9. Have children sit in a circle. Say a rhyming word such as *spin.* Throw a soft ball to one of the children. The child who catches the ball should say a word that rhymes with *spin* such as *win.* That child should toss the ball to another child or back to you. The person who has the ball should think of another rhyme. Continue until no one can think of additional words that rhyme with the original word. Then begin with a new word.

10. Gather pairs of objects or pictures of objects whose names rhyme. Place the objects in a bag and have a child pick an object without looking. A second child also picks an object and decides if the names of the objects rhyme. If they rhyme, two new children are chosen. If the words do not rhyme, another child picks an object and decides if it rhymes with either of the words. Continue the process until all objects have been paired correctly.

11. Provide pictures and/or objects that rhyme and have children sort them into groups that rhyme. Begin, if possible, with actual objects.

12. Read a rhyming couplet and have children supply the missing word.

    If you are *bad,* mom will be _____ .

    If you see a *bee,* get me a cup of _____ .

    I saw a *rat;* you saw a _____ .

Activities, tips, & Center Ideas for Sound Blending

1. Tell the children that you are thinking of an animal. Give them a sound clue, segmenting each of the sounds of the word and saying the sounds slowly and deliberately. If the animal is a wolf, for example, say the sounds /w/ /o/ /l/ /f/. Ask children to blend the sounds together to tell you the name of the animal. Then repeat the process with the name of another animal.

2. Collect pictures from magazines that have a subject that is identifiable to children. For example, a picture of a dog would be one that children could identify. Cut the picture into the number of sounds in the word. For example, cut the picture of the dog into three pieces. Have children put the picture puzzle together saying the sounds of the subject of the picture.

3. Tell children that you will be saying the sounds of a word and they will need to guess the word and draw a picture of it. Give children paper and crayons. Then say a word that can easily be drawn such as *bat*. Say the sounds in the word *bat*, /b/ /a/ /t/. Have children say the word and then draw a bat. Repeat this activity with other words.

4. When you have an extra minute between activities or when your class is lining up to leave the room, say the sounds of a word that you have used during class. If you have been discussing wind in a lesson on the weather, for example, say the sounds /w/ /i/ /n/ /d/. Have the children blend the sounds to form the word *wind*.

5. Sing or chant songs that could be adapted as a blending activity. For example, adapt the song *Bingo* (Ericson & Juliebo, 1998). Sing or chant the song using the sounds of the child's name. Then repeat the name you used in the song. Tell children that the sounds can be put together to make a name. Repeat with another child's name. An example of the song follows.

   There was a teacher

   who had a student

   And Maria was her name

   /M/ /ar/ /i/ /a/, /M/ /ar/ /i/ /a/, /M/ /ar/ /i/ /a/

   And Maria was her name.

6. Say word parts of compound words such as *base* and *ball* for *baseball*. Have two children stand in front of the room. Tell the children that baseball has two word parts. Have the first child say the first word, *base,* and the second child say the second word, *ball*. Tell children that some words have two words in them and that they should listen for words within other words.

7. Place several objects in a bag or a box. Select one object. Say the name of the object and say, "I see a carrot." Say the word in its syllables or individual sounds. Have the children blend the sounds of the word together and say the word.

8. Take a large rubber band and stretch it. Tell children that you want them to stretch a word. Say a word slowly as you stretch the rubber band. Then have children pretend to stretch a rubber band as they stretch words with you.

Activities, tips, & Center Ideas for Sound Isolation

1. Ask children to listen to you saying three words: *kite, kitten,* and *Ken.* Tell children that these words begin with the same sound, the sound /k/. Tell children that you will be saying three more words and that they should listen for the beginning sound. Say three more words and have children tell you the sound that they hear. As children become proficient at hearing beginning sounds, repeat the activity using ending sounds.

2. Tell children that you will be saying a sound and that they should think of as many words that begin (or end) with that sound as they can. Say a sound (not a letter) such as /s/ for the letter *s*. Have children think of words that begin with that sound.

3. Say a child's name. Have the children repeat the name with you clapping the number of syllables. For example, say the name *Kristen.* Clap two times, one for each syllable. Say the names of other children who have two-syllable names. Have children clap with you as you say the names. Repeat with names of one syllable, two syllables, and so on.

4. Say words that have parts that are the same or different such as the words *ball* and *tall.* Have children say the words with you. Ask children which parts of the words are the same and which parts are different. Guide children to understand that the sounds /b/ and /t/ are different but the sound /all/ is the same in both words. Repeat using other pairs of words.

5. Read books of rhymes to children. After reading, say two of the rhyming words. Have children say the rhyming words with you several times. After children have said the rhymes, ask them which of the sounds are alike in the rhymes and which are different.

6. Sing the song "What's the Sound?" to the tune of "Old MacDonald Had a Farm" (Yopp, 1992). Use different sounds each time you sing the song. An example of a verse follows.

    What's the sound that starts these words:

    baby, ball, and bed?

    /b/ is the sound that starts these words:

    baby, ball, and bed.

    With a /b/ /b/ here, and a /b/ /b/ there,

    here a /b/, there a /b/, everywhere a /b/ /b/.

    /b/ is the sound that starts these words:

    baby, ball, and bed.

Activities, tips, & Center Ideas for Sound Substitution

1. Have children select a sound of the day, such as the sound /m/, and then say each of their names with that sound in place of the first sound (Yopp, 1992). Children should say Mina for Gina, Merry for Jerry, and so on.

2. Write the letters of the alphabet on large index cards and place them on a table. Say a word such as *turtle*. Have a child choose a letter from the stack on the table. Say the word *turtle,* beginning with the letter sound the child has chosen. For example, if the child selected the letter j, the new nonsense word would be *jurtle.* Enjoy the fun of creating nonsense words. Repeat the activity with a new letter sound.

3. Have children create a page for a picture book with words that rhyme. For example, say the word *clown* and have children draw a picture of a *clown.* Then say the word *town* and have children draw a picture of a *town.* Repeat with other rhyming words as in *down* and *frown.* Have children read their books of rhyming words. Point out that the rhyming words have different beginning sounds but the same ending sounds. Create other pages with different rhyming words.

4. Play a consonant riddle game. Say a word such as bunny. Then present the riddle by saying, "What rhymes with bunny but starts with an /f/?" Have children guess what the word is. Other words to use are hat-cat, sun-fun, dish-fish, moo-zoo, fat-hat, meet-feet, and wish-dish.

5. Tell children that you want them to listen to the sounds in the words that you say. Tell them that you'll be switching one of the sounds. Say a pair of words with one sound switched. You might switch the beginning consonants as in *hill* and *Bill,* you might switch the vowels such as *ball* and *bell,* or you might switch the ending sounds as in *game* and *gate.* After saying the new words, have the children say them with you. Continue with several pairs of words.

6. Tell children that you will be singing a song that they know but that you will be changing some of the words (Yopp, 1992). Write a section of a song on the chalkboard or an overhead transparency. Sing or chant the song as it was written. Then suggest a new sound to use to sing the song. Sing the song with the new sound. Repeat with additional verses. The following song is sung to the tune of *Someone's in the Kitchen with Dinah.*

> I have a song that we can sing
> I have a song I know.
> I have a song that we can sing
> Strumming on the old banjo.
>
> Fe-Fi-Fiddly-i-o
> Fe-Fi-Fiddly-i-o
> Fe-Fi-Fiddly-i-o
> Strumming on the old banjo.
>
> Ke-Ki-Kiddly-i-o
> Ke-Ki-Kiddly-i-o
> Ke-Ki-Kiddly-i-o
> Strumming on the old banjo.

RHYMES

Dear Families,

When children learn to pick words that rhyme or think of rhyming words, they are building skills that will help them as readers. Examples of rhyming words are *cat* and *hat;* *ball* and *call;* and *run* and *sun.* Here are some simple activities you can do with your children to help them practice their rhyming skills.

- Share nursery rhymes, poems, and songs that contain rhyming words. Some familiar ones you might share are "Jack and Jill," "Hickory Dickory Dock," and "Mary Had a Little Lamb." Share these nursery rhymes, poems, and songs often and be sure to talk about the rhyming words with your children.

- Say two words and ask your children if they rhyme. Here is a list to get you started with this activity.

Word	Word	Do they rhyme?
Top	Pop	Yes
Race	Face	Yes
Big	Boy	No
Ring	Sing	Yes
Made	Good	No
Bit	Sit	Yes
Noodle	Poodle	Yes

- Say a word to your children and ask them to think of a rhyming word. It's okay if they make up pretend words. For example, if you pick the word *bubble,* your children might say *gubble.* This type of language play is a fun way to practice rhyming.

I hope you and your children have fun with these rhyming activities.

Sincerely,

3.3

Phonics

> **Goal:** To help children develop phonics skills.
>
> **Assessment Strategy 5** Auditory Discrimination, page 148
>
> **Assessment Strategy 6** Phonics: Consonants, page 151
>
> **Assessment Strategy 7** Decoding, page 163

Background

Reading is a complex process, and children use many tools and techniques to construct meaning. Phonics is one of the cueing systems that children use when they encounter unknown words. The other cueing systems focus on semantics (meaning) and syntax (structure of language). Effective readers use these cueing systems flexibly and in combination as they attempt to construct meaning from printed materials. While phonics is an important part of beginning reading instruction, it is not the only component (Cunningham, 2005). Within a sound reading program, teachers provide instruction in each of the various components of word identification: structural analysis, use of context, sight vocabulary, and phonics.

Phonics is not a method of teaching reading (Heilman, 2005); rather, it is an important tool for decoding unfamiliar words and making sense of what is read. Many different teaching methods and approaches include phonics instruction. What these methods and approaches have in common is their focus on teaching children the letter-sound associations in our language (Strickland, 1998). Because approximately 84% of the words in the English language are phonetically regular, instruction in phonics is essential in helping beginning readers break the code and make sense of reading (Anderson, Hiebert, Scott, & Wilkinson, 1985).

Adams (2001, pp. 67–68) also notes that "a serious goal of any responsible program of beginning reading instruction" is to ensure children's grasp of the basics of phonics. According to the National Reading Panel (2000), those basics involve the systematic teaching of a prespecified set of letter-sound relationships. What seems to be important is the teaching of phonics in an intentional and systematic manner in kindergarten and first grade.

The following teaching strategies and activities offer a wide variety of suggestions for helping beginning readers develop phonics skills. Some of the strategies and activities provide explicit instruction of phonics, and other ideas focus on more contextualized approaches to phonics instruction. By using a variety of systematic approaches and strategies, you will be able to help children develop the phonics skills necessary to progress in reading.

EXPLICIT PHONICS

Explicit Phonics focuses on teaching phonics one element at a time, building systematically from individual elements to larger pieces of text. Children first learn letters and sounds, then blend words, and then read these components in connected text. Some children who have difficulty learning from more indirect methods benefit from the explicit nature of this type of phonics instruction (Adams, 1990).

DIRECTIONS

1. Select a letter, digraph, or other phonic element to be taught.

2. Present the phonic element by writing the graphemes that represent it on the chalkboard (e.g., sh).

3. Tell the children, "The letters *sh* stand for the /sh/ sound."

4. Ask the children to make the /sh/ sound as you point to the letters.

5. Have the children write the letters *sh* on their papers. Ask them to say the sound as they point to the letters.

6. Present the children with several words that contain the target phonic element. Have the children sound out the words and say them together. Emphasize the target phonic element. For example, you might use the following words for the /sh/ sound.

   shoe
   sheep
   she

7. This type of lesson can be extended to include writing sentences for the words, reading the words in other materials, or playing a word game.

8. Guidelines for teaching phonics appear on the following page.

Guidelines for Teaching Phonics

General Guidelines

»» Teach common consonant sounds first.

»» Teach short vowel sounds before long vowel sounds.

»» Teach consonants and short vowels in combination so words can be made as soon as possible.

»» Use a sequence in which the most words can be generated. Teach higher frequency sound-spelling relationships before less frequent ones.

»» Progress from simple to more complex sound-spellings.

»» Time spent on phonics instruction should be 10 to 15 minutes daily (Gunning, 2000).

Recommended Phonic Skills for Grades K–3

Kindergarten
phonemic awareness
alphabet recognition
consonants

Grade 1
phonemic awareness
blending and word building
short vowels (CVC pattern)
consonants
final e (CVCe pattern)
long vowel digraphs (ai, ay, ae, ee, oa, ow, etc.)
consonant clusters (br, cl, st, etc.)
other vowels such as oo, ou, ow, oi, oy

Grades 2–3
grade 1 skills review
more complex vowel spellings (ough)
structural analysis (compound words, common prefixes, common suffixes)
multisyllable words

2

WHOLE-PART-WHOLE PHONICS

Whole-Part-Whole Phonics focuses on teaching phonics within the context of meaningful text. This approach allows children to see the use of phonics skills in real reading situations. Typically, a Big Book is used as the focus of this strategy.

⏵ DIRECTIONS

1. Select a story or Big Book that contains a phonic element you want to emphasize. For example, you might use the Big Book *I Went Walking* (Williams, 1989) to teach the initial /w/ sound.

2. Read the story aloud to the children. Discuss the story.

3. Write several sentences from the story or Big Book that contain words with the target phonic element. For example, you might show the children the following sentence and question.

    I went walking.

    What did you see?

4. Read the sentences to the children. Invite the children to reread the sentences with you.

5. Point out the words with the target phonic element. Ask the children to read these words with you. For example, you might draw the children's attention to the following words.

    went

    walking

6. Ask the children to figure out what these words have in common. Lead the children to discover that the words contain the same beginning letter and sound.

7. Ask the children to brainstorm other words that have the target letter and sound.

8. Reread the sentences containing the target words.

9. Return to the story or Big Book and ask the children to read along with you as you reread the story.

Aa Bb Cc   Tips for English Language Learners

Peregoy and Boyle (2001) note that although there is little research on phonics instruction for English Language Learners, several principles developed for native English speakers should apply to teaching phonics to English Language Learners. Those principles follow.

1. Teach spelling patterns rather than rules. Word families (see Appendix B on the CD-ROM) should be helpful for such teaching.

2. Teach phonics within a meaningful context. Teaching Strategies 2 and 3 in this section may be especially relevant.

3. Provide sufficient time for children to read and write to enhance the development of phonics skills taught.

4. Use informal assessments to help determine needed areas for instruction. Then provide responsive instruction that will lead to greater independence.

PHONICS IN CONTEXT

Phonics in Context stresses teaching target words in the context of sentences and passages. In this approach, consonants are generally not isolated but taught within the context of whole words. This approach is very common in many basal anthology programs (Gunning, 2004).

DIRECTIONS

1. Make a list of words that contain the target phonic element. Limit your list to four or five words. For example, you might teach the initial /d/ sound using the following words.

    dad

    door

    dog

    do

2. Write one sentence for each word on the chalkboard. Try to make the sentences link together to form a short story or passage. For the target words listed above, you might use the following sentences.

    My <u>dad</u> came home from work.

    We ran to the <u>door.</u>

    He had a big <u>dog</u> with him.

    "<u>Do</u> we get to keep him?" we asked.

3. Underline the target words.

4. Read the sentences aloud to the children.

5. Have the children echo read the sentences with you. To do this, you read the sentence first, and the children read the sentence immediately after you.

6. Have the children read each target word after you read it aloud.

7. Ask the children what letter or letters all of the target words have in common. Discuss their responses.

8. Say the target words again and ask the children to listen carefully to determine what sound or sounds the words have in common. Discuss their responses.

9. Ask the children to brainstorm other words that have the same sound or sounds in them. Write these words on the chalkboard.

10. Ask the children to make the sound that all of the target words contain. Then ask them what letter or letters make that sound. Invite the children to state the generalization they learned (e.g., the letter *d* makes the /d/ sound).

11. Return to the sentences and ask the children to read them chorally.

WORD SORTS

The human brain is a pattern detector that seeks to categorize or sort information to make it more meaningful. Such categorizing or sorting "allows us to find order and similarities among various objects, events, ideas, and words that we encounter" (Bear, Invernizzi, Templeton, & Johnston, 2004, p. 61). The word sorting strategy allows students to engage in this process as they search, compare, and contrast words to identify meaningful patterns and generalizations about letters and sounds.

DIRECTIONS

1. Determine the purpose of your word sorting activity. Is it to focus the children's attention on sounds, or do you want to target patterns such as word families? This lesson will focus on a sound sort for beginning sounds.

2. Prepare picture cards for the words you want the children to sort. You can create these cards yourself or you may wish to use the pictures provided in the book *Words Their Way* (Bear, Invernizzi, Templeton, & Johnston, 2004). Also prepare a letter card for each beginning sound students will sort for in the activity. For example, if you are targeting the letters *b* and *c* you would prepare a letter card for each as well as approximately 6–8 picture cards for each letter. For the letters *b* and *c* you could include the pictures:

    b - ball, boy, bat, box, bed, bug, bell, bus

    c - cat, cow, cup, coat, corn, can, car, cake

3. Explain to the children that they will be looking at pictures, saying the word the picture represents, and figuring out the beginning sound for the word. Model the process by saying the following.

    This is a picture of a ball. *Ball* begins with /b/.

4. Tell the children that you will put the picture of the ball under the letter *b* because *ball* begins with /b/.

5. Continue with several more cards to ensure the children understand the process.

6. Provide a set of letter cards and picture cards for children to sort the words at their desks or in small groups.

7. Word sorts can be adapted to match various phonics instructional goals. Some examples of other types of word sorts are listed in the box below.

WORD SORTS

Picture sorts for beginning blends (e.g., bl, cl, sp, dr)
Picture sorts for beginning digraphs (i.e., wh, ch, sh, th)
Picture sorts for beginning short vowels
Picture sorts for medial short vowels
Picture sorts for long vowels
Word sorts for CVC words
Word sorts for CVCe words
Word sorts for r-controlled vowels
Word sorts for hard and soft *c* or *g*

WORD FAMILIES

Almost all words are composed of an onset and a rime. The onset is the first letter or letters before the vowel, and the rime is the vowel to the end of the word or syllable. For example, in the word *top* the onset is *t* and the rime is *-op*. There are 37 common rimes in the English language that account for over 500 words used in the primary grades (Wylie & Durrell, 1970). By teaching these rimes to children, they will be able to read and spell many words very quickly and easily.

DIRECTIONS

1. Select one of the rimes in the box below. Write the rime on the chalkboard, on chart paper, or on an overhead transparency.

COMMON RIMES

-ack	-ain	-ake	-ale	-all	-ame	-an	-ank	-ap	
-ash	-at	-ate	-aw	-ay	-eat	-ell	-est	-ice	
-ick	-ide	-ight	-ill	-in	-ine	-ing	-ink	-ip	
-ir	-ock	-oke	-op	-or	-ore	-uck	-ug	-ump	-unk

---

2. Explain to the children that this word part is called a spelling pattern. Tell the children that you will use the spelling pattern to create a word family by adding letters to the beginning of the rime.

3. For example, if you selected the rime *-all,* you could demonstrate how adding the letter *b* forms the word *ball* and adding the letter *t* forms the word *tall*. Ask the children to think of other words you can form using the rime *-all*. Write the words as the children share them.

4. Once you have made a list of all the words for the rime, give the children a sheet with a blank house on it and have them copy the words into the word family house. You can display the word family houses on a bulletin board or in the reading corner of the room.

5. Repeat the strategy throughout the school year to teach and review the rimes you want to teach to the children in your class.

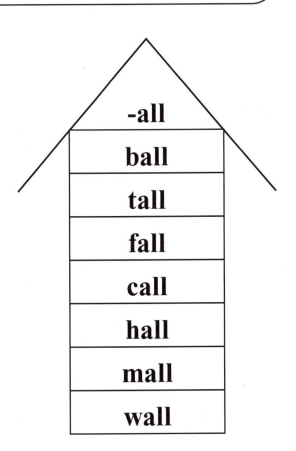

-all
ball
tall
fall
call
hall
mall
wall

Word Families

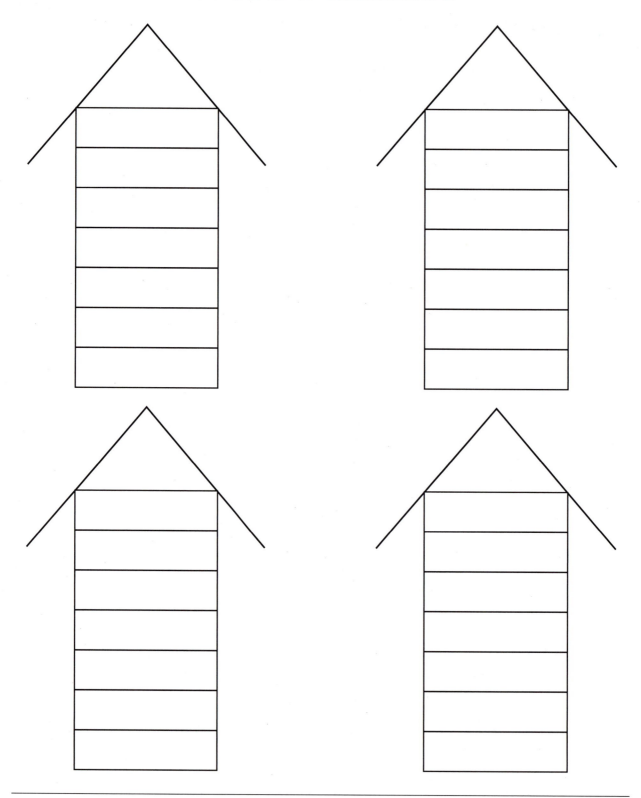

From Laurie Elish-Piper, Jerry L. Johns, and Susan Davis Lenski, *Teaching Reading Pre-K–Grade 3* (3rd ed.).
Copyright © 2006 by Kendall/Hunt Publishing Company (1-800-247-3458, ext. 4). May be reproduced for
noncommercial educational purposes.

MAKING WORDS

Making Words is a hands-on phonics strategy that helps children see patterns in words as they manipulate letter cards or tiles (Cunningham & Hall, 1998). This strategy helps children understand letter and sound associations as they work with word families or onsets and rimes. An onset is the beginning part of a word that comes before the vowel. For example, in the word *cat,* the onset is *c.* A rime is the part of the word from the vowel to the end. For example, in the word *cat,* the rime is *at.* Rimes are sometimes referred to as phonograms, spelling patterns, or word families. In the Making Words strategy, children manipulate letter cards or tiles to build words that start out small and get longer as the lesson progresses. Typically, a Making Words lesson focuses on one or more rimes or spelling patterns that the children are learning. Refer to Appendix B on the CD-ROM for a list of rimes or word families. For lists of words and sample lessons for the Making Words strategy, consult Cunningham and Hall (1998).

DIRECTIONS

1. Choose the word that will be the longest word made in the lesson (e.g., splash).

2. Make a list of other words that can be made using the letters in the word *splash.* Arrange these words to show how changing letter order or adding a new letter can form a new word. An example follows.

a	ash
Al	lash
as	splash
has	

3. Select the words you will include in your lesson. Consider the patterns and words that can be made by rearranging letters in a previous word. Proper nouns can be included to help children learn about using capital letters correctly.

4. Make letter cards on large index cards for each letter needed for the lesson. Write each consonant in black and each vowel in red. Write each word for the lesson on a small index card. Place the large letter cards in a pocket chart.

5. Make individual letter cards for each child. This can be done by writing letters on index cards or small squares of paper. Letter tiles can also be used.

6. Distribute a set of letters to each child. Provide a few minutes for the children to explore the letters and words they can make with their letter cards.

7. Say, "Use two letters to make the word *as.* I am *as* tall *as* Bill." Remind the children that each word must have a vowel (red letter).

8. Pause for a moment while the children make the word with their letter cards. Ask for a volunteer to come to the front of the class and make the word using the large letter cards in the pocket chart. Provide time for the children to self-check the words they made.

9. Say, "Add one letter and make the word *has.* He *has* a pet dog."

10. Ask for a volunteer to make the word in the pocket chart. Have children self-check their own words.

11. Continue the lesson using the same steps with the other words.

12. When you have used all of the words on your list except the last word (splash), challenge the children by saying, "See what word you can make using all of your letters."

Activities, tips, & Center Ideas

1. Use poetry to teach common rimes and other target phonic elements. Read the poem first for enjoyment. Then direct the children's attention to the rime or phonic element you want to teach. Ask the children to say the sound with you. Invite the children to identify words in the poem that contain the rime or sound. Make a list of the words and underline the rime or target phonic element. Brainstorm other words that also contain the rime or sound.

2. Engage the children in shared reading of Big Books or other enlarged texts such as chart stories. After reading the texts for enjoyment and meaning, direct the children's attention to specific phonic elements. Ask the children to identify words from the text that contain that element.

3. Use shared writing to model phonics strategies for children. For example, as you are writing a list in front of the class, think aloud as you use phonics strategies to spell a word. You might say, "I need to make a list of things to buy at the store. First I need to get milk. How does *milk* begin? It sounds like the beginning of *money* and *Mark*. That means I need to use the letter *m*." Continue with this pattern for the remainder of the word. Model this type of sounding out strategy frequently for children through shared writing.

4. Write letters or spelling patterns you want to review on large note cards or pieces of tagboard. Give one card to each child. Have several children stand in front of the class and ask them to sequence themselves in an order that spells a word. For example, if you gave the children *c, a,* and *t* cards, they could spell the word *cat*. Ask the children how they can change one letter and make a new word. For example, the *c* can be changed to an *h* to form *hat*, a *b* to form *bat,* and an *r* to form *rat*. Continue forming new words until you have run out of words. Then introduce a new spelling pattern or rime.

5. Write an incomplete sentence on the chalkboard, a sheet of chart paper, or an overhead transparency. For example, you might write. "I like to play _____ ." Then write a word that is one letter away from being correct. For example, you might write *hall*. Ask the children to change a letter to form a word that makes sense in the sentence. Have a child write the correct word *ball* in the blank. Continue this pattern with additional sentences.

6. Have children play sound bingo to practice their phonics skills. Using pieces of tagboard or large index cards as the bingo game board, divide the board into five rows and five columns. Write one letter in each box. Put the letters in different order on each card. Distribute cards and markers to each child. Use picture cards or a word list to call out words. Ask the children to listen for the beginning sound of the word. If the children's game board contains the beginning letter of the word, they should cover the letter on the game board. When a child has a vertical, horizontal, or diagonal row covered, the child must read the covered letters and their sounds to verify that he or she has bingo. Variations of this game can focus on ending sounds, vowel sounds, or blends.

7. Play sound hunt with the children. Divide the class into small groups and assign each group a letter or spelling pattern that you want to review. Then ask the children to search for objects in the classroom that contain the sound represented by the letter or spelling pattern. Have children make lists of the objects they find. Provide time for groups to share their findings.

8. Use word ladders (Blevins, 1998) to help children see how changing one letter can change a word. Draw a word ladder on the chalkboard, a piece of chart paper, or an overhead transparency. Write a word on the bottom rung of the word ladder. Say the word with the children. Ask if the children can change one letter to form a new word. Write the new word on the second rung. Continue until the ladder is full. A sample word ladder is shown below.

sun
bun
fun
run

9. Display a picture of an animal or object. Write its name on the chalkboard, leaving out one letter. For example, show a picture of a cat and write c __ t on the chalkboard. Ask the children what is missing. Write the missing letter in the space. Continue with other picture and word combinations. You can use this activity to focus on beginning, ending, or vowel sounds.

10. Teach children to play sound checkers to reinforce specific phonic elements. Write a word on each square of an old checkerboard. The game is played like checkers, but the children must read the words on each space they land on. If they cannot read the words correctly, they must return to their original space.

11. Use the children's names to point out similarities and differences in the way the names look and sound. Invite children to notice the sounds with which their names begin and end. For example, you might say, "Natalie's name begins with the /n/ sound. It is written with the letter *n*. Who else has a name that begins with the /n/ sound?"

12. Use children's books to teach vowel sounds. Share the book, discuss the vowel sound, and ask children to identify examples of the vowel sound. See pages 128–129 for recommended children's books for teaching short and long vowel sounds.

ă ĕ ĭ ŏ ŭ

Children's Books with Specific Short Vowel Sounds

Short a

Baker, K. (1999). *Sometimes.* New York: Harcourt Brace.

Cameron, A. (1994). *The cat sat on a mat.* Boston: Houghton Mifflin.

Flanagan, A. K. (2000). *Cats: The sound of short a.* Elgin, IL: The Child's World.

Griffith, H. (1982). *Alex and the cat.* New York: Greenwillow.

Kent, J. (1970). *The fat cat.* New York: Scholastic.

Most, B. (1980). *There's an ant in Anthony.* New York: Morrow.

Short e

Ets, M. H. (1972). *Elephant in a well.* Bergenfield, NJ: Viking.

Flanagan, A. K. (2000). *Ben's pens: The sound of short e.* Elgin, IL: The Child's World.

Galdone, P. (1973). *The little red hen.* New York: Scholastic.

Lionni, L. (1994). *An extraordinary egg.* New York: Knopf.

Short i

Lankford, M. D. (1991). *Is it dark? Is it light?* New York: Knopf.

Leonard, M. (1998). *Get the ball, Slim.* Brookfield, CT: Millbrook.

McPhair, D. (1984). *Fix-it.* Bergenfield, NJ: Viking.

Sanfield, S. (1995). *Bit by bit.* East Rutherford, NJ: Viking.

Short o

Anholt, C., & Anholt, L. (1992). *All about you.* Bergenfield, NJ: Viking.

Flanagan, A. K. (2000). *Hot pot: The sound of short o.* Elgin, IL: The Child's World.

Freeman, D. (1955). *Mop top.* Bergenfield, NJ: Viking.

Hutchins, P. (1968). *Rosie's Walk.* New York: Simon & Shuster.

Seuss, D. (1965). *Fox in socks.* New York: Random House.

Short u

Marshall, J. (1984). *The cut-ups.* Bergenfield, NJ: Viking.

Seuss, D. (1982). *Hunches and bunches.* New York: Random House.

Udry, J. M. (1981). *Thump and plunk.* New York: Harper & Row.

āēīōū

Children's Books with Specific Long Vowel Sounds

Long a

Aardema, V. (1981). *Bringing the rain to Kapiti Plain.* New York: Dial.

Flanagan, A. K. (2000). *Play day: The sound of long a.* Elgin, IL: The Child's World.

Henkes, K. (1987). *Sheila Rae, the brave.* New York: Greenwillow.

Munsch, R. (1987). *Moira's birthday.* Buffalo, NY: Firefly.

Long e

Chardiet, B., & Maccarone, G. (1992). *We scream for ice-cream.* New York: Scholastic.

Cowley, J. (1994). *The screaming mean machine.* New York: Scholastic.

Keller, H. (1983). *Ten sleepy sheep.* New York: Greenwillow.

Long i

Cameron, J. (1979). *If mice could fly.* Riverside, NJ: Atheneum.

Gelman, R. (1979). *Why can't I fly?* New York: Scholastic.

Gordh, B. (1999). *Hop right on.* New York: Golden Books.

Minarik, E. E. (1978). *No fighting! No biting.* New York: Harper Collins.

Long o

Buller, J., & Schade. S. (1992). *Toad on the road.* New York: Random House.

Johnston, T. (1972). *The adventures of Mole and Troll.* East Rutherford, NJ: Viking.

Wild, M. (1994). *Going home.* New York: Scholastic.

Long u

Lobel, A. (1966). *The troll music.* New York: Harper & Row.

Segal, L. (1977). *Tell me a Trudy.* New York: Farrar, Straus & Giroux.

Slobodkin, L. (1959). *Excuse me—certainly!* New York: Vanguard Press.

LETTER SOUNDS

Dear Families,

Here is a fun activity called word families that you can try at home. This activity will help your child review some of the spelling patterns we have been learning in school.

Help your children make words using letter cards or magnetic letters. You can make letter cards on index cards or by cutting a sheet of paper into pieces. Magnetic letters can be found in the toy aisle at most grocery stores, discount stores, drug stores, and many "dollar stores." You can use the word families below (-at, -ack, -ip, -ug) to make many words with your children. Begin by forming the pattern using the letter cards or magnetic letters. Then ask your children to put another letter card or magnetic letter in front of the pattern to form a new word. Tell your children you want to see how many words you can find that fit into the word family. Four word families (-at, -ack, -ip, and -ug) are shown below.

Word Families

-at	-ack	-ip	-ug
bat	back	dip	bug
cat	jack	hip	dug
fat	pack	lip	hug
hat	sack	rip	jug
mat	tack	sip	mug
pat	black	tip	plug
sat	crack	zip	rug
brat	snack	chip	slug
chat	stack	flip	smug
flat	track	grip	snug
that	whack	ship	
		skip	
		slip	
		trip	
		whip	

Other patterns you can use for this activity are listed below in the box

-ain	-ake	-ale	-all	-ame	-an	-ank	-ap	ash	-ate	-aw
-ay	-eat	-ell	-est	-ice	-ick	-ide	-ight	-ill	-in	-ine
-ing	-ink	-ir	-ock	-oke	-op	-or	-ore	-uck	-ump	-unk

I hope you and your children enjoy making word families.

Sincerely,

Assessments of Alphabet Knowledge, Phonemic Awareness, and Phonics

Goal: To help assess children's knowledge of the alphabet, various aspects of phonemic awareness, and phonics.

Background

There is probably no need to use all of the assessments in this section. Through your daily instruction, you can informally evaluate children's progress in the areas of alphabet knowledge, phonemic awareness, and phonics. Children's writing can also be used to give you insights into how they are using their knowledge of letter-sound associations (phonics) to help spell words. If you wish to more systematically assess one or more of the major topics in this chapter, choose the most appropriate assessment. Use it before instruction to help determine which students could profit from instruction in the area. You can also use an assessment after instruction in a specific area to help assess the effectiveness of your instruction and whether additional instruction is warranted. There are two forms of each assessment in this section to provide greater flexibility in use.

Section 3.4 **ASSESSMENT STRATEGY**

ALPHABET KNOWLEDGE

OVERVIEW	This assessment contains uppercase and lowercase letters of the alphabet in nonsequential order to help assess letter-naming ability. Lowercase *a* and *g* appear in both manuscript and print forms. There are two forms of the test. You may want to use Form 1 at the beginning of the year and Form 2 later in the year.
MATERIALS NEEDED	1. Child's copy, either Form 1 (page 134) or Form 2 (page 136): two 5″ × 8″ cards 2. A copy of the Record Sheet (page 135 or page 137) that corresponds to the form selected for use
PROCEDURES	1. Duplicate the appropriate Record Sheet. 2. Place the alphabet page before the child. Use the 5″ × 8″ cards to block off everything but the line being read. If necessary, point to each letter. Say, "Here are some letters. I want to see how many you know." Encourage the child to say "pass" or "skip it" if a particular letter is not known. Stop if the child becomes frustrated or has little or no knowledge of the letters. *(continued)*

3. As the child responds, use the Record Sheet to note correct (+) responses. When responses are incorrect, record the actual response or *DK* (child doesn't know) above the stimulus letter. If the child self-corrects, write *s/c;* self-corrections can be made at any time. Some sample markings for the letter o are given below.

Marking	Meaning of Marking	Marking	Meaning of Marking
+ O	Identified correct	C O	Said C for O
DK O	Don't know	C s/c O	Said C for O but self-corrected

SCORING AND INTERPRETATION

Count the correct number of responses for the uppercase letters and the lowercase letters. Self-corrections are counted as correct. Note the scores in the boxes on the Record Sheet on page 135 or 137. Based on the number of correct responses and your observations, make a judgment about the child's alphabet knowledge. Unknown letters or incorrect responses may help form the basis for instruction. Refer to Section 3.1.

Additional Ways of Assessing Alphabet Knowledge

1. Observe the child's responses to ongoing instruction to teach the letters. Make mental notes about any particular letters that cause confusion and provide appropriate instruction. Remember that children often confuse *b, d, p,* and *q* in the early stages of reading instruction.

2. Use children's writing for indications of letters that may be confused or unknown. Provide additional instruction as needed,

3. Be alert for children whose knowledge of the alphabet appears to lag behind other children in your classroom. Use this information to help decide if special instruction may be needed.

B T R Z F N K

X V I M J D L

Y Q W C U A

O H S E G P

s d o a k w g

l u r t q h y

i p v f n z g

b x e c j m a

Form 1—Alphabet Knowledge—Child's Copy

RECORD SHEET

Form 1

Alphabet Knowledge

Name _____ Date _____

Teacher's Directions   132
Child's Copy   134

✒ BRIEF DIRECTIONS

Present the alphabet sheet to the child. Use 5″ × 8″ cards to block off everything but the line being read. If necessary, point to each letter with a finger. Then say, "Here are some letters. I want to see how many you know." Place a plus (+) above correctly identified letters. Record the child's responses for incorrect letters. Total correct responses and record the score in the boxes. Note that lowercase *a* and *g* appear in both manuscript and print forms.

B	T	R	Z	F	N	K
X	V	I	M	J	D	L
Y	Q	W	C	U	A	
O	H	S	E	G	P	

☐ **Total Correct**

s	d	o	a	k	w	g
l	u	r	t	q	h	y
i	p	v	f	n	z	g
b	x	e	c	j	m	a

☐ **Total Correct**

From Laurie Elish-Piper, Jerry L. Johns, and Susan Davis Lenski, *Teaching Reading Pre-K–Grade 3* (3rd ed.). Copyright © 2006 by Kendall/Hunt Publishing Company (1-800-247-3458, ext. 4). May be reproduced for noncommercial educational purposes.

I   S   K   H   Q   V   L

A   G   P   J   N   D   M

T   C   Z   E   F   U

B   O   X   Y   R   W

r   x   z   k   t   e   y

w   q   c   g   h   m   a

i   p   s   v   d   l   j

u   o   f   b   a   n   g

Form 2—Alphabet Knowledge—Child's Copy

RECORD SHEET

Form 2

Alphabet Knowledge

Name _____ Date _____

Teacher's Directions	132
Child's Copy	136

➤ BRIEF DIRECTIONS

Present the alphabet sheet to the child. Use 5″ × 8″ cards to block off everything but the line being read. If necessary, point to each letter with a finger. Then say, "Here are some letters. I want to see how many you know." Place a plus (+) above correctly identified letters. Record the child's responses for incorrect letters. Total correct responses and record the score in the boxes. Note that lowercase *a* and *g* appear in both manuscript and print forms.

I	S	K	H	Q	V	L
A	G	P	J	N	D	M
T	C	Z	E	F	U	
B	O	X	Y	R	W	

☐ **Total Correct**

r	x	z	k	t	e	y
w	q	c	g	h	m	a
i	p	s	v	d	l	j
u	o	f	b	a	n	g

☐ **Total Correct**

RHYME DETECTION

OVERVIEW	This assessment will help determine the child's ability to hear whether or not words rhyme. This skill is helpful in learning phonics. It is also often taught early in phonemic awareness instruction. Form 1 may be used as a pretest early in the school year. Form 2 may be used later in the year or after specific instruction in rhyming.
MATERIALS NEEDED	1. A copy of the Record Sheet for Form 1 (page 139) or Form 2 (page 140).
PROCEDURES	1. Practice saying the words on the list. 2. Say the following to the child, "I want you to tell me if two words rhyme. When words sound the same at the end, they rhyme. *Hat* rhymes with *cat*. Does *look* rhyme with *book?* Yes. Does *mat* rhyme with *bat?* Yes. But not all words rhyme. *Mice* does not rhyme with *soon* because *mice* ends with *ice* and *soon* ends with *oon*. Does *cat* rhyme with *pig?* No. Does *sick* rhyme with *pick!* Yes. Now, listen carefully. I'm going to say some words, and I want you to tell me if they rhyme." 3. Say all the words distinctly but in a normal voice. 4. Place a ✓ in the appropriate column to indicate whether the child's response was correct or incorrect.
SCORING AND INTERPRETATION	Count the number of correct items and record the total on the appropriate Record Sheet on page 139 or page 140. Informally judge the child's ability to detect rhymes. If the child could profit from additional instruction in rhyme detection, refer to the instructional strategies and activities in Section 3.2.

Additional Ways of Assessing Rhyme

1. Many poems and nursery rhymes provide an informal opportunity to assess the child's ability to rhyme. Note the child's ability to predict a rhyming word at the end of a line of a poem or rhyme.

2. Listen to children's language play in the classroom and on the playground. Watch for evidence of rhyming as children play a variety of games (e.g., jump rope).

RECORD SHEET

Form 1

Rhyme Detection

Teacher's Directions   138
Child's Copy   None

BRIEF DIRECTIONS

Say to the child: "I want you to tell me if two words rhyme. When words sound the same at the end, they rhyme. *Hat* rhymes with *cat.* Does *look* rhyme with *book?* Yes. Does *mat* rhyme with *bat?* Yes. But not all words rhyme. *Mice* does not rhyme with *soon* because *mice* ends with *ice* and *soon* ends with *oon.* Does *cat* rhyme with *pig?* No. Does *sick* rhyme with *pick?* Yes. Now, listen carefully. I'm going to say some words, and I want you to tell me if they rhyme." Place a ✓ in the appropriate column, total correct responses, and record the score in the box.

			Correct	Incorrect
1. bee	—	see	_____	_____
2. tall	—	call	_____	_____
3. jet	—	dog	_____	_____
4. can	—	man	_____	_____
5. him	—	gym	_____	_____
6. hen	—	bag	_____	_____
7. rat	—	sat	_____	_____
8. room	—	zoom	_____	_____
9. back	—	sing	_____	_____
10. bake	—	rake	_____	_____

Total Correct

Observations, Comments, Notes, and Insights

Form 2

Rhyme Detection

Name _____ Date _____

Teacher's Directions   138
Child's Copy   None

➤ BRIEF DIRECTIONS

Say to the child: "I want you to tell me if two words rhyme. When words sound the same at the end, they rhyme. *Hat* rhymes with *cat.* Does *look* rhyme with *book?* Yes. Does *mat* rhyme with *bat?* Yes. But not all words rhyme. *Mice* does not rhyme with *soon* because *mice* ends with *ice* and *soon* ends with *oon.* Does *cat* rhyme with *pig?* No. Does *sick* rhyme with *pick?* Yes. Now, listen carefully. I'm going to say some words, and I want you to tell me if they rhyme." Place a ✓ in the appropriate column, total correct responses, and record the score in the box.

			Correct	Incorrect
1. me	—	he	_____	_____
2. ball	—	mall	_____	_____
3. hog	—	let	_____	_____
4. than	—	ran	_____	_____
5. skim	—	trim	_____	_____
6. rag	—	men	_____	_____
7. that	—	fat	_____	_____
8. green	—	broom	_____	_____
9. ring	—	sack	_____	_____
10. shake	—	bake	_____	_____

Total Correct ☐

Observations, Comments, Notes, and Insights

PHONEME SEGMENTATION

OVERVIEW	Phoneme segmentation refers to the child's ability to segment phonemes (sounds) in words. Phoneme segmentation is strongly related to success in reading and spelling acquisition. This assessment was designed for use with English-speaking kindergartners. It may also be used with older children experiencing difficulty in literacy acquisition. Two forms of the assessment are included. Use one form to help determine if the child needs instruction in phoneme segmentation. The second form can be used later to help assess the child's growth in phoneme segmentation.
MATERIALS NEEDED	1. A copy of the Record Sheet for Form 1 (page 142) or Form 2 (page 143).
PROCEDURES	1. Say to the child, "Today we're going to play a word game. I'm going to say a word, and I want you to break the word apart. You are going to tell me each sound in the word in order. For example, if I say *old,* you should say /o/-/l/-/d/. Be sure to say the sounds, not the letters, in the word."
	2. Then say, "Let's try a few together." The practice items are *ride, go,* and *man.* If necessary, help by segmenting the word for the child. Encourage the child to repeat the segmented sounds.
	3. During practice provide feedback after each response. You can nod or say "Right" or "That's right." If the child is incorrect, correct him or her and provide the appropriate response.
	4. Proceed through all of the items. Put a plus (+) beside those items that the child correctly segments. Incorrect responses may be recorded on the blank line following the item.
SCORING AND INTERPRETATION	The child's score is the number of items he or she correctly segments into all constituent phonemes. No partial credit is given. For example, *she* (item 5 on Form 1) contains two phonemes /sh/-/e/; *grew* (item 7 on Form 1) contains three phonemes /g/-/r/-/ew/: and *three* (item 4 on Form 2) contains three phonemes /th/-/r/-/ee/. If the child says letter names instead of sounds, code the response as incorrect and note the type of error on the Record Sheet on page 142 or page 143. Such notes are helpful in understanding the child's literacy development. Some children may partially segment, simply repeat the stimulus item, provide nonsense responses, or give letter names.
	Total the number of correct responses. Place the score in the box on the Record Sheet. Then make an overall judgment of the child's phoneme segmentation abilities. A wide range of scores is likely. Yopp (1995) reported that two samples of kindergartners achieved mean scores of 11.78 and 11.39 when all 22 words were administered.
	The child's responses may help form a basis for instructional interventions. Refer to Section 3.2.

Form 1

Phoneme Segmentation

Name _____ Date _____

Teacher's Directions   141
Child's Copy   None

▶ BRIEF DIRECTIONS

Say to the child: "Today we're going to play a word game. I'm going to say a word, and I want you to break the word apart. You are going to tell me each sound in the word in order. For example, if I say *old,* you should say /o/-/l/-/d/. Be sure to say the sounds, not the letters, in the word. Let's try a few together."

PRACTICE ITEMS

ride, go, man *(Assist the child in segmenting these items as necessary.)*

TEST ITEMS

(Put a plus (+) beside those items that the child correctly segments; incorrect responses may be recorded on the blank line following the item.) The correct number of phonemes is indicated in parentheses.

1. dog (3) _____   7. grew (3) _____

2. keep (3) _____   8. that (3) _____

3. fine (3) _____   9. red (3) _____

4. no (2) _____   10. me (2) _____

5. she (2) _____   11. sat (3) _____

6. wave (3) _____

Total Correct ☐

Observations, Comments, Notes, and Insights

Form 2

Phoneme Segmentation

Name _____ Date _____

Teacher's Directions   141
Child's Copy   None

✎ BRIEF DIRECTIONS

Say to the child: "Today we're going to play a word game. I'm going to say a word, and I want you to break the word apart. You are going to tell me each sound in the word in order. For example, if I say *old,* you should say /o/-/l/-/d/. Be sure to say the sounds, not the letters, in the word. Let's try a few together."

PRACTICE ITEMS

ride, go, man *(Assist the child in segmenting these items as necessary.)*

TEST ITEMS

(Put a plus (+) beside those items that the child correctly segments; incorrect responses may be recorded on the blank line following the item.) The correct number of phonemes is indicated in parentheses.

1. lay (2) _____
2. race (3) _____
3. zoo (2) _____
4. three (3) _____
5. job (3) _____
6. in (2) _____

7. ice (2) _____
8. at (2) _____
9. top (3) _____
10. by (2) _____
11. do (2) _____

Total Correct ▢

```
Observations, Comments, Notes, and Insights



```

PHONEME DELETION AND SUBSTITUTION

OVERVIEW	Two assessments are included in this area. Phoneme Deletion assesses the child's ability to produce a word part when the initial phoneme (sound) is deleted. Phoneme Substitution assesses the child's ability to make a new word by substituting a phoneme (sound). These phonemic awareness tasks can be assessed to determine whether children "can already perform the manipulations being taught as determined by pre-tests" (National Reading Panel, 2000, p. 2–31). If you assess the areas of phoneme deletion and phoneme substitution, be certain that children will be expected to make use of the two skills in your instructional program. There are two forms of each assessment. Form 1 could be used to determine if the child can already perform these phonemic awareness tasks. Form 2 could be used after instruction to help evaluate progress.
MATERIALS NEEDED	1. A copy of the Record Sheet for Form 1 (page 146) or Form 2 (page 147).
PROCEDURES	1. For Phoneme Deletion, practice the words before you administer the assessment. Then say to the child, "Listen to me say the word *fun*. I can say the word *fun* without the /f/. *Fun* without the /f/ is *un*. Now I'll say some words, and I want you to tell me what is left when the first sound is taken away." Use another example if you think it is needed. "Listen to me say the word *make*. I can say the word *make* without the /m/. *Make* without the /m/ is *ake*."
	2. Use the words on the Record Sheet. The general prompt for each word is, "What is _____ without the / __ /?" Place a ✓ in the appropriate column after each word. Then total the correct responses and record the score in the box.
	3. For Phoneme Substitution, practice the words before you administer the assessment. Then say to the child, "Listen to the word *fun*. I can make a new word. I can take the /f/ off *fun* and put on a /r/ and make *run*. Now you say the word *car*." (Have the child say the word.) "Take the /c/ off *car* and put on a /j/ to make a new word. The word is _____ (jar)." Use another example if you think it is needed. "Take the /b/ of *bunch* and put on a /l/ to make a new word. The new word is _____ (lunch)."
	4. Use the words on the Record Sheet. Use the general prompt above. Place a ✓ in the appropriate column after each word. Then total the correct responses and record the score in the box.

SCORING AND INTERPRETATION	Count the number of correct items for each assessment administered and record the total on the Record Sheet on page 146 or page 147. Informally judge the child's ability to delete and substitute phonemes. If the child could profit from additional instruction in one area or both of the areas assessed, refer to the appropriate instructional strategies and activities in Section 3.2.

Additional Ways of Assessing Phonological Awareness

1. Use ongoing instruction to make informal judgments about the child's abilities in the areas assessed as well as other areas of phonemic awareness.

2. As you read children's literature containing language play (such as rhyming words), you can judge by the responses which children seem to be learning how sounds make up words.

3. A number of commercially published tests are available. Consult resources such as Salvia and Ysseldyke (2001) or Gillet, Temple, and Crawford (2004).

Form 1

Phoneme Deletion and Substitution

Name _____ Date _____

Teacher's Directions   144
Child's Copy   None

✎ BRIEF DIRECTIONS: PHONEME DELETION

Say to the child, "Listen to me say the word *fun*. I can say the word *fun* without the */f/*. *Fun* without the */f/* is *un*. Now I'll say some words, and I want you to tell me what is left when the first sound is taken away." Use another example if you think it is needed. "Listen to me say the word *make*. I can say the word *make* without the */m/*. *Make* without the */m/* is *ake*."

Use the words on the Record Sheet. The general prompt for each word is. "What is _____ without the /__/?" Place a ✓ in the appropriate column after each word. Then total the correct responses and record the score in the box.

		Correct	Incorrect
1. dad without /d/	ad	_____	_____
2. cheek without /ch/	eek	_____	_____
3. sock without /s/	ock	_____	_____
4. fin without /f/	in	_____	_____
5. nose without /n/	ose	_____	_____

Total Correct [ ]

✎ BRIEF DIRECTIONS: PHONEME SUBSTITUTION

Say to the child, "Listen to the word *fun*. I can make a new word. I can take the */f/* off *fun* and put on a */r/* and *run*. Now you say the word *car*," (Have the child say the word.) "Take the */c/* off *car* and put on a */j/* to make a new word. The new word is _____ (jar)." Use another example if you think it is needed. "Take the */b/* off *bunch* and put on a */l/* to make a new word. The new word is _____ (lunch)."

Use the words on the Record Sheet. Use the general prompt above. Place a ✓ in the appropriate column after each word. Then total the correct responses and record the score in the box.

		Correct	Incorrect
1. /m/ off mad and put on an /s/	sad	_____	_____
2. /f/ off fish and put a /d/	dish	_____	_____
3. /b/ off bell and put a /f/	fell	_____	_____
4. /p/ off pup and put on a /c/	cup	_____	_____
5. /s/ off see and put on a /w/	weed	_____	_____

Total Correct [ ]

Form 2

Phoneme Deletion and Substitution

Name _____ Date _____

Teacher's Directions   144
Child's Copy   None

BRIEF DIRECTIONS: PHONEME DELETION

Say to the child, "Listen to me say the word *fun*. I can say the word *fun* without the */f/*. *Fun* without the */f/* is
un. Now I'll say some words, and I want you to tell me what is left when the first sound is taken away." Use
another example if you think it is needed. "Listen to me say the word *make*. I can say the word *make* without
the */m/*. *Make* without the */m/* is *ake*."

Use the words on the Record Sheet. The general prompt for each word is, "What is _____ without the
/_/?" Place a ✓ in the appropriate column after each word. Then total the correct responses and record the
score in the box.

		Correct	Incorrect
1. team without /t/	earn	_____	_____
2. made without /m/	ade	_____	_____
3. sat without /s/	at	_____	_____
4. race without /r/	ace	_____	_____
5. leg without /l/	eg	_____	_____

Total Correct ☐

BRIEF DIRECTIONS: PHONEME SUBSTITUTION

Say to the child, "Listen to the word *fun*. I can make a new word. I can take the */f/* off *fun* and put on a */r/*
and make *run*. Now you say the word *car*." (Have the child say the word.) "Take the */c/* off *car* and put on a
/j/ to make a new word. The new word is _____ (jar)." Use another example if you think it is needed.
"Take the */b/* off *bunch* and put on a */l/* to make a new word. The new word is _____ (lunch)."

Use the words on the Record Sheet. Use the general prompt above. Place a ✓ mark in the appropriate column after each word. Then total the correct responses and record the score in the box.

		Correct	Incorrect
1. /c/ off cat and put on an /f/	fat	_____	_____
2. /s/ off sing and put on a /w/	wing	_____	_____
3. /r/ off red and put on a /b/	bed	_____	_____
4. /d/ off duck and put on a /l/	luck	_____	_____
5. /p/ off pack and put on a /b/	back	_____	_____

Total Correct ☐

AUDITORY DISCRIMINATION

OVERVIEW	Auditory Discrimination will help evaluate the child's ability to distinguish between words that differ in one phoneme (sound). Children typically engage in auditory discrimination activities as part of initial instruction in phonics. Two forms are available so one form can be a pretest and the second form could be used as a posttest.
MATERIALS NEEDED	1. A copy of the Record Sheet for Form 1 (page 149) or Form 2 (page 150).
PROCEDURES	1. Practice the words on the list, saying them clearly in a normal voice. 2. Do not rush the child during the assessment. 3. If the child misses a pair of items or asks for one to be repeated, move on to the next item and return to any such items at the conclusion of the test. If the child responds correctly, give credit. 4. Face the child away from you and say: "Listen to the words I am about to say: *fair-far.* Do they sound exactly the same or are they different? (For young children, the teacher may prefer the words "alike" and "not alike" in place of the words "same" and "different.") Yes, they are different. Listen to these two words: *cap-cap.* Are they the same or different? Now I am going to read you pairs of words. I want you to tell me if they are the same or different. Do you understand what you are to do? Please turn your back to me and listen very carefully." 5. Say all the words distinctly but in a normal voice. 6. Mark + for correct responses and – for incorrect responses.
SCORING AND INTERPRETATION	Note the number of correct "same" and "different" responses and enter the total on the Record Sheet on page 149 or page 150. Based on the error scores, make a judgment about the child's auditory discrimination ability. A child who misses two or more of the "same" pairs may not have understood the concepts "same" and "different." Such results may mean that the test was not valid. Areas of concern can be strengthened by the instructional strategies and activities in Section 3.2.

Form 1

Auditory Discrimination

Name _____ Date _____

Teacher's Directions   148
Child's Copy   None

			Same	Different
1. though	—	show		❏
2. moss	—	moth		❏
3. jump	—	jump	❏	
4. luck	—	lock		❏
5. sing	—	sing	❏	
6. light	—	sight		❏
7. set	—	sit		❏
8. rap	—	rack		❏
9. bed	—	bad		❏
10. sit	—	sick		❏
11. duck	—	duck	❏	
12. can	—	tan		❏

Total Correct [ ]

Observations, Comments, Notes, and Insights

RECORD SHEET

Form 2

Auditory Discrimination

Name _____ Date _____

Teacher's Directions   148
Child's Copy   None

			Same	Different
1. debt	—	get		❑
2. tick	—	tip		❑
3. touch	—	touch	❑	
4. disk	—	desk		❑
5. mall	—	mall	❑	
6. came	—	tame		❑
7. sew	—	saw		❑
8. lass	—	laugh		❑
9. duck	—	dock		❑
10. mud	—	mug		❑
11. thing	—	thing	❑	
12. nice	—	mice		❑

Total Correct ☐

Observations, Comments, Notes, and Insights

From Laurie Elish-Piper, Jerry L. Johns, and Susan Davis Lenski, *Teaching Reading Pre-K–Grade 3* (3rd ed.).
Copyright © 2006 by Kendall/Hunt Publishing Company (1-800-247-3458, ext. 4). May be reproduced for
noncommercial educational purposes.

PHONICS: CONSONANTS

OVERVIEW	This strategy will help assess the child's knowledge of the beginning and ending sounds of words. The tasks are of the recognition (not writing) type for beginning sounds and ending sounds. Two forms are included for use as a pretest and posttest. In addition, you could use only a portion of the assessment (e.g., initial sounds or final sounds) to help evaluate your instruction.
MATERIALS NEEDED	1. The child's pages in this book containing the pictures and letters for Form 1 (pages 153–154) 2. Two 5″ × 8″ cards 3. A copy of the Record Sheet for Form 1 on pages 155–156
PROCEDURES	**Part 1 (p. 153 in Form 1)** 1. Show the child the page containing the pictures and letters. Cover everything but the first row of pictures. 2. Point to the pictures and say, "Look at the pictures and tell me what they are." If the child does not say *ball, cat, leg,* and *wagon,* say the correct words. Be sure the child knows the names of the pictures before continuing. 3. Then say, "I will say a word, and I want you to point to the picture that begins with the same beginning sound as the word I say." Then say the words one at a time and circle the child's responses on the Record Sheet. The correct responses are in bold type. The words for Form 1 are *came, wolf, box, look,* and *went.* After the last word, cover the pictures with one of the 5″ × 8″ cards. **Part 2 (p. 153 in Form 1)** 4. Cover the letters except the first row (*o, x, d, n, k*). Then say, "I will say a word. I want you to point to the letter that you hear at the beginning of the word I say. Be sure to listen for the sound at the beginning of the word." Then say the word and circle the child's response on the appropriate page of the Record Sheet. The correct response is in bold type. Then cover the line of letters, expose a new line of letters, and say the next word. If necessary, repeat the basic instruction: "Point to the letter you hear at the beginning of _____." The words for Form 1 are *duck, hand, kitten, mouse,* and *table.* *(continued)*

Part 3 (p. 154 in Form 1)

5. Cover everything but the picture of the sun and the row of letters following it. Say, "Now I want you to name the picture and then point to the letter that begins the first sound of the picture. What's this picture? Good, now point to the letter that begins the first sound of the picture." Circle the child's response on the Record Sheet. The correct response is in bold type. Continue to the next item. If the child does not say the correct name for the picture, say the correct word and repeat the directions: "Point to the letter that begins the first sound of the picture." Continue giving the remaining items in a similar fashion. The pictures for Form 1 are *sun, fish, giraffe, net,* and *pen.*

Part 4 (p. 153 in Form 1)

6. Return to the top of the page and cover everything but the first row of pictures. Then say, "You probably remember the names of these pictures. Please say them for me."

7. Then say, "This time I want you to listen to the ending sound of the word I say. Then I want you to point to the picture with the same ending sound as the word I say." Say the words one at a time and circle the child's responses on the Record Sheet. The correct responses are in bold type. The words for Form 1 are *flat, pen, bag, street,* and *tall.* The basic direction is, "Point to the picture that ends with the same ending sound as _____." When the last item is completed, cover the pictures with one of the 5″ × 8″ cards.

8. Then cover the letters except for the first line. Say, "I will say a word. I want you to point to the letter that has the same ending sound as the word I say." The basic direction is, "Point to the letter that ends with the same sound as _____." Then say the word and circle the child's response on the Record Sheet. The correct response is in bold type. Then cover that line of letters, expose a new line of letters, and say the next word. If necessary repeat the basic instruction. The words for Form 1 are *duck, band, went, house,* and *win.*

SCORING AND INTERPRETATION

1. Count the number of initial sounds recognized and record the total on the Record Sheet on page 155.

2. Count the number of ending sounds recognized and record the total on the Record Sheet on page 156.

Informally judge the child's recognition of initial and final sounds. If the child's initial and final phonic skills need to be strengthened, refer to the instructional strategies and activities in Section 3.3.

o x d n k

n d a g h

f k r x t

m s p t h

l v t j n

Form 1—Phonics: Consonants—Child's Copy

m s r o g

h y f b c

f k g s t

w c r d n

r h j n p

Form 1—Phonics: Consonants—Child's Copy

RECORD SHEET

Form 1

Phonics: Consonants

Name _____ Date _____

Teacher's Directions   151–152
Child's Copy   153–154

INITIAL CONSONANT SOUND RECOGNITION

Part 1

1. came	ball	**cat**	leg	wagon
2. wolf	ball	cat	leg	**wagon**
3. box	**ball**	cat	leg	wagon
4. look	ball	cat	**leg**	wagon
5. went	ball	cat	leg	**wagon**

Part 2

6. duck	o	x	**d**	n	k
7. hand	n	d	a	g	**h**
8. kitten	f	**k**	r	x	t
9. mouse	**m**	s	p	t	h
10. table	l	v	**t**	j	n

Part 3

11. sun	m	**s**	r	o	g
12. fish	h	h	**f**	b	c
13. giraffe	f	k	**g**	s	t
14. net	w	c	r	d	**n**
15. pen	r	h	j	n	**p**

Total Correct [ ]

Form 1

Phonics: Consonants (cont.)

Name _____ Date _____

FINAL CONSONANT SOUND RECOGNITION

Part 4

1. flat	ball	**cat**	leg	wagon	
2. pen	ball	cat	leg	**wagon**	
3. bag	ball	cat	**leg**	wagon	
4. street	ball	**cat**	leg	wagon	
5. tall	**ball**	cat	leg	wagon	
6. duck	o	x	d	n	**k**
7. band	n	**d**	a	g	h
8. went	f	k	r	x	**t**
9. house	m	**s**	p	t	h
10. win	l	v	t	j	**n**

Total Correct ☐

Observations, Comments, Notes, and Insights

PHONICS: CONSONANTS

OVERVIEW	Consonant phonic elements will help assess the child's knowledge of the beginning and ending sounds of words. The tasks are of the recognition (not writing) type for beginning sounds and ending sounds. Two forms are included for use as a pretest and posttest. In addition, you could use only a portion of the assessment (e.g., initial sounds or final sounds) to help evaluate your instruction.
MATERIALS NEEDED	1. The child's pages in this book containing the pictures and letters for Form 2 (pages 159–160) 2. Two 5″ × 8″ cards 3. A copy of the Record Sheet on pages 161–162.
PROCEDURES	**Part 1 (p. 159 in Form 2)** 1. Show the child the page containing the pictures and letters. Cover everything but the first row of pictures. 2. Point to the pictures and say, "Look at the pictures and tell me what they are." If the child does not say *ball, cat, leg,* and *wagon,* say the correct words. Be sure the child knows the names of the pictures before continuing. 3. Then say, "I will say a word, and I want you to point to the picture that begins with the same beginning sound as the word I say." Then say the words one at a time and circle the child's responses on the Record Sheet. The correct responses are in bold type. The words for Form 1 are *coat, wood, book, leaf,* and *wet.* After the last word, cover the pictures with one of the 5″ × 8″ cards. **Part 2 (p. 159 in Form 2)** 4. Cover the letters except the first row (*o, x, d, n, k*). Then say, "I will say a word. I want you to point to the letter that you hear at the beginning of the word I say. Be sure to listen for the sound at the beginning of the word." Then say the word and circle the child's response on the Record Sheet. The correct response is in bold type. Then cover the line of letters, expose a new line of letters, and say the next word. If necessary, repeat the basic instruction: "Point to the letter you hear at the beginning of _____ ." The words for Form 2 are *door, head, mother,* and *toy.* *(continued)*

Part 3 (p. 160 in Form 2)

5. Cover everything but the picture of the sun and the row of letters following it. Say, "Now I want you to name the picture and then point to the letter that begins the first sound of the picture. What's this picture? Good, now point to the letter that begins the first sound of the picture." Circle the child's response on the Record Sheet. The correct response is in bold type. Continue to the next item. If the child does not say the correct name for the picture, say the correct word and repeat the directions: "Point to the letter that begins the first sound of the picture." Continue giving the remaining items in a similar fashion. The pictures for Form 2 are *man, fork, giraffe, nose,* and *pencil.*

Part 4 (p. 159 in Form 2)

6. Return to the top of the page and cover everything but the first row of pictures. Then say, "You probably remember the names of these pictures. Please say them for me."

7. Then say, "This time I want you to listen to the ending sound of the word I say. Then I want you to point to the picture with the same ending sound as the word I say." Say the words one at a time and circle the child's responses on the Record Sheet. The correct responses are in bold type. The words for Form 2 are *hat, hen, log, feet,* and *call.* The basic direction is, "Point to the picture that ends with the same ending sound as ." When the last item is completed, cover the pictures with one of the 5″ × 8″ cards.

8. Then cover the letters except for the first line. Say, "I will say a word. I want you to point to the letter that has the same ending sound as the word I say." The basic direction is, "Point to the letter that ends with the same sound as _____ ." Then say the word and circle the child's response on the Record Sheet. The correct response is in bold type. Then cover that line of letters, expose a new line of letters, and say the next word. If necessary, repeat the basic instruction. The words for Form 2 are *truck, land, bend, mouse,* and *pin.*

SCORING AND INTERPRETATION

1. Count the number of initial sounds recognized and record the total on the Record Sheet on page 161.
2. Count the number of ending sounds recognized and record the total on the Record Sheet on page 162.

Informally judge the child's recognition of initial and final sounds. If the child's initial and final phonic skills need to be strengthened, refer to the instructional strategies and activities in Section 3.3.

o   x   d   n   k

n   d   a   g   h

f   k   r   x   t

m   s   p   t   h

l   v   t   j   n

Form 2—Phonics: Consonants—Child's Copy

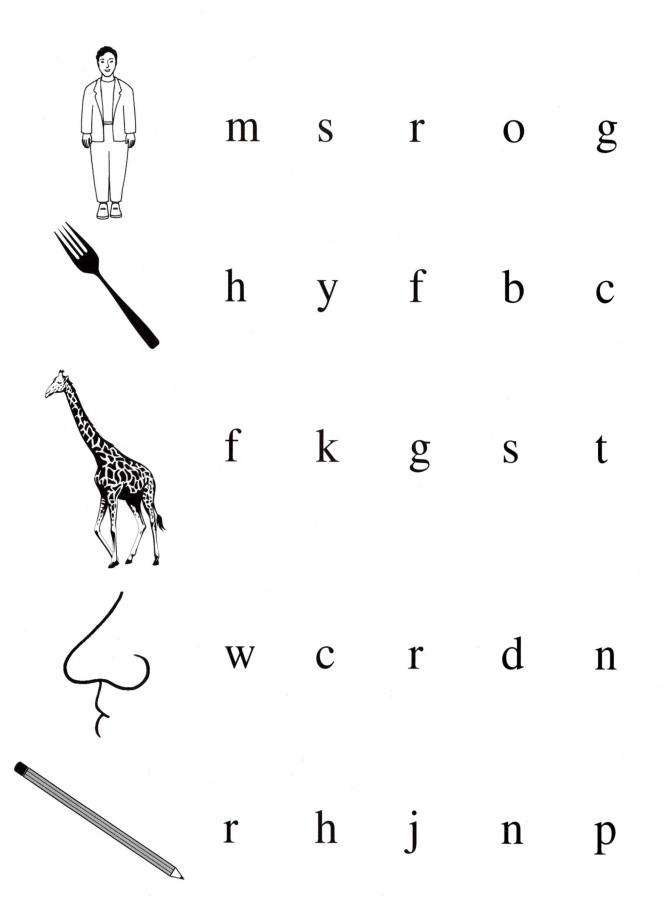

m	s	r	o	g
h	y	f	b	c
f	k	g	s	t
w	c	r	d	n
r	h	j	n	p

Form 2—Phonics: Consonants—Child's Copy

RECORD SHEET

Form 2

Phonics: Consonants

Name _____ Date _____

Teacher's Directions   157–158
Child's Copy   159–160

INITIAL CONSONANT SOUND RECOGNITION

Part 1

1. coat	ball	**cat**	leg	wagon
2. wood	ball	cat	leg	**wagon**
3. book	**ball**	cat	leg	wagon
4. leaf	ball	cat	**leg**	wagon
5. wet	ball	cat	leg	**wagon**

Part 2

6. door	o	x	**d**	n	k
7. head	n	d	a	g	**h**
8. keep	f	**k**	r	x	t
9. mother	**m**	s	p	t	h
10. toy	l	v	**t**	j	n

Part 3

11. man	**m**	s	r	o	g
12. fork	h	y	**f**	b	e
13. giraffe	f	k	**g**	s	t
14. nose	w	c	r	d	**n**
15. pencil	r	h	j	n	**p**

Total Correct ☐

From Laurie Elish-Piper, Jerry L. Johns, and Susan Davis Lenski, *Teaching Reading Pre-K–Grade 3* (3rd ed.).
Copyright © 2006 by Kendall/Hunt Publishing Company (1-800-247-3458, ext. 4). May be reproduced for
noncommercial educational purposes.

Form 2

Phonics: Consonants (cont.)

Name _____ Date _____

FINAL CONSONANT SOUND RECOGNITION

Part 4

1. hat	ball	**cat**	leg	wagon
2. hen	ball	cat	leg	**wagon**
3. log	ball	cat	**leg**	wagon
4. feet	ball	**cat**	leg	wagon
5. call	**ball**	cat	leg	wagon
6. truck	o	x	d	n **k**
7. land	n	**d**	a	g h
8. bent	f	k	r	x **t**
9. mouse	m	s	p	t **h**
10. pin	l	v	t	j **n**

Total Correct ☐

Observations, Comments, Notes, and Insights

DECODING

OVERVIEW	This assessment is adapted from the work of Cunningham (1990) and Duffelmeyer, Kruse, Merkley, and Fyfe (1994). It is intended to provide an easy and appealing way to assess the child's ability to decode words. It is possible to analyze the results to help determine the child's strengths and weaknesses in phonics. There are two forms of the assessment. To get an overview of the child's decoding skills, administer one of the forms and analyze the results. A more complete picture of the child's decoding will result if you administer both Form 1 and Form 2, because there will be a greater number of items upon which to base your analysis.
MATERIALS NEEDED	1. The child's page in this book containing the list of names, either Form 1 (page 165) or Form 2 (page 168) 2. A 5″ × 8″ card 3. A copy of the Record Sheet on page 166 or page 169 that corresponds to the form selected for use 4. A copy of the Scoring Chart on page 167 or page 170 that corresponds to the form selected for use
PROCEDURES	1. Place the list of names before the child and say something like, "I'd like you to pretend to be a teacher who must read the names of students in a class—just as I have done in our class. Do the best you can and make a guess if you're not sure." Use a 5″ × 8″ card to expose one name at a time and say, "Begin with this one." 2. Encourage the child to read the entire list but be sensitive to a child who may find the task too difficult or frustrating after several names. Be supportive and encouraging; however, use your professional judgment to decide whether to discontinue the assessment. 3. As the child responds, use the Record Sheet to note correct (+) responses. When responses are incorrect, write phonetic spellings (e.g., Rit for Rite, Chook for Chuck, Prostin for Preston) for names that are mispronounced.
SCORING AND INTERPRETATION	Use the child's responses on the Record Sheet along with the corresponding Scoring Chart to analyze the child's responses and gain insights into the child's strengths and weaknesses in phonics. The Scoring Chart contains eight categories to help you analyze the results. On the Record Sheet, mark the child's responses by circling the corresponding items on the Scoring Chart that are *(continued)*

correct. Total the items for each category. Then you will have an indication of how well the child performed in relationship to the total number of items for the category. For example, if the child knows 12 of the 14 initial consonants in Form 1, you could reasonably conclude that the child knows most of the initial consonants assessed. You could also decide if the two "missed" consonants should be taught. If there is an area where only a few items are known, that particular area of phonics may need to be taught to the child.

Remember that identified areas of strength and weakness should be verified through ongoing instruction. There are also some categories that contain only a few items. For these categories, any possible weaknesses should be viewed as tentative.

Based on data obtained from Cunningham (1990), it is reasonable to expect children in second grade to obtain an average score of less than 50%. By fifth grade, the average child will achieve a score of greater than 90%. Another study by Dufffelmeyer, Kruse, Merkley, and Fyfe (1994) using a longer version of Cunningham's test found that the average child in second grade received a score of 63% correct. By fifth grade, the average score was 92%. Keep these percentages in mind as you interpret the results. In addition, use the results to help decide which phonics skills and patterns should be taught within your curriculum.

Additional Ways of Assessing Phonics and Decoding

1. As children orally read instructional materials in the classroom, informally analyze their miscues or errors. Look for patterns of miscues and plan appropriate responsive instruction. For example, a child who has difficulty with the middle of words may have problems with certain vowels. Determine which specific vowels or vowel combinations need to be taught to the child.

2. Use the graded passages found in Section 6.4, Assessment Strategy 4. As the child reads the passages, mark any miscues made. Analyze the miscues to find patterns of specific sounds that may be unknown. Base your instruction on this type of analysis. Be open to change your instruction if additional information suggests another course of action.

3. Use an informal reading inventory (Johns, 2005) in the ways noted above to help determine the child's strengths and weaknesses in phonics. Many informal reading inventories have provisions to analyze miscues in a systematic manner to help determine instructional needs.

Bertha Murphy

Tim Cornell

Yolanda Clark

Roberta Slade

Gus Quincy

Ginger Yale

Patrick Tweed

Wendy Swain

Fred Sherwood

Dee Skidmore

Ned Westmoreland

Troy Whitlock

Thelma Sheperd

Form 1—Decoding—Child's Copy

Based on Cunningham, P. (1990) and Duffelmeyer, F. A., Kruse, A. E., Merkley, D. J., & Fyfe, S. A. (1994).

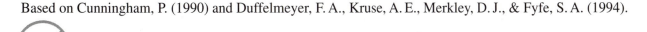

RECORD SHEET

Form 1

Decoding

Name _____ Date _____

Teacher's Directions	163–164
Child's Copy	165
Scoring Chart	167

BRIEF DIRECTIONS

Present the sheet with the names to the child. Say, "I'd like you to pretend to be a teacher who must read the names of students in a class—just as I have done in our class. Do the best that you can and make a guess if you're not sure." Use a 5″ × 8″ card to expose one name at a time and say, "Begin with this one." Note correct responses with a plus (+) and use phonetic spellings for names that are mispronounced. Total correct responses and record the score in the box.

	First Name	Last Name
Bertha Murphy	_____	_____
Tim Cornell	_____	_____
Yolanda Clark	_____	_____
Roberta Slade	_____	_____
Gus Quincy	_____	_____
Ginger Yale	_____	_____
Patrick Tweed	_____	_____
Wendy Swain	_____	_____
Fred Sherwood	_____	_____
Dee Skidmore	_____	_____
Ned Westmoreland	_____	_____
Troy Whitlock	_____	_____
Thelma Sheperd	_____	_____

Total Correct [ ]

Scoring Chart for Decoding

Name _____ Date _____

Name	Initial Con.	Initial Con. Blends	Con. Digraphs	Short Vowels	Long Vowels/ VC-e	Vowel Digraphs	Controlled Vowels	Schwa
Bertha Murphy	B M		th ph		y		er ur	a
Tim Cornell	T C			i e			or	
Yolanda Clark	Y	Cl		a	o		ar	a
Roberta Slade	R	Sl			o ade		er	a
Gus Quincy	G			u i	y			
Ginger Yale	G Y			i	ale		er	
Patrick Tweed	P	Tw		a, i		ee		
Wendy Swain	W	Sw		e	y	ai		
Fred Sherwood		Fr	Sh	e		oo	er	
Dee Skidmore	D	Sk		i		ee	or	
Ned Westmoreland	N W			e e			or	a
Troy Whitlock		Tr	Wh	i, o		oy		
Thelma Sheperd			Th Sh	e e			er	a
Totals	14	7	6	17	7	5	10	5

Jay Conway

Chuck Hoke

Kimberly Blake

Homer Preston

Cindy Sampson

Chester Wright

Stanley Shaw

Glen Spencer

Flo Thorton

Grace Brewster

Ron Smitherman

Vance Middleton

Bernard Pendergraph

Form 2—Decoding—Child's Copy

Based on Cunningham, P. (1990) and Duffelmeyer, F. A., Kruse, A. E., Merkley, D. J., & Fyfe, S. A. (1994).

Form 2

Decoding

Name _____ Date _____

Teacher's Directions 163–164
Child's Copy 168
Scoring Chart 170

▶ BRIEF DIRECTIONS

Present the sheet with the names to the child. Say, "I'd like you to pretend to be a teacher who must read the names of students in a class—just as I have done in our class. Do the best that you can and make a guess if you're not sure." Use a 5″ × 8″ card to expose one name at a time and say, "Begin with this one." Note correct responses with a plus (+) and use phonetic spellings for names that are mispronounced. Total correct responses and record the score in the box.

	First Name	Last Name
Jay Conway	_____	_____
Chuck Hoke	_____	_____
Kimberly Blake	_____	_____
Homer Preston	_____	_____
Cindy Sampson	_____	_____
Chester Wright	_____	_____
Stanley Shaw	_____	_____
Glen Spencer	_____	_____
Flo Thorton	_____	_____
Grace Brewster	_____	_____
Ron Smitherman	_____	_____
Vance Middleton	_____	_____
Bernard Pendergraph	_____	_____

Total Correct ☐

Based on Cunningham, P. (1990) and Duffelmeyer, F. A., Kruse, A. E., Merkley, D. J., & Fyfe, S. A. (1994). From Laurie Elish-Piper, Jerry L. Johns, and Susan Davis Lenski, *Teaching Reading Pre-K–Grade 3* (3rd ed.). Copyright © 2006 by Kendall/Hunt Publishing Company (1-800-247-3458, ext. 4). May be reproduced for noncommercial educational purposes.

Form 2

Scoring Chart for Decoding

Name _____ Date _____

Name	Initial Con.	Initial Con. Blends	Con. Digraphs	Short Vowels	Long Vowels/ VC-e	Vowel Digraphs	Controlled Vowels	Schwa
Jay Conway	J C			o		ay ay		
Chuck Hoke	H		Ch	u	oke			
Kimberly Blake	K	Bl		i	y ake		er	
Homer Preston	H	Pr		e	o		er	o
Cindy Sampson	C S			i a	y			o
Chester Wright			Ch	e	i		er	
Stanley Shaw		St	Sh	a		ey aw		
Glen Spencer		Gl Sp		e e			er	
Flo Thorton		Fl	Th		o		or	o
Grace Brewster		Gr Br			ace	ew	er	
Ron Smitherman	R Sm		th	i	o	er	a	
Vance Middleton	V M			a i				o
Bernard Pendergraph	B P		ph	e, a			er, ar er	
Totals	12	9	6	16	8	5	10	5

chapter *four*

Fluency and High-Frequency Words

Overview

If fluency was once considered a neglected reading goal (Rupley, 2005), that is no longer the case. In 2000, the *Report of the National Reading Panel* identified fluency as one of the five critical components of effective reading instruction. One of the necessary foundations to help children read fluently is the ability to recognize many words at sight. Additional foundations (e.g., oral language, letter familiarity, phonemic awareness, decoding) for fluency are presented in other chapters, so this chapter will offer strategies to help children learn high-frequency words and develop fluency.

Questions/Answers

What is fluency?

Over the last two decades, the concept of fluency has evolved to include four essential components: 1) speed or rate, 2) accuracy, 3) prosody (appropriate expression), and 4) comprehension (Johns & Berglund, 2006). Basically, fluency means that the child does not have word-identification problems that would hinder the speed, accuracy, or comprehension of what is read (Harris & Hodges, 1995). It also means that the child reads with proper expression and groups words that belong together. The following sentence provides an example of what good phrasing looks like when a child reads it aloud (slashes indicate groupings): The spotted cat/ sat quietly/ under the tree.

How do high-frequency words fit with fluency?

There is a small core of words that occur over and over again in English. These words have been identified as basic, core, essential, or high frequency and have been presented in lists such as the Revised Dolch List included in this chapter. If children are unable to recognize these words automatically, they will have great difficulty becoming fluent readers. A mastery of high-frequency words is a necessary, but not sufficient, foundation for fluency. Although these words comprise over 60 percent of the words on a page of text, children also need to know many additional sight words if they are to become efficient and effective readers.

Why is fluency important?

Fluency is the bridge between decoding and reading comprehension (Pikulski & Chard, 2005). Children who experience difficulty in reading, for the most part, are not fluent readers (Klenk & Kibby, 2000). When children gain fluency, they can focus more of their attention on constructing meaning during reading.

What conclusions about fluency can be drawn from research and expert opinion?

After reviewing numerous studies, the contributors to the Report of the National Reading Panel (2000) noted that fluency can be improved for both good readers and for readers who struggle. "Classroom practices that encourage repeated oral reading with feedback and guidance lead to meaningful improvements in reading expertise for students" (National Reading Panel, 2000, p. 3-3). This finding is supported by Klenk and Kibby (2000) who also reviewed fluency research and found that repeated reading was a common method of developing fluency, especially in the primary grades. They also found that teacher modeling of the text that children were about to read was another effective practice to promote fluency.

How can fluency be assessed?

Several procedures can be used to assess fluency. Informal reading inventories (e.g., Johns, 2005) permit you to time a child's reading and then calculate the number of words read per minute. Similar calculations can be done using materials from classroom instruction or by using running records (Clay, 1985). Informal fluency rubrics may also be used. Some of these methods will be described in this chapter so you will have multiple ways to assess a child's fluency if you desire to do so.

High-Frequency Words

> **Goal:** To help children learn high-frequency words by sight.
>
> **Assessment Strategy 1** High-Frequency Words, page 214
>
> **Assessment Strategy 2** Common Nouns, page 220

Background

There are two major ways that words are identified: automatically and through mediated strategies. The automatic method of word identification is referred to as sight words, and high-frequency words are the focus of this section. (Mediated strategies refer to using phonics, structural analysis, and context. These strategies can help children identify words that are not known at sight so that the words can ultimately become sight words. Some of these strategies are introduced in chapters 3 and 4).

Knowledge of high-frequency words is critical for fluent reading. When children know these words by sight, they are pronounced quickly and easily. A number of words in our language occur very frequently, and these words, called high-frequency words, are important for children to learn at sight. Did you know that 13 words account for nearly 25% of the words children (and adults) encounter in their reading? The 13 words are listed below.

a   and   for   he   in   is   it   of   that   the   to   was   you

In addition to the 13 high-frequency or basic words, there are word lists that contain additional words that children need to learn if their reading is to become fluent (Fry, Fountoukidis, & Polk, 2000; Johns & Lenski, 2005; Zeno, Ivens, Millard, & Duvvuri, 1995). These sight words are a necessary, but insufficient, basis for fluent reading. That is because words like those contained in the Revised Dolch List (Johns, 1981) comprise only 50% to 60% of the words children encounter in their reading. Many other words also need to be learned at sight. You will also need to teach words related to units of study and those found in books used for instruction.

Children need to learn to automatically read and write words by sight for two major reasons. First, by knowing words at sight, children can devote their attention to decoding less common words and focusing on the meaning of what they are reading and writing. Second, because a number of these words are not pronounced or spelled in predictable ways (Hiebert & Martin, 2001), decoding them can be difficult and confusing. Third, children will often see these words in their reading and use them in their writing, so they will benefit greatly from knowing basic words automatically.

The teaching strategies, along with the ideas and activities presented in this section, offer a range of options for helping children learn to recognize high-frequency words at sight so their reading can become more automatic and fluent. Easy-to-use strategies for assessing sight word knowledge are also provided at the end of this chapter.

EXPLICIT INSTRUCTION

Explicit Instruction of high-frequency words allows teachers to help children learn important sight words in an efficient manner. By providing focused instruction on targeted sight words, children can learn to read, spell, and write the words in a relatively short period of time.

DIRECTIONS

1. Select several targeted sight words. Two lists of basic sight words are provided at the end of this strategy. The high-frequency words on these lists should be learned at sight (automatically) by children. The words *take* and *make* will be exemplified in this lesson.

2. Say each word aloud and use it in a sentence.

   take   I will take my dog for a walk.

   make   My dad will make my favorite snack.

3. Encourage children to use each word in a sentence and then write the sentences on the chalkboard. Underline each target word.

   Help me <u>take</u> out the garbage.

   I would like to <u>make</u> a kite.

4. Discuss each word's use and special features. You might want to emphasize that the words rhyme, that they differ in only one letter, only the first letter in each word differs, and the *e* is "silent" (not pronounced).

5. Ask the children to spell each word aloud as you point to each letter. Be sure that each word is clearly written on the chalkboard. Children can also chant the spelling of each word as you point or a child points to each letter.

6. Invite children to spell the words in the air with their fingers as they orally recite the spelling of each word.

7. Have children write each word on paper and spell it aloud as they write.

8. Invite children to write each word on a note card and place it in their personal word banks. You can also have children hold up a card to indicate which of the words you say in a sentence. Some possible sentences appear below.

   I <u>take</u> out the ball for recess.

   Do you know how to <u>make</u> the toy?

   I must <u>make</u> my bed.

   Will you <u>take</u> me with you?

9. Make copies of the words so they can be placed on the Word Wall (see Teaching Strategy 2). Use a similar procedure as additional high-frequency words are introduced.

REVISED DOLCH LIST

a*	could	he*	might	same	told
about*	cut	heard	more	saw	too
across	did	help	most	say	took
after	didn't	her*	much	see	toward
again	do	here	must	she*	try
all*	does	high	my	short	turn
always	done	him	near	should	two
am	don't	his*	need	show	under
an*	down	hold	never	six	up*
and*	draw	hot	next	small	upon
another	eat	how	new	so*	us
any	enough	I*	no	some*	use
are*	even	I'm	not*	soon	very
around	every	if*	now	start	walk
as*	far	in*	of*	still	want
ask	fast	into	off	stop	warm
at*	find	is*	oh	take	was*
away	first	it*	old	tell	we*
be*	five	its	on*	ten	well
because	for*	just	once	than	went
been	found	keep	one*	that*	were*
before	four	kind	only	the*	what*
began	from*	know	open	their*	when*
best	full	last	or*	them	where
better	gave	leave	other	then	which
big	get	left	our	there*	while
black	give	let	out*	these	white
blue	go	light	over	they*	who
both	going	like	own	think	why
bring	gone	little	play	this*	will
but*	good	long	put	those	with*
by*	got	look	ran	thought	work
call	green	made	read	three	would*
came	grow	make	red	through	yes
can*	had*	many	right	to*	yet
close	hard	may	round	today	you*
cold	has	me	run	together	your
come	have*	mean	said*		

*one of the 50 most common words.

The rationale and research for this list is described in Johns, J. L. (1981). The development of the revised Dolch list. *Illinois School Research and Development, 17,* 15–24. From Laurie Elish-Piper, Jerry L. Johns, and Susan Davis Lenski, *Teaching Reading Pre-K–Grade 3* (3rd ed.). Copyright © 2006 by Kendall/Hunt Publishing Company (1-800-247-3458, ext. 4). May be reproduced for noncommercial educational purposes.

High-Frequency Nouns

air	girl	nothing
back	group	people
book	hand	place
boy	head	road
car	home	room
children	house	school
city	man	side
day	men	table
dog	money	thing
door	morning	time
eye	mother	top
face	Mr.	town
father	Mrs.	tree
feet	name	water
friend	night	way
		year

The rationale and research for this list is described in Johns, J. L. (1981). The development of the revised Dolch list. *Illinois School Research and Development, 17,* 15–24. From Laurie Elish-Piper, Jerry L. Johns, and Susan Davis Lenski, *Teaching Reading Pre-K–Grade 3* (3rd ed.). Copyright © 2006 by Kendall/Hunt Publishing Company (1-800-247-3458, ext. 4). May be reproduced for noncommercial educational purposes.

Tips for English Language Learners

- High-frequency words are abstract and difficult for many children to learn. Use plenty of oral language activities with these words. Children will use high-frequency words when they speak, even if the utterance is incomplete. Use children's language to create phrase cards and illustrations to help children expand their reading vocabularies.

José <u>and</u> Mike

Chandy <u>runs</u>.

Cal <u>is</u> small.

- Label objects in the classroom using high-frequency words and a noun. For example, the door to the classroom can be labeled "the brown door." Use a similar approach with other objects: a big clock, the white wall, our library, the teacher's desk, our reading corner, and so on. Link these phrases to ongoing lessons when appropriate.

Section 4.1   *TEACHING STRATEGY*   **2**

WORD WALL

The Word Wall strategy is helpful for teaching high-frequency words. The words are taught to children, and then they are posted on the Word Wall for future reference. A variety of hands-on activities are also incorporated into Word Wall instruction to help children learn and remember the high-frequency words (Cunningham, 2000). Typically, teachers will spend a few minutes each day teaching and reviewing new Word Wall words over the course of a week. The following directions provide suggestions for teaching Word Wall words over a period of several days.

DIRECTIONS

1. Select up to five target high-frequency words to teach in a week. Word lists containing high-frequency words, children's spelling errors, and grade-level curricula are sources of words for the Word Wall.

2. Introduce each word to students by writing it on an index card and using the word in a sentence. Write the sentence on the chalkboard and underline the Word Wall word.

3. Ask children to suggest other sentences that use the Word Wall word. Discuss the meaning or use of the word.

4. Point to each letter of the word as you spell it aloud. Invite children to spell the word with you as you point to each letter.

5. Trace around the configuration of the word using another color of chalk. Discuss the shape of the word.

6. Follow this pattern for each of the new Word Wall words. Place the index cards for the five new words on the Word Wall. Arrange the words alphabetically and use a different color of index card or ink for each new word.

7. Engage children in the Clap, Chant, and Write activity. Ask children to number a piece of scratch paper from one to five. Say each word, using it in a sentence. Ask children to write each word on their paper. Then have children clap and chant the spelling of each word as you lead the process. Have children correct their own spellings.

8. On another day, select five words appropriate for rhyming. Ask children to review rhymes using the Word Wall. Have children number a sheet of scratch paper from one to five. Ask them to write a Word Wall word that rhymes with the word you give to them. Give children the rhyming word and the first letter as clues. For example, you might say the word begins with *m* and rhymes with *by*. Continue this pattern for all five Word Wall words.

9. Guide children to check their own words. Ask them to say the word they wrote and to spell it aloud when you call each number and restate the clues. For example, after you say, "Number 1. The word begins with /m/ and rhymes with *by*," children should respond, "My, m-y." Continue with this pattern until all five words have been checked. Ask children to correct their work as you complete this step.

10. On another day, engage children in a cross-checking activity with the Word Wall words. Tell the children that they will need to select the Word Wall word that makes sense in a sentence and begins with a certain letter. For example, tell the children, "The word begins with *t* and fits in the sentence I went to _____ store yesterday." Continue with this pattern with all five Word Wall words.

11. Have children check their own words by reading each sentence again and restating the beginning letter of the word. Ask children to chant the word and then the spelling for each of the five Word Wall words.

12. Remind children that the Word Wall is an important resource to help them with their reading, writing, and spelling. For additional Word Wall activities, consult Cunningham (2000).

ASSOCIATIVE LEARNING

Associative Learning for high-frequency words is a strategy designed for use with children who have difficulty learning high-frequency words because the words lack meaning clues. The associative learning technique helps children develop concrete associations for abstract high-frequency words such as *for, of* and *the* (Cunningham, 2000).

✍ DIRECTIONS

1. Select one or two targeted high-frequency words for this strategy, for example, *of.* Present the word by using it in a phrase accompanied by an illustration. The word should be underlined as shown in the example below.

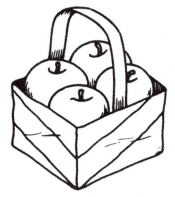

a box <u>of</u> apples

2. Have children brainstorm other possible ways to use *of* in a phrase or sentence. After several oral examples have been shared, distribute index cards and invite children to make their own picture cards and label them. Ask children to write the targeted sight word using a red crayon or marker. Have children underline their word. Be ready to assist children with the spelling of the other words that are part of their phrase. Some sample cards are shown below.

a glass <u>of</u> juice   two <u>of</u> my friends

3. Provide time for children to share their picture cards with other children. The phrase cards can become part of children's word banks.

CREATING PHRASES AND SENTENCES

To help children move their learning of single high-frequency words into context, phrases and sentences can be created with the high-frequency words children are learning. Children should also be given an opportunity to help create phrases and sentences using high-frequency words. Multiple practice opportunities are needed to help children recognize the words automatically.

DIRECTIONS

1. Select high-frequency words and some nouns that students have been learning. The Revised Dolch List and the High-Frequency Nouns found in Teaching Strategy 1 in Section 4.1 are useful resources for creating phrases and sentences. The words below are used to exemplify a typical lesson.

boy	girl	and	is	big	see
the	have	water	by	can	run

2. Display the words on individual cards on a wall chart or on the chalkboard tray. Tell the children that they have been learning these words. Point to each word and have the class pronounce it.

3. Then say, "I can put some of these words together and make a short phrase. Watch while I choose three words and make a phrase." Put the phrase *boy and girl* on the wall chart or chalkboard tray. Have the children say the phrase. Create other phrases and have the children repeat them. Some possible phrases are listed below.

the big boy	the little girl	by the water	the little boy	the little girl
can run	can see	boy and girl	have water	girl can run
boy can run	run and see	run by water	by water	can see water

4. Invite children to make additional phrases from the words. Stress that the phrases should make sense. As children suggest phrases, write them on the chalkboard and have the class read them together.

5. During this lesson or a future lesson, focus on making sentences. Use a procedure similar to steps 3 and 4 above. Some possible sentences are listed below.

The girl and boy are big.	The boy and girl are little.
The little girl can see.	The girl is by the water.
The boy can run.	See the girl run by the water.
See the girl.	See the water.
The boy is big.	The boy and girl see the water.
See the little girl run.	The girl is by the water.

6. As children become more familiar and comfortable with the activity, have them write the words for the lesson on strips of paper and individually make phrases and sentences. Encourage the children to work individually, with partners, and then in small groups.

7. Children can be given additional opportunities for practice by reading the phrases and sentences on the following pages. All the phrases and sentences are made from the Revised Dolch List and the High-Frequency Nouns. Once children master all these words, they will be able to recognize over 60 percent of the words in reading materials typically used in the primary grades.

PHRASES WITH HIGH FREQUENCY NOUNS

through the air	give some money
back again	in the morning
saw the book	with my mother
boy can play	Mr. Green
car went fast	Mrs. White
small children	your name
the big city	every night
a long day	nothing better
their old dog	many good people
open the door	the only place
close one eye	a long road
see your face	my own room
with my father	his new school
two feet	by my side
one good friend	under the table
a small girl	which small thing
four in a group	how much time
in your hand	over the top
on her head	through some town
going home	up in the tree
around the house	in the warm water
an old man	one way to go
two mean men	every year

PHRASES WITH REVISED DOLCH LIST

a big green tree	been going to play	didn't know which one	gave some away
about that girl	before she said	do go to town	get one through
across her face	began to hold	does keep his dog	give him one
after this morning	best place	done with that	go with them
again today	better book	don't leave now	going away
all around my house	big green house	down and up	gone for good
always going together	long black road	draw some people	good enough for me
I am not	cold blue water	eat in the morning	got close to it
an old school	both good and bad	enough to keep	green and blue
father and mother	bring a friend	even though	grow up
another friend	but then	every little thing	had to help her
any old place	by the tree	far away	hard to do
are going	to call him	fast enough for me	has a cold
around the room	came into the room	find out which one	have to go
as he heard	can go together	first thing	he and she
ask to help	close the door	high five	heard a dog
at another city	cold water	not for long	help find out
going away	come together	found out	her own town
over here	be open	could read a book	four more

(continues)

PHRASES WITH REVISED DOLCH LIST

high up	because he heard her	cut through it	from here to there
with him	did look away	full of light	his small feet
hold my hand	make another friend	old red school house	see a tree
hot enough for me	she and I	how long	many more
on top of that	short walk around	she and I	may it be
once there was	should have been	why I'm small	find me first
one of those feet	show how big	if I can	big and mean
only two more	five or six	in its house	might leave now
open the right one	small enough to	into the road	more than that
or you might not	so short that	is enough	most of all
other than that	some of that	before it was	much more than that
our little children	group	its own place	out the door
soon enough	just enough	must have been	over the tree
start to go	keep near	my new dog	our own house
still more than	what kind of thing	near the door	play with you
to stop	know how to read	need to go	put that away
some more	last one out	never tell	ran from me
to tell me	leave again	next one	read with
ten more than that	left or right	new day	red and black

(continues)

From Laurie Elish-Piper, Jerry L. Johns, and Susan Davis Lenski, *Teaching Reading Pre-K–Grade 3* (3rd ed.). Copyright © 2006 by Kendall/Hunt Publishing Company (1-800-247-3458, ext. 4). May be reproduced for noncommercial educational purposes.

PHRASES WITH REVISED DOLCH LIST

not more than this	let it go	no one around	right down there that
while they play	light and fast	not now	his round face
the big thing	like any other	now we go	run away
their own home	little green me	one of those	said to me
not all of them	long gone	off the road	same as her
then there was	look around	oh stop	saw an eye
over there	made a friend	say nothing	these two people
took a car	they should start	very long road	your white house
toward the town	think about	to walk with me	try to run
turn around	this red table	want to go	two or three
under the table	those good children	a warm day	up and out
upon the door	was well done	with us	to use it
thought to leave	as we go	white and black	who one is
three more than that	well enough	why both can go	will go away
went around	with both of them	work every day	through an old door
were never so small	would like to go	yes, there is	yet another one
you and she	to the town	what once was	before today
when we walk	together again	where you go	told to do
which one	too much help		

SENTENCES WITH HIGH FREQUENCY NOUNS

The air is cold.

Can you bring it back?

Mr. Green read a book.

The boy ran away.

A car is going fast.

The children read.

The city is big.

Another day went by.

The dog can play.

Close the door.

Keep one eye open.

I see your face.

Ask your father.

Put those on your feet.

Who is your friend?

This girl can draw.

The group went to town.

He can hold her hand.

Put that on your head.

Let us go home.

I like our little house.

That man is Mr. Black.

Some men left town.

Do you have any money?

I get up in the morning.

My mother is short.

Mr. Black is going home.

Mrs. Green read this book.

What is your name?

I read at night.

Nothing can stop you.

The people sit at the table.

Which place will you go?

The car is in the road.

I have my own room.

She is going to school.

Come over by my side.

The dog is under the table.

Which thing do you have?

How much time is left?

Look at the top of the tree.

I'm going to town.

Can he go up the tree?

Turn off the water.

Which way did he go?

Every year I grow.

SENTENCES WITH REVISED DOLCH LIST

A dog is my friend.

I like to read about children.

She ran across the room.

We went after they did.

He heard me again.

All children can come.

I always try my best.

I am your friend.

They saw an open door.

I draw with blue and green.

We saw another city.

Do you have any water?

They are going home.

We went around the tree.

It was as big as a house.

What did you ask?

We read at school.

He is going away.

I want to be your friend.

I'm better because you are here.

You have been near me.

He saw her before.

We began to play.

Our dog is better than before.

His house is big.

Her dog is black.

Our book is blue.

I like both of you.

She could bring you too.

She went away but came back.

We were by the tree.

I heard mother call me.

He came with me.

Father can draw a tree.

Would you close the door?

Mother has a cold.

Would you come with me?

She could run very fast.

He cut down the tree.

I did not eat enough.

She didn't look away.

Do you play together?

She does have a dog.

We are done with that.

We don't go away.

Come down the road.

(continues)

SENTENCES WITH REVISED DOLCH LIST

This is the best school.

They might eat after I do.

I have had enough.

You have even more of that.

I like to read every day.

She ran far away.

He ran fast.

Can you find my friend?

She is always first.

Five children play together.

Come here for me.

We found a new thing.

She has four children.

We came from our house.

This room is full.

She gave him a hand.

We get into the city.

Would you give me a hand?

We go to school together.

The dog is going away.

My money is gone.

Most children are always good.

She got to go home.

Can you draw a face?

The book was hard to read.

She has been here before.

We have left town.

He will play today.

I heard you say that.

Will you help me?

Her friend will help you.

My mother is here.

The book is high up.

She saw him.

I took his hand.

We hold our money.

I will eat a hot dog.

How are you?

I like to eat.

I'm going home.

I will go if you do.

The book is in my hand.

Come into my house.

She is home.

Bring it here.

The group took its turn.

(continues)

SENTENCES WITH REVISED DOLCH LIST

My room is green.

The tree can grow.

He had some help.

I know which thing you took.

We went out last.

Don't leave me out.

He left last night.

She let us call her.

Turn off the light.

I like your dog.

He is little.

This morning is long.

Look over there.

I made this.

She can make room for you.

They have many children.

You may keep this.

Look at me.

They are mean.

He might find it.

I draw more than she does.

He has the most money.

I don't have much money.

He had just enough money.

Keep your dog away.

My mother is kind.

I want to go next.

This house is new.

There is no room here.

I am not going to leave.

He is done now.

It is full of water.

Turn off the light.

Oh, what a day this is!

This town is old.

Turn on the light.

We have been there once.

She is one year old.

There is only enough for me.

Open the door.

We can take this or that.

She will give me one or the other.

Our house is hot.

Get out.

Get over it.

I own the house.

(continues)

SENTENCES WITH REVISED DOLCH LIST

My dog must eat.

My friend is short.

She is near me.

I need to go.

She will never tell me why.

I am right.

Our table is round.

We can run around.

They said we could.

These are the same.

I saw the school.

She could say so much.

I see many people.

She is a girl.

My father is short.

He should grow up.

Can you show me?

There are six people here.

My dog is small.

Her feet are so small.

I would like some water.

We can eat soon.

When did you start?

We can go play.

She put it on her head.

He ran out the door.

We read the book.

We read the red book.

The morning is here.

Their time has come.

Give it to them.

What do we do then?

The city is over there.

These people like to read.

They can stay.

I like to think about you.

This is my father.

Those people must go away.

We thought about it.

He saw three children.

I am through with this.

She is going to go home.

I will go to the city today.

We can be together.

She told him to leave.

They like you too.

(continues)

SENTENCES WITH REVISED DOLCH LIST

Keep still.

Nothing can stop her.

Take some money over there.

Go tell your mother.

Five people have ten feet.

That is more than four.

What do you think of that?

Once upon a time the house was green.

You could come with us.

He could use some air.

The city is very big.

I want to go home.

It was cold.

She took water from the well.

We were going to go.

When is the next time?

Which one is he?

My dog is white.

Why do I have to do this?

He could go with you.

Would you like to play?

We took a look at the book.

Don't look toward the light.

You can do it if you try.

Is it my turn?

I have two feet.

She is under the table.

Don't go up there.

I am not done yet.

You are going to play now.

I like your name.

We like to go for a walk together.

My house is warm.

We can think about it.

He went with her.

What do you think of that?

Where could we see you?

I am here while she is there.

Who are you?

She will take your place.

We have work to do.

Yes, I would.

From Laurie Elish-Piper, Jerry L. Johns, and Susan Davis Lenski, *Teaching Reading Pre-K–Grade 3* (3rd ed.).
Copyright © 2006 by Kendall/Hunt Publishing Company (1-800-247-3458, ext. 4). May be reproduced for
noncommercial educational purposes.

PATTERN BOOKS

Pattern Books provide a meaningful way for children to master high-frequency words in the context of real text. As you connect word instruction and children's literature, children are able to see the words in the story, understand how they are used, and practice identifying the words in a meaningful context. The following strategy can be used with any pattern book, and it serves as an excellent introduction to teaching high-frequency words to young children (May & Rizzardi, 2002). An extensive list of pattern books can be found in Johns and Lenski (2005).

DIRECTIONS

1. Prior to beginning the lesson, select a pattern book that emphasizes the targeted high-frequency word(s). For very young children, you will want to select only one or two words for study. For older children, three to five different words can be targeted.

2. Prepare teacher-made charts that contain the text, but not pictures, from the book.

3. Write target word(s) on chart paper. Prepare cards containing the high-frequency words.

4. To teach the lesson, read the book aloud to the children. Read the book again, inviting the children to chime in when they can predict what comes next.

5. Invite the children to take turns with echo reading. For echo reading, the teacher reads a line or phrase, and then the children echo it back.

6. Provide opportunities for the children to engage in choral reading of the story. For choral reading, have a group of children read a section of text in unison. You can provide support by reading along with the children and then fading your voice at the points in the text when they are able to take on more of the reading responsibility. Use a pointer to point to each word during choral reading to help children track the words as they read them.

7. Next, have children read the text from teacher-made charts that do not contain pictures.

8. Invite children to engage in echo and choral readings of the text as described above in steps 5 and 6.

9. Next show children the targeted high-frequency word(s) on index cards and read them with the children.

10. Ask children to place matching word cards on the chart containing the text. Have children say each word as they match their cards with the words on the chart paper. This can be done by taping the word cards to the chart paper, using a pocket chart, or using magnets on a magnetic chalkboard.

11. After children place their word cards on the chart paper, read the entire text chorally with the children.

12. Next, place the word cards in random order and invite children to match the cards to the text on the chart paper. Have children say the words as they match them to the text.

13. Discuss the new words the children learned during the activity.

14. Have the children add the high-frequency words to their word banks or personal Word Walls. You can also post the targeted word(s) on the classroom Word Wall.

Activities, tips, & Center Ideas

1. Tell children that they will learn high-frequency words best if they practice them in many different ways. Use the See, Write, Point, Say, and Spell cycle to help children practice new words. Guide the children through the following steps.

   • See the word in your head. Visualize or picture what it looks like.

   • Write the word on paper; write it again using different colors; write it in different sizes; write it in the air with your finger; and write it on a friend's back using your pointing finger.

   • Point to the word and say it. Point to the word and spell it aloud, then silently.

2. Help children create personal Word Walls using file folders. Draw a grid on the file folder and label each section with a letter of the alphabet. Have children add high-frequency words to their personal Word Walls. Children can use these resources at their desks or at home as they read and write (Cunningham, 2000).

3. Wordo is a variation of Bingo that focuses on practicing high frequency words (see Revised Dolch List on page 175). For young children, divide the Wordo card into 9 blocks, and for older children use 25 blocks. You will also need to supply plastic counters, beans, or other small objects to be used to cover words as the children fill in their blocks. Make a list of high-frequency words to practice, write each word on an index card, and call out the words one at a time. Have the children chant the spelling of each word and cover it with a counter. The first child to cover an entire row of words is the winner of the game. Ask the winner to read the words aloud to check that the words have been called. The winner can then serve as the caller. Continue the game for several rounds to provide additional practice with the high-frequency words. A sample Wordo card is shown below.

WORDO

and	for	in
that	it	you
was	to	is

4. Select a children's book, poem, or chart story that contains a high-frequency word you have been teaching. Using small sticky notes or removable correction tape, cover the sight word in the text. Present the book, poem, or story to the children. When you reach the covered word, ask the children what would make sense in the blank. Reveal the first letter of the covered word. Ask the children which of their guesses will still work. Continue this pattern until all letters of the word are revealed.

5. Play word games and puzzles such as hang-man, concentration, and go fish to provide opportunities for children to practice words.

6. Use the Language Experience Approach (LEA) to teach sight words in children's spoken vocabulary. The LEA is discussed in detail in Section 2.1. Teaching Strategy 2 (pages 52–53). Draw children's attention to specific high-frequency words in the text they dictated. Have children read the high-frequency words, spell them, and discuss the words' meanings or functions in that context.

7. Trace words in salt trays, sand trays, or shaving cream to help children get multiple opportunities to write, see, and remember high-frequency words.

8. Wide reading of easy texts supports sight word development because children have many opportunities to see high-frequency words used in meaningful contexts. Provide daily time for children to read from self-selected materials.

9. Make high-frequency words in clay or play dough to allow children to feel the words and letters as they shape the clay or play dough. Ask children to point to each letter as they chant the spellings aloud. Pretzel dough or cookie dough can also be used so children can eat their baked sight words when the activity is over.

10. Go on a word hunt in the classroom or school. Ask children to identify target words as you tour the classroom or school. Discuss how the words are used and spelled. Discuss the importance of children knowing the words in their daily lives.

11. Play the grab bag game with children to reinforce word knowledge. Write high-frequency words on cards and place them in a bag. Have the children take turns selecting a card, reading it aloud, chanting the spelling, and using the word in a sentence. If the child is correct, he or she gets to keep the card. The winner has the most cards.

12. Scrambled words provide children with an opportunity to manipulate letter cards to spell high-frequency words. Write words to be practiced on different colors of construction paper or index cards. Use one word per color. For each word, have the children arrange the letters in proper order, chant the spelling, read the word, and use it in a sentence.

SIGHT WORDS

Dear Families,

Learning words at sight is an important part of becoming a good reader. Here are some suggestions for helping your child learn sight words.

- Play scavenger hunt with your child by looking for a specific sight word in the newspaper, in junk mail, or as you and your child do errands in the community.

- Help your child master the 20 most frequently used words in the English language:

the, of, and, to, a, in, is, that, it, was, for, you, he, on, as, are, they, with, be, his.

Six ideas are given below.

1. You can print the words on cards or cut the words from the attached sheets. Begin by showing each card to your child to see if the word is known. For words that are unknown, have your child look at the word while you say it and use it in a sentence.

2. Encourage your child to use the word in a phrase or sentence. Then you and your child can spell the word together out loud.

3. Have your child write the word on paper.

4. Many different experiences with these words will help your child learn them. As you read to your child, make the connection that some of the words in the book are the same as those on the cards. You can show your child the word on the card and connect it to the word on the page. Have your child also make these connections by showing you the words on the cards that match the words on a page of a book.

5. You can use these 20 words with a few other words to write phrases and sentences for your child to read. Be sure to use your child's name in the phrases and sentences.

6. Carry the cards with you so you can practice the words with your child when you have a minute or two. Practice over time will help your child master these very basic words.

I hope you and your child enjoy these activities.

Sincerely,

the	of
and	to
a	in
is	that
it	was

for	you
he	on
as	are
they	with
be	his

Fluency

Goal: To help children read smoothly and easily.

Assessment Strategy 3 Words Per Minute, page 226

Assessment Strategy 4 Fluency Scale Checklist, page 230

Background

Good readers are fluent readers. "They read words accurately, rapidly, and efficiently" (National Reading Panel, 2000, p. 3-3). When you listen to children read orally, you can spot the fluent readers. Fluent readers are able to read text in a normal speaking voice with appropriate intonation and inflection. Fluent readers are able to read texts smoothly and easily using various strategies to construct meaning from print (Duffy & Roehler, 1989). They use their knowledge of word decoding, stories, and the world to understand the meaning of new texts. A goal of reading instruction in the primary grades is for children to read fluently with good comprehension.

Many times young children are not fluent readers. Think about the children you teach. Some children may be choppy readers, reading with many stops, starts, and hesitations. They may be monotonous readers who read with little or no expression. Or children may be hasty readers and race through the passage ignoring phrasing and punctuation. When children are choppy, monotonous, or hasty readers, they are not reading fluently (Wilson, 1988).

Primary-grade children need to learn how to read fluently while they are learning other reading skills. But you need to remember that developing fluency takes time and practice. While children are building fluency, they are also expanding their sight vocabulary, learning word-identification strategies, and learning how to use their background knowledge to construct meaning from texts. As children become proficient with these reading strategies, they are able to read the words in a passage more automatically. As children read words more automatically, they can pay closer attention to reading texts smoothly and easily.

Teaching children how to read fluently also enables them to read with better comprehension. When children learn how to read in a way that mirrors spoken language, as fluent readers do, they are better able to understand the meaning of texts (Rasinski, 1989).

Pikulski and Chard (2005) identify nine areas that should be included in a comprehensive fluency program. Our adaptation of their ideas follows:

1. graphophonic (phonological awareness, phonics) foundations,

2. extending oral language skills and building sight vocabulary,

3. providing instruction in the acquisition of high-frequency words,

4. teaching common word and spelling patterns,

5. teaching, modeling, and providing practice in helpful decoding strategies,

6. using appropriate (instructional level) texts to teach fluency,

7. using repeated reading procedures (echo reading, readers theater, structured repeated reading, etc.),

8. encouraging wide independent reading, and

9. using appropriate assessment procedures to monitor fluency development. Because other chapters contain some of these strategies, the remainder of this chapter will present other helpful strategies, ideas, and activities to support the teaching of fluent reading. In addition, a number of ways to assess fluency are provided at the end of this chapter.

Section 4.2   *TEACHING STRATEGY*

ECHO READING

Echo Reading is especially useful for young children who do not know how to read. It can also be used for children who are able to read connected text. The procedure involves modeling fluent reading to children and having them echo the same text with appropriate phrasing, stress, and intonation.

DIRECTIONS

1. Initially, select a fairly easy selection to have children echo read with you. Poetry, nursery rhymes, and texts with patterns are especially good choices for very young children.

2. Invite children to tell what it means to hear an echo. Explain the concept if necessary. Help children understand that when you say something the very same words you said can be echoed or repeated back to you. Try a few simple words and phrases and have the children echo them back to you. You might use the following words and sentences:

    Hello.

    How are you?

    I'm fine.

    It's fun to echo!

3. Tell the children that you would like them to echo *One, Two, Buckle My Shoe* or another selection that will capture their interest. Say a sentence and have the children echo it back to you. After the selection is completed, show the children the text on chart paper or on an overhead transparency. Highlight punctuation marks that help cue how the text should be read.

4. Have the children look at the text and echo it, mirroring your rate, expression, and accuracy. Repeat any sentences that may need additional practice.

5. Older children can be invited to read a text and have the other children echo their reading. The same text can be echo read several times with different stress and emphasis.

6. Be on the lookout for especially engaging selections to use for echo reading with the children.

CHORAL READING

Choral reading occurs when children read poetry or other short passages together or in groups. Choral reading facilitates fluency because children are able to read print along with other children. When reading in groups, children who have trouble reading fluently are carried along with the pace and expression of the other readers. All of the readers are able to read more smoothly and easily because they are able to listen to more proficient readers as they match speech and print in a smooth, steady reading pace.

DIRECTIONS

1. Identify a poem, a short book, or a passage that would be of interest to the children who will be choral reading.

2. Note words that may be new to the children or that the children may have difficulty reading. Write the words on the chalkboard or on chart paper. Highlight and read the difficult words to the class, paying special attention to sounds or patterns in the words that the children have learned.

3. Have the entire group read the passage silently.

4. Read the passage aloud or ask one of the children to read it aloud. As the passage is read, track the print with a pointer or your hand.

5. Discuss the passage, asking children to retell the poem or story.

6. Decide on the method of choral reading. The following varieties of choral reading have been suggested by Trousdale and Harris (1993).

   • Two-part arrangement. One group of voices reads alternately with another group.

   • Soloist and chorus. One voice reads and the rest of the group joins in on the refrain.

   • Line-a-child. One child or a pair read alone. Then the next child reads the next line, and so on.

   • Increasing or decreasing volume. Voices are added or subtracted, building up to and moving away from the high point of the story.

   • Increasing or decreasing tempo. The rate of reading is increased or decreased as the passage is read.

   • Unison. The whole group reads as one.

   • Accompaniment by music, movement, or sound effects. The reading is accompanied by instruments, hand motions, or sound effects (such as snapping fingers or clapping).

   • Combination. A combination of any of the above ideas.

7. Experiment with volume, tempo, and expression. Have fun.

8. Perform the choral reading for an audience. Have a leader read the title and give the first beat so the group begins together. Tape-record or videotape the performance and replay it, listening for fluent reading.

PHRASE-CUED TEXT

At the beginning stages of reading, it is not unusual for children to read word by word. Children who struggle in second or third grade often have difficulty reading in phrases. "The concept of phrase boundaries can be taught by cueing pauses in text with slashes" (Hudson, Lane, & Pullen, 2005, p. 702). Researchers (Cromer, 1970; O'Shea & Sindelar; Rasinski, 1990) found that segmenting text into phrasal units or making phrase boundaries resulted in improved oral reading performance and comprehension, particularly for children who are slow, but accurate, readers. The strategy is also valuable for children who struggle with reading.

✒ DIRECTIONS

1. Select a familiar selection to read to children. For this lesson, "Jack and Jill" will be used.

2. Read the selection word by word, pausing after each word. For example, Jack . . . and . . . Jill . . . ran . . . up . . . the . . . hill.

3. Ask the children to describe your reading. Ask them how the reading sounded. Guide them as necessary to realize some of the following:
   - It did not sound like talk.
   - The reading was slow.
   - The words were said one at a time. They were not put together.

4. Praise the children for their insights and tell them that fluent readers chunk or group words together when they read and use slight pauses between the phrase chunks. This makes the reading sound more natural and like talk. Point out that some words sound natural when they are chunked together. You could also use a sponge to visually demonstrate how words are "squished" together.

5. Demonstrate how *Jack . . . and . . . Jill* can be "squished" together to make *Jack and Jill.* The sponge could represent *Jack and Jill* and another sponge could represent *ran up the hill.*

6. Write the entire rhyme on the chalkboard or an overhead transparency. Group the words in appropriate phrases. Place a / after a phrase and a // at the end of a sentence. Point out the purpose of the slash marks. You could say, "A single slash mark means that I should make a brief pause. Two slash marks mean that I should pause longer."

7. Then have the children participate in Echo Reading as you model how the phrases should be read. The children may also read the rhyme together several times.

8. Help children transfer phrasing to other sentences in their reading. Some possible sentences with the phrasing marked are provided below.

   All my friends/ were playing.//

   I was inside,/ sick in bed.//

   I really wanted/ to play/ with my friends.//

   The cow/ jumped over the moon.//

   Hickory/ dickory/ dock.// The mouse/ ran up the clock.//

   Winter is/ my favorite time/ of the year.//

9. Older children may be given unmarked text and asked to mark the phrase boundaries. Note that children may not all mark the phrases in the same way. Take time to discuss the way different children marked the phrases and whether some seem more helpful and logical than others.

10. For very young children, use examples that are familiar and perhaps memorized. Then move to sentences that connect to their lives.

READING WITH EXPRESSION AND EMOTION

Children need many opportunities to read with expression and emotion using the cues provided by punctuation, capital letters, and other typographic signals. Prosody is the general term that refers to phrasing, tone, and pitch. Appropriate use of these elements helps oral reading to sound conversational and approximates the emphasis the author probably intended.

✎ DIRECTIONS

1. Choose a brief selection to read aloud to the class. It should contain some of the typographic signals (e.g., all capital letters for a word, italics, dashes, exclamation marks, and question marks) that can influence how the selection is to be read. You can also prepare sentences that focus on the specific goals you have for the lesson. A few example sentences are listed below.

   > I saw a GIANT bear.
   >
   > Put the ball *in* the box, not by it.
   >
   > **"Ooouch!** I stubbed my toe!" yelled Hector.
   >
   > What do YOU like to eat?
   >
   > My friend, a great swimmer, really likes the water.
   >
   > I have collections of rocks, coins, and pencils.
   >
   > "Roger, what time should we leave?" asked Sue.
   >
   > What *color* of apples do you like?

2. Read the selection or sentences to the class, asking the children to listen carefully. Invite the children to comment on your reading: voice changes, stresses on certain words, loudness, softness, and so on.

3. Discuss with the children how you decided how to read the words. Some common typographic signals are listed below. They can be written on the chalkboard or on an overhead transparency to facilitate sharing. Be selective in how many signals are taught in a single lesson. A chart titled "Signals and Punctuation to Remember" could be developed over several lessons.

SIGNALS AND PUNCTUATION TO REMEMBER

!	Exclamation Mark: strong feelings of surprise, joy; fear, anger, etc.
?	Question Mark: raise voice at end of sentence
—	Dash: pause
...	Ellipsis: pause
.	Period: pause
,	Comma: brief pause
HI	All Capital Letters: louder emphasis
<u>see</u>	Underline: stress the underlined word or phrase
Oh	Boldface: stress the word or phrase
" "	Quotation Marks: read the words as you think the character or speaker might have said them
on	Italics: emphasize the word or phrase

---

4. Display the selection or sentences that you read. Use a chart or an overhead transparency. Be sure children see the typographic signals that helped guide your reading.

5. Use Echo Reading (see Strategy 1) with the selection or sentences. Point to the words as they are read to help the children make connections with the typographic signals.

6. Encourage children to be alert to the typographic signals in other reading that they do. Stress that the signals apply to silent reading as well.

7. Point out typographic signals during ongoing reading lessons so children have ample opportunities to practice and solidify their learning. Create additional sentences or use the resource provided on the next page.

Reading with Expression and Emotion

1. Eyeballs for sale!

2. Would you like it?

3. Please pick up the *brown* box.

4. Please, oh **please,** help me lift this box.

5. Can you hear me?

6. Sometimes, I like to read before I go to bed.

7. The dog had l-o-n-g white hair and some brown spots.

8. I heard a tiny bird go *cheep, cheep, cheep.*

9. I like vanilla, chocolate, and strawberry ice cream.

10. I felt the mud squish between my toes!

11. What is your **favorite** computer game?

12. Harry Potter books are great!

13. "Go pick up your clothes," said mom.

14. My teacher joyfully exclaimed, "Great work!"

15. *"Where* did you find that strange object?" inquired Pat.

From Laurie Elish-Piper, Jerry L. Johns, and Susan Davis Lenski, *Teaching Reading Pre-K–Grade 3* (3rd ed.). Copyright © 2006 by Kendall/Hunt Publishing Company (1-800-247-3458, ext. 4). May be reproduced for noncommercial educational purposes.

RADIO READING

Radio Reading (Greene, 1979) helps children focus on communicating a message so it can be understood by listeners. There may be some miscues in the reading, but listeners respond to the reading by discussing it, restating the basic message, and evaluating how the message was delivered.

DIRECTIONS

1. Bring a radio to class and have children listen to it for a few minutes. You should preview a station to identify content that would be appropriate for your class. Before asking children to listen, tell them that they will discuss the message after listening.

2. After listening to the radio for a minute or two, turn it off and invite children to share what was heard. Focus on the message and clarity of what was said.

3. Relate the children's listening to the radio to the strategy called Radio Reading. Tell children that they will have an opportunity to listen to classmates read a brief selection. The material selected for reading should be a paragraph or two at an appropriate level of difficulty (e.g., at the child's instructional level where approximately 95% of the words are known). The goal is to communicate meaning.

4. Select an appropriate passage for a child to read. Stress that the goal is to communicate the meaning of the passage to the other children in the classroom. If a word is unknown during the reading, the child should merely point to the word and ask, "What is that word?" You immediately tell the child the word so the reading can proceed with limited interruption. The other children serve as listeners, and they do not have a copy of the passage.

5. After the passage is read, invite the children who were the listeners to discuss the message that was conveyed. The intent of this discussion is to confirm that an accurate message was sent and received. The reader is responsible for clearing up any confusion by the listeners by rereading selected portions of the passage. In some cases, misread words may cause confusion. In such cases, the listeners must raise questions about the clarity of the content presented. Remember that the basic goal in Radio Reading is to present a message clearly; moreover, it is the goal of the listeners to evaluate the clarity of the message and to help resolve any misunderstandings.

MULTIPAIRED SIMULTANEOUS ORAL READING

At least once a week most primary-grade children will need to practice reading fluently. Some children are naturally fluent readers, but most are not. Most children need guidance and practice in order to read smoothly and easily. Because almost all of the children you teach will need practice reading fluently, all of the children can practice at once with Multipaired Simultaneous Oral Reading (Poe, 1986). During Multipaired Simultaneous Oral Reading, the group is divided into pairs. Each child takes turns reading to a partner. After one child reads, the partners switch roles so that all children practice reading fluently.

DIRECTIONS

1. Identify a passage that would lend itself to building fluency. For older readers, select a passage from a chapter book that has dialogue in it. Write the page number of the passage on the chalkboard or on an overhead transparency.

2. Tell children that they will be reading the passage to a partner. Explain that the goal of their reading will be to read fluently with a steady pace and good expression.

3. Model reading the passage with fluency. Read the passage expressively at a pace that moves quickly.

4. Ask children to read the passage with you. If there are any challenging sections containing dialect or difficult words, help the children say the difficult words.

5. Have children choose a partner for reading or choose partners for the children. Each time you use this strategy, have children choose different partners so that no one becomes dependent on another reader. At times, have children of the same reading ability work together. At other times, pair children of differing abilities. If a pair does not work well together, ask the children to change partners.

6. Let the pairs of children set their own rules about how much each child will read—one page, one paragraph, two paragraphs, and so on—before switching to the second reader.

7. Have children read the selection aloud. Monitor the activity and provide guidance as needed.

8. When a pair finishes reading, give each child a silent activity to complete.

9. After everyone has completed the paired oral reading, discuss the children's success at reading fluently. Occasionally, have a child volunteer to read a passage to the class. Congratulate all children on learning to read more smoothly.

Section 4.2 **TEACHING STRATEGY**

TEACHER-ASSISTED READING (NEUROLOGICAL IMPRESS METHOD)

For children to learn how to read fluently, they need to hear and practice fluent reading. Sometimes beginning readers can identify fluent reading, but they are unable to produce it. To help students learn how to read fluently, you can use Teacher-Assisted Reading, or the Neurological Impress Method (Heckleman, 1966). The Neurological Impress Method (NIM) is a technique in which the teacher (or another trained individual) and child simultaneously read aloud from the same book. The teacher reads slightly faster than the child in order to keep the child reading at a fluent pace. The child hears the reading and tries to read with the same pace and expression. The Neurological Impress Method is a useful strategy when you are helping one child or a small group of children improve fluency. Flood, Lapp, and Fisher (2005) have added a comprehension component (a retelling and comprehension questions) to the NIM that they call Plus (NIM PLUS). In the first study with NIM PLUS, they found statistically significant gains in words correct per minute in oral reading, silent reading, and comprehension for students in grades three through six after 3.3 hours of training. In the second study, 20 students in grades three through six who were reading below grade level received NIM PLUS instruction with intervention tutors. Statistical results revealed significant gains in the three areas mentioned above. Especially noteworthy was the fact that child gains were achieved without being taught by the teacher. In addition, the method "seems to work as well with second language students as it does with native English speakers" (p. 158).

✒ DIRECTIONS

1. Identify an interesting short book or passage that is at the child's reading level. You might identify several books and ask the child to choose one for the lesson.

2. Have the child sit slightly in front of you so that your voice is close to the child's ear.

3. Tell the child to follow your voice during the reading.

4. Read the material out loud with the child, but a little louder and faster than the child. Read only a short passage.

5. Run your finger under the words as you read.

6. Reread the same passage several times. Drop your voice behind the child's as the child begins to read fluently. Place the child's hand on your hand so that both of you can use your fingers to follow the lines of print.

7. As the child reads, do not correct any miscues. Your goal is to help the child build fluency. You should mentally note miscues so you can work on needed word-identification strategies at another time.

8. Have the child read alone while the child follows the print with a finger. Support the child's reading as needed by saying the words aloud.

9. Read the passage with the child once more, speeding up the pace. Encourage the child to read fluently at a faster pace.

10. Use this strategy for approximately 10 minutes per day, four days per week. Plan on using this strategy for at least five weeks. Fluency needs to be developed over a period of time.

Section 4.2   **TEACHING STRATEGY**

STRUCTURED REPEATED READING

Structured Repeated Reading (Samuels, 1979) is a motivational strategy that engages children in repeated readings of text. A Reading Progress Chart helps monitor the child's growth in fluency, which results, in part, from the automatic recognition of words and the reduction of miscues. We have found this strategy to be especially effective with children who struggle in reading.

✎ DIRECTIONS

1. Select a brief passage or story of 50 to 200 words for the child to read aloud. For beginning readers, or readers who struggle, a passage of approximately 50 words is sufficient for the first time the strategy is used. The passage should be at an appropriate level of difficulty. That means that the child should generally recognize more than 91% of the words. If the passage contains 50 words, the child should generally recognize about 46 of the words. If the child misses more than 6 words in a 50-word passage, it is probably not suitable for repeated reading.

2. Ask the child to read the passage orally. Using a copy of the passage (optional), note the child's miscues and keep track of the time (in seconds) it took the child to read the passage.

3. Ask the child to tell you something about the passage or ask a question or two. Be sure that the child is not just calling words.

4. Record the time in seconds and the number of miscues on a chart like that provided on page 208. In the example below, the child read a 45-word passage in 58 seconds and made 4 miscues. To convert seconds into rate in words per minute (WPM), multiply the number of words in the passage by 60 and then divide by the time (in seconds) it took the child to read the passage. As noted in the example below, the rate is approximately 46 words per minute (WPM).

$$
\begin{array}{r}
46\,\text{WPM} \\
58)\overline{2700} \\
\underline{232} \\
380 \\
\underline{348}
\end{array}
$$

5. Encourage the child to practice rereading the passage independently for a day or two. The reading can be done both orally and silently. It can also be done at home. The idea is to have the child practice the passage several times before you next meet with the child to repeat the process described in step 2.

6. Repeat the process of having the child read the passage to you. Record the time in seconds and the number of miscues on the chart under reading 2. Continue this general procedure over a period of time until a suitable rate is achieved. You can use your professional judgment to determine a suitable rate or refer to the norms for oral-reading rates provided on page 227. The chart below shows the 5 readings for a second-grade child over a 10-day period. The initial rate of 46 WPM was increased to approximately 87 WPM by the fifth reading. According to the norms provided for second graders in the spring of the year (p. 227), this child's rate is slightly below average. Use the information in the chart on page 227 to help determine target reading rates.

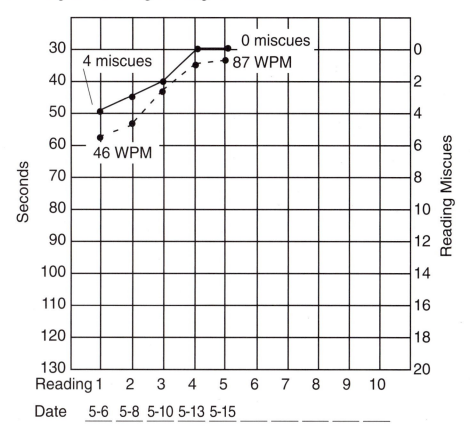

7. Repeat the strategy with a new selection. As you use the Reading Progress Chart on page 208, note that space is provided to record the date and to chart up to 10 readings. You should base the actual number of readings on the child's progress in fluency. Some children will achieve a satisfactory level of fluency after a few readings; other children may need six or seven readings. Be flexible and responsive to individual differences. The Reading Progress Chart was designed to show visible evidence of gains. Children are reinforced with the charts and are motivated to improve their rate and accuracy. The charts can be a meaningful way to gather evidence of fluency development over time with a variety of passages. As a chart is completed for a passage, it can be placed in the child's work folder or portfolio.

8. Samuels (2002) simplified the method so it does not require charting or computation of the time it takes the child to read the passage. In brief, the strategy involves pairs of readers (a better reader and a poorer reader). One child reads while the other child follows the words in the text. Then the children reverse roles. The process is repeated so each child reads the passage four times. Research by O'Shea, Sindelar, and O'Shea (1985) found that most of the gains in reading speed, word recognition error reduction, and expression in oral reading were acquired by the fourth reading.

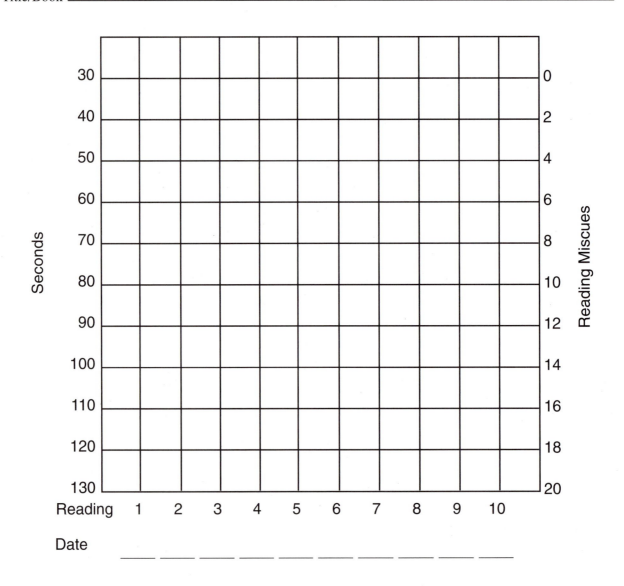

Reading Progress Chart
for _____

Title/Book _____

Seconds (left axis, top to bottom): 30, 40, 50, 60, 70, 80, 90, 100, 110, 120, 130

Reading Miscues (right axis, top to bottom): 0, 2, 4, 6, 8, 10, 12, 14, 16, 18, 20

Reading   1   2   3   4   5   6   7   8   9   10

Date   ___ ___ ___ ___ ___ ___ ___ ___ ___ ___

- Prepare backpacks with a tape recorder, storybook, and audiotape of the storybook. Include a letter explaining how to use the materials in the home language of the parents. Allow children to use the backpack at home for three to five days. Take time to teach the children how to use the tape recorder and consider color-coding the *stop, play,* and *rewind* buttons on the tape recorder. The child and parent can be encouraged to follow along in the storybook as the audiotape is played. Financial assistance to help support projects of this type may be available from school, business, community agencies, and professional organizations. A parent may also be recruited to assist with various aspects of the backpack project.

- Encourage children to take home attractive books that they can read independently to their parents. If possible, secure books that are written in the home language as well as English. Enclose a piece of paper that parents can sign indicating that they listened to their children read. Children can also be encouraged to talk about the pictures and illustrations with their parents.

Activities, tips, & Center Ideas

1. Recognize that reading is a developmental process and that fluency will develop as children increase their sight vocabularies and acquire a flexible repertoire of word-identification strategies. Children in the primary grades generally will increase fluency as they gain more experience reading.

2. Encourage the repeated readings of pattern books. Pattern books are books that have repetitive phrases like "Brown Bear, Brown Bear, what do you see?" When children read books with repetition, they quickly become familiar with the repeated phrases, making the book easier to read with fluency. Consult Johns and Lenski (2005) for a list of pattern books.

3. Model good reading fluency by reading aloud to children. Occasionally point out that when you read books to the class, you are reading in a way that is similar to the spoken language children hear. Tell children that good readers try to read so their reading sounds like talking.

4. Encourage frequent reading of easy books where children recognize about 98% of the words. Children have more trouble reading fluently when they are trying to read books that are difficult for them. If a book is difficult, children have to devote attention to word identification and can't put as much effort into fluent reading. Try to have children read easy books several times each week.

5. Use flashlight reading of Big Books (Rennick & Williams, 1995). Place a Big Book on a chalkboard ledge or an easel. Tell children that you will be shining a flashlight on the words and that the children should read along with the flashlight. Move the flashlight along the sentences at a smooth, steady pace. Invite children to read the words as the flashlight shines on them.

6. Provide opportunities for children to listen to talking books on audiotapes or to use computer programs with sound. Capitalize on children's interests when a particularly popular book is played repeatedly by allowing children to listen and read their favorite books again and again.

7. Use daily dictated stories for fluency practice. Have children dictate one or more sentences that you write on the chalkboard or on chart paper. Read the sentences to the class with expression and good phrasing. Then have the class read along with you. Tell children that you want them to read with expression.

8. Make a videotape or audiotape of yourself reading an easy book. Send the book and the tape home with the children to practice reading outside of school. You could also ask other adults who are familiar to children to participate in videotape or audiotape reading. A school principal, a head teacher, a librarian, a crossing guard, a bus driver, and a lunchroom worker are all adults who children see on a regular basis and would be good role models for reading. You may have to supervise the reading of other adults so that their reading is a good example for the children, but having a variety of reading models is worth your time and energy.

9. Develop a reading pals program with older children: students in intermediate grades, middle schools, high schools, or colleges. Suggest books for the reading pals to read with your children. Ask the pals to practice reading the books several times and to aim for fluent, conversational reading. Have the reading pals read the books to your children; then have the children read along with their reading pals.

10. Identify songs and poems that children enjoy. Print the songs or poems on the chalkboard or on chart paper. Read or sing them with the children. Repeat the process several times a day. Encourage children to practice independently so they can read the words fluently.

11. Have children read fluently by performing Readers' Theater scripts. Readers' Theater scripts are similar to play scripts except they do not have stage directions. Children read the lines while sitting or standing rather than acting. When asking children to perform a Readers' Theater script, assign lines; then have children read their lines several times. Children should practice their lines aloud several times. After children have practiced their lines, they can read the script for an audience. Consult www.aaronshep.com/rt for free scripts.

12. Provide children with many opportunities to read to an audience. Have children identify favorite passages of books, practice them, and read them to the class. Use a small microphone to encourage fluent reading. Inexpensive microphones can be purchased at many toy stores.

READING OUT LOUD

Dear Families,

We have been working on oral reading fluency in school. Fluency is when reading is done smoothly, at a good pace, and with expression. Here are some ideas to help your child practice oral reading fluency at home.

• Encourage your child to read and reread books to you. Read along with your child at a pace that helps the child maintain reading that is reasonably smooth. Feel free to repeat sentences to help your child develop greater fluency and confidence. If the story has people or animals talking, make the dialog come alive by using different voices. Always take time to listen to your child's reading—even if your child wants to read the book again and again. Take advantage of your child's interest in rereading.

• Provide a good model of oral reading by reading to your child. Ask your child's teacher or a librarian for appropriate books. Reread books when asked and praise your child's efforts to read along. Enjoy the experience with your child each and every time the book is read.

I hope you and your child find these ideas useful.

Sincerely,

Assessments of Fluency and High-Frequency Words

Goal: To help assess children's knowledge of high-frequency words and the ability to read fluently.

Background

You may already have a variety of formal and informal ways to assess your children's progress in fluency and knowledge of high-frequency words. If you feel the need to expand or supplement your assessment strategies, we have provided a variety of assessments that correspond to the major topics in this chapter. Use those that will help you examine a particular area to identify what specific instruction is warranted or whether your instruction resulted in the outcomes you desired. There is no single way to use the assessments. Our goal is to provide you with easy-to-use assessments to help you evaluate or monitor children's progress in reading.

HIGH-FREQUENCY WORDS

OVERVIEW	The purpose of this assessment is to ascertain the child's ability to automatically identify a sample of the most common words in English. The words on the Revised Dolch List (see page 175) occur frequently in all types of printed materials. If you want to assess children's knowledge of these basic words, use one of the forms provided. The words selected for these assessments are the 50 most frequently used words in English. You could also make your own assessments by selecting other words from the Revised Dolch List if children know the basic words in these assessments. How children perform on the assessments will inform you about what words you may want to target for instruction to the entire class, small groups, or individual children.
MATERIALS NEEDED	1. Child's copy, either Form 1 (page 216) or Form 2 (page 218) 2. A copy of the Record Sheet that corresponds to the form selected for use, either Form 1 (page 217) or Form 2 (page 219) 3. Two blank sheets of paper
PROCEDURES	1. Duplicate the Record Sheet corresponding to the form selected for use. 2. Choose one form of the assessment. Cover the words with the two sheets of paper so only one word will be uncovered at a time. Place the page containing the covered words before the child. Say, "I want you to say some words for me. Let's begin with this one." 3. Move one of the blank sheets of paper below the first word and ask the child to say the word. If the child says the number, cover it up and point to the word. As the child says words, note correct responses with a plus (+) in the appropriate place on the Record Sheet. Record any incorrect responses by using the following markings (or your own system).

Marking	Meaning of Marking	Marking	Meaning of Marking
man men	Substitution	m— men	Partial Pronunciation
		<u>men</u>	Repeated word
man s/c men	Self-correction	small ʌmen	Insertion
~~men~~	Omitted word	the/small	Pause

4. Encourage the child to say "pass" or "skip it" for any unknown words. Say, "Just do the best you can." Stop the assessment if no response is given to the first four words.
5. Proceed through the words until the assessment is completed. If you observe anxiety, frustration, or reluctance on the part of the child, use your professional judgment to determine if the assessment should be stopped.

SCORING AND INTERPRETATION	Count the number of words pronounced correctly and record the score in the box on the Record Sheet. Self-corrections are counted as correct, but make a note about any words that were not known automatically. The intent of this assessment is to determine if the child knows the most common words in English at sight. Mispronunciations, partial words, refusals, saying "don't know," and self-corrections are evidence that the words are not known automatically. These words may become the basis for instruction using the teaching strategies described in Section 4.1. The same form of the assessment could be used after targeted instruction to note gains in basic sight word knowledge. Form 2 of the assessment could be used after the child had near mastery of the words on Form 1 or as a further assessment of the child's knowledge of the most common words in English.

1. the

2. and

3. a

4. is

5. it

6. for

7. he

8. as

9. they

10. be

11. at

12. from

13. I

14. have

15. but

16. were

17. all

18. when

19. their

20. her

21. we

22. about

23. said

24. if

25. would

Form 1—High-Frequency Words—Child's Copy

High-Frequency Words

Name _____ Date _____

Teacher's Directions   214–215
Child Copy   216

BRIEF DIRECTIONS

Present one word at a time for the child to pronounce. Say, "I want you to say some words for me. Let's begin with this one." Use a plus (+) for correct responses. Record the child's responses for incorrect words. Total correct responses and put the score in the box.

1. the _____

2. and _____

3. a _____

4. is _____

5. it _____

6. for _____

7. he _____

8. as _____

9. they _____

10. be _____

11. at _____

12. from _____

13. I _____

14. have _____

15. but _____

16. were _____

17. all _____

18. when _____

19. their _____

20. her _____

21. we _____

22. about _____

23. said _____

24. if _____

25. would _____

Total Correct [   ]

1. of

2. to

3. in

4. that

5. was

6. you

7. on

8. are

9. with

10. his

11. or

12. had

13. not

14. this

15. by

16. one

17. she

18. an

19. there

20. can

21. what

22. up

23. out

24. some

25. so

Form 2—High-Frequency Words—Child's Copy

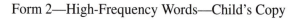

RECORD SHEET

Form 2

High-Frequency Words

Name _____ Date _____

Teacher's Directions   214–215
Child Copy   218

BRIEF DIRECTIONS

Present one word at a time for the child to pronounce. Say, "I want you to say some words for me. Let's begin with this one." Use a plus (+) for correct responses. Record the child's responses for incorrect words. Total correct responses and put the score in the box.

1. of _____
2. to _____
3. in _____
4. that _____
5. was _____
6. you _____
7. on _____
8. are _____
9. with _____
10. his _____
11. or _____
12. had _____
13. not _____

14. this _____
15. by _____
16. one _____
17. she _____
18. an _____
19. there _____
20. can _____
21. what _____
22. up _____
23. out _____
24. some _____
25. so _____

Total Correct [   ]

COMMON NOUNS

OVERVIEW	The purpose of this assessment is to ascertain the child's ability to identify automatically a sample of the most common nouns. There are a number of nouns that occur frequently in printed materials. The nouns in these assessments are based on the work of Johns (1975), Zeno, Ivens, Millard, & Duvvuri (1995) and Gunning's (1998) list of 500 words that occur with the highest frequency in first-grade texts and children's books that are on a first-grade level. The words selected for these assessments use some of the most common nouns in English that are likely to be among the spontaneous speaking vocabulary of children in kindergarten and first grade, appropriate to young children's interests, and related to first-grade activities. How children perform on the assessment should give you helpful indications of nouns known as well as nouns that you may want to teach. Remember that these nouns occur frequently in various types of printed materials and need to be recognized automatically if students are to become fluent readers.
MATERIALS NEEDED	1. Child's copy, either Form 1 (page 222) or Form 2 (page 224) 2. A copy of the Record Sheet that corresponds to the form selected for use, either Form 1 (page 223) or Form 2 (page 225) 3. Two blank sheets of paper
PROCEDURES	1. Duplicate the Record Sheet corresponding to the form selected for use. 2. Choose one form of the assessment. Cover the words with the two sheets of paper so only one word will be uncovered at a time. Place the page containing the words before the child. Say, "I want you to say some words for me. Let's begin with this one." 3. Move one of the blank sheets of paper below the first word and ask the child to say the word. If the child says the number, cover it up and point to the word. As the child says the words, note correct responses with a plus (+) in the appropriate place of the Record Sheet. Record any incorrect responses by using the following markings (or your own system).

Marking	Meaning of Marking	Marking	Meaning of Marking
man men	Substitution	m— men	Partial Pronunciation
man s/c	Self-correction	men	Repeated word
~~men~~	Omitted word	small ∧men	Insertion
		the/small	Pause

4. Encourage the child to say "pass" or "skip it" for any unknown words. Say, "Just do the best you can." Stop the assessment if no response is given to the first four words.
5. Proceed through the words until the assessment is completed. If you observe anxiety, frustration, or reluctance on the part of the child, use your professional judgment to determine if the assessment should be stopped.

SCORING AND INTERPRETATION	Count the number of words pronounced correctly and record the score in the box on the Record Sheet. Self-corrections are counted as correct, but make a note about any words that were not known automatically. Mispronunciations, partial words, refusals, saying "don't know," and self-corrections are evidence that the words are not known automatically. These words may become the basis for instruction using the teaching strategies described in Section 4.1. The same form of the assessment could be used after targeted instruction to note gains in knowledge of common nouns. Form 2 of the assessment could be used after the child has near mastery of the words on Form 1 or as a further assessment of the child's knowledge of some of the most common nouns in English.

Additional Ways of Assessing Sight Words and Nouns

1. Observe the child's oral reading of materials being used for instruction to informally assess if the most common nouns in English are known automatically.
2. Use an informal reading inventory (Johns, 2005) or running records to help determine the number of words known at sight.
3. Observe the child's writing to note growth in the child's ability to spell the most common nouns correctly.

1. people

2. years

3. man

4. house

5. school

6. mother

7. father

8. head

9. room

10. city

11. name

12. group

13. face

14. door

15. air

16. girl

17. nothing

18. back

19. place

20. book

21. side

22. egg

23. car

24. farm

25. train

Form 1—Common Nouns—Child's Copy

Form 1

Common Nouns

Name _____ Date _____

Teacher's Directions   220–221
Child Copy   222

➤ BRIEF DIRECTIONS

Present one word at a time for the child to pronounce. Say, "I want you to say some words for me. Let's begin with this one." Use a plus (+) for correct responses. Record the child's responses for incorrect words. Total correct responses and put the score in the box.

1. people _____	14. door _____
2. years _____	15. air _____
3. man _____	16. girl _____
4. house _____	17. nothing _____
5. school _____	18. back _____
6. mother _____	19. place _____
7. father _____	20. book _____
8. head _____	21. side _____
9. room _____	22. egg _____
10. city _____	23. car _____
11. name _____	24. farm _____
12. group _____	25. train _____
13. face _____	Total Correct [ ]

1. water

2. things

3. home

4. children

5. men

6. hand

7. eye

8. night

9. money

10. day

11. feet

12. boy

13. road

14. dog

15. time

16. morning

17. friend

18. top

19. place

20. table

21. way

22. tree

23. frog

24. town

25. truck

Form 2—Common Nouns—Child's Copy

RECORD SHEET

Form 2

Common Nouns

Name _____ Date _____

Teacher's Directions   220–221
Child Copy   224

➤ BRIEF DIRECTIONS

Present one word at a time for the child to pronounce. Say, "I want you to say some words for me. Let's begin with this one." Use a plus (+) for correct responses. Record the child's responses for incorrect words. Total correct responses and put the score in the box.

1. water _____   14. dog _____

2. things _____   15. time _____

3. home _____   16. morning _____

4. children _____   17. friend _____

5. men _____   18. top _____

6. hand _____   19. place _____

7. eye _____   20. table _____

8. night _____   21. way _____

9. money _____   22. tree _____

10. day _____   23. frog _____

11. feet _____   24. town _____

12. boy _____   25. truck _____

13. road _____   Total Correct [   ]

WORDS PER MINUTE

OVERVIEW	The purpose of this assessment is to determine the child's rate of reading in words per minute. Basically, you ask the child to read new material at an appropriate level of difficulty. While the child reads, note miscues and time the reading. Then you perform a few simple calculations to determine the child's rate of reading in words per minute. The child's rate can be compared to other students in the classroom or the norms provided on page 227. The nice thing about this assessment strategy is that it can be repeated at regular intervals using instructional materials to help gauge the child's growth in fluency.
MATERIALS NEEDED	1. A reading passage at the child's instructional level (at least 95% word accuracy and 75% comprehension) 2. A copy of the passage being read 3. A stopwatch or a watch with a second hand 4. A Reading Rate Class Record Sheet on page 229
PROCEDURES	1. Select a reading passage at the child's instructional level. Make a copy of the passage so that you can note any miscues the child makes. Get a stopwatch or use a watch with a second hand. 2. Present the passage to the child. Say, "I would like you to read me this passage. When you have finished reading, I'd like you to tell me about what you've read. You may begin." When the child begins reading, begin your timing. 3. Note any miscues the child makes. Use your own coding system or the one presented below.

Marking	Meaning of Marking	Marking	Meaning of Marking
man men	Substitution	m— men	Partial Pronunciation
man s/c men	Self-correction	men	Repeated word
~~men~~	Omitted word	small ∧men the/small	Insertion Pause

4. When the child completes the reading, note the number of seconds that elapsed. Then invite the child to tell you a bit about what was read. You might want to say, "Tell me about what you've read." You may prefer to ask a question or two to be sure that the child was not calling words without any understanding of the passage.

5. To determine the child's rate of reading, follow the steps below.
   - Count or estimate the number of words in the passage (e.g., 150).
   - Multiply by 60. The resulting numeral becomes the dividend (e.g., 9000).
   - Divide by the number of seconds (e.g., 100) it took the child to read the passage (e.g., $9000 \div 100 = 90$).
   - The resulting numeral (e.g., 90) is the quotient, which is in words per minute (WPM).
6. Record the child's reading rate on the Reading Rate Class Record Sheet found on page 229.

SCORING AND INTERPRETATION

There are at least three ways to interpret the results. First, you can time the child's reading at various points throughout the school year to note changes in rate of reading. Second, if you enter each child's scores on the Reading Rate Class Record Sheet, you can make informal comparisons among children. Third, there are norms for oral reading rates for students in the primary grades.

The chart below contains these rates for over 120,000 children and provides words correct per minute (WCPM) at the 90th, 75th, 50th, 25th, and 10th percentiles for students in grades one through three for three time periods (fall, winter, and spring) of the school year. You may choose the words per minute rates in the charts for comparison purposes. Keep in mind that the figures in these charts should be used informally to help you monitor the progress of children within a particular grade and compare growth to these established standards.

Oral Reading Norms for Students in Grades One through Three

Grade (N)	Percentile	Fall N	Fall WCPM	Winter N	Winter WCPM	Spring N	Spring WCPM
1 (38,239)	90		32		69		101
	75		14		40		75
	50	2,847	7	16,416	21	18,976	48
	25		2		11		26
	10		1		5		13
2 (45,446)	90		98		122		140
	75		74		98		115
	50	13,738	49	15,454	72	16,254	89
	25		23		46		64
	10		12		20		37
3 (43,717)	90		128		144		160
	75		101		117		136
	50	12,844	73	14,988	90	15,883	107
	25		48		58		78
	10		26		37		45

If you believe one or more of the children in your class have reading rates that warrant strengthening, consider the teaching strategies presented earlier in this chapter. Keep in mind that a limited sight vocabulary could be a major contributing factor to a slow rate of reading.

Additional Ways of Assessing Fluency

1. Refer to the assessments in Chapter 5. There are five passages ranging in difficulty from the beginning stages of reading through third grade.

2. Use an informal reading inventory (Johns, 2005) or running records to determine rate of reading. If running records are used, refer to the procedure described in step 5 on page 227 to calculate rate of reading.

3. Use one-minute reads. This procedure is essentially the same as Assessment Strategy 3 except that all children read for only one minute. The number of words read in one minute becomes the child's WPM.

    A word of caution: Some teachers have every child in the room read the same material for one-minute reads. While this technique provides a common baseline for the data gathered, the range of reading levels in most classrooms makes this procedure less accurate for children who read above or below grade level.

Reading Rate Class Record Sheet

CHILD	DATE	WPM	COMMENTS

FLUENCY SCALE CHECKLIST

OVERVIEW	Many teachers informally assess the child's fluency during the course of instruction. That informal assessment may result in a mental note or a brief comment in the child's progress folder or portfolio. There are a number of fluency scales that may be used to keep the process informal but systematic. We offer a basic four-point fluency scale arranged so it can be used with an individual child or a class of children.
MATERIALS NEEDED	1. Duplicate sufficient copies of the Individual Fluency Scale Record Sheet from page 232 if the scale is to be used with an individual child 2. Duplicate sufficient copies of the Class Fluency Scale Record Sheet from page 233 if the scale is to be used with the entire class
PROCEDURES	1. Duplicate sufficient copies of the Record Sheet for the scale you intend to use. 2. Review the four levels of fluency described on the fluency scale. 3. When you decide to focus on a child's oral reading fluency, note the date on the Record Sheet and indicate the level of fluency. Use your professional judgment to arrive at a level. 4. Repeat the process from time to time or at regularly scheduled intervals. Record the date and level of fluency.
SCORING AND INTERPRETATION	The four-point fluency scale is scored informally. Make numerous observations of the child's oral reading and judge the fluency. Over time, you should expect to see some improvement in fluency. If fluency for a child appears to be static compared to other children in your room, consider what in the child's reading behavior may be contributing to the situation. Then develop appropriate instructional interventions using your experience along with the strategies suggested in this chapter. Ensure that the child is given appropriate instructional materials. There may be times when a lack of fluency is actually an indication the instructional materials are too difficult for the child.

Additional Ways of Assessing Fluency

1. Use an informal reading inventory (Johns, 2005). Most informal reading inventories are designed to permit the assessment of fluency by determining rate of reading.

2. Use running records to note miscues, time the child's reading, and refer to step 5 in Assessment Strategy 3 (page 227).

3. Observe the child's oral reading and note particular behaviors that may be having a negative influence on fluency. Some of these behaviors are listed below.

   • many repetitions

   • excessive use of phonics

   • numerous unknown words

   • word-by-word reading

   • inappropriate phrasing

Individual Fluency Scale

Child _____ Teacher _____ Grade _____

LEVEL	DESCRIPTION
1	Reads almost entirely word by word; monotone; little or no use of punctuation
2	Reads mostly in 2- to 3-word phrases with some word by word; monotone with some expression; some evidence of punctuation
3	Reads mostly in phrases; appropriate expression; uses punctuation most of the time
4	Reads fluently; good expression; consistently attends to punctuation

DATE	LEVEL	COMMENTS

Class Fluency Scale

LEVEL	DESCRIPTION
1	Reads almost entirely word by word; monotone; little or no use of punctuation
2	Reads mostly in 2- to 3-word phrases with some word by word; monotone with some expression; some evidence of punctuation
3	Reads mostly in phrases; appropriate expression; uses punctuation most of the time
4	Reads fluently; good expression; consistently attends to punctuation

CHILD	DATE	LEVEL	COMMENTS

chapter *five*

Vocabulary

Overview

Vocabulary knowledge is important for understanding text. Vocabulary words are labels for concepts, and children must understand the meaning of key vocabulary words in order to understand what they read (Beck, McKeown, & Kucan 2002). While incidental word learning allows children to learn many words during their daily lives (Brett, Rothlein, & Hurley, 1996), it is important for children to be taught key vocabulary as well as strategies for understanding new words independently.

Beck, McKeown, and Kucan (2002) have identified three tiers of words that help teachers determine which words to target for vocabulary instruction. Tier One consists of the most basic words such as *sit, hat,* and *walk.* These words rarely require instruction related to their meanings. Words in Tier Two are considered high-frequency words for mature language users and consist of words such as *eager, manage,* and *fortunate.* Words in Tier Two play a large role in the verbal functioning of adults and children; therefore, most vocabulary instruction should be directed toward words in this tier (Beck, McKeown, & Kucan, 2002). Tier Three is comprised of words that are used infrequently and are often linked to a specific domain or discipline such as the words *peninsula, quadrilateral,* or *pulmonary.* "These words are probably best learned when a specific need arises, such as introducing *peninsula* during a geography lesson" (Beck, McKeown, & Kucan, 2002, p. 8). This chapter contains useful teaching strategies and activities to help children strengthen and expand their vocabularies so they may become skilled language users.

Teachers often ask important questions about how they can help children build their vocabularies and understand the words they read. Some of those frequently asked questions are listed and answered on the next two pages.

Questions/Answers

How do young children learn vocabulary?

Children learn vocabulary first through hearing words and connecting them to the related concepts. For example, children hear the word "helicopter" and relate it to the vehicle they have seen in the past. Once children have words in their listening and speaking vocabularies, they can connect this knowledge to the written word. When children encounter new vocabulary words in their reading for which they do not have a concept or personal experience, such connections are necessary to help them understand and remember the vocabulary words. For example, the word "rapidly" will be unfamiliar to many children, but the teacher can demonstrate how he or she moves "rapidly" across the room and the children can be invited to march "rapidly" around the room. The teacher can also help children make connections by discussing how the word "rapidly" is very similar to other words such as "quickly."

What does it mean to know a word?

Knowing a word can be considered on a continuum rather than an "all or nothing" proposition. Word knowledge can be divided into three main levels: no knowledge of the word, limited knowledge, and much knowledge (Dale, 1965). Multiple exposures to words are necessary for children to develop in-depth knowledge of words.

How should I select vocabulary words for instruction?

Children encounter many words during a typical school day. Clearly, you can't and shouldn't try to teach all of them explicitly because that would not leave time for other instruction or activities. Beck, McKeown, and Kucan (2002) suggest that teachers direct their vocabulary instruction to Tier Two words that are commonly used by mature language users. Such words are used in many contexts and domains (e.g., *certain, complete,* and *repeat*). To be more specific, Beck, McKeown, and Kucan (2002) estimate that providing vocabulary instruction on approximately 400 vocabulary words per year will result in meaningful improvements in word knowledge and comprehension. The selection of Tier Two words for instruction can be completed by using three criteria offered by Beck, McKeown, and Kucan (2002).

1. Importance and utility of words: "words that are characteristic of mature language users and appear frequently across a variety of domains" (p. 19).

2. Instructional potential: words can be taught in a variety of ways to help children understand and connect words and concepts.

3. Conceptual understanding of words: "words for which children understand the general concept but provide precision and specificity in describing the concept" (p. 19).

I can't teach all of the words the children in my class need to know and understand. Is there anything else I can do to help them build their vocabularies?

Providing explicit instruction for important vocabulary words is a key component of vocabulary instruction; yet it is not possible to teach children all of the words they will encounter in your classroom. You can, however, teach children to develop word learning strategies such as using context, identifying meaningful word parts such as prefixes and suffixes, and consulting word learning references such as picture dictionaries or glossaries. In addition, teachers can promote word learning by helping children develop a curiosity about words by promoting word play, immersing them in interesting words through read alouds and rich discussions, and providing opportunities for wide reading in the classroom. By creating this type of classroom climate, you can help children develop their independent words learning skills so they are able to enhance their vocabularies.

section 5.1

Word Consciousness and Word Play

> **Goal:** To help children develop an interest in words.

Background

When children are immersed in rich verbal environments, they have many opportunities to explore and play with words (Ganske, 2000). This type of rich vocabulary environment helps children develop an awareness of words and a desire to learn new words to use in their listening, speaking, reading, and writing (Beck, Perfetti, & McKeown, 1982). Many children find the use of games, riddles, puzzles, and other types of word play an extremely motivating and successful way to learn new words.

Section 5.1   *TEACHING STRATEGY*

TEXT TALK

The Text Talk strategy is based on research that shows that providing rich discussions in relation to teacher read-alouds contributes to children's language and vocabulary development (Beck & McKeown, 2001). By selecting quality texts that provide "extended, connected content for building meaning" (Beck & McKeown, 2001, p. 14), teachers are able to provide high quality read-aloud experiences for the children in their classrooms. In this strategy, the teacher targets two to four words for explicit instruction. If a teacher shares one read-aloud per day with an average of three words per book for instruction, the children can potentially learn over 500 words just through teacher read-alouds using Text Talk.

DIRECTIONS

1. Select a trade book to read aloud. Beck and McKeown (2001) offer the following suggestions for selecting books for use with the Text Talk strategy.

   • Texts should be intellectually challenging.

   • Texts should provide "grist for children to explore ideas and to use language to explain ideas" (p. 14).

   • Texts should rely on the words rather than the pictures to communicate meaning.

2. Select two to four words for instruction from the read-aloud book. Words for instruction should be unfamiliar to the children but related to a concept the children could identify with and find useful in normal conversation. For example, if the book *Trouble with Trolls* (Brett, 1992) was selected, the following words could be targeted for instruction.

> squealed
>
> boasted
>
> reluctantly

3. Read the story aloud to the children and discuss their understanding of the key ideas in the story.

4. Draw the children's attention to one of the target vocabulary words. For example, the word *squealed* is used in the story in this sentence. "The troll *squealed* and growled. 'I want dog!'"

5. Ask the children to say the target vocabulary word aloud with you.

6. Explain the meaning and use of the word. For example, for the word *squealed* you might say the following.

> The troll *squealed* which means he made a loud, high-pitched cry or sound like this [make sound]. A person, animal, or even a troll might squeal when very excited or surprised like the troll in the story was.

7. Engage children in thinking about the target word. For example, you might say the following.

> Think about something that might make you squeal with excitement or surprise. Start your sentence with "I *squealed* because _____ ." After a child responds, call on another child to explain the response. For example, if Lucas says, "I *squealed* because it was my birthday, and I opened a present that was exactly what I wanted," you would ask the next child, "What does it mean that Lucas *squealed* because it was his birthday, and he opened a present that was exactly what he wanted?" Provide opportunities for several children to share and respond before moving on to the next word.

8. Create a chart that lists the target vocabulary words. Each time a child uses one of the words, mark a tally on the chart to show how children are adding new words to their vocabularies. Add new target vocabulary words to the chart as you complete additional read-alouds using the Text Talk strategy. A sample chart is provided below.

WORD	NUMBER OF TIMES WE'VE USED THE WORD
squealed	✓
boasted	✓✓
reluctantly	✓
fortunate	✓✓✓
eager	✓

IN/OUT

IN/OUT is an exclusion brainstorming strategy that focuses on having children decide which words presented by the teacher will be IN the text they will read and which will be OUT of the text. This strategy helps children make predictions about text content and activate background knowledge prior to reading a text (Fisher, 1998).

DIRECTIONS

1. Select six to eight words in a book you will be reading with children. The words should be important for understanding the book.

2. Add four to six words that will not be found in the book but will be familiar to the children. These words can be taken from a book the children have recently read or from a topic or theme being studied in the classroom.

3. Write the words on the chalkboard or on a sheet of chart paper. For example, with the book, *Bumblebee, Bumbleebee, Do You Know Me?* (Rockwell, 1999), it is important for children to be aware of the names of common insects and garden flowers. The teacher might select the following words from the book: *bumblebee, butterfly, cricket, ladybug, daffodil, tulip, rose,* and *daisy.* Distracters might be selected from a recent unit on pets to include *fish, cat, dog,* and *hamster.* Words that are IN the book and those that are OUT of the book should be mixed together to form one list. For example, the list for *Bumblebee, Bumbleebee, Do You Know Me?* (Rockwell, 1999) might be as follows:

bumblebee	cricket
daffodil	rose
fish	dog
butterfly	ladybug
tulip	daisy
cat	hamster

4. Show the cover and title of the book you will be reading. Ask the children to predict what they think the book will be about and why. If the children's predictions are not accurate or complete, provide a brief statement about the contents of the book. For example, with the book *Bumblebee, Bumbleebee, Do You Know Me?* (Rockwell, 1999), you might say something like the following.

   This book is a garden guessing game. On the cover I see a bumblebee and some flowers. I know that a bumblebee is an insect, and I know that flowers grow in a garden.

5. Guide the children through the list of words by reading each word aloud and asking the children, "Will this word be IN the book or OUT of the book? Why?" When children correctly identify words that will be IN the book, ask them follow-up questions such as, "What color is a daffodil?" or "What sound does a bumblebee make?" to help build and activate the children's background knowledge prior to reading the book.

6. Read the book aloud to the children or use a shared reading format. As you read the book, direct the children's attention to the words from your list that are IN the book.

7. After reading the book, review the list of words to see if the children correctly predicted which words would be IN and OUT of the book.

- Provide a picture, photo, or an object to represent each word being taught. Display the picture, photo, or object as you say the word. The use of a visual for each word will help English Language Learners identify the concepts being discussed.

Section 5.1   **TEACHING STRATEGY**   3

OLD TEACHER

Word games are a fun way to motivate children to build their vocabularies. Word games should be simple so children can play them without teacher guidance. Old Teacher, a variation on the traditional game Old Maid, is a simple card game that can be played by children during center time, independent work time, or while the teacher works with guided reading groups (Blachowicz & Fisher, 2006).

DIRECTIONS

1. Prepare a deck of Old Teacher cards. The deck should contain one card with the picture of an Old Teacher on it. The remaining cards should be divided evenly between word cards and definition cards. The deck should contain at least 12 word cards and 12 definition cards. Word cards contain just the word, and definition cards contain a short definition. A set of word cards is shown below.

Tremble	To shake from fear or worry.

2. The words for Old Teacher should come from words the children have read or heard recently in the classroom. Words may also come from books the children have read or units the children have studied.

3. Old Teacher is played by two to four children at a time. Children shuffle the cards and deal out all of the cards.

4. Each child takes a turn by picking one card from the hand of the player on his or her left. If the child has a pair (word card matches the definition card), he or she places the pair on the table and reads the word and definition aloud. If another child in the game does not agree with the pair, the children can use a dictionary to resolve the challenge. If the challenge is correct, the challenger gets to take an extra turn. If the challenger is incorrect, the player gets to take an extra turn.

5. The game continues until all of the pairs are played. The child left with the Old Teacher card is declared the "Old Teacher," and he or she serves as the dealer for the next game.

- Word cards for Old Teacher can include a picture to help clarify concepts.
- Definition cards should include a picture, example, or translation into the child's home language if possible.
- The game can be sent home for children to practice on their own or with a family member as a fun way to review vocabulary words and their meanings.

Section 5.1   *TEACHING STRATEGY*

WORD STORMING

Word fluency is the ability to name words easily. This skill is an important foundation for reading, writing, and speaking development. Because the brain sorts or organizes ideas and information for later retrieval, using categories to organize words helps children develop their word fluency (Readence & Searfoss, 1980).

DIRECTIONS

1. Explain to the children that Word Storming is like brainstorming, but the focus of the strategy is on listing as many words as possible related to a specific category. Tell children that when they Word Storm, they are trying to build their word fluency which is their ability to name words quickly and easily.

2. Assign each child to a partner. Have one child in each pair serve as the word stormer and the other child will serve as the recorder. Provide a category such as *vehicles, animals,* or *community helpers,* depending on what you have been studying in the classroom.

3. Tell the word stormer to say as many words related to the category as he or she can in one minute. The recorder in each group tallies each word that the word stormer says, providing one point for each word. Repetitions and words that are unrelated to the category do not count.

4. Have partners switch roles and complete step 3 again. (The teacher may wish to change the category for the second partner so he or she must name new words rather than relying on the words previously listed by the partner.)

5. Provide time for Word Storming several times per week. Record children's progress to show their growth in word fluency.

- Pair an English Language Learner with a native English speaker for this activity. Have the ELL serve as the recorder first. Then use the same category when the ELL is the word stormer so the child can build on the words identified by the partner.

- Do not initially time the ELL on this activity. Have the ELL identify a specific number of words related to the category rather than focusing on the time element.

- Use pictures related to the category and have the ELL name the picture to promote growth in word knowledge in English.

Section 5.1   **TEACHING STRATEGY**

VOCABULARY SORTS

Vocabulary Sorts are based on the word sort strategy (see Teaching Strategy 4 in Section 3.3), but the focus is on meanings rather than phonic elements or spelling patterns. In a Vocabulary Sort, children sort word cards into categories based on meaning. As children complete a closed sort (categories are provided by the teacher), they gain additional practice with vocabulary words which results in greater understanding of the words and how they are related.

DIRECTIONS (CLOSED SORT)

1. Select 10 to 12 words that children have been learning in the classroom. Write each word on an index card or print the words on tag board and cut them apart.

2. Explain to children that they will be sorting their words into categories that you will provide to them. For example, if the children just read the book *Eating the Alphabet* (Ehlert, 1989), the words for the activity might be: *cherry, pear, potato, radish, carrot, watermelon, beet, strawberry, corn, okra, melon,* and *lime*. The categories for the Vocabulary Sort would be *fruits* and *vegetables*.

3. Working with a partner, ask the children to sort the word cards into the correct categories. Ask children to explain why they sorted the word cards as they did.

Modifying the Strategy to an Open Sort

4. To modify the strategy to an Open Sort, ask the children to sort the word cards into categories based on common features or properties. Then explain that they should label the category with a word or phrase that describes what all of the word cards in the stack have in common. In the example discussed in step 2, the children might develop categories based on color (red, green, and other colors), on taste (sweet, sour), and on type of food (fruit, vegetable).

- Include both the word and a picture on each word card to provide an additional resource to English Language Learners.
- If you know some or all of the words on the word cards in the child's home language, add those words to the cards to help the child make connections between the home language and English.

Section 5.1 *TEACHING STRATEGY*

WORD RIDDLES

Young children are very interested in jokes, riddles, and puns. These types of word play contribute to children's interest in words. The development of vocabulary riddles "is a way to stimulate exploration of words and to build interest and flexibility in word learning" (Blachowicz, 1998, p. 10).

DIRECTIONS

1. Share several riddles with the children. For example, you might share some of these old favorites.

    What is black and white and read all over? A newspaper!

    How did the sick pig get to the hospital? He took a hambulance!

    What do you call a duck that gets all A's in school? A wise quacker!

2. Explain to the children that you can write your own word riddles by following a few simple steps (Thaler, 1988). First, choose a subject for the riddle. For example, you might select *plant* because the children have been studying this topic in science.

3. Tell the children you will take the word *plant* and remove the first part to leave you with *ant*.

4. You will then make a list of words that begin with *ant*. Your list might include

    antonym

    antenna

    anticipate

5. Explain to the children that you will then add back the missing letters *pl* and make up riddles for the words. The riddles you create might include

    What is the opposite of a plant? A plantonym!

    How does a tree feel where it's going? It uses its plantenna!

    How does a tree know what is going to happen next? It can planticipate things!

6. Provide time for the children to write and share other word riddles.

Activities, tips, & Center Ideas

1. Read aloud to children each day. Select books, poems, and other texts that contain interesting words and rich language. By reading to children daily, many will become increasingly interested in new words.

2. Create a bulletin board or large poster where children can write new and interesting words they have learned. Provide time for children to share their words with the class.

3. Introduce a new word each day by writing it on the chalkboard, reading it to the children, discussing its meaning, sharing examples of how it can be used, and inviting the children to use the word during the day. To be a good word model, try to use the new word at least five times during the day to help the children learn and remember it.

4. Enrich the verbal environment in the classroom by using mature language such as *exhausted* rather than *tired* or *fundamental* rather than *main*. By using such language in your teaching and conversations with children, you will build their interest in words (Beck, McKeown, & Kucan, 2002).

5. Have children go on a Word Hunt to locate interesting words in their reading, as they watch television, or as they have conversations. Provide time for children to share the words they found on their Word Hunts. Challenge the children to use each word they found on their word hunt as a way of expanding their vocabularies.

6. Play concentration using vocabulary words and their definitions. Have children copy a vocabulary word on half of the index cards. Have them write a definition for each word on each remaining index card. Divide the class into groups of two. Tell children to place all of the cards face down on the floor or table. One child begins the game by selecting two cards. If the child draws a word and its definition, he or she keeps the cards and continues drawing until he or she misses. If the child does not draw a match, the next child gets a turn. Once all of the cards have been matched, the children count the cards in their stacks to see who the winner is.

7. Play Vocabulary Bingo to help children practice the vocabulary words they are learning. Make Bingo cards with one vocabulary word in each box. Read aloud a definition or a sentence with the vocabulary word deleted. Ask children to mark the appropriate vocabulary word on their cards using pennies, beans, or plastic counters. Once a child has Bingo, ask him or her to say each vocabulary word and give a definition or use it in a sentence. The child who is able to do so is the winner and becomes the caller for the next game.

8. Introduce the Gift of Words approach to the children by explaining that some authors use such interesting words, phrases, and sentences that they are gifts to the reader (Scott & Nagy, 2004). Share some of your favorite words, phrases, or sentences from books you have read recently with children. Write these on sentence strips and display them in the classroom. Discuss the words, phrases, and sentences to ensure that children understand them. Periodically, invite children to suggest words, phrases, or sentences to add to the Gift of Words display. Be sure to provide time for discussion before adding words to the display. Encourage children to use these words, phrases, and sentences in their speaking and writing.

WORD PLAY

Dear Families,

Words are an important part of reading. As your children learn new words, they are able to use them in their reading and writing. Playing word games is a great way to build your children's interest in words. Here are some fun word games you might enjoy playing with your children.

Board Games	*Scrabble Junior* *Up Words* *Boggle Junior* *Alpha Bug Soup* (These board games are available at most discount stores and toy stores. Some libraries also have games available for people to check out.)
20 Questions	Two players are needed for this game. One player thinks of an object. The other player can ask up to 20 questions that can be answered with a "yes" or a "no." If the player guesses the object correctly in 20 questions or less, he or she wins. Switch roles and play again.
Pencil and Paper Games	Pencil and paper games such as crossword puzzles and jumbles can be found in most newspapers. You can also print crossword puzzles for free from the Fun School Website located on the Internet at http://www.funschool.com/printables/print_cwp.php

I hope you and your children have fun playing these word games!

Sincerely,

Context

Goal: To help children use context to identify and understand unknown words.

Background

Children learn approximately 4,000 new words each school year (Nagy & Anderson, 1984). Because all of these words cannot be taught directly, it is clear that learning words from meaningful contexts is an important part of vocabulary development (Armbruster, Lehr, & Osborn, 2001). By helping children understand how to use context to identify and understand unknown words, they are able to be problem solvers who can figure out challenging words when they read (Bear, Invernizzi, Templeton, & Johnston, 2004).

Section 5.2   **TEACHING STRATEGY**

TEACHING ABOUT CONTEXT

 **DIRECTIONS**

1. Explain to the children that sometimes authors provide hints about unknown words through the use of context.

2. Write a sentence on the chalkboard or on a piece of chart paper. For example, you might use the following sentence.

    The *potter,* the person who makes clay pots and jugs, worked hard from sunrise until sunset.

3. Explain to children that one type of context clue the author may provide is the use of a definition. Tell them that the author might provide a short definition of the word right in the sentence as in the example above. Ask the children what the word *potter* means in the example. Invite children to explain how they figured out the meaning for the word. Clarify as necessary.

4. Provide additional practice using examples of words that are defined by context. Remind children to look at and think about the context when they encounter an unknown word in their reading.

5. Other types of context clues are listed below. If you intend to teach various types of context clues to children, plan to target one type of context clue at a time until children understand it before moving on to other types of context clues.

TYPE OF CONTEXT CLUE	EXAMPLE
Synonym	**Marta was in *despair;* she had never felt such sadness before.** (The synonym sadness is more familiar than the word despair; therefore, it should be helpful to young readers.)
Antonym	**The willow tree bent with the breeze, but the old oak tree stood rigid.** (The antonym phrase *bent with the breeze* is opposite the word *rigid.* This comparison should be helpful to children who are unfamiliar with the meaning of the word *rigid.*)
General	**David was an *industrious* student who always did his home-work, studied for his tests, and paid complete attention in class.** (The phrases, *always did his homework, studied for his tests,* and *paid complete attention in class* should help clarify the meaning of the word *industrious.*)

Section 5.2   *TEACHING STRATEGY*   **2**

PREVIEW IN CONTEXT

Preteaching vocabulary enhances children's comprehension as they read. By selecting a few key vocabulary words to preteach in the context of the story or text, teachers can help children understand these words and the underlying concepts before they begin reading.

DIRECTIONS

1. Select two or three important vocabulary words children will encounter in their reading. Identify the sentences that contain these words in the text.
2. Copy the words and sentences onto an overhead transparency, chart paper, or the chalkboard.
3. Explain to the children that there are several new vocabulary words in their reading and you want them to understand what they mean before they read the story or passage.
4. Direct the children's attention to one of the words and the sentence containing it that you have written on an overhead transparency, chart paper, or chalkboard. For example, you might display the following sentence before reading a science passage on amphibians.

    A frog is an *amphibian* that lives in the water and on land.

5. Assist the children with figuring out the meaning of the word by using the context. You may need to ask questions to guide their observations and insights. For example, you might say, "What do you know about the word *amphibian* from this sentence?" The children may offer responses such as, "A frog is an amphibian," and "It lives in the water and on land."
6. Expand the children's understanding by asking questions such as, "Can you think of other animals that are like frogs and live in the water and on land?" and "What characteristics does a frog have that help him live on both land and in the water?"

- Provide pictures, concrete objects, or other visuals to accompany each word. Point to the appropriate visual when you read the sentence to help the English Language Learners make the connection between the visual and the English words.

Section 5.2   *TEACHING STRATEGY*   **3**

CONTEXTUAL REDEFINITION

The Contextual Redefinition strategy helps children figure out the meaning of an unknown word by using information in the surrounding sentences (Readence, Bean, & Baldwin, 2001). This strategy may incorporate one or more of the different types of context clues listed in Teaching Strategy 1 in this section.

DIRECTIONS

1. Select two or three unfamiliar words in a text that children will be reading.

2. If the sentence containing the unfamiliar word provides useful context clues, it can be used for the activity. If it does not, write a sentence for the word that provides the meaning or gives clear hints about the meaning of the word.

3. Present the sentences to the children by writing them on the chalkboard or on a piece of chart paper. For example, you might share this sentence with the children.

    The *timid* mouse ran and hid in his hole.

4. Ask children to explain or define the vocabulary word using the context. For the word *timid*, the child might say, "The mouse ran and hid so it must have been afraid." Then restate the child's words, adding the vocabulary word. For example, you might say, "Jordan said the mouse must have been afraid. The word *timid* means afraid, and we know that because the author provided good context clues to help us understand."

5. Follow up by asking other children to explain how they figured out the meaning of the word *timid*. By providing multiple opportunities to hear the word and its meaning, the children will be more likely to remember it and add it to their vocabularies.

6. Complete a similar process with other vocabulary words.

MAZE

In the Maze strategy, the teacher deletes a key word from a sentence that contains useful contextual information. Three words are provided as possible choices to fill in the blank, and the children select the word that makes sense in each sentence. This strategy is useful for teaching context clues to children "who might have word-finding problems or who might have limited English-recall vocabularies" (Blachowicz & Fisher, 2006, p. 34).

➤ DIRECTIONS

1. Select a sentence and delete a key word. Be sure the sentence provides clear context clues to help the children identify the missing word.

2. List three choices for the deleted word. One of the choices should be correct, and the other two choices should not make sense in the sentence.

3. Write the sentence on the chalkboard or on an overhead transparency.

4. Read the sentence with the children. Tell them that a word has been removed from the sentence and that they are to choose from the list the word that makes sense in the sentence.

5. For example, you might use the following sentences and choices.

    The dog wagged his _____.

            car

            tail

            nose

    It was a hot and _____ day.

            sunny

            snowy

            hungry

6. Discuss each word and whether it makes sense in the sentence. For example, you might say, "The dog wagged its car. Does that make sense? Can a dog wag a car?"

7. Continue through this process for several sentences to provide additional practice. When the children are consistently able to identify the correct word using the Maze strategy, move on to use the Hidden Word strategy (Teaching Strategy 5).

Aa Bb Cc Tips for English Language Learners

- This strategy is very supportive of English Language Learners because they are able to use the list of words to complete the task rather than having to think of the words on their own.

- Providing only two choices for each blank will make the task easier for English Language Learners.

HIDDEN WORD

In the Hidden Word strategy, specific words are deleted from a text to focus the children's attention on using context to figure out what word makes sense in each blank. The teacher selects one or more words to cover in a passage and guides the children to predict what word(s) would make sense in the passage by using the context.

DIRECTIONS

1. Select a passage and copy it onto an overhead transparency. You may need to enlarge the passage so children can easily see it.

2. Identify two or three words to teach in the passage. When selecting the words to teach, be sure there are sufficient context clues to help the children figure out the missing words. Cover the target words using "sticky notes" or masking tape.

3. Display the transparency and tell the children you will be working together to figure out what words would make sense in the blanks.

4. Read the passage aloud with the children. Discuss the gist of the passage to ensure that children have grasped the major ideas.

5. Point out that some of the words have been covered. Then tell the children that you will be using the context to make predictions about what words could fit into the blanks.

6. Ask the children to predict what words would make sense in the first blank. As they share predictions, ask them to explain how they used the context to come up with their ideas.

7. After several children have shared and supported their predictions, pull the "sticky note" or masking tape off to reveal the actual word in the passage. Discuss the actual word in comparison to the children's predictions.

8. Follow steps 6 and 7 until all of the blanks in the passage have been discussed.

C(2)QU

This strategy provides children with both contextual and definitional information to help them predict word meaning in a systematic manner (Blachowicz & Fisher, 2006). Words selected for the C(2)QU strategy should be new labels for already-known concepts or partially known words so children will be able to complete the task. C(2)QU is comprised of four steps: (1) choose and present the word in a general context, (2) present the word in a more explicit context, (3) pose a question to clarify the word's meaning, and (4) ask children to demonstrate understanding by using the word in a sentence or explaining the meaning in their own words.

🐦 DIRECTIONS

1. Choose a word to be taught that is important to a text the children will be reading or a unit they will be studying. Develop a broad but meaningful context for the word by writing one or two sentences. Display the sentences on the chalkboard or an overhead transparency. This is step C1 (choose) in the strategy. For example, you might present the following sentence for the word *regret*.

    C1   I *regret* that I did not tell the truth.

2. Ask the children to make predictions about what they think the word means. Ask them to explain their predictions using the information in the sentence and from their own experiences.

3. Provide a more explicit context for the word by presenting a sentence that contains some definitional information. This is step C2 (context) in the strategy. For example, you might present the following sentence for the word *regret*.

    C2   I was so sorry for what I had done that I began to *regret* my actions.

4. Ask a question that clarifies the meaning of the word. For example, you might ask, "If I *regret* something, does that mean I'm sorry too?" This is the Q (question) step in the strategy.

5. Ask the children to use the word in a meaningful sentence or to explain it in their own words. This is the U (understanding) step of the strategy.

6. Continue this process with several other target words to help the children strengthen their use of context clues.

Activities, tips, & Center Ideas

1. Cover words on classroom posters, bulletin boards, and/or signs. Have the children predict what words are missing. Uncover the words and have children discuss how they used context to figure out the missing words.

2. Have children draw word posters to provide a personal visual context for new or challenging words. On their posters, children should draw a picture that helps them remember the word. They should also write the word and a brief explanation. A sample word poster is shown below.

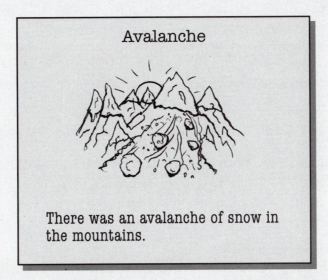

Avalanche

There was an avalanche of snow in the mountains.

3. Before reading a Big Book with the children, cover a word with a "sticky note." Read the sentence or passage with the children. Discuss what words would make sense and why. Then remove the "sticky note" to reveal the actual word. Compare the appropriateness of the predicted words with the actual word.

4. Delete a word in your verbal directions to the children. For example, you might say "Boys and girls, please put your books _____." Ask the children what word makes sense in the blank. Ask them to explain their ideas. Tell them the word. Discuss it in relation to their predictions.

5. Write a sentence on a sentence strip. Cut it apart into separate words. Remove one of the words and replace it with a blank piece of sentence strip. Give each set of words to a pair of children. Ask the children to put the sentence together and figure out what would make sense in the blank. This activity can be also placed in a learning center for independent practice.

6. Make a flip booklet that contains a sentence with one word covered by a flap. Working independently, the child guesses what word makes sense. The child then lifts the flap to reveal the actual word. This activity works well in a learning center. A sample flip booklet is shown below. The covered word is *ball*.

The puppy chased the bouncing _____ .

CONTEXT CLUES

Dear Families,

We have been learning how to use context clues to figure out difficult words in our reading. This is a skill that good readers use. You can help your child practice using context clues at home. Here are several activities you can try.

• Write a sentence on a sheet of paper. Leave one word out. Ask your child what words make sense in the blank.

• Choose one of your child's books and place a "sticky note" or piece of masking tape over a word in one sentence. Read the sentence and discuss what would make sense in the blank. Pull off the "sticky note" or masking tape to show the word.

• Play Guess My Word with your child. Say a sentence but say "blank" for one of the words. Ask your child what words would make sense in the blank. Tell your child the word you were thinking of. Then switch roles so your child tells you a sentence.

Enjoy these activities. Thank you for your help in supporting your child as a reader.

Sincerely,

From Laurie Elish-Piper, Jerry L. Johns, and Susan Davis Lenski, *Teaching Reading Pre-K–Grade 3* (3rd ed.). Copyright © 2006 by Kendall/Hunt Publishing Company (1-800-247-3458, ext. 4). May be reproduced for noncommercial educational purposes.

Word Parts

Goal: To help children use word parts to identify and understand unknown words.

Background

The structural analysis of words is a helpful strategy for understanding the meaning of words (Bear, Invernizzi, Templeton, & Johnston, 2004). Words are made up of basic meaning units called morphemes. There are two types of morphemes—bound and free. Bound morphemes must be attached to a root word (sometimes called a base word) to have meaning. Prefixes such as *pre-, un-,* and *dis-* and suffixes such as *-ed, -ing,* and *-es* are examples of bound morphemes. Free morphemes, often called root words or base words, can stand alone and have meaning. As children develop as readers, they encounter words that are longer and more complex. By having a basic understanding of how to analyze unknown words by looking for prefixes, suffixes, root words, and compound words, children are able to figure out the meanings of many words they encounter in their reading (Edwards, Font, Baumann, & Boland, 2004).

Section 5.3 **TEACHING STRATEGY**

KEYWORD METHOD

The Keyword Method uses auditory and visual cues to help children learn and remember the meanings of words (Pressley, Levin, & Delaney, 1983). The basic procedure for the Keyword Method focuses on three steps: recoding, relating, and retrieving (Mastropieri, 1988). This strategy has been found to be particularly effective with children who have special learning needs.

DIRECTIONS

1. Identify a target vocabulary word for the strategy.
2. Display the word on the chalkboard or on an overhead transparency.
3. The first step in the strategy is to recode the word, meaning the children identify a part of the word that looks like or sounds like a word they already know. For example, if the key word is *willpower,* the teacher might guide the children to select the word *power* because they understand that word and can easily picture that word as a superhero (with powers) with his fist raised in the air. This is the keyword.
4. The second step is relating the recoded word (keyword) to the definition of the target word using imagery. For example, because the definition of the word *willpower* is determination, self-control, or strength of mind, the teacher could guide children to relate the keyword *power* to the definition by imagining or visualizing a superhero with his fist raised in the air, saying, "I'm strong and determined!"

5. The last step in the strategy is retrieving. In this step, children recall the meaning of the target word by first thinking of the recoded word, picturing the image related to the word, and then relating it to the definition. For example, with the word *willpower,* children are guided to think of the keyword *power* and to then visualize the superhero with his raised fist who is saying, "I'm strong and determined!"

6. Model the strategy several times with different vocabulary words to ensure the children understand the process.

Aa Bb Cc | Tips for English Language Learners

- The Keyword Strategy provides both visual and auditory cues to help children understand and remember word meanings. This combination of cues is very helpful for English Language Learners.

- If there is a cognate (a word in the home language and in English that has comparable form and meaning) such as *carro* in Spanish and *car* in English, the child could use this cognate to serve as the keyword for *carnivore.* For example, *carro* is the keyword, and to relate the word the child visualizes a person driving in a car to get a hamburger because a carnivore eats meat. Be cautious about using false cognates or words in the home language that seem to be comparable but are not.

Section 5.3 **TEACHING STRATEGY** 2

COMPOUND WORD CUT-APART

Compound words can be challenging for children to identify and understand because they are multisyllabic and composed of many letters. The compound words *baseball, hotdog,* and *backpack* are likely to be in the listening and speaking vocabularies of many young children; however, these words are long and might be difficult to identify without the use of structural analysis. By breaking compound words into the two root words (free morphemes), children can easily identify the meaning of these words.

DIRECTIONS

1. Identify several compound words from reading materials and units of study the children have encountered in your classroom.

2. Write each compound word on a sentence strip.

3. Select one word to demonstrate the Compound Word Cut-Apart strategy. This strategy works best when implemented with a small group of children who are seated around a table on in a circle on the floor.

4. Show the children the strip containing the compound word. For example, if the compound word is *baseball,* tell the children,

   This special word is called a compound word. It is made from two smaller words. If a compound word is cut into the two smaller words, we can figure out the word and its meaning. Then ask children, "What small word do you see in this compound word? I see *ball* at the end of the word."

   Using scissors, cut the word *ball* from the strip. The word *base* will remain.

5. Tell the children, "The other small word in this compound word is base. You can see that I cut the compound word into the two small words *base* and *ball.*"

6. Explain that by looking at the meanings of the two small words, you can often figure out the meaning of the compound word. Discuss the meaning of the words *base* and *ball* and how they combine to form the meaning of the compound word *baseball*.

7. Guide children through the strategy again with the several other compound words such as *popcorn, lunchbox,* and *backpack.* Hand a strip to each child in the group. Discuss each compound word one at a time by following this process.

   What small word do you see in this compound word?

   Using the scissors, cut that small word from the strip.

   What other small word do you see in your compound word?

   What does each small word mean?

   How do the words combine to make the meaning of your compound word?

8. After the children understand the process, you may wish to introduce compound words that do not hold the literal meaning of each of the root words so the children can develop a more advanced understanding of compound words. For example, if you select the compound word *butterfly,* the children will begin to understand that compound words are comprised of two small words but that each may not retain the literal meaning of the root word. In the case of *butterfly,* the root word *fly* retains its meaning, but the word *butter* is not represented in the meaning of the compound word.

Section 5.3 **TEACHING STRATEGY** 3

PREFIX REMOVAL AND REPLACEMENT

Prefixes are worth teaching because a relatively small number of prefixes are used in a large number of words. More specifically, the three most common prefixes *un-, re-,* and *in-* account for 51% of the words in the English language with prefixes (Graves, 2004). Prefixes are also consistent in their spelling and meaning which is helpful when children are trying to identify and understand unknown words.

DIRECTIONS

1. Select a word with a common prefix. For example, you may choose *unknown, remove,* or *incomplete* because these words contain the most common prefixes (*un-, re-,* and *in-*).

2. Display the word on the chalkboard. Tell children that the word *unknown* contains a prefix and a root word. Point out that the prefix is *un-.*

3. Ask the children if what is left is a real word. In this example, it is the root word *known.*

4. Tell the children that if they try to remove a prefix and a real word is left, they have found a prefix.

5. Tell the children that the prefix *un-* means not. Discuss the meaning of the root word *known* (understood clearly).

6. Explain that the meaning of the word *unknown* is a combination of the meaning of the prefix *un-* and the root word *known.*

$$
\begin{array}{ll}
\text{un} & = \text{not} \\
\underline{+ \text{known} =} & \underline{\text{understood clearly}} \\
\text{unknown} = & \text{not understood clearly}
\end{array}
$$

7. Put the word in a sentence and ask the children if it makes sense using the meaning you identified.

   There was an *unknown* amount of money missing after the bank robbery.

8. Repeat the process with several other words. A list of the most common prefixes and their meanings is provided below to assist you with planning instruction on prefixes.

PREFIX	MEANING	EXAMPLE
un-	not	unlucky
re-	again	rewrite
in-	not	incomplete
dis-	not	disappear

9. This lesson can also be adapted for use with suffixes. A list of common suffixes is provided in the box below.

SUFFIX	MEANING	EXAMPLE
-s or -es	plural	cats; dishes
-ful	full of	powerful
-ist	someone who does	scientist
-less	without	hopeless
-ness	state of being	happiness
-ly	in the manner of	kindly

4

ADDING UP WORDS

Root words hold the bulk of the meaning of words; therefore, it is important for children to be able to identify and understand root words. By stripping off affixes (prefixes and suffixes), children will be able to locate root words and focus their attention on their meanings (Paynter, Bodrova, & Doty, 2005). The strategy Adding Up Words focuses on understanding the concept, importance, and meanings of common root words, prefixes, and suffixes in English.

DIRECTIONS

1. Write several sentences on the chalkboard that contain root words with affixes (prefixes and/or suffixes). For example, you might write these sentences.

    I had to *rewrite* my homework paper because it was too messy.

    Maria was *restless* as she waited for the bell to ring.

    He felt much *unhappiness* after his pet dog ran away.

2. Read each sentence with the children. Direct their attention to the underlined word in each sentence.

3. Read the underlined word aloud. Ask the children to repeat it after you.

4. Tell the children that the underlined word is a root word with a prefix at the beginning. Write this equation on the chalkboard.

    prefix + root word = rewrite

5. Explain that the prefix at the beginning of the word is *re-* and the root word is *write*. Tell the children that when you add together the parts of the word, you can figure out its meaning.

6. Write the following equation on the chalkboard

    re + write = rewrite

7. Tell the children that by looking at the meaning of the prefix and root word, you can identify the meaning of the word. Explain that the prefix *re-* means again; therefore, the word *rewrite* means to write again.

8. Continue this process for the remaining words. The equations for *restless* and *unhappiness* are listed below.

    Root word + suffix = restless

    Rest + less = restless

    Prefix + root word + suffix = unhappiness

    Un + happy + ness = unhappiness
    (This example requires a discussion of the spelling change in the root word *y* changes to *i* before adding -*ness*.)

9. Repeat this lesson with new words to help the children understand how to identify and use root words, prefixes, and suffixes to understand word meanings.

Tips for English Language Learners

- To make the activity more meaningful for English Language Learners, provide each word on a sentence strip. Have the children cut each word apart to identify the prefix, root word, and suffix. Then have the children put them back together to show how the parts are combined to make the word.

Section 5.3 **TEACHING STRATEGY** **5**

WORD FAMILIES

Using word families (sometimes called word neighborhoods or phonograms) to teach vocabulary helps children learn a number of related words easily (Nagy & Anderson, 1984). This approach to teaching vocabulary is based on the theory that if children know and understand the meaning of the root word, this knowledge can serve as a bridge to other forms of the word (Edwards, Font, Baumann, & Boland, 2004). For example, if the children know the meaning of the word *photo,* they can apply it to other words in the same word family (photograph, photographer, photography, photographic).

DIRECTIONS

1. Select a word family that will be useful for the children to know for reading a text or completing a unit of study in the classroom. For the purpose of this teaching strategy, a word family is defined as a group of words that share a common root word.

2. For example, you may select the word family listed below.

   sum

   summary

   summarize

3. Explain to the children that learning about word families will help them understand and remember words that are related because they share a common root word.

4. Write the word family on the chalkboard. Ask the children what root word all of the words have in common. In the example, the common root word is *sum.*

5. Underline the root word in each of the words in the word family. Explain that this group of words is called a word family because they all share a root word.

6. Invite children to predict the meaning of the root word *sum.* Remind them that they have probably seen the word *sum* in their math books and activities.

7. Clarify that the meaning of the root word *sum* is to total something or add it together.

8. Discuss the remaining words in the family, focusing on how their meanings are all related to the root word *sum.*

   sum = to total something or add it together

   summary = the key points put together in a short format (e.g., write a summary)

   summarize = to put the key points together in a short format (e.g., to write a summary)

9. Periodically introduce new word families as they connect to the texts the children are reading or the units they are studying in the classroom.

Activities, tips, & Center Ideas

1. Play word-building games on the chalkboard. Write a root word on the chalkboard and ask the children to make as many new words as they can using the root word. Tell the children that they can use different forms of the word from the same family and they can also add prefixes and suffixes to the root word. For example, if you select the word *set,* the children might suggest the following words: *setting, setter, settle, settler, reset, resetting,* and *preset.*

2. Create a bulletin board or poster in the classroom where children can write all of the words they encounter that contain prefixes. Provide time each week to discuss the new words that were added to the bulletin board or poster. The same idea can be applied to suffixes.

3. Make a list of compound words and write each part on an index card. Pass one card out to each child. Ask the children to find the other word that combines with theirs to form a compound word. Have the children stand with their partner and say their compound word and its meaning aloud.

4. Take the children on a word walk in the classroom or school to look for a specific type of word. For example, you might take them on a compound word walk, a prefix walk, or a suffix walk. Provide time for the children to share the words they found.

5. Have the children work with partners to create silly compound words. After they develop their silly compound word, have them write a definition for it. Ask the children to share their silly compound word. A sample silly compound word created by a pair of first-grade children is provided below.

> dogwindow
> The window where my dog hangs his head out in our car.

COMPOUND WORDS

Dear Families:

We have been learning about compound words in our class. We have learned that a compound word is formed by adding two smaller words together to make a new word. Some of the compound words we learned are listed below.

base + ball = baseball
back + pack = backpack
sun + flower = sunflower

We are having a scavenger hunt for compound words so we can make a bulletin board in our class.

Please help your child look for compound words at home, in your neighborhood, as you read together, and as you watch television or videos. You and your child can write the words you find in the chart below. Please return the chart by _____ so we can add your words to the bulletin board.

Happy compound word hunting!

Sincerely,

Compound Words We Found	

section 5.4

Connecting and Extending Word Meanings

Goal: To help children deepen their knowledge of vocabulary words.
Assessment Strategy 1 Three-Minute Conferences, page 292
Assessment Strategy 2 Teacher Checklist of Vocabulary Use, page 294

Background

Vocabulary knowledge is directly related to children's comprehension of text (McKeown & Beck, 2004). Vocabulary can be learned in a variety of ways, including listening, reading, instruction, and student-centered activities (Blair-Larsen & Williams, 1999). Vocabulary instruction is an important part of the curriculum, regardless of subject area. For example, in addition to learning vocabulary in conjunction with reading, children must learn key vocabulary words in math to understand important concepts. Beck and McKeown (1991) offer four principles for effective vocabulary instruction across the curriculum.

1. All approaches to teaching vocabulary are more effective than no instruction.
2. No one approach has been shown to be consistently best.
3. Multiple approaches and activities yield the best gains in vocabulary knowledge.
4. Repeated exposures to vocabulary words increase understanding.

The following strategies are designed to help children strengthen their vocabulary knowledge.

Section 5.4 **TEACHING STRATEGY** *1*

VOCABULARY CONNECTIONS

Children can understand and remember new vocabulary words best when those words are connected to the children's experiences and knowledge (Biemiller, 2004). The Vocabulary Connections strategy introduces a new word using a synonym the children will already know.

✎ DIRECTIONS

1. Select a key vocabulary word that is important for children to know to understand a story or passage. Identify a synonym or phrase for the word that will be familiar to the children. For example, if the vocabulary word is *rehearse,* you might select *practice* as your synonym. Ask the children, "What do you do to get ready to perform a play?"

2. Provide time for the children to share their ideas. List their ideas on an overhead transparency or the chalkboard. Discuss the connections among their ideas. For example, children may say, "I practice my lines by saying them over and over," "I learn my parts and memorize them," and "We do the play over and over until it is ready." You may respond, "Your ideas all talk about doing something over and over until you learn it very well. When you do this, you *rehearse* for the play."

3. Show the children a sentence from the story that contains the vocabulary word. Display this sentence on an overhead transparency or the chalkboard.

> We will *rehearse* for the play today after school so we will be ready to perform on Saturday.

4. Have children turn to a partner and brainstorm sentences and situations when they could use the word *rehearse*. Provide time for sharing and write these sentences and situations on an overhead transparency or the chalkboard.

Aa Bb Cc | Tips for English Language Learners

- If the vocabulary word is an action word, invite several children to pantomime the word. This process will help English Language Learners visualize the meaning of the word.

- If the vocabulary word is a concrete object, provide a visual or example or invite children to draw the object. Write the vocabulary word on a card to display with the object, visual, or drawings.

Section 5.4 **TEACHING STRATEGY** 2

WORD FRAMES

To help students fully understand important conceptual vocabulary, a Word Frame can be used (Tompkins, 2002). For maximum effectiveness, this activity should focus on a very small number of key vocabulary words rather than a long list of words. An appropriate number of words for this activity is two or three. The Word Frame allows students to identify synonyms and/or examples as well as antonyms and/or nonexamples of the target vocabulary word.

DIRECTIONS

1. Select two or three key vocabulary words that are essential to understanding the unit or reading. For example, you might select the words *community* and *citizen* from your social studies book.

2. Demonstrate the procedures for completing the Word Frame using the example listed below for the word *community*.

Community is _____. It is _____, _____, and

_____. It is never _____ or _____.

Community is _____.

Explain to children that they can fill in the blanks with one word or with a phrase. A sample completed Word Frame for *community* is provided below.

Community is <u>a neighborhood</u>. It is <u>family</u>, <u>friends</u>, and <u>neighbors</u>. It is never <u>far away</u> or <u>unfriendly</u>. Community is <u>where you live.</u>

3. Provide time for children to offer multiple responses to the Word Frame. Discuss the children's responses.

4. Present another vocabulary word to the children. Ask them to complete the Word Frame for the vocabulary word with a partner or as a whole class.

Section 5.4   *TEACHING STRATEGY*   **3**

FOUR-SQUARE VOCABULARY

This strategy helps students develop personal understandings for key vocabulary words and concepts (Johns & Lenski, 2005). Students fill out a grid that contains key information about the word. To be effective, this strategy should focus on no more than two or three key vocabulary words.

DIRECTIONS

1. Draw a sample Four-Square Vocabulary grid on the chalkboard or overhead transparency to model the process for students. Select a word they will already know. For example, if you use the word *happy*, their Four-Square Vocabulary grid might look like this.

Word	Makes me think of . . .
Happy	Playing with friends, birthday parties, and cartoons
Meaning	Opposite
Glad	Sad

2. Have children fold a sheet of paper in half in length and then in width to form four boxes. Have them label each of the boxes using the words *Word, Makes me think of . . . , Meaning,* and *Opposite*. If you prefer, you can give children grids that already contain the labels. Be sure children understand the meanings of the words used for labels.

3. Give the children key words from the unit they are studying. It is important to select words they have already encountered in their reading, discussion, and activities.

4. Have children fill out the Four-Square Vocabulary grids.

5. Provide time for children to share their grids with their peers. Discuss how and why children may have made different personal associations as part of their grids. Discuss the importance of "making new words their own" by connecting them to their life experiences.

Four-Square Vocabulary

Name _____ Date _____

Word	Makes me think of . . .
Meaning	**Opposite**

Word	Makes me think of . . .
Meaning	**Opposite**

Tips for English Language Learners

- Modify the Four-Square Vocabulary grid so it contains a box for the word in the child's home language and a drawing related to the word. A sample Four-Square Vocabulary grid is provided below.

Word in English	Word in Home Language
Meaning	Picture

VOCABULARY MAPPING

The Vocabulary Mapping strategy helps children brainstorm and associate words that are related to a key concept (Stahl & Vancil, 1986). By discussing and visually mapping a key concept and associated words, children are able to understand relationships among words and develop a deep understanding of the key concept. Research on Vocabulary Mapping has revealed that it improves children's recall of key concepts and passage comprehension (Stahl, 1997). In addition, the Vocabulary Mapping strategy has been found to be particularly useful for children with limited vocabularies and poor reading skills.

DIRECTIONS

1. Select a word that represents a key concept children must understand in a text they will be reading.

2. Write the word on the chalkboard, an overhead transparency, or a piece of chart paper.

3. Explain to children that the word is very important for a text they will be reading and that you will be creating a Vocabulary Map to represent this key concept.

4. Ask the children to brainstorm any words they can think of that are related to the key concept. For example, if the key concept is *plants,* the children could brainstorm words such as *flowers, roots, stem, vegetables, trees, grass, grow, water,* and *dirt.* Write these words on the chalkboard, overhead transparency, or chart paper. As children share words related to the key concept, ask them to define or explain the word. Then invite other children to share additional information they know about the brainstormed word. Continue in this manner until the children have shared the words they know related to the key concept.

5. After the children have shared all of the words they can think of that are related to the key concept, add any related words you want the children to know. For example, with the key concept of *plants,* you may share the words *stamen, pistil, seed, bud,* and *oxygen.*

6. Next, work with children to create a Vocabulary Map that shows the key concept and related words. As you complete this step, ask the children to define, explain, or give an example for each of the words placed on the map. Group related words together under a heading such as *Kinds of plants* to show how words are connected. After you have completed the Vocabulary Map, invite children to share other words they can think of related to the headings on the map. A sample is shown on the next page for the key concept of *plants.*

Completed Vocabulary Map for *Plants*

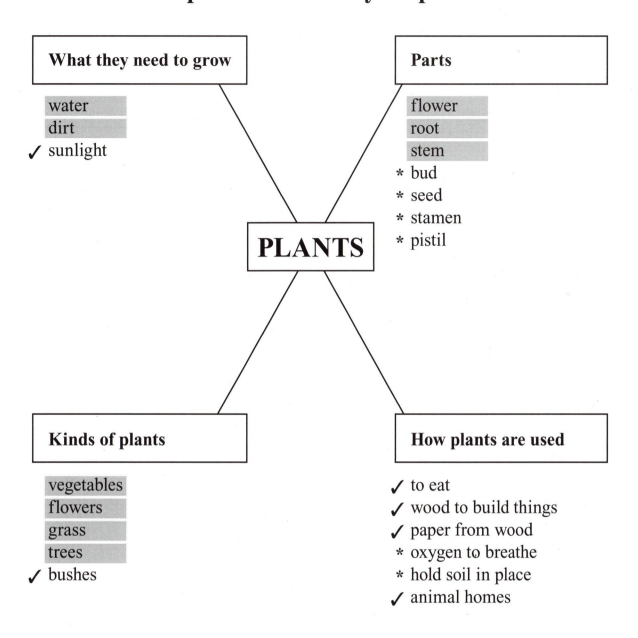

What they need to grow

water
dirt
✓ sunlight

Parts

flower
root
stem
* bud
* seed
* stamen
* pistil

PLANTS

Kinds of plants

vegetables
flowers
grass
trees
✓ bushes

How plants are used

✓ to eat
✓ wood to build things
✓ paper from wood
* oxygen to breathe
* hold soil in place
✓ animal homes

Note: Words that are highlighted were brainstormed by children. Words that are marked with an asterisk *
were added by the teacher, and words that are marked with a ✓ were added by children after the Vocabulary
Map was created.

VOCABULARY ANCHORS

Vocabulary Anchors (Winters, 2001) uses a graphic organizer to help children understand vocabulary words clearly by connecting their prior knowledge to new ideas. Vocabulary Anchors work best for concepts that are concrete and already somewhat familiar to children (Johns, Lenski, & Berglund, 2006).

DIRECTIONS

1. Show the Vocabulary Anchor sheet by displaying it on an overhead transparency. Ask children if they have ever seen a boat floating on a lake, river, or even in their bathtub. Point to the anchor and explain to the children how an anchor can be used to keep the boat in one place. Also discuss how a chain or rope is used to attach the anchor to the boat.

2. Explain to children that when they learn something new it is helpful to connect the new learning to something they already know. Tell them that doing so will keep the new learning connected to ideas they already know so they can remember the new information.

3. Tell children that they will be using the Vocabulary Anchor to learn and remember important information related to a vocabulary word they will be studying. For example, if the target vocabulary word is *tornado,* write *tornado* in the bottom of the boat.

4. Then ask the children to think of a word that is related to *tornado* that they already know a lot about. They may suggest the word *thunderstorm.* Tell the children that the word *thunderstorm* is the anchor word because a tornado and a thunderstorm are similar because they are both types of weather with wind and rain.

5. Explain to children that you will write the things that are similar between a tornado and a thunderstorm next to the rope that connects the anchor to the boat. These words will be *weather, wind,* and *rain* for the example *tornado.*

6. Tell the children that while a tornado and a thunderstorm are similar, they are not exactly alike. Then explain to the children some ways they are different. With the example *tornado,* you may say they are different because "tornados have a small funnel of quickly spinning air, tornados form only in the most violent thunderstorms, and tornados may reach speeds of 800 kilometers per hour."

7. Write these phrases near the right side of the boat to show they are not connected to the anchor word *thunderstorm.* Place a minus sign (–) next to each of them to show that they are not related to the anchor word.

8. Direct the children's attention to the sail on the boat and ask them, "What can I write on the sail to help us remember our new word *tornado?*" Explain that some of the children may choose different words to write on the sail, but they should be sure to choose something that will help them remember the word and its meaning. For example, you might share the following ideas with the children to show how you remember the word *tornado.*

> I am going to write the word *terrible* because a tornado is a terrible storm. I have seen pictures of tornados that do terrible damage to houses, trees, and buildings. I am also going to writing *turning* because the funnel cloud in a tornado is turning very fast and can cause a lot of damage. When I look at my Vocabulary Anchor, those words *terrible* and *turning* will help me remember what is important to know about a tornado.

9. Review the Vocabulary Anchor with the children to help them understand how to use it to remember the target word. For example, you may say the following.

> The word we want to learn and remember is *tornado*. It is the word in our boat. The anchor word is *thunderstorm,* and it is related to *tornado*. They are similar because they are both types of weather with wind and rain. I put those words near the rope that holds the anchor to show that they are related to both tornados and thunderstorms. I also know that tornados and thunderstorms are different so I wrote "small funnel of quickly spinning air," "only form in most violent thunderstorms," and "reach speeds of 800 kilometers per hour" away from the anchor and rope to show that these ideas are only related to tornados. I also put a minus sign (–) next to these ideas to show that they don't apply to the anchor word *thunderstorms*. Finally, I chose two words *terrible* and *turning* to put in the sail because a tornado is a terrible, turning funnel cloud that does terrible damage. The words *terrible* and *turning* will help me remember the meaning of *tornado*.

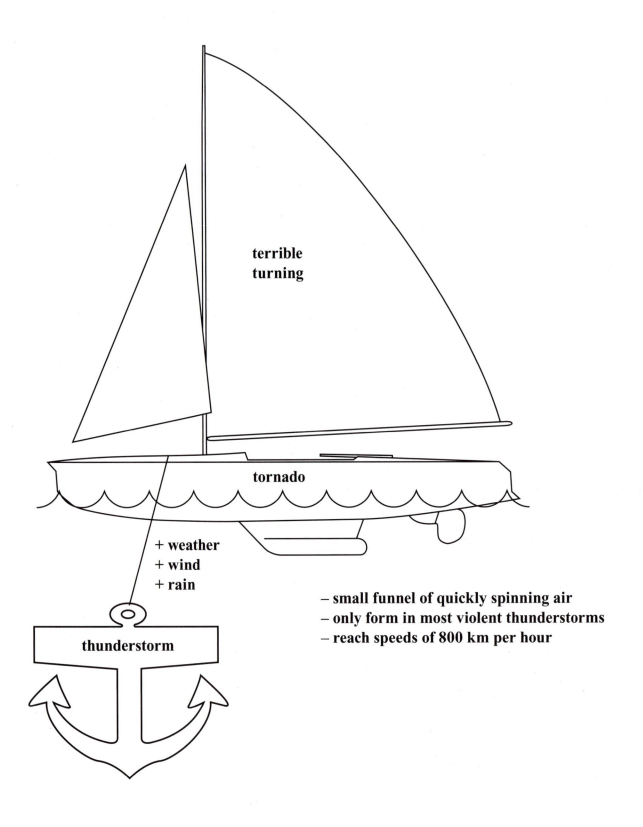

terrible
turning

tornado

+ weather
+ wind
+ rain

– small funnel of quickly spinning air
– only form in most violent thunderstorms
– reach speeds of 800 km per hour

thunderstorm

Vocabulary Anchor

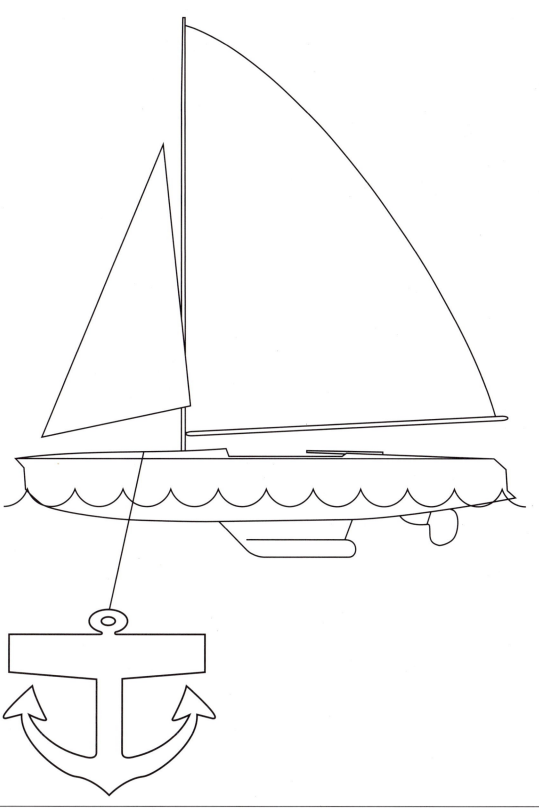

CONCEPT OF DEFINITION MAP

The Concept of Definition Map is an excellent strategy for teaching key concepts and vocabulary (Buehl, 2001). Through the use of a structured graphic organizer, children can develop a deeper understanding of a word, including the category of the word, its characteristics or properties, and examples. By having a deeper understanding of a word, children are more likely to remember the word and add it to their working vocabulary (Schwartz & Raphael, 1985).

DIRECTIONS

1. Select a key concept you have been studying, such as *mammals.*

2. Tell the children that it is important to understand the whole definition or meaning of the word and the Concept of Definition Map will help them do so.

3. Display a blank Concept of Definition Map on an overhead transparency or draw one on the chalkboard.

4. Write the target word *mammal* in the box labeled *Concept.*

5. Ask the children, "What is a mammal? What group or category does it belong to?" If the children have difficulty responding to this question, tell them, "A mammal is a type of animal, so *animal* is the category it belongs to. I will write *animal* in the box with the label *Category* on it."

6. Tell the children that there are important characteristics or properties of a mammal that they should know. Pose the question, "What is a mammal like?" or "What makes a mammal a mammal?" to help the children identify characteristics or properties of mammals. Write these in the ovals under the heading *Properties / Characteristics.*

7. Explain to the children that knowing examples is another important part of understanding a definition fully. Ask them to suggest examples of mammals. Write these in the ovals at the bottom of the Concept of Definition Map above the label *Examples.*

CONCEPT OF DEFINITION MAP FOR MAMMALS

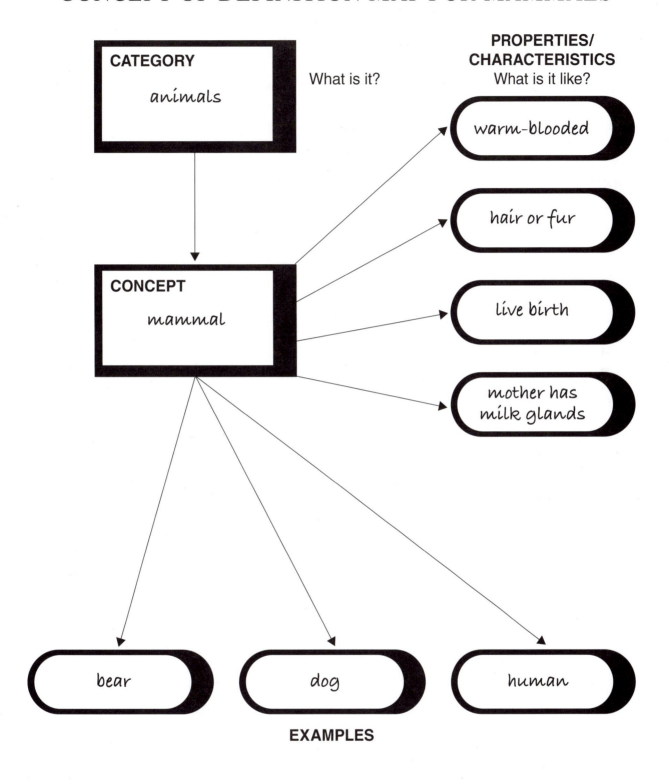

CATEGORY

animals

What is it?

**PROPERTIES/
CHARACTERISTICS**
What is it like?

warm-blooded

hair or fur

CONCEPT

mammal

live birth

mother has
milk glands

bear

dog

human

EXAMPLES

Name _____ Date _____

CONCEPT OF DEFINITION MAP

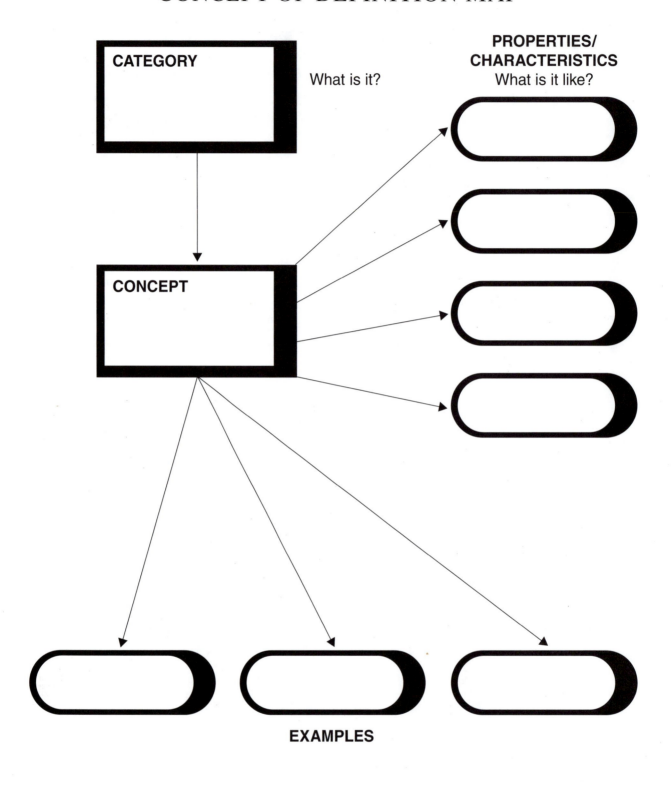

CATEGORY

What is it?

**PROPERTIES/
CHARACTERISTICS**
What is it like?

CONCEPT

EXAMPLES

From Laurie Elish-Piper, Jerry L. Johns, and Susan Davis Lenski, *Teaching Reading Pre-K–Grade 3* (3rd ed.). Copyright © 2006 by Kendall/Hunt Publishing Company (1-800-247-3458, ext. 4). May be reproduced for noncommercial educational purposes.

Activities, tips, & Center Ideas

1. Have children keep a vocabulary box using a card file box and index cards. Instruct children to write each vocabulary word on a card and the definition or sentence on the other side. Provide time for children to review the cards independently or with a partner. Children can also take the cards home to review words with their parents or other family members.

2. Have children keep a vocabulary notebook that contains target vocabulary words with their definitions, examples, drawings, and personal associations. Encourage children to add their own vocabulary words to their notebooks. Provide time for children to discuss and compare their vocabulary notebook entries.

3. Use the List-Group-Label strategy (Readence & Searfoss, 1980) to activate children's background knowledge about a target vocabulary word. For example, for the word *tornado,* ask children to brainstorm words that come to mind. List these words on the chalkboard or chart paper. Next, have children group the words according to common aspects. This step can be done as a whole group or in small groups or dyads once children have learned the strategy. After the words have been grouped, ask children to label each group.

4. To help children expand their vocabularies and use interesting adjectives and adverbs, have them create semantic maps to show how the words are all related (Buis, 2004). Select a commonly used word such as *nice* or *fast.* Write the word in the middle of a sheet of chart paper or on the chalkboard. Under the word, write a sentence that uses the word such as "That boy runs fast." Ask the children to brainstorm words that could replace the word *fast* in the sentence. Write the words they suggest in the form of a web on the chart paper or chalkboard (see sample below). For each word, discuss whether it fits in the sentence or if the sentence would need to be modified to accommodate the synonym. Tell the children that using the synonyms in their writing and speech will make their language more interesting and descriptive.

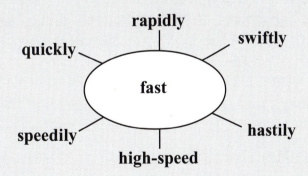

The boy runs fast.

5. Have children act out or pantomime new vocabulary words as a way of making the new words come alive. Provide the children with a list of five to seven vocabulary words they have been studying. Have them pantomime the words with a partner to review the words.

6. Share riddles with children to help them learn and understand vocabulary. For example, for the word, *sum* you might say, "I'm less than all and more than none. I add up in math like 1 + 1. What am I?" After sharing riddles with children, invite them to develop their own and share them with their peers.

WORD LEARNING

Dear Families,

Here are some tips for helping your children learn new words and build their vocabularies.

- Try to teach your child one new word every few days by using interesting words as you and your child talk and do daily activities. For example, instead of saying, "Are you hungry?" you could ask your child, "Are you famished?" Give your child hints about the meaning of the word so he or she can understand it. Try to use the word many times to help your child remember it. Encourage your child to use the word also.

- Talk about new and interesting words your child encounters while reading with you, watching television or videos, listening to the radio, using the computer, or talking with others.

- Encourage your child to describe the things he or she sees, hears, and experiences. For example, as you are traveling to the grocery story, ask your child to find something that has wheels. If your child says "a bus," ask him or her to describe the bus using color, size, and other descriptive words.

- As you are reading with your child, point out words that may be new to him or her. Discuss what they mean. After you are done reading the story, go back and make up sentences with your child to use the new words.

I hope you and your children have fun with these word learning ideas.

Sincerely,

section 5.5

Resources for Vocabulary Learning

Goal: To help children learn to use resources to support vocabulary learning.

Background

A rich verbal environment includes resources that children can use to locate, identify, and understand new words (Beck, McKeown, & Kucan, 2002). Resources include picture dictionaries, dictionaries, glossaries, and word files. Vocabulary resources offer many benefits; however, children must be taught how, why, and when to use such resources. For example, in order for children to be able to use a dictionary or picture dictionary effectively, they must know when to use a dictionary, how to locate a word in the dictionary, what the parts of a dictionary entry are, how to choose between multiple meanings, and how to apply the meaning (Blachowicz & Fisher, 2006). While this process is too complex for the youngest learners, children in the early elementary grades can learn to use dictionaries that are specially designed for children. In addition, by creating their own picture dictionaries and word files, young children will have access to valuable vocabulary resources and also begin to develop the skills needed for future dictionary use.

Section 5.5 **TEACHING STRATEGY**

MAKING A PICTURE DICTIONARY

A picture dictionary is a useful vocabulary resource for the youngest learners. Words are organized alphabetically, and pictures accompany each word in the dictionary. By making their own picture dictionaries, children are able to create vocabulary resources that are personally meaningful and useful (Blachowicz & Fisher, 2006). In addition, by creating their own picture dictionaries, children are beginning to learn the skills necessary for using published dictionaries.

DIRECTIONS

1. Explain to the children that they will be creating a picture dictionary that contains new and interesting words they want to know.

2. Show a sample page from a picture dictionary. For example, you might show the following entry for the word *bumblebee*.

B b

Bumblebee

3. Tell the children that they will be making their own picture dictionaries. Explain that you will help them make the first two pages for the picture dictionary. They will then add more pages during the upcoming days and weeks.

4. Write a target vocabulary word for the picture dictionary on the chalkboard. The word should come from a book the children have read recently or a unit they are studying. For example, if the children are studying a unit on frogs, you might select the word *tadpole*.

5. Tell the children that you will put the word *tadpole* on the *T* page in the picture dictionary because dictionaries are organized by letters or alphabetically.

6. Next, explain that you will add a picture of a tadpole to help you remember what the word means. Tell the children that they can draw a picture, use clip art pictures, or cut pictures from magazines for their picture dictionaries.

7. Construct the tadpole entry to demonstrate how children should go through the process of making a picture dictionary entry. Use the sheet on page 281 for each page of the picture dictionary. It is suggested that each page be three-hole punched, so the pages can be assembled into a 1-inch three-ring binder. This format will allow for pages to be added easily during the year.

8. Provide time for the children to make their own entry for *tadpole*.

9. Invite the children to suggest several other choices of vocabulary words to add to their picture dictionaries. Write these words on the chalkboard so the children see them spelled correctly. Discuss what illustration could be drawn for each of the words.

10. Instruct the children to select one of the words on the chalkboard and make a picture dictionary entry for it by writing the beginning letter at the top of the page, writing the word at the top of the page, and drawing or cutting and gluing a picture to represent the word. Provide drawing materials, magazines, clip art pictures, scissors, and glue or glue sticks so children can illustrate the word.

11. Provide time for the children to share their picture dictionary entries.

12. At least twice a week, provide time for the children to add one or more new entries to their picture dictionaries. Children can also be encouraged to add entries when they have completed their work.

13. As children read and write in the classroom, encourage them to use their picture dictionaries as resources.

Aa Bb Cc Tips for English Language Learners

- English Language Learners will benefit from making bilingual dictionaries that contain new words in both English and their home language.

Picture Dictionary Page

_____ _____

_____

WORD RING

A Word Ring is a helpful vocabulary resource that children can use for their reading and writing. By having children construct their own word rings, they get practice with new words. Words can easily be added to the ring over time so this resource can grow with children over the year.

DIRECTIONS

1. Provide each child with a small stack of 3 × 5 inch index cards. Each card should have a hole punched in the upper left corner. Each child should also be given a 1-inch metal ring fastener.

2. Explain to children that they will be making a word ring of interesting words they want to learn and remember.

3. Display a sample word ring card by making a copy on an overhead transparency. Explain to the children that the word ring card contains the letter the word begins with, the word, and something related to the word's meaning (i.e., a picture, definition, or example). A sample word ring card is provided below.

S   scamper

to run playfully

The puppy will *scamper* after a toy.

4. Have the children brainstorm possible words to include in their Word Rings. List these words on the chalkboard. For each word, discuss a possible drawing, definition, or example that could be written on the card.

5. Provide time for the children to create several cards for their Word Rings.

6. Show the children how to hook the cards onto the metal ring. Remind the children to organize the cards in ABC or alphabetical order on their rings.

7. Periodically provide time for the children to add cards to their Word Rings.

Aa·Bb·Cc Tips for English Language Learners

- Encourage English Language Learners to write the word in both English and their home language on each Word Ring card. Provide a choice if the children want to write a definition or example in English or in the home language.

- Using the Word Ring cards as flash cards may be useful for some English Language Learners because this activity provides repeated exposure to new words.

Section 5.5   **TEACHING STRATEGY**   3

USING A DICTIONARY

Using a dictionary involves several steps. First, children must understand when and why to use a dictionary. Second, they must understand alphabetical order and the use of guide words in order to locate a word in a dictionary. Next, they must understand the parts of a dictionary entry. They must also know how to choose between multiple meanings. Finally, they need to understand how to apply the meaning from the dictionary entry to their reading, writing, or speaking. The process of using a dictionary must be taught over time so children can acquire the necessary skills and knowledge to do so successfully. Because of the complexity of the process of using a dictionary, Teaching Strategy 3 is most appropriate for children in late first grade through third grade.

DAY 1

 **DIRECTIONS**

1. Select a picture dictionary or children's dictionary that is appropriate for the level of the children you are teaching. Be sure a copy of the dictionary is available for each child.

2. Gather the children together in a circle on the carpet or other meeting area in the classroom. Ask them what they can do when they don't know the meaning of a word. Their ideas may include asking someone for help, looking at pictures, or skipping the word to see if the passage makes sense without it.

3. Tell children that they can also use a dictionary to find the meaning of a word.

4. Show the dictionary the children will be using. Tell the children that the dictionary contains useful information about words, including their meanings or definitions.

5. Open to the A section of the dictionary. Tell the children, "The dictionary starts with the words that begin with A, and it continues through the alphabet. This means that the words are organized in ABC or alphabetical order. In other words, the dictionary puts the A words first, followed by the B words, then the C words, D words, and so on through the letter Z." If children have not mastered the concept of alphabetical order yet, additional instruction may be necessary in this area.

6. Hand out a dictionary to each child. Tell the children, "Open your dictionary to the beginning. Turn pages until you get to the first A word. In my dictionary the first word is *aardvark*. See if you can find the page with *aardvark*. When you find it, leave your dictionary open to that page." Provide time and assistance so each child finds the appropriate page.

7. Explain that at the top of each page there are guide words that help children know what words will be found on that page. Tell the children that if the guide words start with the same letter as the word they are looking up, they are in the right section of the dictionary. Also point out if their dictionary uses a thumb index on the side edges of the pages to allow for locating a letter easily. If the children are not able to alphabetize through the third letter, additional instruction may be necessary for the children to use guide words effectively.

8. Continue this process with several other words so the children learn how to locate words in the dictionary.

DAY 2

🕊 DIRECTIONS

1. Hand out dictionaries to the children. Remind them how the words are organized in a dictionary. Provide time for the children to locate several words to give them additional practice locating words.

2. Explain to the children that once they find a word in the dictionary, they will need to read the entry that tells about the word.

3. Ask the children to look up the word *falcon.*

4. Once they locate the word in the dictionary, guide them through the entry. You may wish to display the entry on an overhead transparency so you are certain that the children are all looking at the correct entry. For *falcon,* the following entry could be displayed.

Falcon /ˈfal-kən/ *n*

Any of several small hawks
with long wings and swift flight

5. Read the entry. Explain that first the pronunciation of the word is given. Then the part of speech is provided. Tell children that the meaning or definition of the word is provided next. Explain that some words only have one definition but others have two or more. Finally, tell children that some entries include a picture of the word.

6. Discuss the meaning of the word *falcon.* Help the children restate the definition in a way that makes sense to them. For example, they may say, "It's a small hawk with long wings and it flies fast."

7. Finally, ask the children to suggest sentences that use the word *falcon.* Explain that the sentence should demonstrate an understanding of the word. Possible sentences the children suggest may include:

    The *falcon* flew quickly into the forest.

    The *falcon* had long wings that made it easy to fly fast.

8. Complete the process in steps 4–7 several times with different words to allow the children practice time using the dictionary. Additional instruction in identifying the correct definition from multiple choices will likely be necessary.

THE DICTIONARY GAME

The Dictionary Game is a useful instructional strategy to implement after children have received initial instruction on the use of the dictionary (See Teaching Strategy 3 in this section). The Dictionary Game focuses on having children predict which words will appear in a definition of another word (Koeze, 1990). The game format of this strategy provides a fun context for having children practice using the dictionary.

DIRECTIONS

1. Place children into groups of three to four members. Have children in each group sit together in a circle. Each group will need one dictionary.

2. One child chooses a familiar word that all of the group members are likely to know. For example, the child may suggest *globe*.

3. The child to the left of the one who chose the word predicts a word that will appear in the definition of the word *globe*. For example, the child may predict that *earth* will appear in the definition.

4. The remaining children in the group must also make a prediction of a different word that will be in the definition. The children may not predict common words such as articles (e.g., *a, the, an*) or conjunctions (e.g., *and, or*).

5. The child who chose the word globe then looks up the word in the dictionary and reads the definition aloud. The child awards a point to each child who correctly predicted a word that appeared in the definition. Points are tallied on a sheet of paper.

6. A new round then begins with the child to the left choosing a word. The game continues for as many rounds as desired.

PAVE

Selecting the correct definition for a specific context is a complex and important dictionary skill. PAVE is designed to help children cross-check a word's meaning in the dictionary with the context in which the word appeared (Bannon, Fisher, Pozzi, & Wessel, 1990). The word PAVE stands for the components in the strategy: Prediction, Association, Verification, and Evaluation.

DIRECTIONS

1. Display the PAVE template on an overhead transparency (see the reproducible on page 287). Tell the children that they will be learning the PAVE strategy to gain more practice with choosing the correct dictionary definition.

2. Tell the children that PAVE has four steps, each represented by one of the letters in the word PAVE.

   P = predict a meaning from the context where the word appears

   A = associate the meaning with an image

   V = verify the meaning by using the dictionary

   E = evaluate the prediction

3. Model the PAVE strategy using a familiar word such as *eager*. To model the process, you may wish to say the following.

> I saw the word *eager* in the sentence, "John was eager to meet his father at the train after the long trip."
>
> I will write the word in the sentence on the PAVE sheet.
>
> I will also write the word in the box on the sheet.
>
> Using the sentence, I will make a prediction of the definition for the word *eager*. I think it means *excited for something to happen*. I will write that in the space on the sheet.
>
> Now I need to predict a good sentence that uses *eager* and shows my meaning. I will write the sentence, *I am eager to go to the birthday party this Saturday*. I thought of that sentence because it is something I'm excited to have happen.
>
> I now need to look up the word *eager* in the dictionary. The definition in my dictionary says, *desiring very much; impatient*. I need to write that definition on my sheet.
>
> Now I need to look back at the sentence I wrote and see if it makes sense using the dictionary definition. I think it does because the dictionary definition of *desiring very much; impatient* fits into my sentence.
>
> The last thing I need to do is to create an image related to the word *eager* to help me remember what the word means. I think I'll do a sketch of a child holding a present thinking about going to a birthday party. That is related to the meaning and to my sentence, and it will help me remember the word's meaning.

4. Distribute a copy of the PAVE sheet to each child. Guide the children through completing the process with a word you have selected. Be sure the word is familiar to the children so they will have adequate background knowledge to complete the task.

5. Provide practice with several additional words before asking children to complete the PAVE process with a partner or individually.

Name _____ Date _____

PAVE

Sentence where I found the word: _____

_____

Word	Association (add a drawing to help you remember the word)

Predicted definition _____

My sentence _____

_____

Verified definition (from dictionary) _____

_____

Another sentence (if my first sentence did not use the word correctly) _____

_____

Activities, tips, & Center Ideas

1. Create a class Big Book picture dictionary. Add new or interesting words from books the class has read. Place the big book dictionary in the classroom library center so all children have access to this resource.

2. Conduct a dictionary scavenger hunt. Have children work with a partner, sharing one dictionary. Provide a list of words and have children record the page number in the dictionary where each word is located.

3. Create a vocabulary resource center in the classroom that contains picture dictionaries, spelling dictionaries, and antonym/synonym dictionaries. Encourage the children to use the vocabulary resources to support their reading and writing.

4. Provide dictionary resources on CD-ROMs in the classroom computer station. These electronic dictionaries contain many visuals, video clips, and audio clips to help children understand words. Several children's dictionaries available on CD are listed below.

   American Heritage Children's Dictionary (Pearson Software)

   Eyewitness Children's Encyclopedia (Dorling Kindersley)

   My First Incredible, Amazing Dictionary 2.0 (DK Multimedia)

5. Make a bulletin board in the classroom related to key content vocabulary the children have been studying. For example, during the study of weather, you may make a bulletin board that contains the words *storm, cloud, cold front, warm front, hail, tornado,* and *hurricane.* For each word, you can display a picture and brief definition. Encourage children to use the bulletin board as a vocabulary resource for their reading and writing.

PICTURE DICTIONARY

Dear Families:

The children in our classroom have been making a picture dictionary. This dictionary contains important and interesting words we have been learning about at school. Your child should have brought home his or her picture dictionary with this letter. Take a few minutes to have your child show you the words he or she has put in the picture dictionary so far.

Please work with your child to create a page to add to the picture dictionary. You can choose any word that you and your child think is interesting. Use the attached page to complete this activity. Please return the completed page by _____ so we can share the pages in class. Thank you for your support. Your help makes a difference in your child's development as a reader!

Sincerely,

Picture Dictionary Page

_____   _____
capital letter   lower case letter

_____
word

Picture (you can draw it or cut and glue a picture from a magazine)

5.6

Assessments of Vocabulary

Goal: To assess the child's ability to understand and use vocabulary that was taught in school.

Background

The best way to assess a child's vocabulary development is through on-going observations, activities, and discussions in the classroom. Some teachers keep a checklist or use anecdotal records to document if and how children are using recently-taught vocabulary words (Blachowicz & Fisher, 2006). Another common approach used for assessing taught-vocabulary is the use of teacher-made tests or quizzes where children must use target vocabulary words in sentences, match them with appropriate synonyms, choose corresponding examples, or match them with their definitions. You will likely find that using a variety of assessment approaches is a helpful way to assess the children's vocabulary knowledge and use.

1

THREE-MINUTE CONFERENCES

OVERVIEW	Select up to 10 words that the children have been taught and provide a list to the children. When you meet with each child for the Three-Minute Conference, ask the child to use each word in a meaningful way. By meeting with three children per day, you should be able to meet with all of the children in the class over approximately a two-week period.
MATERIALS NEEDED	1. A pencil or pen 2. Record Sheet on page 293
PROCEDURES	1. Tell the children you will be holding Three-Minute Conferences to assess their knowledge of vocabulary words they have recently studied. Provide the list to the children. 2. Begin holding the Three-Minute Conferences the next day. 3. Say one of the vocabulary words and ask the child to use it in a meaningful way (give a sentence, explain meaning in own words, or give a clear example). 4. Record the child's performance. 5. Continue through the remaining words on the list.
SCORING AND INTERPRETATION	Evaluate the child's performance by checking the appropriate column on the record sheet: C = complete and indicates that the child understands the word fully and can use it in a meaningful manner; P = partial and indicates that the child has some knowledge of the word but does not have a full understanding; and N = no, the child does not have meaningful knowledge related to the word.

RECORD SHEET
Three-Minute Conferences

Name _____ Date _____

WORD	NOTES ON CHILD'S PERFORMANCE	KNOWLEDGE OF WORD C = complete P = partial N = no

From Laurie Elish-Piper, Jerry L. Johns, and Susan Davis Lenski, *Teaching Reading Pre-K–Grade 3* (3rd ed.). Copyright © 2006 by Kendall/Hunt Publishing Company (1-800-247-3458, ext. 4). May be reproduced for noncommercial educational purposes.

Chapter Five   Vocabulary   **293**

2

TEACHER CHECKLIST OF VOCABULARY USE

OVERVIEW	The checklist can be used to assess and keep a record of children's knowledge and use of vocabulary words that were taught in school (Blachowicz & Fisher, 2006).
MATERIALS NEEDED	1. A pencil or pen 2. Record Sheet on page 295
PROCEDURES	1. As children participate in class discussions, writing activities, and lessons, note when they use vocabulary words. 2. Note which children use the words in their speaking and in writing by circling a S for speaking and a W for writing
SCORING AND INTERPRETATION	Informally analyze each child's performance by reviewing the record sheet periodically. You can also note words that are problematic for many children in the class by looking for patterns on the record sheet.

Additional Way of Assessing Vocabulary Knowledge and Use

1. The Passage Reading Assessment (see Section 6.4) contains a vocabulary question for each level. The vocabulary questions can be analyzed to determine if a child knows vocabulary words at a specific level.

Teacher Checklist of Vocabulary Use

CHILD'S NAME	WORD 1		WORD 2		WORD 3		WORD 4		WORD 5	
_____	S	W	S	W	S	W	S	W	S	W
_____	S	W	S	W	S	W	S	W	S	W
_____	S	W	S	W	S	W	S	W	S	W
_____	S	W	S	W	S	W	S	W	S	W
_____	S	W	S	W	S	W	S	W	S	W
_____	S	W	S	W	S	W	S	W	S	W
_____	S	W	S	W	S	W	S	W	S	W
_____	S	W	S	W	S	W	S	W	S	W
_____	S	W	S	W	S	W	S	W	S	W
_____	S	W	S	W	S	W	S	W	S	W
_____	S	W	S	W	S	W	S	W	S	W
_____	S	W	S	W	S	W	S	W	S	W
_____	S	W	S	W	S	W	S	W	S	W
_____	S	W	S	W	S	W	S	W	S	W
_____	S	W	S	W	S	W	S	W	S	W
_____	S	W	S	W	S	W	S	W	S	W
_____	S	W	S	W	S	W	S	W	S	W
_____	S	W	S	W	S	W	S	W	S	W

S = Used in Speaking
W = Used in Writing

chapter *six*

Comprehension

Overview

Reading is the process of constructing meaning; therefore, teaching children to understand what they read and to respond to their reading are important goals of literacy instruction at all grade levels. Comprehension of text involves having children connect their prior knowledge to what they are reading and responding to what they have learned (Rosenblatt, 1978). Because reading is a cognitive process, children need to be actively engaged in reading in order to comprehend what they have read.

The strategies that children will use to construct meaning could be different based on the type of text they are reading. Texts can be either narrative or informational. Narrative texts tell a story and are commonly used in primary classrooms and are the types of texts that parents read most often at home (Duke, 2000; Duke & Purcell-Gates, 2003).

The primary purpose of informational texts is to inform the reader. Although some informational texts have elements of narratives, such as the *Magic School Bus* books, most are written using expository text structures such as comparison-contrast, problem-solution, and cause-effect (Kletzien & Dreher, 2004).

Teachers often ask questions about ways they can help children comprehend their reading. Some of these frequently asked questions follow.

Questions/Answers

What are key factors in comprehension?

Comprehension is the process of constructing meaning from text. What this means is that each child brings his or her background knowledge and previous experiences to the text to make meaning. For example, a child who lives on a farm will likely understand a passage about cows with a different degree of comprehension than a child who lives in the city and has never had a firsthand experience with cows. It is important to note that there is not a single, correct interpretation of a story. A rich bank of background knowledge and previous experiences will greatly enhance a child's comprehension. When children come to school with limited background knowledge or experiences in certain areas, teachers can provide a variety of hands-on and vicarious experiences to assist children with comprehension. In addition, explicit instruction in various aspects of comprehension will help children understand what they read.

What is listening comprehension and how is it related to literacy development?

Listening comprehension refers to a child's ability to understand a story or passage that is read aloud to him or her. By determining a child's listening comprehension level, a teacher can determine a child's potential for growth in reading.

Do children respond differently to narrative and informational texts?

The stance readers use for narrative text is often different from than of informational text (Rosenblatt, 1978). When reading narrative text, readers tend to read from an aesthetic stance. In other words, they look for the story and respond in a more personal way. When reading informational text, readers tend to read from an efferent stance. They read to gather information. In studies of children responding to text, however, researchers have found that children's responses tend to be mixed, rather than from one perspective (Moss, 2003; Tower, 2002). As a teacher, you should teach children how to respond in different ways, but you should also accept the types of responses children give you.

I teach kindergarten. Should children this young be asked to respond to stories and informational text?

Yes, children of all ages should be given the opportunity to respond to both types of texts. If you teach young children who are unable to read and write their own responses, you can read stories aloud to the class and write their responses for them on a Language Chart. In addition, young children can share their responses orally, through art, and by dramatization.

My English Language Learners seem to have difficulty understanding how narrative texts work. Is there a reason for this?

Texts are organized in culturally accepted ways. Narrative texts from English-speaking North America tend to follow a plot that directs the narrative toward a goal. Informational texts can be divided in a number of ways but most state a main idea and list supporting details. Students who have been raised in mainstream English-speaking families and have heard stories told to them or read to them will have a good understanding of narrative texts. When students have not been exposed to the text structures common in the United States and Canada, they may have a difficult time following the story line. For example, many Spanish stories follow a more circular route than do English stories, and Spanish informational texts tend to follow non-linear reasoning rather than being direct (Lenski & Ehlers-Zavala, 2004). The exception to this generalization is books written in English and translated into another language. These books, for the most part, will still contain a story line that is more typical of English texts than Spanish texts.

Comprehension of Narrative Texts

> **Goal:** To help children understand what they read.
>
> **Assessment Strategy 1** Retelling a Story, page 340
>
> **Assessment Strategy 4** Caption Reading, page 347
>
> **Assessment Strategy 5** Passage Reading, page 354

Background

Reading is the process of comprehending text. As children read, they construct meaning from texts or passages. The meaning each child constructs is typically a bit different from the way other readers understand the story. That's because there is not one single, correct interpretation of any story. Comprehension is based on a number of factors, one of which is prior knowledge. As a result, no two readers will produce the same meaning from a text, and no reader's understanding of a text will exactly match what the author had in mind while writing (Goodman, 1996).

As children read, they rely on their background knowledge to make sense of the ideas and concepts in the story. Children also use their knowledge of word identification strategies to identify the words of the text. As they read, children set purposes for reading and monitor their reading progress. Finally, children summarize what they have read and apply those summaries to other situations (Flood & Lapp, 1990). The result of these mental activities is a construction of meaning of the passage.

As you can see, comprehending text is a complex thinking process. Because comprehension is so individual, children will vary in their ability to comprehend different stories. For example, children with a great interest in and knowledge about dogs may closely attend to the Clifford books and read with rich comprehension. Other children may not have that interest and may not comprehend Clifford stories as easily.

The way children apply strategies as they process text also has an impact on reading comprehension. Children who apply many strategies will probably have rich comprehension. Children who do not apply the reading strategies they have learned may not have as deep an understanding of the story. Therefore, you need to teach children how to use thinking strategies to comprehend the stories and books they read. Several teaching strategies, ideas, and activities follow that can help you teach children how to construct meaning as they read.

STORY BOARDS

A Story Board is a series of frames that describe a narrative. Story Boards show events in a series and can be written and/or illustrated. Children read or listen to a story and determine the beginning, middle, and end or the events that take place in the plot. Story Boards can help children learn how narrative texts are organized.

DIRECTIONS

1. Identify a story that has a clear beginning, middle, and end or that has events in a series that can be easily discerned. An example of such a story is *Miss Bridie Chose a Shovel* (Connor, 2004).

2. Teach children about the organization of narrative texts. Younger children should learn that narratives have a beginning, middle, and end. Children who understand those basic concepts can learn that stories have events that take place in order.

3. Read the story or have children read the story in groups. As children are listening to the story, have them think about the events that occurred.

4. Provide children with a copy of the Story Board. One group of three frames is sufficient for children who are drawing a beginning, middle, and end. Children who are drawing a series of events should be given more than one set of frames.

5. Guide children to think about the way the beginning of the story as in the example that follows.

   Teacher: What happened first in the story *Miss Bridie Chose a Shovel?*

   Charlie: Miss Bridie was getting on a ship.

   Teacher: Yes, she was. What did she do before she got on the ship?

   Charlie: She decided what to take with her.

   Teacher: What did she take?

   Charlie: She took a shovel.

   Teacher: Let's draw a picture of Miss Bridie choosing a shovel before she gets on the ship. This is the beginning of the story.

6. Have children draw a picture of the beginning of the story. You might have some children label the picture. Older children can write a sentence or two under the illustration.

7. Guide children in determining the middle and end of the story. Ask them to illustrate these parts of the story and to label or write sentences about them. Older children can write several events that occurred in the story. Make sure children write them in the order that occurred in the book.

8. Have children share their Story Boards with others in the class.

9. Remind children that narrative texts have a beginning, middle, and end and include a series of events.

10. Ask children to find other stories that exemplify these characteristics. A blank copy of a Story Board follows.

Name _____

Date _____

Story Board

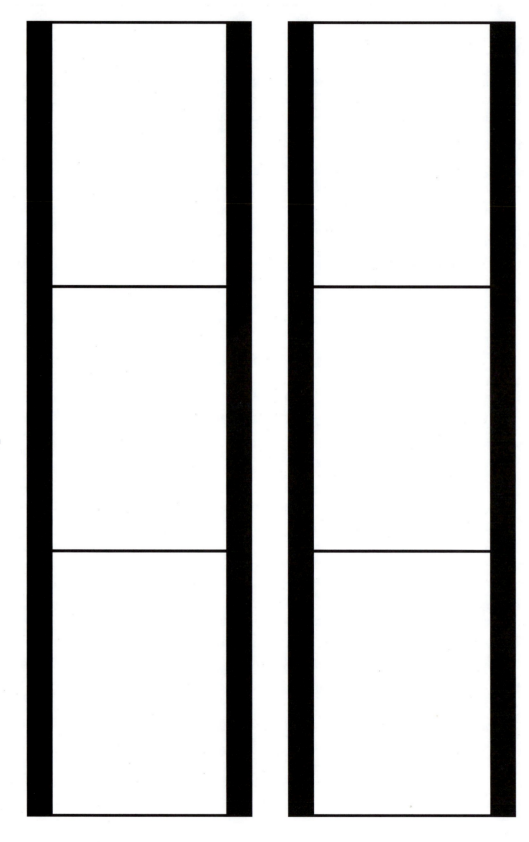

From Laurie Elish-Piper, Jerry L. Johns, and Susan Davis Lenski, *Teaching Reading Pre-K–Grade 3* (3rd ed.). Copyright © 2006 by Kendall/Hunt Publishing Company (1-800-247-3458, ext. 4). May be reproduced for noncommercial educational purposes.

STORY FRAME

A Story Frame is a summary outline of an entire story. After reading a story, children can fill in the blanks of a Story Frame to improve their comprehension (Fowler, 1982). You can create a general Story Frame as in the example below or write one specifically for a story or passage.

DIRECTIONS

1. Identify a story or a passage that has a plot that children can easily identify. Read the story aloud or have the children read it independently or with partners.

2. Encourage children to construct meaning from the story by reminding them to use comprehension monitoring strategies. Remind them to use fix-up strategies if they lose track of the story's plot.

3. After the children have finished reading, remind them of the elements of the story. Explain that every story has a problem but that the problem might be something the main character wants done. For example, the problem in the story *Rainy Day Fun* (Palazzo, 1988) is that the children are trying to think of what they could do on a rainy day. Explain that this is the problem of the story and that events will happen through the story to solve the problem. Have children identify the solution to the problem. In *Rainy Day Fun* (Palazzo, 1988), the children decided to put on a play.

4. After children have identified the problem in the story, remind them that stories are told by events in sequential order. Have them identify the events in the story they have read.

5. Ask children to retell the story they read. Remind them to state the problem of the story, the events in the plot, and how the problem was solved. If they forget any part of the plot, direct the children to reread that portion of the story.

6. Provide children with a copy of a Story Frame. Tell them that they should fill in the blanks so that the entire paragraph tells part of the story. Children can work with a partner or independently.

7. Identify one of the children's Story Frames that correctly tells the story. Read it aloud to the children. Have children check their Story Frames to determine if they understood the story. A copy of a Story Frame is on the following page.

Story Frame

Name _____ Story Title _____

In this story, the problem starts when _____

_____.

After that, _____

_____.

Next, _____

_____.

Then, _____

_____.

The problem is finally solved when _____

_____.

The story ends _____

_____.

STORY MAP

A Story Map is a graphic that shows the relationship among the parts of the story. Understanding the key components of a narrative can help children comprehend the story.

⚓ DIRECTIONS

1. Select a narrative that has obvious story elements such as setting, characters, narrator, conflict, major events, and outcome such as the book *Punctuation takes a Vacation* (Pulver, 2003).

2. Identify the story elements and complete a Story Map to use as an example. In *Punctuation takes a Vacation,* the elements listed below are present.

    Setting: Present time in a school

    Narrator: Someone who is observing the plot or a main character

    Key Conflict: The problem understanding written work without punctuation

    Major Events:

    - Mr. Wright was teaching punctuation.
    - He decided to let punctuation take a vacation.
    - The students wrote stories and messages without using punctuation.
    - Students were frustrated because they couldn't understand the meaning of the stories and messages.
    - The students asked to be able to use punctuation again.

    Outcome of the Conflict:

    The students in Mr. Wright's class appreciated the role of punctuation in writing.

3. Before reading the story to children, review the elements of a story. Tell children that the setting is the time and place that the action occurred, that the narrator can be part of the story or someone observing the action, that the key conflict or problem is the issue that the story is about, that the major events occur in a sequence, and that the outcome of the conflict is how the story ends.

4. Read the story to children or have them read it in groups.

5. Provide children with copies of the Story Map.

6. Make a transparency of the Story Map and place it on an overhead projector. Invite children to provide answers to each section of the Story Map. If children are unable to answer a section, tell them your answer. As children gain experience with Story Maps, they will become more confident in their answers.

7. Tell children to think about the components of a narrative whenever they read or hear a story. A blank copy of a Story Map follows.

Story Map

Name _____ Date _____

Story Title _____

➤ DIRECTIONS

A story map is a diagram that shows the relationship among the major parts of a story and helps you chart the events. Fill out the story map below for the story you are reading.

Setting

Place _____

Time _____

Narrator or Character (describe)

_____

_____

Key Conflict or Problem

_____

_____

Major Events

1. _____

   _____

2. _____

   _____

3. _____

   _____

4. _____

   _____

Outcome of the Conflict

_____

_____

CHARACTER WEB

Children can get a deeper understanding of a story if they identify the character traits of the main character (Roser & Martinez, 2005). One way to encourage children to think about character traits is by using a Character Web. A Character Web is a graphic organizer that focuses on the facets of a character in a story. Most children will need guidance to identify character traits that can be listed on a Character Web.

◥ DIRECTIONS

1. Identify a narrative text that has a main character with easily identifiable character traits such as *Mr. Lincoln's Way* (Polacco, 2001). In this story, Mr. Lincoln, the principal of a school, spends time with a troubled boy in order to engage him in school and in learning.

2. Write the term "Character Web" on the chalkboard. Ask children if they have heard the term before and if they know what a character in a story is.

3. Build on children's existing knowledge about characters in stories by providing examples from past stories you have read to the class. Tell children that characters in stories have a variety of traits just like real people do. Identity some traits of characters in stories that are familiar to the class.

4. Read the selected story reminding children to think about the main character. After reading, ask children to tell you what they remember about the main character, in this case Mr. Lincoln.

5. Read the story a second time. Children often concentrate on the plot during the first reading of a story. Rereading can help children focus on other aspects of the narrative.

6. After rereading the story, instruct children to think about one aspect of Mr. Lincoln's character. Tell the class that character traits are revealed by what a character thinks, says, and does so that remembering parts of the plot can help them understand the main character. Many traits must be inferred by children from information in the text.

7. Invite children to volunteer to tell the class what they remember about Mr. Lincoln. As children express their thoughts, guide them to think about ways the ideas express a character trait as in the following example.

   Teacher: What can you remember about Mr. Lincoln?

   Stacey: He was cool.

   Teacher: Can you tell me why he was cool?

   Stacey: He remembered to celebrate Kwanzaa and Christmas too.

   Teacher: Let's think about a character trait for this. Can we say he was considerate of different people? Let's put that down as a character trait. What else?

   Jeremy: He kept helping Eugene even though Eugene was a bully.

   Teacher: Yes, Mr. Lincoln was persistent. Do you know what persistent means? It means he kept on trying. Let's put that down as a second character trait.

8. Continue developing a list of character traits through discussion of the story. If children have difficulty remembering appropriate sections of the story, reread the parts that reveal the character's main trait. Then ask children what they think about the character.

9. Write the character traits that you have discussed on the Character Web. Tell children that developing a Character Web can help them understand more about the story.

10. Remind children to look for character traits as they read narrative texts independently. A blank Character Web follows.

Character Web

Name _____ Date _____

Character

STORY QUILT

A Story Quilt helps children identify the theme, or message of a story. Narrative texts typically have a point that the plot portrays. Sometimes the point of the story, which is called the theme, is easy to understand and sometimes it is subtle. Children can learn to identify the theme of a story by developing a Story Quilt.

DIRECTIONS

1. Select a story that has an easily identifiable theme. Many picture books have themes, or messages, that the author is trying to portray to the reader. One such book is *Ruby the Copycat* (Rathman, 1997). In this story, the main theme is that everyone is special and has talents.

2. Write the word *theme* on the chalkboard. Tell children that the theme is not the plot but is the main point of the story. Have children say the word with you and write it on slates or paper.

3. Explain to children that they can identify the theme of a story through the plot. Review the term *plot* and remind children that the plot is what happens in the story.

4. Tell children that the theme for *Ruby the Copycat* is that everyone is special and has talents. Explain to children that they will be trying to find parts of the story that relate to the theme.

5. Read the selected book to children.

6. Provide children with the blank copy of the Story Quilt. Write the theme on the chalkboard and have children write the theme in the center circle on their sheets. Provide assistance if necessary.

7. Have children think about parts of the story that explain the theme. For example, the fact that Ruby is a good hopper illustrates one of the ways that Ruby is special. Have children write or draw that idea in one of the sections of the Story Quilt.

8. Encourage children to think of other ways the story portrayed the theme. Have them write those ideas in a second section.

9. Tell children that the theme of a story is something that they can connect to their lives. In the example of *Ruby the Copycat,* for instance, they can think about ways they are special or have special talents. Invite children to write or draw ways the theme relates to their lives in the remaining two sections of the Story Quilt as in the example.

10. Have children color their Story Quilts and display them on a bulletin board. You can also develop a larger Story Quilt with more sections for a display.

11. Remind children that they can look for the theme of a narrative text when they read independently. A blank copy of a Story Quilt follows.

Aa Bb Cc Tips for English Language Learners

- Invite English Language Learners to work with a partner, draw their responses and label them, or share their connections orally.

Ruby the Copycat
by Peggy Rathmann

Ruby is a great hopper.

Angela was good at lots of things.

Everyone is special and has talents.

I am a good artist.

My sister is good at singing.

Story Quilt

Name _____ Date

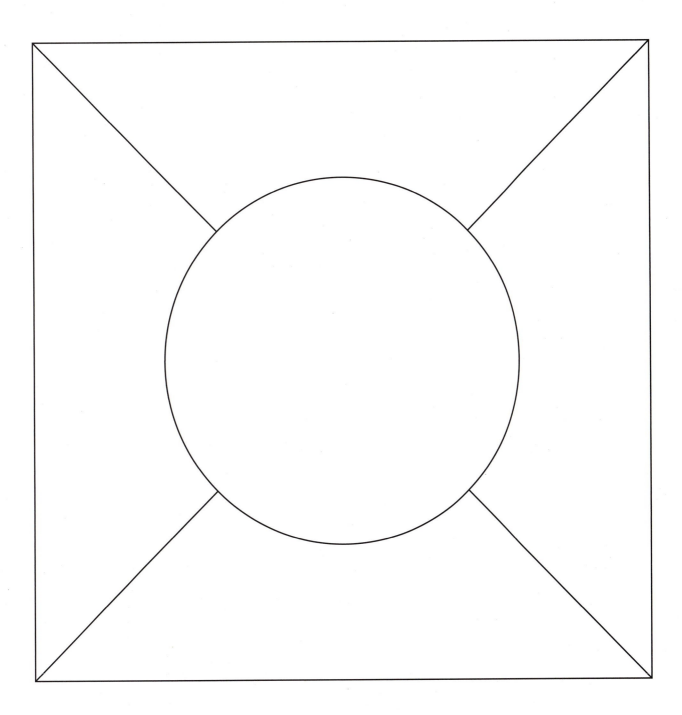

From Laurie Elish-Piper, Jerry L. Johns, and Susan Davis Lenski, *Teaching Reading Pre-K–Grade 3* (3rd ed.). Copyright © 2006 by Kendall/Hunt Publishing Company (1-800-247-3458, ext. 4). May be reproduced for noncommercial educational purposes.

Activities, tips, & Center Ideas

1. Have children read a story independently. They may read silently, with a partner, or out loud. After they have finished reading the story, ask one child to begin to retell the story. Encourage the first child to retell only one or two sentences. Write the sentences on the chalkboard or on an overhead transparency. Then invite another child to continue retelling the story. Write that child's retelling and continue until the story is completed. Read the retold story aloud inviting children to read with you. Explain that after they finish reading a passage they should retell the story to themselves to help them remember it.

2. Have children create a literature time line after reading a story. Tell children that as they are reading the story they should pay particular attention to the events in the story. After children have finished reading, have them draw a horizontal line at the center of a long piece of paper. Under the line, they should write information about the time the event took place. They may have information about days of the week, months, seasons, or years. Above the time, they can draw a picture of the event that took place. Display the literature time lines around the room.

3. Encourage children to read books in a series. After they begin a series, have children write journal entries that record the main events of the story and other information about the main characters. As they get to know characters that are repeated in series books, children can begin writing questions to the characters. Another child reading the same series can answer the questions.

4. Help children identify the main idea of a story. Cut passages from old books or articles that are at a variety of reading levels. Fasten the passages to index cards. On the back of each card write several possible phrases or sentences that describe the main idea. Have children read the passage, write their answers on a separate sheet of paper, and then compare them with the answers on the back of the cards.

5. Before children read a story, list several words from the passage on the chalkboard or an overhead transparency. Add other words to the list that are not included in the story. For example, if you were reading *Sam's Sandwich* (Pelham, 1990), you might include the following words: *horse, lettuce, cake, picnic, cucumber, salami, ants, swim,* and *ketchup.* Before children read the story, have them predict what words they think they will encounter as they read. Ask children for reasons for their choices. As children read, have them write down the words that they found in the text. After children read, encourage them to retell the story using the words that were part of the original list.

6. Have children act out a story after reading with a tableau (Purves, Rogers, & Soter, 1990). Tell children that they will be creating a tableau, or a frozen scene, from a story they have read. Explain that a tableau is a scene much like a photograph. A tableau captures a scene and, unlike a videotape, it does not show movement. Explain that to create a tableau children will have to discuss which event they want to portray. Then have children decide how to arrange themselves and their props so that the audience will understand the event. Have children practice creating the tableau several times before presenting it to an audience.

7. Help children form mental images as they read by asking them to describe images as they are reading. For example, if children are reading a Curious George story, have them describe what George is seeing and what George is doing. Then have them draw a picture of a scene from the story. Explain that when they are reading, they should try to picture what they are reading.

8. Encourage children to identify sequence as they read. Explain that stories have a beginning, a middle, and an end and that the events are in a specific order. To reinforce the concept of sequence, gather several comic strips that children can read independently. Cut the comic strips into their frames. Scramble the order of the frames and have children put them in order.

9. Have children complete paper bag retellings to enhance their comprehension. First, ask children to identify key items from a story, then make paper cutouts of these items, and finally put them in a paper bag they have decorated and labeled with the title of the book. Children can then do their retellings by using the items in the bag. Children can share their retellings with partners, the class, or their families.

SHARING BOOKS

Dear Families,

Reading and sharing books is a great way to help your child become a good reader. Your child's class is doing a book bag program to make connections between home and school. Please read the enclosed book with your child and complete the activities listed below. Return the book bag to school as soon as possible so it can be shared with other families.

Sincerely,

Book Bag Program

1. Read the book with your child.
2. Talk about your favorite parts.
3. Draw something about the book in the notebook.
4. Write a sentence to explain your picture.
5. Sign your name and have your child write his or her name.
6. Return the bag, book, notebook, and crayons to school by _____ .

Responding to Literature

Goal: To help children learn to discuss and write about literature.

Background

A natural extension of reading or hearing stories is to discuss or write about them. When children read or listen to stories, they form a provisional interpretation of the text. That interpretation deepens if they respond to the story in some way—through talk, writing, drama, or art. As children respond to stories, they learn that they can make their own meanings from text.

Section 6.2 **TEACHING STRATEGY** **1**

LANGUAGE CHARTS

Language Charts are a useful tool for young children who cannot write independently. They are a collection of the reflections, extensions, and creations of meaning in which children talk about books and teachers save their ideas on a large chart (Roser & Hoffman, 1995).

DIRECTIONS

1. Select a book to read aloud to the class. Some picture books that are especially thought-provoking follow.
   - Bunting, E. (1992). *Summer wheels.* San Diego: Harcourt Brace.
   - Cronin, D. (2000). *Click, clack, moo: Cows that type.* New York: Simon & Schuster.
   - Lionni, L. (1967). *Frederick.* New York: Pantheon.
   - Viorst, J. (1971). *The tenth good thing about Barney.* New York: Atheneum.

2. Before reading, tell children that you will be asking them to respond to the story after you are finished. Be specific about the type of response that you will elicit. For example, you might have children tell you how the book made them feel, what the book reminded them of, or what they thought about a story. If you read *Click, Clack, Moo: Cows That Type,* for example, you might say, "I'm going to read you a story today that I think you will like. It's about some cows that get a typewriter. You're going to find out what the cows do with the typewriter. Do you think this story could be real? No, cows can't really type, so the story is made up. After I finish reading, we're going to talk about what you liked most about the *Click, Clack, Moo: Cows That Type.*"

3. Read the story aloud to children. After reading, ask children to remember the part they liked best and to share that part.

4. Write the children's responses on a large piece of chart paper that can be displayed in the classroom. At the top of the chart write the title of the story and the names of the author and illustrator. Then write the heading "Parts we liked best." List the children's responses with their names under the heading as in the example that follows.

Click, Clack, Moo: Cows That Type
Author: Doreen Cronin
Illustrator: Betsy Lewin

Parts we liked best:
- when the cows went on strike (Samantha)
- when the farmer read the first note (Carlos)
- when the duck asked for blankets (Brett)

5. Reread the entire Language Chart with children, frequently pointing to the words as you read. Encourage children to read their own ideas independently. Emphasize that the Language Chart is a place for children to record their own thoughts about stories.

Aa Bb Cc Tips for English Language Learners

- When English Language Learners talk about stories, they should be allowed to discuss the stories in their native language if at all possible (Battle, 1995). Children who are learning English may have difficulty forming their ideas into English words and may have an easier time responding to the stories using their first language. Encourage young children to talk about stories with others who speak the same language. If you know the children's first language, record their ideas on the Language Chart using that language.

Section 6.2   **TEACHING STRATEGY**   **2**

GETTING THE FEELING

One way to respond to literature is to identify the feelings you get from the story. Young children often have difficulty identifying feelings that go beyond mad, sad, and glad. Helping children identify feelings from stories gives them an opportunity to develop their own personal interpretations of text.

DIRECTIONS

1. Tell children that stories can make them feel lots of different ways and that responding to stories should include how they feel. Provide an example from your own adult reading as in the example that follows. "Last night I was reading *The Africa Diaries* by Dereck and Beverly Joubert (2001). (Show book to children.) As I read the book, I had lots of different feelings. First, I was totally *amazed* at the vivid photographs the authors took of elephants. Then in the chapter on lions, I was *afraid* for the authors. They put themselves in really dangerous situations. Later in the book, I was *angry* at the poachers who killed the wild animals, and, finally, I was *anxious* to see those African animals before they become extinct."

2. Develop a list of emotions that children could feel from stories or use the list that follows. Over the course of several days, describe each of the emotions on the list so that children have a clear idea what each emotion means. A list of emotions follows.

3. Select a book to read aloud to children or have them read independently. Before reading, tell children that you will be asking them how the story made them feel and to identify the part that made them feel that way. Use your own personal example and list your feelings along with the appropriate part of the story. An example follows.

Feelings	Part of story
amazed	photographs of elephants
afraid	taking pictures of lions
angry	people who kill animals
anxious	to see animals before they're extinct

4. Read the selected book to the class or have them read independently. After reading is completed, ask children to think about how the story made them feel. List their feelings and the part of the story on a Language Chart (see Section 6.2, Teaching Strategy 1).

EMOTIONS

afraid
alone
amazed
angry
anxious
awful

bashful
blue
brave
bright

cheerful
clumsy
confident
courageous

daring
delighted
depressed
despised
downcast
downhearted
dreadful

fantastic
foolish
friendly
furious

glad
gloomy
good
grand
great

happy
hated

important

joyful

mysterious

nervous

overjoyed

pleased
powerful
proud

relaxed

sad
scared
sharp
shy
silly
small
starved
strange
stressed
strong
superb

terrific
thrilled
timid
tough

uneasy
unsure

warm
weak
wise
wonderful
worried

LITERARY LETTERS

Children can respond to the characters in a narrative text through a Literary Letter. A Literary Letter is a letter written by children to one of the characters in the story. When children respond to characters, they develop a deeper insight into the story and become more engaged in reading.

DIRECTIONS

1. Select a story that has a character with whom children can relate. An example is the book My *Diary from Here to There* (Pérez, 2002), a story about a young girl who immigrates to the United States from Mexico.

2. Remind children that many narrative texts are fiction which means they are not true. Tell children that even though the stories are not true they should imagine the characters in the books to be real people. Tell children that they will be writing a letter to the main character from this story.

3. Ask children if they have received letters (or e-mails) from relatives or friends. Discuss the content of the letters. Tell children that the letter they will write to the main character should contain the elements of good letters—that they should have lots of details, be personal, ask questions, and follow letter format.

4. Read the story to children or have them read it independently.

5. Have children brainstorm ideas about what to write to the main character. Some examples follow.
   - Welcome Amada to the United States.
   - Tell Amada about your family.
   - Ask Amada how she likes it here.
   - Ask Amada specific questions about her family or their lives in Mexico.

6. Provide children with blank copies of the Literary Letter or have them write a letter on different paper. Encourage them to write letters that are interesting to read.

7. Have children share their Literary Letters with each other and with the class. After reading the letters, discuss the kinds of ways different children responded to the character in the story. Remind children that responses are individual and unique.

8. Tell children to think of the characters as real people when they read independently. A blank copy of the Literary Letter follows.

Literary Letter

Date _____

Dear _____ ,

_____

_____

_____

_____

_____

_____

_____

_____

_____

_____

_____

_____

_____

_____

_____

_____

Sincerely,

_____

RESPONDING TO PLOT

Children can respond to stories in a number of ways when they react to the plot of the story (Moss, 1995). They can respond to the characters, the events in the story, and the problem. When children respond to the plot, they can even make connections to their own lives.

DIRECTIONS

1. Select a book to read to children or that children can read independently that has a clear plot and interesting characters. The plot should have an identifiable problem, events in a sequence, and a resolution to the problem. Characters can be humans or animals, but they should be developed so that children can form an opinion.

2. Explain to children that they will be responding to the plot or the characters in the story after reading.

3. Read the book aloud or have children read independently.

4. Duplicate and distribute the response questions on page 321. Read the questions with children, explaining terms as needed.

5. Tell children that they should select one question to answer as a response to the story. Emphasize that no response is incorrect but that responses reflect individual ideas. Provide children with adequate time for writing.

6. After children have finished writing their responses, invite them to share their responses with their peers.

7. Encourage children to write responses using the Response Questions when they read on their own.

Aa Bb Cc Tips for English Language Learners

- In order for children to respond to text, they need to have some background knowledge about the topic or some connection to parts of the story. Children who do not speak English may have similar backgrounds to the English speakers in your classroom, or they may have very different experiences. Au (2000) reminds us that, as educators, we need to connect instruction to children's experiences rather than connecting children to instruction. Therefore, as you select books for children's responses, choose books that have themes that are familiar to all children.

Response Questions

1. Who was your favorite character? Why?

2. Was there a character you did not like? Why?

3. What was your favorite part of the story? Why?

4. Who was the hero or heroine? How do you know?

5. Who was the villain? How do you know?

6. Was there a helper? What did this character do?

7. What was the problem in the story? How was it solved?

8. What do you think is the most important thing to remember about this story?

9. Does this story remind you of any other story you have read or heard?

10. What did you think of the illustrations? Did you find anything in the pictures that was not included in the words?

Adapted from Moss, J.F. (1995). Preparing focus units with literature: Crafty foxes and authors' craft. In N.L. Roser & M.G. Martinez (Eds.), *Book talk and beyond: Children and teachers respond to literature* (pp. 53–65). Newark, DE: International Reading Association.

DISCOVERING THE MESSAGE

Stories have a message, or a theme, that children can identify through response (Martinez & Roser, 1995). Identifying the message of a story takes the ability to think conceptually, so very young children may have difficulty with this strategy. However, even young children should be exposed to the message of the story as they learn different ways to respond to literature.

DIRECTIONS

1. Select a book to read to children or have children read independently something that has a clear message. A list of appropriate books follows.
   - Blume, J. (1974). *The Pain and the Great One.* New York: Dell.
   - Hutchins, P. (1968). *Rosie's walk.* New York: Aladdin.
   - Rylant, C. (1995). *Dog heaven.* New York: Simon & Schuster.
   - Sendak, M. (1963). *Where the wild things are.* New York: Harper and Row.

2. Before reading, tell children that they should listen to the story for the message. Explain that a message is a main point that the author is describing by means of a story. Provide an example similar to the following one.

   > Juan was new to Mrs. White's second grade classroom. He moved to the school from San Salvador where he had been a good student in school and an excellent soccer player. Juan didn't speak much English. He was trying to learn, but he made lots of mistakes. Some of the children in the class laughed at him, but Juan laughed right along with them. His favorite time of the day was recess where he kicked a soccer ball all by himself. One day a group of boys who had been playing kickball asked Juan to teach them how to play soccer. Juan didn't understand right away, but after the boys pantomimed kicking the soccer ball, Juan understood. Every day after that Juan and his friends played soccer with Juan teaching the boys the rules of the game—in Spanish.

3. Tell children that this story has several messages. Ask children to think about what some of the messages could be. After several minutes, have children volunteer possible messages from the story. List them on a chalkboard or on chart paper. Some messages that children could glean from the story follow.
   - Moving to a new class is difficult.
   - A good nature helps make friends.
   - Speaking different languages doesn't have to prevent friendships.
   - We can all learn from each other.

4. Tell children that this story illustrates how several messages can be discovered from the same story. Explain to children that not everyone will agree on the messages for a story but that each child can interpret the story's message in different ways.

5. Read a story to children or have them read independently. After reading, have them list the messages they discovered in the story on a Language Chart (pages 315–316).

Activities, tips, & Center Ideas

1. Children can respond to stories through drama. Choose a story that has a clear plot and more than one important character. Tell children that they will be acting out the story after you read it to them. Read the story to children while dramatizing the action. Then list the names of the important characters on the chalkboard or on chart paper. Ask students to volunteer for the roles. After choosing volunteers, ask them to restate the plot. If necessary, write sentences describing the plot on the chalkboard or on chart paper. Read the sentences and encourage the children to act out the story.

2. Some children like to draw pictures in response to stories. After reading a story, provide children with paper, markers, crayons, and paint. Ask children to draw a picture in response to the story. Tell them that they can draw a picture about how the story makes them feel, or they can draw about events or characters in the story. After the pictures are completed, have children tell or write about their pictures. Display the pictures in the classroom.

3. For children who can write independently, have them write character journals. To write a character journal, children need to pretend to be the character and write about the character's life. Provide an example of a character journal from a story that is familiar to children such as the three little pigs. Remind children that the first little pig built his house of straw and the wolf blew it down. Then write the event from the pig's point of view as in the following example. After the children have heard the example, tell them to write a journal entry from a character's point of view.

   I am so embarrassed! My brothers and I decided to build separate houses, and we had a bet about who could be finished first. I decided to build my house of straw because our neighbor had just mowed his field and straw was lying all over the place. I just gathered up the straw and started building my house. I was finished in no time, but before I could find my brothers to tell them I had won, a huge wolf came to the door and said he'd blow my house down. And that's exactly what he did! He blew and blew, and my house came tumbling down. I made a mad dash for it, and, luckily, I got to my brother's house before he could catch me. I'm going to have nightmares about this day for a long time, and I'll never again do anything as foolish as building a straw house.

4. Children can also respond to literature by writing to authors. You can write to any author in care of the publisher or on the author's web site. Before having children write to an author, brainstorm ideas for their letters. Remind children to be kind and to ask specific questions in their letters. Tell children they can tell the author how well they liked a book, but that they need to be polite. Model writing a letter to an author for children before they write.

RESPONDING TO READING

Dear Families,

When you read to your children, give them time to respond to the story through talking or through writing. Instead of asking specific questions about the story, ask your children how they felt or what they thought about the story. Here are four important ideas for having children respond to stories.

- Choose books carefully. Make sure books are interesting to your child and worth the time to read.

- Encourage your child to talk about the book during and after reading. Any conversation about books should be encouraged.

- Help your child understand the story if necessary. While reading, ask your child what is happening in the story. If your child doesn't know, reread parts of the book.

- Praise your child for all attempts to discuss books.

I hope your family enjoys these ideas for reading and responding to stories.

Sincerely,

section 6.3

Comprehension of Informational Texts

> **Goal:** To comprehend of informational texts.
>
> **Assessment Strategy 2** Informational Text Retelling, page 342

Background

There are many reasons why preschool and elementary teachers should use informational texts. According to Palmer and Stewart (2003), some young children prefer informational books to narrative texts and are more motivated to read them. Using both informational texts and narrative texts can help children become better readers (Duke, Bennett-Armisead, & Roberts, 2002).

Children in the primary grades read mainly fictional texts in school, but teachers are becoming increasingly aware of the need for young children to experience informational texts (Yopp & Yopp, 2000). Informational texts are organized differently from fictional texts, so they are unfamiliar to many children. Informational texts are organized in five patterns: description, sequence, comparison, cause-effect, and problem-solution. The patterns of description and sequence are the most commonly used patterns for informational texts young children might read and, therefore, should be taught in school. A variety of strategies, ideas, activities, and assessments follows.

Section 6.3   **TEACHING STRATEGY**

GRAPHIC ORGANIZERS

Graphic Organizers are visual representations of text. They can be drawn in any number of ways that depict the organization of the text.

➷ DIRECTIONS

1. Identify a piece of informational text for children to read or to hear such as *Elephant* by Mary Hoffman (1986).

2. Determine whether the book could be represented by a graphic organizer that depicts description or sequence. A copy of each graphic organizer follows at the end of this strategy.

3. Duplicate and distribute copies of the graphic organizer to each student. Then remind children, as in the example below, that nonfictional texts are organized differently from fictional texts.

    You remember how stories are organized. They have settings, characters, a sequence of events, and a solution. These stories are called fiction. Some books don't have these elements because they are not stories. They are books that give us information rather than tell a story.

    You can remember the difference by thinking of stories you have heard at bedtime. Bedtime stories are often made-up stories with settings, characters, and plots. When you are told how to build a kite, it's *explaining* something. That's like an informational book. It explains something rather than telling a story.

    Informational books won't have a plot. Instead, they will have a main point and details that explain that point, or they will tell you how to do something. When we read the book *Elephants,* listen for the main point of the book and the details.

4. Read the book aloud or have children read individual copies of the book.
5. Have children identify the main point of the book. Write it in the center of the circle as in the following example.

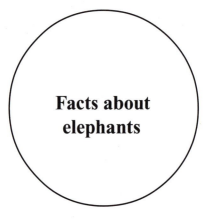

6. Ask children to brainstorm the details that they learned in the book. List the details on the spokes that radiate out from the center of the circle as in the example that follows.

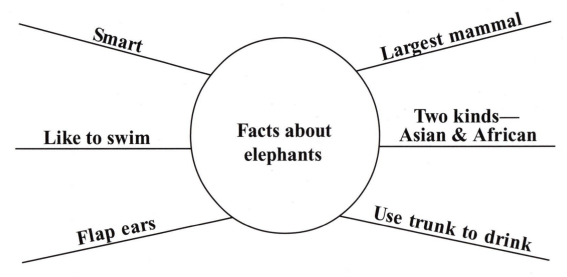

7. Tell children that they have completed a "picture" of the organization of the book *Elephant.* Remind children that this type of book is different from stories that they read.
8. Use a future lesson to model different organizations of informational text.

Name _____ Date _____

Graphic Organizer
Informational Text: Description

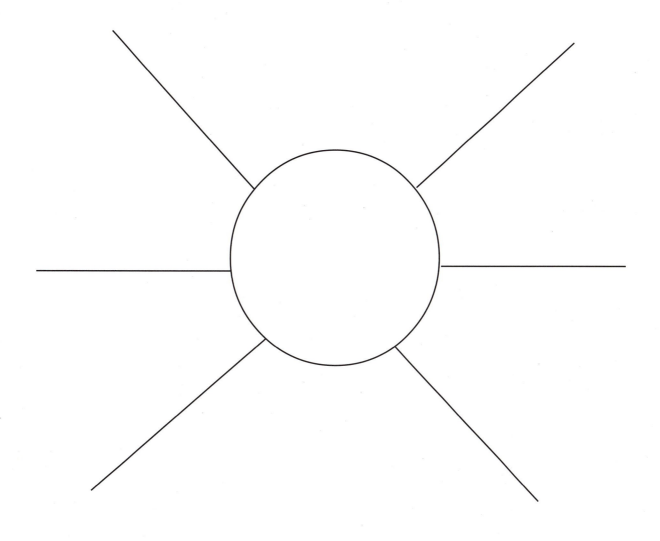

Name _____ Date _____

Graphic Organizer
Informational Text: Sequence

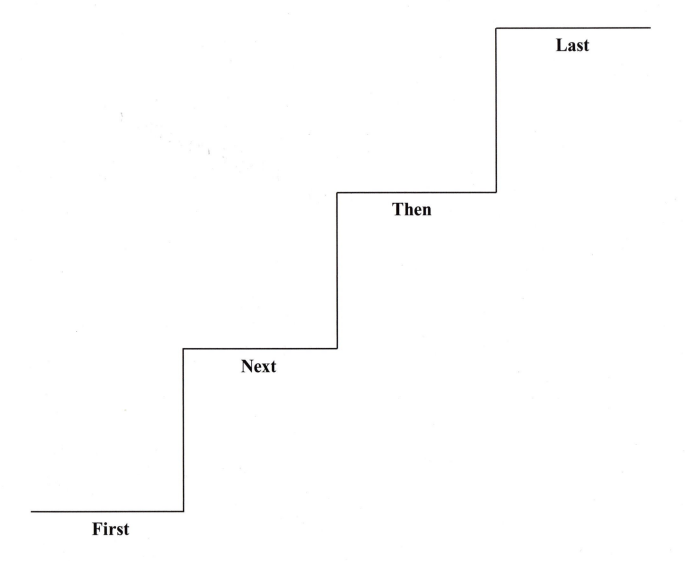

Last

Then

Next

First

From Laurie Elish-Piper, Jerry L. Johns, and Susan Davis Lenski, *Teaching Reading Pre-K–Grade 3* (3rd ed.). Copyright © 2006 by Kendall/Hunt Publishing Company (1-800-247-3458, ext. 4). May be reproduced for noncommercial educational purposes.

EXPOSITORY FRAMES

Expository Frames are another method to teach children how informational text is organized. An Expository Frame synthesizes an entire text in a few sentences that mirror the organizational pattern of the whole text. The sentences in an Expository Frame have blanks for children to fill in specific details.

✎ DIRECTIONS

1. Choose an informational text for children to read or to hear such as *Rain Forest Babies* (1996) by Kathy Darling.

2. Read the book to children or have children read text sets in small groups. Remind children to look for the way the text is organized.

3. Ask children to discuss the organizational pattern of the book. Remind children that informational text is organized differently from stories and that the book will not have a setting, characters, and a plot. They might say something like the following.

   > The book begins with a map of the rain forests of the world. Then it describes 14 different animals, taking 2 pages for each animal. Each animal is pictured with a description. After the animals are described, the book ends with one page of general information about the rain forest.

4. Develop an Expository Frame to reinforce the pattern of the text. An example for *Rain Forest Babies* follows.

Rain Forest Babies

The rain forest spans the earth near the _____ . In every location, animal babies are

born. Three of the types of animals that live in the rain forest are _____ ,

_____ , and _____ . The babies live in either the canopy, the

understory, or the _____ of the rain forest. The number of rain forests is shrinking

because the trees are being cut down.

SCRAMBLED TEXT

The Scrambled Text strategy helps focus children's attention on the organizational pattern of the text by having them recreate the text. The Scrambled Text strategy can be used with fictional stories as well as informational texts.

✎ DIRECTIONS

1. Select an informational book that has a clear organizational pattern. Read the book to children or have them read copies of the text in small groups. Remind children to look for the organizational pattern of the text while reading.

2. List the main points of the text on chart paper or on index cards. Tell children that you are writing each of the book's main points in the order that they occurred in the book. The following example uses the book *So You Want to Be President* by Judith St. George (2000).

> The President lives in the White House.
>
> The President has a swimming pool, a bowling alley, and a movie theater.
>
> The President always has lots of homework.
>
> People get mad at the President.
>
> It's hard to be elected President.

3. Scramble the ideas from the text so that they are not listed in the order that they were written. Tell children the following.

> "You can see how this book is organized by looking at the ideas from the book that I have written. For example, the book told us that the President lives in the White House, and then it described the kinds of fun things the President has in his house. Informational books sometimes describe things from general ideas to specific ones as is the case in this example. Rearrange the items in this list so they match the way the book was written."

4. Check the children's lists to determine whether they have remembered the book's organization. It may take more than one attempt for some children to arrange the list correctly.

Aa Bb Cc   Tips for English Language Learners

- Children who do not speak English as their first language may have difficulty reading informational text. English Language Learners master content vocabulary, such as that used in informational text, more slowly than they learn "playground language." You might think that an English Language Learner is fluent in English because he or she is able to converse with his or her classmates. However, this child may have little understanding when reading informational text. To scaffold English Language Learners' instruction, have them read informational text with a partner, and provide them with visuals or concrete objects when appropriate.

BOOK TOUR PREVIEWING GUIDE

Informational texts have different features than narrative texts. Some informational texts have such features as graphs, pictures, inserts, and tables. Book Tour Previewing Guides can help children identify text features before reading.

DIRECTIONS

1. Tell children to conduct a Book Tour of informational books before reading so they know what to expect. Explain to children that it is useful for them to be aware of what is coming up in a book before they begin reading.

2. Ask children if they know what a *tour* is. Conduct a class discussion about the use of the word *tour* in this situation.

3. Select an informational book that has external features appropriate for the age level of the children. For example, *The Truth about Animal Builders* (Stonehouse & Bertram, 2003) is a good example. This book is organized like an encyclopedia or website entry and has several features.

4. Show the features to children by holding up the book and pointing to some of the pictures with captions and the inserts. Explain to children that this book has some "features" that are not like the narrative texts that they read. Tell children that these features are common in informational texts and that they will need to become aware of the features of each individual book.

5. Tell children that other books will have different features and that they should conduct a Book Tour so that they are aware of the features.

6. Make an overhead transparency of the example of the Book Tour Previewing Guide that follows. It is completed for *The Truth about Animal Builders*. Discuss each of the questions with children and elicit their replies before showing them the suggested answer. Encourage students to think of a variety of answers.

7. Duplicate and distribute the blank Book Tour Previewing Guide reproducible. Model this strategy several times before expecting children to complete it independently.

8. Remind children that they should conduct Book Tours before reading informational books independently. A blank copy of a Book Tour Previewing Guide follows.

Book Tour Previewing Guide

Name ___Stacey_____ Date ___October 1___

1. Write the title of the book and the name of the author.

    The Truth About Animal Builders by Bernard Stonehouse and Esther Bertram
    _____

2. Does the book look like a work of fiction or is it an informational text? Why do you think so?

    This book looks like an informational book because of its pictures and the way the print is set up.
    _____

3. Page through the book. What do you notice about the book's pictures, headings, subheading, and graphics?

    This book has a different animal on each page. The first page has a huge pictures and the second

    one has the print with lots of smaller pictures.
    _____

4. Place a check by any features of the book. Write any others on the lines.

✓ Pictures with captions		_____ Graphs or charts
✓ Inserts		_____ Cartoons
_____ Table of Contents		_____ Index
_____ Maps		_____ Diagrams
_____ Glossary		_____ Tables
_____ Illustrations		✓ Realistic pictures

    _____
    _____
    _____
    _____
    _____
    _____

Book Tour Previewing Guide

Name _____ Date _____

1. Write the title of the book and the name of the author.

   _____

   _____

2. Does the book look like a work of fiction or is it an informational text? Why do you think so?

   _____

   _____

   _____

3. Page through the book. What do you notice about the book's pictures, headings, subheading, and graphics?

   _____

   _____

   _____

4. Place a check by any external features of the book. Write any others on the lines.

_____ Pictures with captions		_____ Graphs or charts
_____ Inserts		_____ Cartoons
_____ Table of Contents		_____ Index
_____ Maps		_____ Diagrams
_____ Glossary		_____ Tables
_____ Illustrations		_____ Realistic pictures

   _____

   _____

   _____

WHAT'S THE POINT?

Informational texts often have a main point, sometimes called a main idea. The main point of an informational text is not usually stated in one sentence but is prevalent through the text. Ellery (2005) suggests having children find the main point of an informational text through finding the point and then having children answer the question, "How did you know it was important?" Asking children to determine why a point was important helps them distinguish between important and unimportant ideas in the text.

❧ DIRECTIONS

1. Select an informational text that is of interest to children. One such text is *Buildings in Disguise: Architecture that Looks Like Animals, Food, and other Things* (Arbogast, 2004).

2. Determine the main point of the book. In this example, the main point is that there are many buildings in the United States that are built like other things. Architects call them mimetic buildings because they mimic things other than buildings.

3. Read the book to children or have them read it in groups. Ask children to think about the main point of the book.

4. Discuss what the children think is the main point. Guide them to state a main idea sentence such as the following:

   Some buildings look like other objects. They are called mimetic buildings.

5. Provide children with a copy of the What's the Point? sheet. Have children write the main idea statement in the box at the bottom of the page.

6. Ask children what else they can tell you about the main point of the book. For example, they might say that some buildings look like animals, some gas stations look like tee pees, some buildings are built to get attention so that people stop, some restaurants look like tea pots, and so on.

7. Tell children that these other ideas are also important but that they support the main idea statement. Have children write these ideas in the circles at the top of the page.

8. Once children have practice with this strategy, begin with the ideas that support the main idea and then have children generate a main idea statement.

9. Encourage children to think about main points of informational texts as they read independently. A blank What's the Point? page follows.

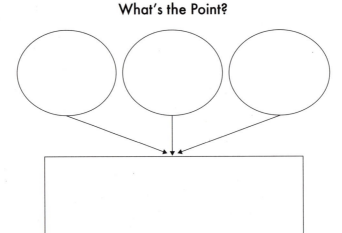

What's the Point?

What's the Point?

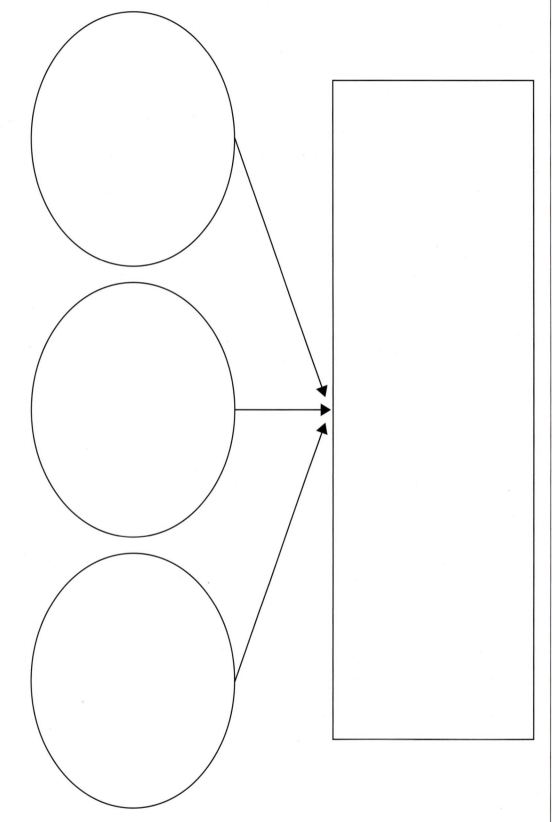

Activities, tips, & Center Ideas

1. Encourage children to read informational texts by giving book talks about informational books. A book talk is a one-to-two-minute "commercial" about a book. After the book talk, display the books in a book center so that children can read them during independent reading time.

2. Read informational picture books to children frequently. Before reading, remind children that the book you are reading does not have a plot but that it describes or explains something.

3. Encourage children to embed "how to" stories in traditional stories in their speaking and writing. For example, a child talking or writing about a family camping trip could describe how they put up their tent. Tell children that including "how to" sections provides readers with information inside a story.

4. Tell children that some television programs and movies are informational rather than fictional. Have children brainstorm a list of television programs that they typically watch. Have children predict which type of programs they watch more frequently. Write the names of the programs on cards that can be placed on a chart. Give children the names of two categories: fictional programs and informational programs. Have children sort the cards into the two categories. Discuss the differences between the types of television programs.

5. Pair fictional texts with informational texts to read aloud to children. Select books that are of similar topics such as *Owl Moon* by Jane Yolen and *All About Owls* by Jim Arnosky. Read one book in the morning and one in the afternoon. Discuss books with children and compare how the books were alike and different (Taberski, 2000).

6. Use a content area word wall to help familiarize children with words found in informational texts (Bean, 2001). To create a content area word wall, identify five words that will be found in informational texts the children will be reading in the next week. For example, if you're going to read *Birds* by Gallimard Jeunesse, you might select the words *beak, prey, feathers, nests,* and *grubs.* Print the five words on colorful paper and display them in the room. At least once a day, read the words aloud with children, having children clap and chant each letter of each word. For example, say the word beak and then say each letter, B-E-A-K. At the end of the week read the book aloud to children.

INFORMATIONAL MATERIAL

Dear Families,

You can broaden your child's literacy knowledge by including informational books in your child's bedtime reading. Informational books "explain" something or "tell" about something. Books that present facts about animals, for instance, are informational texts. Another popular type of informational book is a how-to book such as a book on crafts, cooking, projects, and experiments. Many young children like to read books that provide information, so try to alternate stories with informational books.

Sincerely,

Assessments
of Comprehension

Goal: To assess a child's comprehension.

Background

Two major types of assessments in this section include retelling and passage reading. There are two assessments for narrative retelling and an assessment for informational retelling. Passage reading includes two forms of narrative passages ranging from easy sight word reading through third grade. Six passages are included in each form so you can more easily assess the different reading abilities of children. The passages allow you to assess comprehension, note miscues during oral reading, and determine rate or speed of reading. There is much information that can be gained from these assessment to help focus your instruction on the children's individual needs. In addition, the two forms for each level from beginning reading through grade three permit evaluation at different points in the school year.

Section 6.4   **ASSESSMENT STRATEGY**

RETELLING A STORY

OVERVIEW	You can get a good sense of children's knowledge of story structures by their story retelling. Children who have a developed sense of story will be able to retell stories using story grammar, but those who are unclear about story structure will tell unrelated details. Children's retelling of stories can let you know whether they need more instruction in story structure.
MATERIALS NEEDED	1. An age-appropriate story that is new to the child 2. A copy of the Narrative Retelling Record Sheet on page 341
PROCEDURES	1. Choose a short book that is new for the child. The book should have an obvious plot with named characters. You may choose to use props or puppets with the story if you think visual aids could help the child. 2. Before reading the book say, "I'm going to read a story to you. After I am finished reading, I will ask you to tell me the story as if you were telling it to someone who has not read the story. As you listen, try to remember as much of the story as you can." 3. Read the book aloud to the child. 4. After you have read the book say, "Now tell me as much of the story as you can." If the child hesitates, ask probing questions such as "What was the story about?" or "Who was in the story?" or "What happened next?" You may want to tape-record the retelling for future reference.
SCORING AND INTERPRETATION	Use the Narrative Retelling Record Sheet to record how well the child understands narrative story structure and the rubric for a score. If a child scores below a 4, you should continue to teach story structure explicitly. Have the child participate in another retelling within a short time for a second assessment. Some stories are easier for a child to retell than others, and a second retelling may provide different information.

Narrative Retelling

Name _____ Date _____

Name of text _____

CHECK ALL THAT APPLY

_____ Identifies setting of story.

_____ Identifies main characters.

_____ Identifies problem of story.

_____ Identifies sequence of events.

_____ Identifies solution to problem.

RUBRIC FOR NARRATIVE TEXT RETELLING

4   Child correctly retells story using the setting, names of characters, events as they occurred in the story, the problem, and the solution. Events are described thoroughly and events are in correct sequence.

3   Child correctly identifies setting and some of the characters although without exact names, tells the events in sequence, identifies the story's problem and solution. There are some errors in retelling, but most details are accurate.

2   Child identifies the setting and characters and gives some information about the plot. Details may be minimal.

1   Child identifies few story elements correctly.

INFORMATIONAL TEXT RETELLING

OVERVIEW	Children have a more difficult time understanding the organizational patterns of informational text than stories, but you can assess how well children are learning the pattern of informational text by retellings. An informational text retelling is similar to a story retelling—only the type of text is different. Children who have a good understanding of informational text patterns will be able to retell the text using them, but those who are unclear about the text pattern will most likely relate a list of details. Informational text retellings can inform you of children's progress, and you can tailor your instruction to meet their needs.
MATERIALS NEEDED	1. An age-appropriate informational text that is new to the child 2. Copy of the Informational Text Retelling Record Sheet on page 343
PROCEDURES	1. Choose a short informational book that is new for the child. The book should have a clear text pattern such as main idea-detail or steps in a process. 2. Before reading the book say, "I'm going to read a book to you. After I am finished reading, I will ask you to tell me what occurred in the book as if you were telling it to someone who has not heard it. As you listen, try to remember as much of the book as you can." 3. Read the book aloud to the child. 4. After you have read the book say: "Now tell me as much of the book as you can." If the child hesitates, ask probing questions such as "What is the book about?" or "What happened first?" You may want to tape-record the retelling for future reference.
SCORING AND INTERPRETATION	Use the Informational Text Retelling Record Sheet to record how well the child understands informational text structure. The rubric can be used for a quantitative score. If a child scores below a 4, you should continue to explicitly teach text structure. Have the child participate in another retelling within a short time for a second assessment. Some books are easier for a particular child to retell than others are, and a second retelling may provide different information.

Informational Text Retelling

Name _____ Date _____

Name of Text _____

CHECK ONE

_____ Text is at child's reading level.

_____ Text is above child's reading level.

CHECK ONE

_____ All important facts are recalled.

_____ Most of the important facts are recalled.

_____ Some of the important facts are recalled.

CHECK ALL THAT APPLY

_____ Supporting ideas are recalled.

_____ Ideas are recalled in logical order.

_____ Child used pictures, charts, and graphs.

_____ Child recalled important conclusions.

_____ Child made appropriate inferences.

RUBRIC FOR INFORMATIONAL TEXT RETELLING

4   Child fully explains the main points and supporting details.

3   Child provides the main points and supporting details but does not explain them fully.

2   Child explains most of the main points but is not completely accurate. Child provides some, but not all, details.

1   Child does not correctly identify the main points or supporting details. Retelling is mostly inaccurate.

Adapted from B. Harp (2000). *The handbook of literacy assessment and evaluation* (2nd ed.). Norwood, MA: Christopher-Gordon.

Additional Ways to Assess Informational Text Structure

Retellings are the best way to assess text structure knowledge, but you can administer retellings in several different ways.

1. You can read the book to the child, as is detailed in the directions.
2. You can have the child read the book independently.
3. You can have the child give an oral retelling, but you can also have the child write a retelling.
4. You can have the child draw pictures as a retelling.

Whichever way you administer a retelling, the checklist and rubric apply.

STORY RETELLING

OVERVIEW	Retellings can provide a great deal of information about a child's comprehension of a story. Retelling is a learned task; therefore, you are encouraged to use some of the instructional strategies for retelling (see Section 6.1) prior to using retelling as an assessment.
MATERIALS NEEDED	1. A story that is new to the child 2. Story Retelling Record Sheet (page 346)
PROCEDURES	1. Choose a short book that is new to the child. The book should have a clear plot with named characters. You may choose to use props or puppets with the story if you think these visual aids will support the child's retelling. 2. Before reading the book say, "I'm going to read a story to you. After I'm finished reading, I will ask you to tell me the story as if you were telling it to someone who has not read the story. As you listen, try to remember as much of the story as you can." 3. Read the book aloud to the child. 4. After you have read the book say, "Now tell me about the story as if you were telling it to someone who has not read the story." 5. If the child has difficulty getting started or adding information to the retelling, use the following prompts. • What was the story about? • Who was in the story? • Where did the story take place? • What happened next? • Can you tell me anything else about the story? 6. Use the Story Retelling Record Sheet (p. 346) to record the child's performance on the retelling. You may want to tape-record the retelling so you can analyze it more thoroughly at a later time.
SCORING AND INTERPRETATION	Record the child's retelling in the appropriate boxes on the Record Sheet. Rate each part of the retelling using a scale of 0–3 as outlined on the Story Retelling Record Sheet. If a child scores below a 12, he or she should receive additional instruction in retelling and comprehension of stories.

Story Retelling

Name _____ Date _____

Story _____

RETELLING ELEMENT	CHILD'S RESPONSE	SCORE 0-3
Beginning/Setting (How and where does the story begin?)		
Characters (Who are the main characters?)		
Sequence of Major Events (What are the important things that happen in the story?)		
Problem (What was the problem in the story?)		
Solution (How was the problem solved? How did the story end?)		

Scoring: 0 = omitted or inaccurate
              1 = fragmented
              2 = partial
              3 = complete/detailed

CAPTION READING

OVERVIEW	Caption Reading will assess the child's ability to read a brief story with helpful picture clues. This is a helpful assessment to use with children who are just beginning to read.
MATERIALS NEEDED	1. The page in this book containing the caption story, either Form 1 (page 348) or Form 2 (page 351) 2. A copy of the Record Sheet that corresponds to the form selected for use, either Form 1 (pages 349–350) or Form 2 (pages 352–353).
PROCEDURES	1. Show the child the page containing the story. 2. Invite the child to look at frames of the story (pictures and text) in order as numbered. 3. Then ask the child to read the story aloud. Say, "I want you to read the story to me." As the student reads, mentally note any miscues or record them on the appropriate page of the Record Sheet. 4. If the child has difficulty reading the story, have the child listen while you read it aloud. Say, "Listen to me read the story. Then I will want you to read it to me." After your reading, invite the child to read. 5. Encourage the child to talk about the story with you.
SCORING AND INTERPRETATION	Informally note the miscues the child made, the degree of fluency, and other behaviors on the Record Sheet. If the child was able to read the captions, you can informally analyze fluency, miscues, and overall engagement with the task. If you read the story first, evaluate the degree to which the child was able to memorize and repeat the text. Be alert for how the child uses language as you talk about the story.

The cat sleeps.

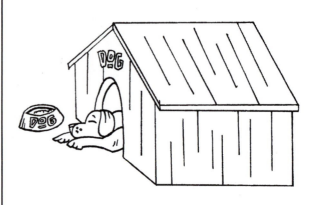

The dog sleeps.

The bird sleeps.

The baby sleeps.

Form 1—Caption Reading—Child's Copy

RECORD SHEET

Caption Reading

Name _____ Date _____

The cat sleeps.

The dog sleeps.

The bird sleeps.

The baby sleeps.

QUALITATIVE JUDGMENTS OF READING

If the child read the story, check the statement that best describes the child's reading.

_____ The child's reading is an exact match with the text.

_____ The child's reading closely matches the text.

_____ The child's reading is somewhat related to the text but is based on the illustrations.

_____ The child's reading is related mostly to the illustrations.

If you read the story first, check the statement that best describes the child's reading.

_____ The child used memory to read the text with high accuracy.

_____ The child used memory and illustrations to read the text with fair accuracy.

_____ The child did not seem to remember your reading and relied almost entirely on the illustrations to read the text.

(continues)

Form 1

Caption Reading (continued)

Record your overall qualitative judgment of reading with an X on the continuum located on this record sheet.

	Not Evident Low Seldom Weak Poor		Some		Evident High Always Strong Excellent

Other Reading Behaviors

Retelling $\vdash\!\!\!\!-\!\!\!\!+\!\!\!\!-\!\!\!\!+\!\!\!\!-\!\!\!\!+\!\!\!\!-\!\!\!\!\dashv$

Reads left to right $\vdash\!\!\!\!-\!\!\!\!+\!\!\!\!-\!\!\!\!+\!\!\!\!-\!\!\!\!+\!\!\!\!-\!\!\!\!\dashv$

Reads top to bottom $\vdash\!\!\!\!-\!\!\!\!+\!\!\!\!-\!\!\!\!+\!\!\!\!-\!\!\!\!+\!\!\!\!-\!\!\!\!\dashv$

Demonstrates letter-sound relationships $\vdash\!\!\!\!-\!\!\!\!+\!\!\!\!-\!\!\!\!+\!\!\!\!-\!\!\!\!+\!\!\!\!-\!\!\!\!\dashv$

Uses monitoring (rereads, corrects) $\vdash\!\!\!\!-\!\!\!\!+\!\!\!\!-\!\!\!\!+\!\!\!\!-\!\!\!\!+\!\!\!\!-\!\!\!\!\dashv$

Points to correct words (if requested by you) $\vdash\!\!\!\!-\!\!\!\!+\!\!\!\!-\!\!\!\!+\!\!\!\!-\!\!\!\!+\!\!\!\!-\!\!\!\!\dashv$

Engagement $\vdash\!\!\!\!-\!\!\!\!+\!\!\!\!-\!\!\!\!+\!\!\!\!-\!\!\!\!+\!\!\!\!-\!\!\!\!\dashv$

Confidence as a reader $\vdash\!\!\!\!-\!\!\!\!+\!\!\!\!-\!\!\!\!+\!\!\!\!-\!\!\!\!+\!\!\!\!-\!\!\!\!\dashv$

Observations, Comments, Notes, and Insights

1

The frog sits.

2

The frog eats.

3

The frog jumps.

4

The frog swims.

Form 2—Caption Reading—Child's Copy

Form 2

Caption Reading

Name _____ Date _____

The frog sits.

The frog eats.

The frog jumps.

The frog swims.

QUALITATIVE JUDGMENTS OF CAPTION READING

If the child read the story, check the statement that best describes the child's reading.

_____ The child's reading is an exact match with the text.

_____ The child's reading closely matches the text.

_____ The child's reading is somewhat related to the text but is based on the illustrations.

_____ The child's reading is related mostly to the illustrations.

If you read the story first, check the statement that best describes the child's reading.

_____ The child used memory to read the text with high accuracy.

_____ The child used memory and illustrations to read the text with fair accuracy.

_____ The child did not seem to remember your reading and relied almost entirely on the illustrations to read the text.

(continues)

Form 2

Caption Reading (continued)

Record your overall qualitative judgment of reading with an X on the continuum located on this record sheet.

	Not Evident Low Seldom Weak Poor	Some	Evident High Always Strong Excellent
Other Reading Behaviors			
Retelling	├────────┼────────┼────────┼────────┤		
Reads left to right	├────────┼────────┼────────┼────────┤		
Reads top to bottom	├────────┼────────┼────────┼────────┤		
Demonstrates letter-sound relationships	├────────┼────────┼────────┼────────┤		
Uses monitoring (rereads, corrects)	├────────┼────────┼────────┼────────┤		
Points to correct words (if requested by you)	├────────┼────────┼────────┼────────┤		
Engagement	├────────┼────────┼────────┼────────┤		
Confidence as a reader	├────────┼────────┼────────┼────────┤		

Observations, Comments, Notes, and Insights

PASSAGE READING

| | OVERVIEW | The Passage Reading assessment strategy is designed to give you information about a child's ability to read connected text. In addition, you can gain insights into a child's comprehension and understanding of vocabulary presented in a passage. Important information on a child's word recognition strategies (See Chapter 3) and fluency (Chapter 4) can also be identified through this assessment. The six passages are based in part on Gunning's (1998) work and descriptions of beginning reading levels. The table below provides some basic information about each of the passages using criteria summarized by Reutzel and Cooteer (2004) and the work of Gunning (2005). |

Passage	Grade Level	Reading Level Code	Words	Approximate Reading Recovery Level
Easy Sight Word	Pre-primer	EEE	25	4–8
Beginning	Primer	EE	50	9–11
Later Beginning	Primer/1	E	75	12–15
Grade 1	1	E7141	100	16–20
Grade 2	2	E8224	100	21–28
Grade 3	3	E3183	100	37–38

MATERIALS NEEDED

1. The pages in this book containing the passages
2. The Record Sheet that corresponds to the passage(s) selected
3. One 5″ × 8″ card

PROCEDURES

1. Duplicate the appropriate Record Sheet(s).
2. Choose a passage that you think the child can read. Place the passage before the child and cover everything but the illustration and the title.
3. Activate the child's background knowledge by saying, "Read the title to yourself and look at the pictures. Then tell me what you think this story will be about." Informally judge the extent of the child's background knowledge and record an X along the continuum on the Record Sheet.

(continued)

Then say, "Read the story to me. I'll ask you to answer some questions when you are finished." As the child reads, note any miscues in the appropriate place on the Record Sheet using the following markings (or your own system).

Marking	Meaning of Marking
man / men	Substitution
man s/c / men	Self-correction
~~men~~	Omitted word
m— / men	Partial pronunciation
men (underlined)	Repeated word
small / ∧men	Insertion

Also, note other behaviors, such as finger pointing, ignoring punctuation, engagement, and strategies used to pronounce words not known at sight. Count the *total* number of miscues or the number of *significant* (those that affect meaning) miscues. Self-corrections need not be included in counting miscues.

4. When the child has finished reading, ask the comprehension questions or invite a retelling of the story. Record a plus (+) for correct responses and a minus (−) for incorrect responses. You may also give half credit. The letter beside the comprehension questions indicates the following types of questions.

Letter	Type of Question
T	Topic—What the passage is about
F	Fact—specific information stated in the passage
E	Experience/Evaluation—making judgments using prior knowledge
I	Inference—putting together information from the passage that is not explicitly stated
V	Vocabulary—explaining a specific word in the passage

5. If the child was successful, present the next passage. Continue administering graded passages until the child has many word recognition miscues (i.e., frustration level) or is unable to answer more than half of the comprehension questions. If the initial passage was too difficult, try an easier passage or go back to Caption Reading.

SCORING AND INTERPRETATION

1. Use the scoring guides on the Record Sheet to evaluate word recognition and comprehension. For word recognition, count the total number of miscues or the number of significant (those that affect meaning) miscues. Record the number of

(continues)

miscues in the appropriate box on the Record Sheet. Then find and circle the level (Independent, Ind./Inst., Instructional, Inst./Frust, or Frustration) on the scoring guide at the bottom of the passage corresponding to the number of total or significant miscues.

2. For comprehension, count the number of comprehension questions missed and record this number in the appropriate box on the record sheet. Then find and circle the level on the scoring guide at the bottom of the questions. If retelling is used to assess comprehension, circle *excellent* for independent level, *satisfactory* for instructional level, and *unsatisfactory* for frustration level.

3. There are also areas of word recognition and comprehension at the bottom of some record sheets that you can evaluate on a scale of 1 to 3. Then make an overall qualitative judgment of the child's word recognition and comprehension abilities on the summary page of the Record Sheet.

4. Throughout the assessment, watch for behaviors often associated with frustration: lack of expression, word-by-word reading, excessive anxiety, and so on. Note such behaviors in the margins of the Record Sheet.

5. Estimate the child's oral reading rate by timing the reading and inserting the seconds required for reading as the divisor in the formula at the bottom of the Record Sheet. Perform the necessary division. The resulting numeral will be an estimate of the child's rate in words per minute (WPM). An example of rate determination is shown below. See Johns (2005, p. 37) for further information about reading rate as well as Chapter 4 in this book.

$$\begin{array}{r} 52\text{WPM} \\ 115\overline{)6000} \\ \underline{575} \\ 250 \\ 230 \end{array}$$

An informal analysis of the child's word recognition and comprehension abilities should help you identify areas for instruction.

My Dog

I have a dog.

My dog is Spark.

Spark is a big dog.

He plays ball.

I play with Spark.

Spark is a fun dog.

Form 1—Passage Reading—Child's Copy   EEE

RECORD SHEET

Form 1

Easy Sight Word Passage Reading

Name _____ Date _____

Teacher's Directions   354–355
Child's Copy   357

Background: Low ├────┼────┤ **High**

My Dog

I have a dog.

My dog is Spark.

Spark is a big dog.

He plays ball.

I play with Spark.

Spark is a fun dog.

EEE (Pre-Primer) Activating Background:

Read the title to yourself and look at the pictures. Then tell me what you think this story will be about.

T   1. ___ What is the story mostly about?
(a dog; Spark)

F   2. ___ What is the dog's name? (Spark)

F   3. ___ What does Spark do? (play ball)

E   4. ___ Why do you think Spark is a fun dog?
(any logical response; because he likes to play ball)

I   5. ___ What other things might Spark like to do? (any logical response)

V   6. ___ What is a dog? (any logical response; an animal; a pet)

Total Miscues [ ]   **Significant Miscues** [ ]   **Questions Missed** [ ]

Word Recognition Scoring Guide		
Total Miscues	Level	Significant Miscues
0	Independent	0
1	Ind./Inst.	—
2	Instructional	1
—	Inst./Frust.	—
3	Frustration	2

Retelling
Excellent
Satisfactory
Unsatisfactory

WPM

)1500

Comprehension Scoring Guide	
Questions Missed	Level
0	Independent
1	Ind./Inst.
1½	Instructional
2	Inst./Frust.
2½+	Frustration

Qualitative Analysis of Word Identification and Comprehension (1 = never; 2 = sometimes; 3 = always)						
Word Identification				**Comprehension**		
Uses graphophonic information	1	2	3	Makes predictions	1	2	3
Uses semantic information	1	2	3	Seeks to construct meaning	1	2	3
Uses syntactic information	1	2	3	Understands topic and major ideas	1	2	3
Knows basic sight words automatically	1	2	3	Remembers facts or details	1	2	3
Possesses sight vocabulary	1	2	3	Evaluates ideas from passages	1	2	3
Possesses numerous strategies	1	2	3	Makes and supports appropriate inferences	1	2	3
Uses strategies flexibly	1	2	3	Stays focused on reading	1	2	3

The Small Fish

There are two small fish. One is red and the other is blue. They live in the sea. They like to play.

One day a big green fish came to the sea. It did not want to play. It wanted to eat the small fish. The big fish was mean.

Form 1—Passage Reading—Child's Copy   EE

Form 1

Beginning Passage Reading

Name _____ Date _____

Teacher's Directions	354–355
Child's Copy	359

Background: Low |———|———| **High**

The Small Fish

There are two small fish. One is red and the other is blue. They live in the sea. They like to play.

One day a big green fish came to the sea. It did not want to play. It wanted to eat the small fish. The big fish was mean.

EE (Primer) Activating Background:

Read the title to yourself and look at the picture. Then tell me what you think this story will be about.

T   1. ____ What is this story about? (fish; two fish who almost got eaten by a big green fish)

F   2. ____ What size was the green fish? (big)

F   3. ____ What do the red fish and the blue fish like to do in the sea? (play)

E   4. ____ What do you think the small fish will do to get away from the green fish? (any logical response; swim fast)

I   5. ____ What do you think the red fish and the blue fish did when they saw the green fish? (any logical response; they swam away quickly)

V   6. ____ What does "play" mean? (any logical response)

Total Miscues [ ]   **Significant Miscues** [ ]   **Questions Missed** [ ]

Word Recognition Scoring Guide		
Total Miscues	Level	Significant Miscues
0	Independent	0
1–2	Ind./Inst.	—
3	Instructional	1
4	Inst./Frust.	2
5+	Frustration	3

Retelling
Excellent
Satisfactory
Unsatisfactory
WPM
)3000

Comprehension Scoring Guide	
Questions Missed	Level
0	Independent
1	Ind./Inst.
1½	Instructional
2	Inst./Frust.
2½+	Frustration

Qualitative Analysis of Word Identification and Comprehension (1 = never; 2 = sometimes; 3 = always)							
Word Identification				**Comprehension**			
Uses graphophonic information	1	2	3	Makes predictions	1	2	3
Uses semantic information	1	2	3	Seeks to construct meaning	1	2	3
Uses syntactic information	1	2	3	Understands topic and major ideas	1	2	3
Knows basic sight words automatically	1	2	3	Remembers facts or details	1	2	3
Possesses sight vocabulary	1	2	3	Evaluates ideas from passages	1	2	3
Possesses numerous strategies	1	2	3	Makes and supports appropriate inferences	1	2	3
Uses strategies flexibly	1	2	3	Stays focused on reading	1	2	3

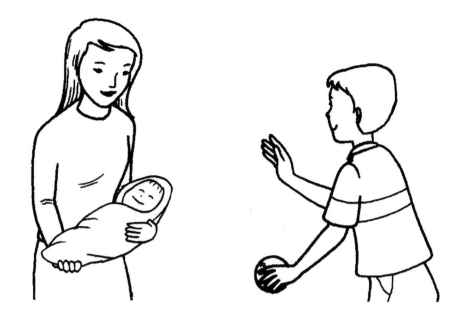

A Big Brother

One day Tim's mother came home with his new baby brother. Tim was very happy. Now he could play with someone. He ran and got his bat and ball. His mother smiled. She said that the baby was too little to play ball. The baby would have to get older. Tim was still glad that he was a big brother. He could help take care of the baby. He felt like a big boy now.

Form 1—Passage Reading—Child's Copy   E

Form 1

Later Beginning Passage Reading

Name _____ Date _____

Teacher's Directions   354–355
Child's Copy   361

Background: Low |———|———| **High**

A Big Brother

One day Tim's mother came home with his

new baby brother. Tim was very happy. Now

he could play with someone. He ran and got his

bat and ball. His mother smiled. She said that

the baby was too little to play ball. The baby

would have to get older. Tim was still glad that

he was a big brother. He could help take care

of the baby. He felt like a big boy now.

E (Later Beginning) Activating Background:

Read the title to yourself and look at the picture. Then tell me what you think this story will be about.

T   1. ___ What is this story about? (Tim and his new baby brother.)

F   2. ___ Why was Tim happy when his mother came home with the new baby? (He could play with someone.)

F   3. ___ What toys did Tim run to get when his baby brother came home? (bat and ball)

F   4. ___ What did Tim's mother do when he went to get his bat and ball? (smiled)

F   5. ___ Why did Tim's mother say the baby couldn't play ball? (He was too little.)

F   6. ___ How did Tim feel about being a big brother? (glad; happy)

I   7. ___ What kind of big brother do you think Tim will be? Why? (any logical response; a good one, a fun one, etc.)

I   8. ___ Why did Tim feel like a big boy? (any logical response; he was bigger than the baby; he could do more things than the baby; he could be a helper.)

E   9. ___ What will Tim probably do to help take care of the baby? (any logical response; talk to him; play with him; give him a bottle)

V   10. ___ What does "glad" mean? (any logical response; happy)

Total Miscues [ ]   **Significant Miscues** [ ]   **Questions Missed** [ ]

Word Recognition Scoring Guide		
Total Miscues	Level	Significant Miscues
0–1	Independent	0
2–3	Ind./Inst.	1
4	Instructional	2
5–7	Inst./Frust.	3
8	Frustration	4+

Retelling
Excellent
Satisfactory
Unsatisfactory

WPM

$\overline{)4500}$

Comprehension Scoring Guide	
Questions Missed	Level
0–1	Independent
1½–2	Ind./Inst.
2½	Instructional
3–4½	Inst./Frust.
5+	Frustration

From Laurie Elish-Piper, Jerry L. Johns, and Susan Davis Lenski, *Teaching Reading Pre-K–Grade 3* (3rd ed.). Copyright © 2006 by Kendall/Hunt Publishing Company (1-800-247-3458, ext. 4). May be reproduced for noncommercial educational purposes.

Paws Visits School

Fred has a big black cat. The cat is named Paws. Fred took Paws to his small school. All of the children loved Paws. They all tried to pet Paws at one time. Paws was very afraid. She jumped out of Fred's arms and ran away. Fred looked all around but could not find Paws. Fred's friend, Anne, looked under the little table. Anne saw Paws under the table. Anne ran and told Fred where she saw Paws. Paws came out when she saw Fred. Fred hugged Paws tightly. Fred took Paws home and gave her some food to eat.

Form 1—Passage Reading—Child's Copy   E 7141

Grade 1 Passage Reading

Form 1

Name _____ Date _____

Teacher's Directions   354–355
Child's Copy   363

Background: Low ├────┼────┤ **High**

Paws Visits School

    Fred has a big black cat. The cat is named Paws. Fred took Paws to his small school. All of the children loved Paws. They all tried to pet Paws at one time. Paws was very afraid. She jumped out of Fred's arms and ran away. Fred looked all around but could not find Paws. Fred's friend, Anne, looked under the little table. Anne saw Paws under the table. Anne ran and told Fred where she saw Paws. Paws came out when she saw Fred. Fred hugged Paws tightly. Fred took Paws home and gave her some food to eat.

E 7141 (Grade 1) Activating Background:
Read the title to yourself and look at the picture. Then tell me what you think this story will be about.

T   1. ____ What is this story about? (Paws; a cat; a boy who takes his cat to school)

F   2. ____ What color was the cat? (black)

F   3. ____ What was the cat's name? (Paws)

F   4. ____ Why did the cat run away? (she was afraid)

F   5. ____ Who helped Fred find his cat? (Anne)

F   6. ____ Where did Anne find Paws? (under the table)

I   7. ____ How do you think Anne felt when she found Paws? (any logical response; happy; excited; glad)

I   8. ____ Why do you think Fred took Paws to school? (any logical response; to show the other children)

E   9. ____ Do you think Fred will take Paws to school again? Why? (any logical response)

V   10. ____ What does "afraid" mean? (scared)

Total Miscues ☐   **Significant Miscues** ☐   **Questions Missed** ☐

Word Recognition Scoring Guide		
Total Miscues	Level	Significant Miscues
0–1	Independent	0–1
2–4	Ind./Inst.	2
5	Instructional	3
6–9	Inst./Frust.	4
10+	Frustration	5+

Retelling
Excellent
Satisfactory
Unsatisfactory

WPM

$\overline{)6000}$

Comprehension Scoring Guide	
Questions Missed	Level
0–1	Independent
1½–2	Ind./Inst.
2½	Instructional
3–4½	Inst./Frust.
5+	Frustration

From Laurie Elish-Piper, Jerry L. Johns, and Susan Davis Lenski, *Teaching Reading Pre-K–Grade 3* (3rd ed.). Copyright © 2006 by Kendall/Hunt Publishing Company (1-800-247-3458, ext. 4). May be reproduced for noncommercial educational purposes.

The Lost Babies

It was getting dark outside. All the animal mothers were looking for their children. Mrs. Turtle found her babies near a tree. Mrs. Toad jumped in the weeds after she found her hungry children. Mrs. Fish found her babies by the rocks in the river. They were safe and happy.

Mrs. Rabbit was very scared. She could not find her babies anywhere. She was afraid that a fox might find her babies first. She looked all over the forest.

Mrs. Mouse helped Mrs. Rabbit look for her lost babies. Mrs. Mouse found them. The lost babies were safe at home.

Form 1—Passage Reading—Child's Copy   E 8224

Grade 2 Passage Reading

Name _____ Date _____

Teacher's Directions   354–355
Child's Copy   365

Background: Low |———|———| **High**

The Lost Babies

It was getting dark outside. All the animal mothers were looking for their children. Mrs. Turtle found her babies near a tree. Mrs. Toad jumped in the weeds after she found her hungry children. Mrs. Fish found her babies by the rocks in the river. They were safe and happy.

Mrs. Rabbit was very scared. She could not find her babies anywhere. She was afraid that a fox might find her babies first. She looked all over the forest.

Mrs. Mouse helped Mrs. Rabbit look for her lost babies. Mrs. Mouse found them. The lost babies were safe at home.

E 8224 (Grade 2) Activating Background:
Read the title to yourself and look at the picture. Then tell me what you think this story will be about.

T 1. ____ What is this story about? (Mrs. Rabbit looking for her lost babies; lost babies)

F 2. ____ Where did Mrs. Turtle find her babies? (by a tree)

F 3. ____ Where were the baby fish? (by the rocks in the river)

F 4. ____ Who couldn't find her babies? (Mrs. Rabbit)

F 5. ____ What was Mrs. Rabbit afraid of? (that a fox might find her babies)

F 6. ____ Who found the baby rabbits? (Mrs. Mouse)

I 7. ____ What time of day did the story take place? Why? (any logical response; night)

I 8. ____ What do you think Mrs. Rabbit did when she heard Mrs. Mouse's news? (any logical response; went right home)

E 9. ____ Why would Mrs. Rabbit be afraid of a fox? (any logical response; it might eat her babies)

V 10. ____ What does "safe" mean? (any logical response; no danger; no harm; protection)

Total Miscues [ ]   **Significant Miscues** [ ]   **Questions Missed** [ ]

Word Recognition Scoring Guide		
Total Miscues	Level	Significant Miscues
0–1	Independent	0–1
2–4	Ind./Inst.	2
5	Instructional	3
6–9	Inst./Frust.	4
10+	Frustration	5+

Retelling
Excellent
Satisfactory
Unsatisfactory
WPM
)6000

Comprehension Scoring Guide	
Questions Missed	Level
0–1	Independent
1½–2	Ind./Inst.
2½	Instructional
3–4½	Inst./Frust.
5+	Frustration

Joe Goes Fishing

One summer day, Joe wished he could go
fishing, but he didn't have a fishing pole. Then
he got a creative idea. He decided to make a
fishing pole out of a stick, some string, and a
paper clip for a hook. Using a shovel, he dug
a hole in the dirt beside the pond and found
some worms. After baiting the hook, Joe tossed
the string into the pond and waited. Suddenly
he felt a tug on the string. He quickly jerked
the string out of the water. Joe was delighted
to find he had caught a little fish.

Form 1—Passage Reading—Child's Copy   E3183

RECORD SHEET

Grade 3 Passage Reading

Form 1

Name _____ Date _____

Teacher's Directions   354–355
Child's Copy   367

Background: Low ├──────┼──────┤ **High**

Joe Goes Fishing

One summer day, Joe wished he could go

fishing, but he didn't have a fishing pole. Then

he got a creative idea. He decided to make a

fishing pole out of a stick, some string, and a

paper clip for a hook. Using a shovel, he dug

a hole in the dirt beside the pond and found

some worms. After baiting the hook, Joe tossed

the string into the pond and waited. Suddenly

he felt a tug on the string. He quickly jerked

the string out of the water. Joe was delighted

to find he had caught a little fish.

E 8183 (Grade 3) Activating Background:

Read the title to yourself and look at the picture. Then tell me what you think this story will be about.

T   1. ____ What is this story about?
(Joe wanting to go fishing; Joe making his own fishing pole.)

F   2. ____ What time of the year was it? (summer)

F   3. ____ What did Joe use for a fishing pole? (a stick)

F   4. ____ What did Joe use for a hook? (a paper clip)

F   5. ____ How did Joe get bait for fishing? (He dug for worms.)

F   6. ____ How did Joe feel when he caught a fish? (delighted)

I   7. ____ How long did Joe have to wait to catch a fish? (not very long)

I   8. ____ What did the tug on his string mean? (He had a fish on his hook.)

E   9. ____ What do you think Joe will do with his fish? (any logical response; take it home to eat; throw it back into the pond)

V   10. ____ What does "delighted" mean? (any logical response; pleased, joyful)

Total Miscues [ ]   **Significant Miscues** [ ]   **Questions Missed** [ ]

Word Recognition Scoring Guide		
Total Miscues	Level	Significant Miscues
0–1	Independent	0–1
2–4	Ind./Inst.	2
5	Instructional	3
6–9	Inst./Frust.	4
10+	Frustration	5+

Retelling
Excellent
Satisfactory
Unsatisfactory

WPM

)6000

Comprehension Scoring Guide	
Questions Missed	Level
0–1	Independent
1½–2	Ind./Inst.
2½	Instructional
3–4½	Inst./Frust.
5+	Frustration

Sam Likes Books

Sam likes books.

He likes big books.

He likes small books.

He likes all kinds of books.

Sam likes to read his books at home.

Form 2—Passage Reading—Child's Copy   EE

Form 2

Easy Sight Word Passage Reading

Name _____ Date _____

Teacher's Directions   354–355
Child's Copy   369

Background: Low |————|————| **High**

Sam Likes Books

Sam likes books.

He likes big books.

He likes small books.

He likes all kinds of books.

Sam likes to read his books at home.

EE (Pre-Primer) Activating Background:

Read the title to yourself and look at the pictures. Then tell me what you think this story will be about.

T   1. ____ What is the story mostly about? (books; Sam)

F   2. ____ Who likes books? (Sam)

F   3. ____ Where does Sam like to read? (at home)

E   4. ____ What do you think Sam reads about? (any logical response)

I   5. ____ Why do you think Sam likes to read? (any logical response; it is fun)

V   6. ____ What is a book? (any logical response; something you read)

Total Miscues [ ]   **Significant Miscues** [ ]   **Questions Missed** [ ]

Word Recognition Scoring Guide		
Total Miscues	Level	Significant Miscues
0	Independent	0
1	Ind./Inst.	—
2	Instructional	1
—	Inst./Frust.	—
3	Frustration	2

Retelling
Excellent
Satisfactory
Unsatisfactory
WPM
)1500

Comprehension Scoring Guide	
Questions Missed	Level
0	Independent
1	Ind./Inst.
1½	Instructional
2	Inst./Frust.
2½+	Frustration

Qualitative Analysis of Word Identification and Comprehension (1 = never; 2 = sometimes; 3 = always)							
Word Identification				**Comprehension**			
Uses graphophonic information	1	2	3	Makes predictions	1	2	3
Uses semantic information	1	2	3	Seeks to construct meaning	1	2	3
Uses syntactic information	1	2	3	Understands topic and major ideas	1	2	3
Knows basic sight words automatically	1	2	3	Remembers facts or details	1	2	3
Possesses sight vocabulary	1	2	3	Evaluates ideas from passages	1	2	3
Possesses numerous strategies	1	2	3	Makes and supports appropriate inferences	1	2	3
Uses strategies flexibly	1	2	3	Stays focused on reading	1	2	3

Ball Game

Bob went to a ball game with his dad. They sat by first base. Dad got two hot dogs and two cold drinks for lunch.

The ball player hit the ball. It came to Bob. He caught the ball with his glove. Bob jumped up and down. He was happy.

Form 2—Passage Reading—Child's Copy   E

RECORD SHEET

Form 2

Beginning Passage Reading

Name _____ Date _____

Teacher's Directions   354–355
Child's Copy   371

Background: Low |——————|——————| **High**

Ball Game

Bob went to a ball game with his dad.

They sat by first base. Dad got two hot

dogs and two cold drinks for lunch.

   The ball player hit the ball. It came

to Bob. He caught the ball with his glove.

Bob jumped up and down. He was happy.

E (Primer) Activating Background:

Read the title to yourself and look at the picture. Then tell me what you think this story will be about.

T   1. ___ What is this story about?
(a boy and his dad at a ball game)

F   2. ___ Where did Bob and his dad sit?
(by first base)

F   3. ___ What did they eat for lunch?
(hot dogs and cold drinks)

E   4. ___ What do you think Bob will do with the ball he caught at the game? (any logical response; keep it in a safe place; show it to his friends)

I   5. ___ Why do you think Bob was happy? (any logical response; he caught the ball; he sat by first base)

V   6. ___ What does "glove" mean? (something that goes over your hand to catch balls)

Total Miscues [ ]   **Significant Miscues** [ ]   **Questions Missed** [ ]

Word Recognition Scoring Guide		
Total Miscues	Level	Significant Miscues
0	Independent	0
1–2	Ind./Inst.	—
3	Instructional	1
4	Inst./Frust.	2
5+	Frustration	3

Retelling
Excellent
Satisfactory
Unsatisfactory

WPM

)3000

Comprehension Scoring Guide	
Questions Missed	Level
0	Independent
1	Ind./Inst.
1½	Instructional
2	Inst./Frust.
2½+	Frustration

Qualitative Analysis of Word Identification and Comprehension (1 = never; 2 = sometimes; 3 = always)							
Word Identification				**Comprehension**			
Uses graphophonic information	1	2	3	Makes predictions	1	2	3
Uses semantic information	1	2	3	Seeks to construct meaning	1	2	3
Uses syntactic information	1	2	3	Understands topic and major ideas	1	2	3
Knows basic sight words automatically	1	2	3	Remembers facts or details	1	2	3
Possesses sight vocabulary	1	2	3	Evaluates ideas from passages	1	2	3
Possesses numerous strategies	1	2	3	Makes and supports appropriate inferences	1	2	3
Uses strategies flexibly	1	2	3	Stays focused on reading	1	2	3

Library Books

Mike was always glad when Friday came. It was library day at his school. He could go and get two new books to read. Mike loved to read. He liked to read about many things. He liked stories about people. When he read about kings, he wished he were a king too. Mike also liked to read about animals. Books about wild animals were his favorite ones to read. He learned a lot by reading.

Form 2—Passage Reading—Child's Copy   E

RECORD SHEET

Later Beginning Passage Reading

Form 2

Name _____ Date _____

Teacher's Directions   354–355
Child's Copy   373

Background: Low |———|———| **High**

Library Books

Mike was always glad when Friday came. It was

library day at his school. He could go and get two

new books to read. Mike loved to read. He liked to

read about many things. He liked stories about

people. When he read about kings, he wished he

were a king too. Mike also liked to read about

animals. Books about wild animals were his

favorite ones to read. He learned a lot by reading.

E (Later Beginning) Activating Background:
Read the title to yourself and look at the picture. Then tell me what you think this story will be about.

T 1. ___ What is this story about?
(Mike liking to read)

F 2. ___ What day of the week did Mike get to go to the school library? (Friday)

F 3. ___ Why was Mike glad when Friday came? (It was library day.)

F 4. ___ How many books could Mike get? (two)

F 5. ___ What did Mike wish he could be? (a king)

F 6. ___ What were his favorite books to read? (books about wild animals)

I 7. ___ What kind of animals might have been in Mike's books? (any logical response; any non-domesticated animals)

I 8. ___ Why do you think Mike loved to read? (any logical response; he liked to learn new things; he could use his imagination.)

E 9. ___ What kinds of things do you think Mike learned about wild animals? (any logical response relating to wild animals)

V 10. ___ What does "favorite" mean? (any logical response; what you really like)

Total Miscues [ ]   **Significant Miscues** [ ]   **Questions Missed** [ ]

Word Recognition Scoring Guide		
Total Miscues	Level	Significant Miscues
0–1	Independent	0
2–3	Ind./Inst.	1
4	Instructional	2
5–7	Inst./Frust.	3
8	Frustration	4+

Retelling
Excellent
Satisfactory
Unsatisfactory

WPM

)4500

Comprehension Scoring Guide	
Questions Missed	Level
0–1	Independent
1½–2	Ind./Inst.
2½	Instructional
3–4½	Inst./Frust.
5+	Frustration

From Laurie Elish-Piper, Jerry L. Johns, and Susan Davis Lenski, *Teaching Reading Pre-K–Grade 3* (3rd ed.). Copyright © 2006 by Kendall/Hunt Publishing Company (1-800-247-3458, ext. 4). May be reproduced for noncommercial educational purposes.

The Pet Shop

Mike ran home quickly from school. He was in a hurry to see his mom. Mike asked, "Are you ready, mom?" Mom just smiled. She was feeding the new baby. Mike jumped up and down saying, "Let's go, mom!" When mom finished, all three of them got into the car. They drove to the pet shop.

Mike looked in all the cages. He saw some brown baby dogs. He saw cats and kittens. Mike also saw birds, hamsters, and turtles. Mike wanted to choose a small pet with only two legs. He knew he would take good care of it.

Form 2—Passage Reading—Child's Copy   E 7141

Grade 1 Passage Reading

Form 2

Name _____ Date _____

Teacher's Directions   354–355
Child's Copy   375

Background: Low |——|——| **High**

The Pet Shop

Mike ran home quickly from school. He was in a hurry to see his mom. Mike asked, "Are you ready, mom?" Mom just smiled. She was feeding the new baby. Mike jumped up and down saying, "Let's go, mom!" When mom finished, all three of them got into the car. They drove to the pet shop.

Mike looked in all the cages. He saw some brown baby dogs. He saw cats and kittens. Mike also saw birds, hamsters, and turtles. Mike wanted to choose a small pet with only two legs. He knew he would take good care of it.

E 7141 (Grade 1) Activating Background:

Read the title to yourself and look at the picture. Then tell me what you think this story will be about.

T	1. ___	What is this story about? (getting a new pet; a trip to the pet shop)
F	2. ___	How did Mike get home from school? (he ran)
F	3. ___	Why did Mike run home from school? (he was in a hurry to see his mom; he wanted to go to the pet shop)
F	4. ___	What was mom doing when Mike got home from school? (feeding the baby)
F	5. ___	How did Mike get to the pet shop? (he rode in his mom's car; mom drove the car)
F	6. ___	What animals did Mike see? (dogs, cats, kittens, birds, hamsters, turtles [any three])
I	7. ___	Which animal do you think Mike will choose to be his pet? Why? (a bird because it has two legs)
I	8. ___	What kind of things will Mike probably have to do to take care of his new pet? (any logical response)
E	9. ___	What animal would you choose for a pet? Why? (any logical response)
V	10. ___	What are "cages"? (a place for animals to sleep; where zoo animals live)

Total Miscues ☐   **Significant Miscues** ☐   **Questions Missed** ☐

Word Recognition Scoring Guide		
Total Miscues	Level	Significant Miscues
0–1	Independent	0–1
2–3	Ind./Inst.	2
4	Instructional	3
5–7	Inst./Frust.	4
8	Frustration	5+

Retelling
Excellent
Satisfactory
Unsatisfactory
WPM
)6000

Comprehension Scoring Guide	
Questions Missed	Level
0–1	Independent
1½–2	Ind./Inst.
2½	Instructional
3–4½	Inst./Frust.
5+	Frustration

Night Time Friend

"It's time to come in the house," Mother called to Joe from the kitchen. "It's getting late and will be dark soon."

Joe did not want to go inside. He sat outside waiting for his friend. Mother watched from the window.

Joe looked up into the sky. He wondered what was taking his friend so long. Then Joe saw something black glide across the night sky. He knew it was his night time friend. Joe watched as it ate insects while flying around the garden.

In the morning, his friend would hang upside down in a cave and fall asleep.

Form 2—Passage Reading—Child's Copy   E 8224

Grade 2 Passage Reading

Form 2

Name _____

| Teacher's Directions | 354–35[ ] |
| Child's Copy | 377 |

Background: Low |———|———|———

[handwritten, on blue note:] Word Fluency Comprehension pg 378–379 Elish-Piper

Night Time Friend

"It's time to come in the house," Mother called to Joe from the kitchen. "It's getting late and will be dark soon."

Joe did not want to go inside. He sat outside waiting for his friend. Mother watched from the window.

Joe looked up into the sky. He wondered what was taking his friend so long. Then Joe saw something black glide across the night sky. He knew it was his night time friend. Joe watched as it ate insects while flying around the garden.

In the morning, his friend would hang upside down in a cave and fall asleep.

[ ] [ ] [ ] ... (the yard) [ ]e to do?

[ ] ...nt to stay outside? ...ting for his friend)

F [ ] ...id Joe's friend sleep? ...upside down)

F [ ] [ ] What did Joe's friend eat? (insects)

I 7. ____ What season do you think it is in this story? Why? (any logical response)

I 8. ____ What is Joe's friend? (a bat)

E 9. ____ Why do you think Mother wanted Joe to come inside? (any logical response; it was time for bed; it is dangerous to be outside after dark)

V 10. ____ What does "glide" mean? (to move smoothly)

Total Miscues [ ]   **Significant Miscues** [ ]   **Questions Missed** [ ]

Word Recognition Scoring Guide		
Total Miscues	Level	Significant Miscues
0–1	Independent	0–1
2–4	Ind./Inst.	2
5	Instructional	3
6–9	Inst./Frust.	4
10+	Frustration	5+

Retelling
Excellent
Satisfactory
Unsatisfactory

WPM

)6000

Comprehension Scoring Guide	
Questions Missed	Level
0–1	Independent
1½–2	Ind./Inst.
2½	Instructional
3–4½	Inst./Frust.
5+	Frustration

Dodge Ball

David did not particularly enjoy gym. He actually wished he could avoid ever attending gym class. Because David was short, he always felt inferior to the other boys. Whenever teams were chosen, he feared he would be picked last. One day, however, David had a great experience. His coach brought out a dodge ball. David had never played this game. As he listened to the rules, his hopes began to rise. He knew he was short, but he was quick. He was not disappointed. The ball never did tag him. For the first time, he felt like a real winner!

Form 2— Passage Reading—Child's Copy   E 3183

RECORD SHEET

Grade 3 Passage Reading

Form 1

Name _____ Date _____

Teacher's Directions   354–355
Child's Copy   379

Background: Low |——|——| **High**

Dodge Ball

David did not particularly enjoy gym. He
actually wished he could avoid ever attending
gym class. Because David was short, he always
felt inferior to the other boys. Whenever teams
were chosen, he feared he would be picked last.
One day, however, David had a great
experience. His coach brought out a dodge ball.
David had never played this game. As he
listened to the rules, his hopes began to rise. He
knew he was short, but he was quick. He was
not disappointed. The ball never did tag him.
For the first time, he felt like a real winner!

E 8183 (Grade 3) Activating Background:

Read the title to yourself and look at the picture. Then
tell me what you think this story will be about.

T	1. ____	What is this story about? (playing dodge ball; David in gym class)
F	2. ____	Why didn't David like to go to gym? (He felt inferior to the other boys.)
F	3. ____	What did David fear about teams in gym? (He would be picked last.)
F	4. ____	What is a word used to describe David? (short; quick)
F	5. ____	How many times had David played dodge ball before? (never; it was his first time)
F	6. ____	How did David feel about his time in the gym at the end of the story? (like a winner)
I	7. ____	Why did David's being short probably make him not like gym? (any logical response; he couldn't jump as high as the others because of his short legs, etc.)
I	8. ____	Why did David's hopes rise? (any logical response; he thought he might be good at dodge ball; he had a chance to prove he could be good at something in gym.)
E	9. ____	How did David's being quick help him to play dodge ball? (any logical response; when he was in the middle, he was able to move fast so the ball didn't hit him.)
V	10. ____	What does "dodge" mean? (any logical response; to move away from something)

Total Miscues [ ]   **Significant Miscues** [ ]   **Questions Missed** [ ]

Word Recognition Scoring Guide		
Total Miscues	Level	Significant Miscues
0–1	Independent	0–1
2–4	Ind./Inst.	2
5	Instructional	3
6–9	Inst./Frust.	4
10+	Frustration	5+

Retelling
Excellent
Satisfactory
Unsatisfactory

WPM

)6000

Comprehension Scoring Guide	
Questions Missed	Level
0–1	Independent
1½–2	Ind./Inst.
2½	Instructional
3–4½	Inst./Frust.
5+	Frustration

From Laurie Elish-Piper, Jerry L. Johns, and Susan Davis Lenski, *Teaching Reading Pre-K–Grade 3* (3rd ed.).
Copyright © 2006 by Kendall/Hunt Publishing Company (1-800-247-3458, ext. 4). May be reproduced for
noncommercial educational purposes.

Additional Ways of Assessing Comprehension

1. Modify the retelling format to match an individual child's preferred approach to learning. For example, you may ask a child to draw a retelling and then explain it to you. A child can also write a retelling or act it out.

2. Develop questions for a story. Ask the child the questions to determine if the child comprehended the story.

3. Use a Story Frame (See Section 6.1, Teaching Strategy 2) to assess if a child understood a story.

chapter *seven*

Strategic Reading

Overview

One of the characteristics of proficient readers is their flexible use of reading strategies. Strategies are the cognitive tools that readers use as they construct meaning from text and that writers use as they produce texts. When children read, they use strategies to make sense of text while reading. A strategy is a sequence of cognitive steps to accomplish a specific goal (Collins, 1998). Good readers selectively and flexibly apply a vast array of strategies to every reading event (Pressley, 1995). In contrast, children who are experiencing difficulty with reading typically use fewer strategies, and their strategy use tends to be rigid rather than flexible. To become a strategic reader, children must be able to plan, monitor, analyze, and regulate their reading (Paris, Lipson, & Wixson, 1983). Many of the strategies that proficient readers use are acquired naturally while others are learned. For example, some children might automatically make predictions when they read but will need instruction on ways to summarize their reading. Reading strategies are frequently learned by purposeful instruction in meaningful social situations. When the strategies in this chapter are taught to children, they can help children in their progress toward becoming strategic readers.

Questions/Answers

What are some examples of strategies that children need to use when reading?

Some of the strategies that good readers use are predicting, monitoring, summarizing, connecting, and visualizing (National Reading Panel, 2000). Good readers use these strategies automatically and very quickly. When you read, for example, you make predictions about what will happen in a split second. You do not need to take a great deal of time to predict; you make predictions throughout your reading. Children may not know these "tricks" of comprehension which is why we need to make reading strategies visible for them during instruction.

What does it mean to monitor understanding while reading?

When readers monitor understanding, they attend to whether the text makes sense as they read it. Because reading is the process of constructing meaning, effective readers are able to determine when they do not understand what they are reading; moreover, they can also apply fix-up strategies to get their comprehension back on track (Pressley & Afflerbach, 1995). For example, children ask themselves, "Do I understand what I'm reading?" If they do not, they apply repair strategies such as rereading, using picture clues, getting a word meaning, or asking for help (Cunningham & Allington, 1998).

How long will I have to teach strategies to children?

You should continue to model strategies throughout the school year, but you also want your students to internalize the strategies so they can use them independently (Almasi, 2003). As you model strategies, begin letting children take on the responsibility for giving examples and explaining their processing. As children take on more responsibility, encourage them to model strategies for their classmates.

Cross-Checking

> **Goal:** To help children use various strategies to cross-check for meaning.
>
> **Assessment Strategy 1** Oral Reading Miscue Analysis, page 418

Background

While reading, children check one kind of information against another, or cross-check, to make sense of the words (Goodman, 1965). To use cross-checking as a strategy, readers use four cues, three from print and one from their background knowledge. The cues that readers use are graphophonic (phonics) cues, semantic (context) cues, syntactic (language) cues, and background knowledge (Wilde, 2000).

When children do not recognize a word in a passage automatically, they must stop to figure it out. They can use graphophonic cues by matching sounds with letters or letter combinations; they can use semantic cues by trying to figure out what word would make sense in the sentence; they can use syntactic cues by deciding what word fits the structure and language of the sentence; and they can use their background knowledge to make sense of the sentences together. These four cues are used simultaneously so that a child can pronounce an unknown word while comprehending the passage (Rumelhart, 1985).

To use cross-checking as a strategy while they read, children need instruction on ways to use each of the cueing systems separately, and they also need instruction and practice using the cueing systems together. To know what cues children are using and what instruction they need, you will need to listen to children read on a regular basis. When you listen to children read, you will hear the types of miscues children make. Miscues are the errors children make when reading aloud. Miscues are not considered mistakes but are a window into children's reading processes (Goodman, 1965). When children make miscues, you learn which cueing systems they are using and which ones they need to strengthen.

For children to become proficient readers, they need a great deal of practice reading materials at their independent and instructional levels. It is through such practice that children can become competent using the four cueing systems. Furthermore, when children use materials that they can read easily, their reading achievement will have a greater likelihood of improving (Adams, 1990). The books children read independently need to be easy enough so that they do not miss more than one or two words per hundred. At the instructional level, students will not miss more than five or six words per hundred (Johns, 2005). When children read books that are more difficult, they have to rely more on their background knowledge and are less able to use the language cues from the print. Strategies, activities, and ideas to guide children in cross-checking follow.

MAKING SENSE

Children are engaged in making sense of the world. For example, they learn how different stores are arranged and where some of their favorite sections are located. They also learn routines at school and what to expect at recess and lunch. Reading should also make sense. In this strategy, children are given opportunities to transfer some of their knowledge of the world to reading.

❧ DIRECTIONS

1. Choose some everyday events to which children can relate. They might include a recent field trip, a walk around the school building, or eating lunch. Select one event, such as eating lunch.

2. Tell children that they have lots of information in their heads that can help them in reading. Have the children close their eyes and picture their lunchroom. Invite them to think of things, people, and food. Have them try to picture what happens when they eat lunch.

3. Ask the children to open their eyes. Write a sentence on the chalkboard such as the following one.

   I saw _____ in the lunchroom.

4. Read the sentence to the class and invite children to offer words that make sense in the sentence. Many words are possible (e.g., names of people and various foods). Reinforce correct responses and suggest some additional words that may or may not make sense (e.g., elephants, chairs, plates, windows, and dad). Invite various children to explain their reasons. For example, a child may say that elephants are too big to fit in the lunchroom. Another child may note that his or her dad has never been to the lunchroom so that doesn't make sense.

5. Transfer the notion of making sense to reading. You might say something like the following. "You have information in your heads that you can use when you read. Reading should make sense. Think of words that make sense when you are reading." Then provide several more sentences and invite children to supply words that make sense or decide if the sentence makes sense. Be sure to have a child explain why a particular sentence does or does not make sense. Some examples follow.

   There is a _____ on the envelope.

   I like to _____ .

   My teacher is wearing a _____ .

   The dog said, "meow."

   We went to the store to buy some kangaroos.

   The game lasted over an hour.

6. Provide other opportunities for children to answer the question, "Does _____ make sense?" Have children explain their answers.

7. For older children, you might want to introduce the term *context*.

PREDICT-SAMPLE-CONFIRM

As children read, they continually use the Predict-Sample-Confirm cycle (Weaver, 1994). When children come to a word they don't know, they make a prediction about the word. While making the prediction, they sample possible words based on the letters of the word, the meaning needed in the sentence, and the type of word that fits the structure of the sentence. From the sampling, children narrow their prediction to a few words. Then children decide which word to try to confirm that prediction, or they change the word. The process of Predict-Sample-Confirm is simultaneous and ongoing. Because this strategy is a key component of reading, it should be explicitly taught to children as in the following example.

DIRECTIONS

1. Tell children that you will be modeling an important strategy that they will be using as they read. Choose a story from a Big Book or a story that children can read and place it on the chalkboard or on chart paper. Cover several of the important words with tape or with sticky notes. A one-sentence example follows.

    When we went to the apple _____ , we saw four types of apple trees.

2. Begin reading the story. When you come to a word that is covered, tell children that you will be making a prediction about the word. Write the word *prediction* on the chalkboard or on chart paper. Ask children for predictions for the covered word. Under the word *prediction,* write the words the children suggested. Explain that when you come to a word you don't know, you make many predictions about what the word could be.

    Predictions

    farm
    orchard
    place
    pie
    yard

3. Tell children that you will choose one of the predicted words to place in the sentence. Choose a word that is not the correct word for the sentence. For example, using the word *farm,* read the sentence to the children.

    When we went to the apple *farm,* we saw four types of apple trees.

4. Tell children that this word may make sense, but you need to confirm its accuracy by looking at the letters of the word. Uncover the first letter in the word *orchard.* Ask children if *farm* could be the correct word and invite a child to explain. Then ask children which word they think fits the sentence based on the first letter. Most children will say the correct word, *orchard.* Explain that if the word didn't fit, you would have to continue predicting more words, sampling the words, and confirming their accuracy.

5. Repeat with additional covered words. Then encourage children to try the Predict-Sample-Confirm strategy while reading independently.

WORD DETECTIVE*

To help children use a variety of strategies to identify unknown words, teach them to become word detectives. Basically, the Word Detective strategy helps children use three cues (sense or context, sounds or phonics, and parts or structural analysis) to help identify unknown words.

1. Introduce the notion of a word detective by dressing in a long coat and a hat and by carrying a magnifying glass. Be creative in your approach. For each of the three cues (i.e., sense, sounds, and parts), develop a visual aid similar to the illustrations below. You may also locate a plastic *brain,* a small *bell,* and a simple *puzzle.*

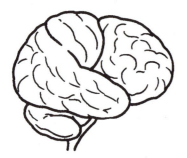 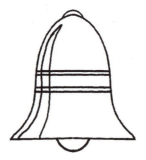 

2. Decide how best to introduce the cues. It is recommended that a different cue be introduced in consecutive lessons and that activities be developed to use the cues in combination. Begin with a cue of your choice and use the basic mode of presentation that is exemplified below for the cue of sense or context.

3. Walk into the classroom dressed in detective attire. Look through your magnifying glass. Invite children to identify who you are (a detective) and what you do (solve mysteries or crimes). Then say something like the following. "You're right! I am a detective. But what you didn't know is that I'm a special kind of detective. I'm a word detective, and I can help you use cues to help figure out or identify unknown words in your reading. Here's the cue I'll share with you today." Hold up a plastic brain or enlarge the illustration of the brain above. You might also prepare a cover for a book titled *Strategies for Young Word Detectives.*

4. Invite children to identify the brain and then explain how they can use their brains to be a word detective. You might say something like the following. "I use my brain when I'm reading to make sure what I read makes sense. If I come to a word I don't know, I use my brain to ask some questions." Invite students to share their ideas and lead them to understand the following strategies. Use examples as appropriate.

    *   I can think about a word that would make sense.

    *   I can say *blank* in place of the unknown word and read to the end of the sentence. Then I can reread the sentence and ask myself, *What word would make sense in the sentence?*

    *   I can read the sentence with the word I put in and ask if it makes sense. (Possible questions might be *Does the word sound right?* or *Is this the way someone might talk?*)

    *   I can look at the pictures or illustrations to get an idea of what the word might be.

---

*Graciously shared by Joan Will, a reading coordinator in West Chicago, Illinois.

5. Tell children that you have some other strategies in your word detective book. In subsequent lessons, introduce strategies for sounds (phonics) and parts (structural analysis). Some of the understandings to develop are presented below. Change the statements as needed to meet the children's needs and to be consistent with your instructional program.

Sounds

- Look at the beginning of the word and make the sound. Ask, "What word begins with that sound and makes sense in the sentence?"
- Put your finger under the word and slowly say the sounds in the word. Then say the sounds faster and try to make a word you have heard before.

Parts

- Look for parts in the word that you know.
- See if the word looks like other words that you know.
- Look for two smaller words that make up the larger word.
- Separate the prefixes and/or suffixes and then try to put the pieces together.

6. Develop classroom charts with the strategies and graphics so children can refer to the cues as needed. Bookmarks with the cues can also be prepared.
7. Refer to the Word Detective strategy throughout the year and add additional strategies as they are taught.

CUE QUESTIONING

As children use cross-checking, they ask themselves questions about the language cues in the sentences. Since most primary-grade children have had limited experience reading independently, they may not know the types of questions to ask. Teaching children about the kinds of questions to ask and providing them with ideas for Cue Questioning will help them as they use cross-checking during reading.

⮞ DIRECTIONS

1. Identify three or four of the questions from the list on page 391 and write them on the chalkboard, a piece of chart paper, or an overhead transparency. Tell children that the questions are ones they should use as they make predictions of words while they read.

2. Ask children to take out their independent reading book and read until they come to a word that is unfamiliar. Give children several minutes to read.

3. Divide the class into groups of two or three children. Tell children that they should ask each other questions about the words. Have one child read a sentence and say "blank" in place of the unknown word. Have the other children in the group ask questions until they can figure out the missing word.

4. Repeat this strategy often using a variety of Cue Questions. Tell children that they should begin asking themselves the same questions when they read and come across an unknown word.

Aa Bb Cc Tips for English Language Learners

- Children who are in various stages of learning English, like all children, will make miscues or errors when they read. Miscues are a natural part of the reading process and should be considered normal. When evaluating the significance of miscues for possible instructional intervention, do not consider dialect differences to be significant. For example, children who speak the Cantonese dialect of Chinese may add an extra syllable to the final sound in a word (e.g., *day offu* for *day off*). Speakers of Spanish may have difficulty pronouncing several English sounds: *d, b, h, m, j, n, ng, r, sh, t, the, v, w, y, z, s*-clusters and end clusters. These examples do not cover the full range of dialect differences; they merely highlight the need for you to be alert and sensitive to pronunciation differences that rarely affect comprehension, so you may ignore them. [For more information see *Dialects in Schools and Communities* (Wolfram, Adger, & Christian, 1999).]

Cue Questions

Questions for Meaning Cues

✓ Did that make sense?

✓ You said _____ . What does that mean?

✓ What would make sense here?

✓ What is happening in the story? Does this word make sense in the story?

Questions for Syntax Cues

✓ Did that sound right?

✓ Can you say it that way?

✓ Would it be correct to say _____ ?

✓ Can you think of a better word that fits?

✓ What word would sound right?

Questions for Visual Cues

✓ Did that look right?

✓ Do you know a word that looks like that?

✓ What do you notice about that word?

✓ Do you notice something familiar about that word?

✓ Do you see a part of the word you know?

Questions for Self-correction

✓ Were you right?

✓ Why did you stop?

✓ What did you notice?

✓ What else could you try?

✓ What else do you know that could help you?

Based on Clay (1993). From Laurie Elish-Piper, Jerry L. Johns, and Susan Davis Lenski, *Teaching Reading Pre-K–Grade 3* (3rd ed.). Copyright © 2006 by Kendall/Hunt Publishing Company (1-800-247-3458, ext. 4). May be reproduced for noncommercial educational purposes.

Activities, tips, & Center Ideas

1. In order for children to be able to use cross-checking strategies, they need to read materials that are at their independent and instructional reading levels. Reading levels change at different rates for different children. Therefore, make frequent assessment decisions about children's reading levels. (See Section 6.4, Assessment Strategy 5, on pages 354–356.)

2. Provide children with many opportunities to read books independently. Young children do not have attention spans that allow for long periods of reading. Therefore, provide children with five to eight minutes to read books at their own reading level at least twice a day.

3. When children read independently, they often choose books that are too difficult. Divide the books in your classroom into reading levels and mark the books with a colored sticker. For example, you might have the easiest books marked with a red sticker, the books that are closer to grade level with a blue sticker, the books at grade level with a green sticker, and the books that are above grade level with an orange sticker.

4. Young children can read many books during an independent reading period because many grade-level books are short with few words. Divide the class into groups of children who read at the same level. Provide each group of children with a small basket of books that are appropriate for the children's reading ability. Tell children that as soon as they finish reading one book they should select another book to read.

5. Create a strategy bookmark for children to use independently. Identify five or six questions from Cue Questioning (see Section 7.1, Teaching Strategy 4) that are most appropriate for the children. Write or print the questions as statements on a bookmark. Give a bookmark to each child in your class and have the children decorate their bookmarks. After bookmarks are decorated, laminate the bookmarks so they are more durable. Give the bookmarks back to the children and tell them that they can use the bookmarks to remind them of cross-checking strategies to use while they are reading independently. A sample bookmark is found on page 394.

6. Tell children that good readers use cross-checking as they read. Model reading an unknown passage. Read it out loud to children, thinking aloud as you come to difficult words. Identify the strategies you use as you read difficult passages.

7. Have children keep a log in which they record unfamiliar words, the context, and the strategies used to pronounce the words and determine their meanings. Provide opportunities for small group sharing.

8. Provide plenty of time for reading, reading, and more reading!

MISTAKES WHILE READING

Dear Families,

- When children read, they make miscues or mistakes. Mistakes are a natural part of reading. For example, a child may read *a* for *the* or *went* for *want*. When your child is reading to you, resist the temptation to correct all your child's mistakes. Instead, ask yourself, "Does the mistake make a change in the meaning?" If the answer is "no," ignore the miscue. You should also know that if your child makes many mistakes while reading, the book being read is probably too difficult. An easy way to judge whether the book is too difficult is to see if your child misses one or more words for every 10 words read (that's 10%). If you count mistakes and get about 10%, help your child choose an easier book.

- There's more to reading than just "sounding it out." To help your child use a variety of strategies to figure out unknown words, cut out the bookmark provided on the next page. Help your child use it to figure out unknown words. Remember not to become worried if your child makes a mistake and it does not significantly change the meaning.

Thanks for your help at home. Your support is important to your child's growth as a reader.

Sincerely,

What's the Word

When I come to a word I don't know . . .

✓ I look at the picture.

✓ I think about the story.

✓ I look at how the word begins.

✓ I get my mouth ready to say the word.

✓ I think about a word I know that has the same sound in it.

✓ I see what I know in the word.

✓ I try a word and see if it makes sense, sounds right, and looks right.

✓ I go back and try again.

section 7.2

Monitoring Reading

Goal: To help children monitor their reading.

Assessment Strategy 2 Monitoring Reading Checklist, page 421

Background

Effective readers monitor their reading to ensure that what they are reading makes sense. One of the keys to becoming an independent reader is the ability to identify and correct one's comprehension problems (Paris, Lipson, & Wixon, 1994). Effective readers ask themselves, "Do I understand what I'm reading?" They also make pictures in their minds, predict from the text, and ask themselves questions as they read. When effective readers detect that what they are reading does not make sense, they realize this and apply appropriate correction or "fix-up" strategies. For example, they may look at pictures, reread to clarify ideas, look up a word in a dictionary, reread for word meaning, or ask for help (Cunningham & Allington, 1998).

Metacognition, or thinking about one's own thinking processes, is an important aspect of monitoring reading (Flavell, 1977). Baker (1991) has identified specific areas that help children develop monitoring strategies for reading. Even young readers can be taught to be on the lookout for the following:

- Words they don't understand.
- Information that doesn't connect with what they already know; and
- Ideas that don't make sense.

While most young children do not automatically monitor their reading, they can be taught simple strategies to help them monitor as they read. The strategies and activities discussed below provide suggestions for teaching children to become active readers who monitor their reading.

CRITTER

The Critter strategy helps children create a visual image to assist them with monitoring their reading (Johns & Lenski, 2005). It serves as a concrete reminder to children that they need to think while they are reading and that their reading should make sense.

DIRECTIONS

1. Draw a cartoon-like Critter and present it to the children on the chalkboard, a piece of chart paper, or an overhead transparency. A sample Critter is shown on the right.

2. Tell children that they can use the Critter to help them think and understand as they read.

3. Ask children to visualize a Critter that they have in their heads that helps them read. Provide time for children to share their ideas.

4. Have children draw and color their Critters.

5. Guide children to develop a list of important questions the Critter can help the children ask themselves as they read. Some possible questions follow.

    - Do I understand what I am reading?

    - What do I already know about the topic?

    - How can I figure out this hard word?

    - Can I use a picture to help me?

    - Do I need to reread?

    - Should I look up the word in a dictionary?

    - Should I ask for help?

6. Laminate the children's Critters and mount them on their desks or reading folders. Post in the classroom the list of questions their Critters can prompt the children to ask themselves. Remind the children to use their Critters to help them think about and understand what they are reading.

MONITORING THINK-ALONG

The Monitoring Think-Along strategy helps children understand the self-monitoring strategies that good readers use. The Monitoring Think-Along can be used to model many different self-monitoring strategies, such as making pictures in your mind, predicting what will come next, asking questions about the text, rereading to clarify ideas, rereading for word meanings, and connecting the text to personal experiences.

DIRECTIONS

1. Select a Big Book or other text that all children will be able to see. Tell children that you are going to show them some strategies that good readers use.

2. Point your index finger to your head to show that you are thinking. Tell children, "I am thinking about what this book might be about."

3. Read the title aloud and, using information from the title, make a comment such as, "That is the name of a girl. I think the story will be about her."

4. Tell the children, "Now, I'll look at the picture on the cover."

5. Make a comment using information from the cover illustration such as, "It looks like a birthday party. I think the book will be about the girl's birthday party."

6. Close your eyes, point your index finger to your head to show you are thinking, and say, "Now I'll try to make a picture in my mind of what might happen at the birthday party." Share with the children some of the things you are visualizing. For example, "I see presents, a chocolate birthday cake, balloons, and lots of children. It looks like everyone is having fun."

7. Begin to read the text aloud. After reading several sentences, stop and ask yourself a question about what you just read. For example, say, "Am I right that the book is about a birthday party? Do I need to change my prediction?" Share your answers with the children.

8. Continue reading the text, stopping periodically to model a monitoring strategy that good readers use. The list below contains possible strategies to model as part of the Monitoring Think-Along.

SELF-MONITORING STRATEGIES

- Make pictures in your mind.
- Predict what will come next.
- Ask questions about the text.
- Reread to clarify ideas.
- Reread for word meanings.
- Connect the text to personal experiences.

Tips for English Language Learners

- Use gestures such as pointing to your head or an actual hat labeled as a thinking cap to clarify that you are sharing thoughts in your head.

- Write the name of the strategy you are using on the chalkboard and display a graphic or icon next to it to clarify its meaning. For example, for rereading, show an arrow pointing back to the beginning of the word.

Section 7.2 **TEACHING STRATEGY** **3**

PAUSE-THINK-RETELL

The Pause-Think-Retell (Robb, 1996) strategy helps children get into the habit of monitoring their comprehension while reading longer texts. This strategy focuses on having children pause at the end of a paragraph, page, or section of text, think about what they have read, and retell the important ideas to themselves. If children are unable to remember enough to retell the text to themselves, they should reread that portion of the text.

DIRECTIONS

1. Select a text that might be challenging for the children. Recopy the text onto chart paper or copy it onto overhead transparencies so all of the children will be able to see it.

2. Tell children that good readers use the Pause-Think-Retell strategy to make sure they understand what they are reading.

3. Model the strategy for children by reading the first paragraph, page, or section of text aloud. Then Pause, point to your head as you Think, and ask yourself, "Can I Retell what I just read?"

4. Retell several of the ideas from the paragraph, page, or section but leave out some important ideas.

5. Tell children, "I think I need to reread that because I can't retell all of the important ideas."

6. Reread the section aloud, emphasizing the important points. Then Pause, point to your head as you Think, and prompt yourself to Retell the important information. Tell children that because you remembered the important ideas from the section, you can go on to the next part of the text. You may also want to remind children how to distinguish among ideas; some are more important than others.

7. Continue modeling this strategy for the next paragraph, page, or section. This time, provide a complete retelling and tell children, "I remembered the important ideas so I can go on to the next part of the book."

8. Continue modeling this strategy for several paragraphs, pages, or sections.

9. Ask children to try the strategy with the next section of the text. Provide prompts such as "Stop and think," "Can you retell what you just read?" and "Did you remember all the important ideas?" to guide them through the process. If children have difficulty distinguishing between important ideas and minor details in their retellings, before conducting further retellings you may want to reteach students how to distinguish minor details from important ideas.

10. Display a poster that has the words Pause-Think-Retell on it. Remind children to use this strategy when they are reading independently.

Tips for English Language Learners

- Encourage English Language Learners to pantomime or draw parts of the retellings they have difficulty verbalizing.
- Provide props to assist English Language Learners do retellings of what they have read. Picture cards with labels can also be used to support retellings for English Language Learners.

Section 7.2   **TEACHING STRATEGY**

MONITORING LOGS

Monitoring Logs allow children to gain insight into how to monitor their independent reading and which monitoring strategies work best in specific situations. When Monitoring Logs are first introduced, the teacher will take on much of the responsibility. Gradually, children will learn to complete the logs on their own.

✎ DIRECTIONS

1. Tell children that good readers monitor their reading. Explain that monitoring means to think about and make sure you are understanding what you are reading. If you are not understanding it, you should go back and try to fix up your understanding.

2. Remind children of fix-up strategies they have learned such as rereading, using picture clues, getting a word meaning, or asking for help. List these on an overhead transparency or write them on the chalkboard or a piece of chart paper.

3. Display a transparency containing a short passage or sentence that may be confusing to the children. Read the passage aloud and think aloud to demonstrate how you handle the difficult text. For example, you could model how to use context to figure out an unknown word by using the following sentence.

   After the dog died, he felt so miserable that he thought he would never stop crying.

   You might say, "If my dog died, I'd cry a lot too. I'd feel so sad. I bet the word *miserable* means sad."

4. Place a transparency containing a page from a Monitoring Log on the overhead projector. Explain to the children that you want to keep track of what strategies you can use to monitor your reading. Fill out the log using the example you just demonstrated.

TITLE	PROBLEM	WHAT I DID	DID IT WORK?
My Dog Sport	I didn't know what miserable meant.	Used context	Yes

5. Tell children that they will be keeping Monitoring Logs. Begin using the Monitoring Logs in conjunction with guided reading groups to provide support for the children. As children begin to understand the process more fully, ask them to add one new entry to their Monitoring Logs at the end of independent reading. Provide time for children to share and discuss their Monitoring Logs with you and their peers.

Monitoring Log

Name _____ Date _____

TITLE	PROBLEM	WHAT I DID	DID IT WORK?

Activities, tips, & Center Ideas

1. Make bookmarks that include monitoring strategies and questions. Provide copies for home and school reading.

2. Develop an I-Need-Help Procedure for children when they realize their reading doesn't make sense and their strategies are not working. Have children copy the I-Need-Help Procedure on the cover of their reading folder or on a bookmark. Also display the I-Need-Help Procedure on a poster in the classroom. A sample I-Need-Help Procedure is listed in the box.

I-NEED-HELP PROCEDURE

1. Think for a minute. Try to solve the problem yourself.

2. Use classroom resources to help you (monitoring log, monitoring posters, World Wall).

3. Ask three students for help.

4. Ask the teacher.

---

3. Explain to the children that good readers create pictures in their minds as they read. Read a passage aloud and ask the children to draw what they saw in their minds. Provide time for the children to share their drawings. Compare their drawings to the text. Explain that good readers create these types of pictures in their minds while they are reading. Read another passage to the children and ask them to close their eyes and visualize a picture in their minds based on the passage. Provide sharing time. Encourage children to use visualization as they read.

4. Have children use partner questioning to support the use of monitoring strategies. Divide the class into partners and have one partner serve as the questioner and the other as the reader. The reader should read a paragraph aloud, and the questioner should ask a question about how the reader monitored his or her reading. For example, the questioner may ask, "Did that make sense to you?" or "Can you retell that in your own words?" or "What did you do when you came to the hard word?" Children can refer to the list of monitoring questions from their Monitoring Logs (Teaching Strategy 4) or the strategy picture cards (Idea 5) to help them with this activity.

5. Use strategy picture cards to provide children with a visual clue regarding the monitoring strategies they can use to help them understand their reading. Post the picture cards in the classroom, provide children with their own copy for their reading folder, and send a copy home for the children and their parents to use for home reading. Sample strategy picture cards are provided on the next page.

Strategy Picture Cards

Does It Make Sense?	What Do You Already Know?
Read On.	Look at Word Parts and Letters.
Reread.	Make a Prediction.
Make a Picture in Your Head.	Retell in Your Own Words.
Look at Picture Clues.	Ask for Help.

This picture makes me think of . . .

In this story, the . . .

Try 3; then ask me for
HELP!

CHECKING UNDERSTANDING

Dear Families,

Good readers use a variety of strategies to monitor their reading to make sure they understand what they are reading. Use this bookmark to prompt your child to use monitoring strategies when you are reading together. Be sure to provide at least five seconds of "thinking time" before prompting your child.

Enjoy your reading!

Sincerely,

Does it make sense?

What do you already know?

Look at word parts and letters.

Make a prediction.

Read on. ⟶

Reread. ⟵

Make a picture in your head.

Look at picture clues.

Retell in your own words.

In this story, the . . .

Engaging with Texts

Goal: To help children become actively involved in reading.

Background

When children are engaged in their reading, they can become so interested in the text that time is meaningless. Engagement is key to reading; in fact, how engaged children are in reading is a key component of reading achievement. There are many ways that teachers can engage children in reading. One of the primary ways is to involve children in thinking, predicting, and connecting activities. A variety of strategies and ideas follow that engage children in reading.

Section 7.3 **TEACHING STRATEGY** *1*

DIRECTED READING-THINKING ACTIVITY (DR-TA)

The Directed Reading-Thinking Activity (DR-TA) (Stauffer, 1969) is a strategy that mirrors the thinking processes good readers use as they construct meaning from texts. The DR-TA can be applied to fiction and nonfiction. The strategy encourages making predictions and monitoring reading comprehension.

DIRECTIONS

1. Select a story or a passage to read aloud to the children. Read the title aloud. Then ask the children to predict the contents of the story by saying, "What do you think the story will be about and why?" Encourage children to suggest many ideas.

2. Read the first few paragraphs or pages. Stop reading after you have introduced a few ideas or events. Ask children to monitor their comprehension by saying, "What just happened in the story?" Tie in their predictions about the title of the story by asking, "Was your first prediction about the story correct?" Allow children time to think; then have them volunteer their answers. If children give a misinterpretation, you may choose to correct them, or you may decide to reread the passage and ask again.

3. After children have a clear understanding of the story thus far, encourage predictions by asking them the following question, "What do you think will happen next?" Allow children to predict many options. After each prediction, ask the follow-up question, "Why do you think so?"

4. After children have made several predictions, tell children that you will continue to read the story and that they should listen to find out if their predictions were correct.

5. Read several more paragraphs or pages. Stop once more and ask children to monitor their comprehension and to make predictions. Use the same questions you asked previously. Allow children time to discuss the story thus far and make additional predictions.

6. Read the rest of the story and ask children to retell the entire story. You may choose to have children retell the story to a partner, to you, or by writing in their journals.

7. Repeat the DR-TA questions frequently to encourage children to ask the same questions as they read independently. Also, use the DR-TA during guided reading lessons. The basic DR-TA questions are listed below.

DR-TA QUESTIONS

What do you think the story will be about? Why do you think so?
What just happened?
What do you think will happen next? Why do you think so?

Section 7.3 **TEACHING STRATEGY** **2**

THINK ALOUD

Since reading comprehension is an internal act, some children have difficulty understanding what you mean when you say, "Make a prediction," or ask "What was the main idea?" Children often do not know the meaning of the language we use in schools (Johns, 1980). To help them understand the meaning of abstract strategies, conduct a Think Aloud. When you conduct a Think Aloud, children are able to understand better how to use comprehension strategies when reading.

DIRECTIONS

1. Select a passage from an informational book or article that contains a few sentences that may be difficult for the children. For example, you might select the following passage from *Earthquakes* by Franklyn M. Branley (1990).

    Large sections of the Earth's crust are always moving. Sometimes two sections push against each other. The place where they meet is called a fault (p. 16).

2. Display the passage on an overhead transparency. Read the passage aloud to the children.

3. Think aloud to model how to deal with the vocabulary word *fault,* which has another more common meaning. You may say, "The word *fault* sounds funny here. I know what fault means. It means you did something and you are responsible for it, but I don't know how fault fits with a book on earthquakes. I think I better reread the section to see if I can find clues to what fault means here." Reread the passage aloud. Think aloud by saying, "It says a fault is where they meet. Since they are talking about sections of the Earth's crust, that must be what a fault is. It sounds like a crack. I bet another word for fault is crack. I can look at the picture in the book to see if it looks like a crack."

4. Explain to children that they can use strategies such as rereading and using pictures to help them with difficult words when reading.

5. Engage in Think Alouds on a regular basis so children can understand how to use strategies in real reading situations.

6. Some important reading strategies and Think Aloud prompts are provided in the following table.

Think Alouds

STRATEGY	THINK ALOUD PROMPTS
Previewing	When I look over this passage, I can see . . . The pictures tell me that . . .
Accessing background knowledge	I know some things about . . . This story reminds me of . . .
Setting a purpose	I want to find out about . . . I'm reading this because . . .
Predicting	From the title I can tell . . . I think . . . will happen next because . . .
Visualizing	The picture I have in my mind is . . .
Identifying new words	If I use the other words in the sentence, this word must be . . . What parts of the word do I know?
Thinking through a confusing point	This might mean . . . I'm not sure I understand this because . . .
Checking for understanding	So far, this story is about . . . The important parts so far are . . .
Using fix-up strategies	I need to reread the part about . . . I need help with . . .
Summarizing the story	The story was about . . . The story means . . .

PROVE-IT PROMPTS

Children become engaged in reading when they have to predict and justify their predictions. One way to help children engage in reading is through Prove-It Prompts (May, 2006). This strategy asks children to make predictions before reading, to provide a rationale for their predictions, and to evaluate the validity of their predictions after reading.

DIRECTIONS

1. Select a book or story that lends itself to making predictions, such as the book *It's Okay to Be Different* (Parr, 2001). Many other books would also be good to model Prove-It Prompts.

2. Show children the cover of the book. Remind children that they have previously learned how to make predictions before reading. Write the word *prediction* on the chalkboard. Ask children what it means to make predictions. You might say something like the following.

   Before I read, I try to guess what the book will be about. That's called making predictions. You know what it means to predict the weather, don't you? [Encourage children to discuss their knowledge about weather prediction.] Forecasters predict the weather because they are not certain what they weather will be like. They are making guesses, but those guesses are based on information they know. For example, before a weather forecaster would predict snow, it would have to be cold outside. When you read, you also make predictions based on things you already know.

3. Duplicate and distribute the Prove-It Prompts Sheet on page 411. Read the title of the strategy to children and tell them that they will have to "prove" their predictions. Ask children if they know what it means to prove something. Provide enough time to discuss a variety of answers and contribute your own knowledge of the word. A sample classroom discussion follows.

Teacher:	If you told your friend that you could throw a baseball from home plate to first base and he said, "Prove it," what would that mean?
Student:	That would mean he would have to actually do it.
Teacher:	What else could it mean?
Student:	Maybe that someone else saw him.
Teacher:	What does it mean to prove something.
Student:	To show it.
Teacher:	In reading you can prove things too. Today you're going to prove your predictions. What do you think that means?
Student:	To explain why a prediction is true.

4. Show children the cover of a book that is new to them and read the title. In the book, *It's Okay to Be Different,* the cover shows a yellow face with green hair, a blue face with purple hair, a green face with red antennae, and a yellow face with a purple bow. Ask children to make predictions about the book. Have children write their predictions on the first blanks. Have children talk about their predictions.

5. Tell children that they need to have good reasons for their predictions. Encourage children to talk about the reasons for their predictions and have them write the predictions in the second group of lines.

6. Read the book to children. After reading, ask children to discuss the predictions that were correct and the ones that were not. Have children discuss parts of the book that "proved" their predictions were correct. A sample classroom discussion follows.

Teacher: What predictions were right?

Student: I predicted that it would be OK to be short.

Teacher: What happened in the book to make that prediction correct?

Student: The book had a page that said it's OK to be small, medium, large, and extra large.

Teacher: Yes, that proves that your prediction was correct.

7. Help children understand that the predictions they make should be based on information. Encourage children to become engaged in reading by making and proving their predictions.

Prove-It Prompts

Name _____ Date _____

Pages _____ to _____

BEFORE YOU READ: What do you think this section will be about?

_____

_____

_____

_____

Why do you think so?

_____

_____

_____

_____

AFTER YOU READ: Prove you were right or wrong.

_____

_____

_____

_____

TALKING DRAWING

Talking Drawing (Wood & Taylor, 2006) is a strategy that engages children by encouraging them to create mental images of a story before and after reading. When children create mental images, they visualize what they are reading and improve their comprehension. Talking Drawing is one of the many strategies that teachers can use to help children visualize when they read. Zeigler and Johns (2005) provide many additional visualization strategies.

DIRECTIONS

1. Select a story or book that is appropriate for visualization, or creating mental images of the reading. One book that works well is *Diary of a Wombat* (French, 2002), but many other books could be used to model the strategy Talking Drawing.

2. Read the title of the story to children and show them the cover. Then ask children to make a picture in their minds of what they think will happen in the story. Some children might have difficulty knowing what you mean. If that is the case, say something like the following.

   When you read, you should make pictures in your mind, just like a movie. You should try to imagine what the characters look like and what they do. In this story, you will be picturing a wombat. I didn't really know what a wombat was until I read the story, so maybe you don't know what a wombat looks like. You can see from the cover of the book that a wombat looks something like a small bear. Now think of what a wombat might do during the day to write in his diary.

3. Duplicate and distribute the Talking Drawing reproducible on page 413. Ask children to draw a picture of what they think will happen in *Diary of a Wombat*. Remind children that there are many good ways to think about the story and that there is not one correct answer.

4. Have children share their drawings with each other. You might consider posting some of the drawings in a public place so that children can see how others have imagined the story.

5. Read the story to the class, showing the pictures. After reading, have children draw a picture of something they heard in the story or something they learned. You might say something like the following.

   Before I read the *Diary of a Wombat* to you, you drew pictures of what you imagined would be in the story. Now you have heard the story. What kinds of things happened to the wombat? Now draw what you have heard.

6. Tell children that what we imagined would be in the story before reading is different from what actually occurs. Have children compare the pictures they drew before reading with the pictures they drew after reading. Discuss the differences.

7. Encourage children to become engaged in reading by visualizing what they have read. Use the strategy Talking Drawing on a consistent basis so that children become accustomed to creating mental images as they read.

Name _____ Date _____

Talking Drawing

Title _____

Before reading: Draw a picture of something you think will happen in the story.

```
┌─────────────────────────────────────────────────────────┐
│                                                           │
│                                                           │
│                                                           │
│                                                           │
│                                                           │
│                                                           │
│                                                           │
└─────────────────────────────────────────────────────────┘
```

After reading: Draw a picture of something that did happen in the story.

```
┌─────────────────────────────────────────────────────────┐
│                                                           │
│                                                           │
│                                                           │
│                                                           │
│                                                           │
│                                                           │
└─────────────────────────────────────────────────────────┘
```

How did your picture change from before reading to after reading?

_____

_____

_____

_____

MAKING CONNECTIONS

Children can enhance their comprehension by making connections from what they are reading to their own experiences, prior knowledge, or other texts with which they are familiar. The Making Connections strategy helps children understand and remember what they are reading by making it personally meaningful. This strategy works well with both fiction and informational text.

DIRECTIONS

1. Introduce the Making Connections strategy to students by explaining how important it is for readers to connect what they are reading to their own experiences, what they already know, and other books they have read or stories they know.

2. Select a story that the children will be able to relate to and read it aloud to them. For example, you might select *Chrysanthemum* by Kevin Henkes (1991). In this story, Chrysanthemum loves her name until the other mice at her school begin to tease her. When a very special substitute teacher tells her how much she loves her name, Chrysanthemum is thrilled and all of her schoolmates want to change their names to flowers, too.

3. Display the Making Connections sheet on the overhead transparency, chalkboard, or chart paper. Explain to the children that you want them to think of a connection the story has to their own lives. If the children are unsure, you may share one of your own connections such as, "When I was younger, a boy at school teased me because I was the tallest one in the class. It made me feel sad and embarrassed." Provide time for children to share their connections to self.

4. Direct the children's attention to the next column: connections to the world. Ask the children what connections they can think of between the story and something else in life and the world. If children have difficulty making a connection, you may share one of your own connections such as, "Chrysanthemum is such an interesting name. I think it is interesting to find out how people and places get their names. I learned that our town is named after the first family that lived here."

5. Direct the children's attention to the next column: connections to other texts. Ask the children what other books, stories, poems, movies, television programs, or other texts the story makes them think of. Invite them to share their reasons.

6. A blank Making Text Connections chart is provided on page 414.

Making Connections

Name _____ Date _____

Title _____

TEXT TO SELF	TEXT TO WORLD	TEXT TO TEXT

Activities, tips, & Center Ideas

1. Help children stay engaged when you read aloud by reading the title of a book or story and having children brainstorm possible words that they might encounter during reading. Encourage children to listen for those words as you read the book or story aloud. Ask children to remember at least one word that you brainstormed before reading that was also in the story.

2. Help children understand some of the purposes for reading so that they know why they are reading. Tell children that there are many reasons to read: for fun, for information, to learn, to become immersed in a story, and so on. Secure a variety of reading materials and place them on a table. Find materials that are familiar to children such as a telephone book, newspaper advertisements, picture books, textbooks, and so on. Talk about the different purposes that readers have for reading each of the texts. As children become involved in setting purposes to read, they become more engaged in reading.

3. Use Book Talks (Johns & Lenski, 2005) to encourage children to read various books. A Book Talk is a brief talk about a book with the purpose of enticing others to read it. Select three or four books each week to describe to children. Tell children about the book and then have it available for children to read.

4. Help children make connections during reading by having a Book Connections Chart. Develop a bulletin board with a place for connections to other books. When reading a book aloud, have children think of connections they could make to other books. When children have a connection, encourage them to write the title of that book on the chart. Leave the chart up in the room so that all of the children remember to make connections during reading.

5. Make sure children have enough time to think during reading. Some children need more time than others, so regularly provide enough quiet time for children to think before they talk about their reading.

PAUSE-THINK-RETELL

Dear Families,

Your children have learned the Pause-Think-Retell strategy at school. Please use this strategy with your child after reading a book or watching a television program. The steps are outlined in the box below.

> ### Pause-Think-Retell
>
> **PAUSE:** Stop near the middle of the story or television program.
> **THINK:** Think what it has been about so far.
> **RETELL:** Tell about the important parts so far.

As your child uses this strategy, his or her reading will improve. Please help your child use this strategy often!

Sincerely,

Assessments of Strategic Reading

Goal: To assess the child's use of reading strategies and monitoring strategies.

ASSESSMENT CHAPTER 7

Background

Teachers can learn a great deal about children's oral reading and monitoring strategies through ongoing observation, often called "kid watching" (Goodman, 1982). The assessment strategies in this section are designed to give you insights about children's reading in the context of real reading. The results of the assessments can help you plan more responsive instruction to support children's reading progress.

ORAL READING MISCUE ANALYSIS

OVERVIEW	When children read orally, you have the opportunity to note their miscues and make observations about their reading strategies. There are several ways to gather such information. You can use the graded passages found in Section 6.4, Assessment Strategy 5, an informal reading inventory (Johns, 2005), or instructional materials from your classroom. Oral Reading Miscue Analysis is similar to Assessment Strategy 3 (Words Per Minute) described in Chapter 4 (pages 226–228).
MATERIALS NEEDED	1. Select one or more reading passages at the child's instructional level. Passages from the pre-primer through the third-grade level can be found on pages 357–380. Additional passages at these and higher levels are available in the *Basic Reading Inventory* (Johns, 2005). You can also use passages from the materials you use for instruction. 2. See pages 357–380 for the copies of the passages from pre-primer through third-grade level. If you decide to use running records, you could use a blank sheet of paper and make a check mark for each word read correctly and note the specific miscues (e.g., substitutions, omissions) and other behaviors such as repetitions and word-by-word reading. 3. Use a stopwatch or a watch with a second hand.
PROCEDURES	1. Invite the child to read the passage you have selected. You might say, "I would like you to read this passage to me. When you have finished reading, I'll ask you some questions (or I'd like you to tell me about what you've read)." When the child begins reading, begin timing with a stopwatch or watch with a second hand. 2. Note any miscues the child makes while reading. In addition, make notations that indicate phrasing and repetitions. Numerous marking systems are available (e.g., Johns, 2005), but you may find the one below easy to use. You may also use your own system.

Marking	Meaning of Marking	Marking	Meaning of Marking
man men	Substitution	m— men	Partial Pronunciation
man s/c men	Self-correction	men	Repeated word
~~men~~	Omitted word	small ^men	Insertion
		the/small	Pause

3. When the child finishes reading, note the number of seconds that elapsed and ask the comprehension questions or invite a retelling. The teacher's copies of the passages and questions on the CD-ROM have provisions for easy notations and record keeping.

SCORING AND INTERPRETATION

Quantitative scores for reading rate, word recognition, and comprehension can be obtained using the procedure described for Assessment Strategy 5 in Section 6.4. Because the focus of Assessment Strategy 1 is related to fluency, you should pay particular attention to reading rate and miscue analysis.

Reading rate can be determined by inserting the seconds required for reading as the divisor at the bottom of the teacher's record sheet for each graded passage. Perform the necessary division. The resulting numeral will be an estimate of the child's rate in words per minute (WPM). An example of this procedure is shown below.

$$
\begin{array}{r}
85.7 \text{ WPM} \\
70\overline{)6000} \\
\underline{560} \\
400 \\
\underline{350} \\
500
\end{array}
$$

For additional information, refer to Assessment Strategy 3 in Chapter 4. You will also find norms tables for possible use. The following questions and comments may provide assistance in formulating ideas for instruction.

- *Does the child read quite accurately but have a slow rate of reading in words per minute?* If the reading is accurate but slow, you will probably want to provide more opportunities for the child to read easy materials and participate in a variety of activities that focus on rereading.
- *Does the child read accurately but in a word-by-word fashion?* The above ideas should be useful. In addition, you can mark phrase boundaries in passages by making light slash marks with a pencil to help the child see how to group words (e.g., the small cat/was sleeping/under the big tree). You could also model phrasing by reading aloud the passage while the child follows. Then have the child model your reading. Read-along audiotapes of favorite books and stories can also be used.
- *Does the child make a number of miscues and read fast (or slow)?* Analyze the nature of the child's miscues. Miscue analysis can be done informally to get insights into the child's general reading strategies and the impact that those strategies can have on fluency and comprehension. Some of the behaviors to look for are related to the following questions. The answers to these questions suggest strategies for instruction.

(continued)

- *Are the child's miscues numerous with no particular pattern?* Many miscues suggest that the reading material may be too difficult. Consider using easier materials for instruction and recreational reading.
- *Is the child's reading generally accurate but characterized by numerous repetitions?* The repetitions may be due mostly to habit. Tape-record the child's reading and have the child listen and comment. Ask the child why he or she repeats so often. Use the child's response to help plan appropriate instruction. Also, as long as the child's comprehension is satisfactory, encourage the child to reduce the repetitions.
- *Is the child's reading characterized by sounding out many words, which reduces fluency?* The child may be overreliant on phonics. Help the child strengthen his or her sight vocabulary and teach how context can be used to help anticipate words. If phonics is the dominant mode of initial instruction, such behavior may be considered normal for some time until the child gains sight words. Be alert for children who seem to be "stuck" on phonics when other children seem to be adding words to their sight vocabularies. Remember to teach a combination of cue systems for word identification and cross-checking. Teaching Strategy 3 (Word Detective) in section 1 of this chapter may be especially helpful.
- *Is the child's reading characterized by a moderate or fast rate and numerous miscues that significantly distort the meaning?* Such reading may seriously impact the child's ability to comprehend the material. You may need to use examples of the child's miscues that distort the meaning to help teach the importance of rereading when the passage doesn't make sense. Teaching the child to use phonics and context as cross-checking strategies may be helpful. Also help the child monitor whether the passage is making sense. Questions like "Am I understanding?" and "Does what I'm reading make sense?" may be used. You may also want to help the child expand his or her sight vocabulary.
- *Is the child's reading characterized by a slow rate and numerous miscues?* Such behavior may be a strong indication that the reading materials are too difficult. Use easier materials. You can also study the nature of the child's miscues to gain insights into the word-identification skills that need to be taught. You may need to teach certain consonant and vowel sounds. If many high-frequency words are unknown (see the Revised Dolch List on page 175), help the child learn those words.

Additional Ways of Assessing Cross-Checking

1. Observe the child's reading to see if a variety of cues are being used (phonics, meaning, language, and background knowledge). Use evidence gathered over time to make your instruction responsive to the child's needs.
2. Invite children to share the strategies they use to identify unknown words. Their sharing can often lead to additional strategies that you will want to teach. Be sure you teach the various cueing systems.

MONITORING READING CHECKLIST

OVERVIEW	You can learn a great deal about a child's use of monitoring strategies through individual reading conferences. This assessment will help you determine which monitoring strategies a child is using when reading as well as which ones you will need to model and instruct the child on in the future.
MATERIALS NEEDED	1. Appropriate book for the child (either fiction or nonfiction is acceptable) 2. A copy of the Monitoring Strategies Checklist Record Sheet (page 422)
PROCEDURES	1. Select a book that is at the child's instructional level. 2. Tell the child, "I want you to read the story aloud. After you are done, I'm going to ask you what strategies you used as a reader." Use the Monitoring Strategies Checklist Record Sheet (page 422). 3. After the child reads the story (or part of it) aloud, ask the child what he or she did before reading. Circle *yes* for the Strategies the child reports using and *no* for those the child does not use. 4. Ask the child what he or she did during reading to make sure the story made sense. Circle *yes* for the strategies the child reports using and *no* for those the child does not use. 5. Ask the child what he or she would typically do after reading the story. Circle *yes* for the strategies the child reports using and *no* for those the child does not use.
SCORING AND INTERPRETATION	Place a ✓ next to the strategies the child reports using. Also, mark any of the strategies you observed the child using that he or she did not report. Based on findings from this assessment, you can determine which monitoring strategies the student needs to learn and apply.

Monitoring Strategies Checklist

Name _____ Date _____

Book _____

Before reading did you:

Think about the title and cover?	Yes	No
Make predictions?	Yes	No
Think about what you already know about the topic?	Yes	No

Notes:

During reading did you:

Ask yourself if the reading made sense?	Yes	No
Pause-Think-Retell?	Yes	No
Make pictures in your mind?	Yes	No
Use strategies to figure out hard words? If yes, what did you do?	Yes	No
Reread to help yourself understand?	Yes	No
Use pictures for clues?	Yes	No
Ask yourself questions?	Yes	No

Notes:

After reading do you usually:

Retell the story?	Yes	No
Think about what you read?	Yes	No
Share what you learned with someone?	Yes	No
Think about what strategies you used to help you read?	Yes	No

Notes:

From Laurie Elish-Piper, Jerry L. Johns, and Susan Davis Lenski, *Teaching Reading Pre-K–Grade 3* (3rd ed.). Copyright © 2006 by Kendall/Hunt Publishing Company (1-800-247-3458, ext. 4). May be reproduced for noncommercial educational purposes.

chapter *eight*

8

Differentiating Reading Instruction

Paula A. Helberg

A typical Pre-K through grade 3 classroom contains children who learned to read before they entered school alongside children struggling to learn the letters of the alphabet. Children with astounding verbal abilities are in the same classroom with children who have difficulty carrying on a conversation. It is the daunting, exciting task for the teacher to meet these children at their varying literacy levels and help each child reach his or her potential. In a differentiated classroom, teachers meet each child's literacy needs in a trusting, supportive, and flexible environment.

Physical Space in a Differentiated Classroom

Before the bell rings for the first day of school, teachers can arrange classrooms with differentiation in mind. In a Pre-K, kindergarten, or first-grade classroom, learning stations may be arranged along the sides of the room. For older children, a leveled classroom library with easy access is essential. A visible daily schedule, with morning message, helps children anticipate their day. A space for small group work is needed, along with space where the class can gather together as a whole. Include a place for children to get supplies and turn in finished work. If you find it difficult to visualize how you might set up your classroom, visit other rooms to gather ideas. Remember, too, that you may start the room with the furniture in one arrangement, but you can always change it as needed. Following is an arrangement to start you thinking about classroom organization.

Organization of Classroom

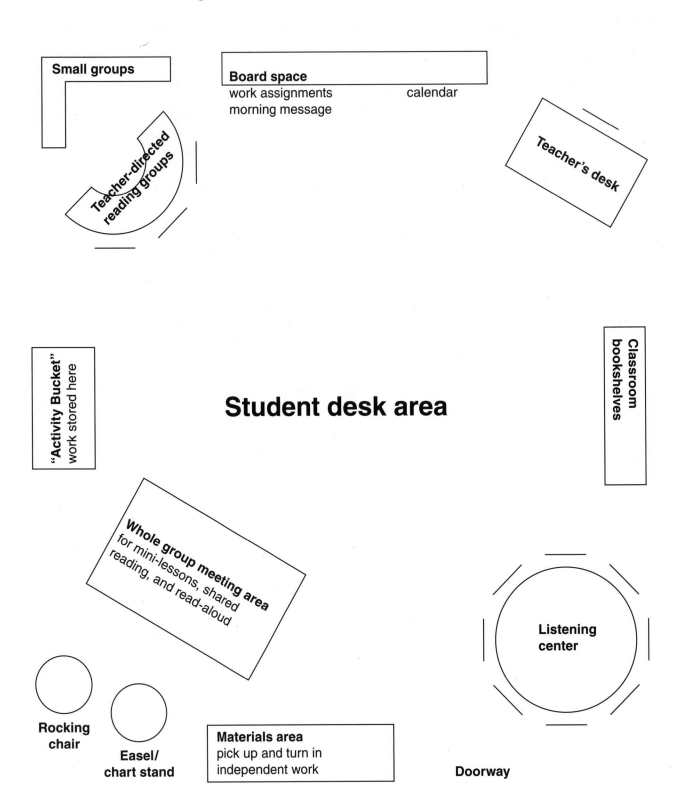

Small groups

Teacher-directed reading groups

Board space
work assignments   calendar
morning message

Teacher's desk

"Activity Bucket" work stored here

Student desk area

Classroom bookshelves

Whole group meeting area
for mini-lessons, shared reading, and read-aloud

Listening center

Rocking chair

Easel/ chart stand

Materials area
pick up and turn in independent work

Doorway

Getting to Know Your Children

From the first day of school until the last, you will continue to learn about your children. Differentiating instruction for them may be as simple as including books about dinosaurs in your classroom library because you know that some of the children are interested in the topic. On the other hand, it can be as difficult as moving children into instructional level reading groups based on their ability when they enter your classroom. The assessment strategies provided in each chapter in this book will be valuable in helping you get to know the children in your classroom. The attitude and interest surveys (section 1.3) will help you collect books for your library that are interesting to your children. Informal reading inventories and running records (section 6.4) will give you information regarding reading levels to assist you in forming your instructional level reading groups. Remember that the assessment strategies included in this book can be used for both formative and summative assessments. For the most part, you will be interested in formative assessments: information that tells you how well the children are learning and how you might alter your instruction to meet each child's needs. Summative assessment is "end-of" information: end of unit, end of school year. This type of assessment informs you of children's sum of learning and can be used to inform parents and perhaps the next-year teacher as well (Harris & Hodges, 1995).

Creating a Positive Classroom Climate

While you may be anxious to begin differentiated instruction on the very first day of school (and interested parents may wish this as well), it is important to remember that differentiation works when children know and understand classroom routines (Tomlinson, 2003). Because differentiation requires that children work independently at times, modeling and practicing independent behaviors is essential. For example, if you expect that children will be reading independently during some portion of your literacy block, make modeling this task one of your earliest lessons. It may sound something like the sharing below.

Teacher: Children, today we are going to practice what you will be doing during independent reading. We are going to talk about what this time will look like and what it will sound like. We will talk about what you should do if you have a problem selecting a book and what you should do if you need help during this time. Now, can anyone tell me what 'independent reading' means?"

Child 1: It means you are reading by yourself.

Teacher: Yes, it means you are reading by yourself. Can anyone else add more?

Child 2: You are reading silently.

Teacher: Reading quietly is important because you will all be reading different books. Let me show you what that looks like. *At this point the teacher picks up a book and begins reading. Later, she whispers a bit to herself, and at another point she appears to be re-reading.* Did you notice what that looked like? Did you notice what that sounded like? One part of the book felt a little bit hard, so I read that part in a whisper-voice. I tried not to disturb my neighbors. After I read that part, I needed to read it again to help me understand. Did you notice that I was really reading? I wasn't looking around the room at what everyone else was doing. Now, can anyone tell me what kind of book is a good book for independent reading?

Child 3: A book that is comfortable to read.

Teacher: Exactly! When I read for fun, I don't like to read my husband's complicated science books, because that's not fun for me. All of us will be reading books at different levels, and that's okay. We are all going to become better readers this year, and the way we will do that is by choosing books that are at our level right now. By the end of this year, we will all be reading harder books, and I might even try a difficult book.

Now, we will talk about what to do if you have finished the book you are working on. It is your job to quickly find two more books at your level. Bring those books to your desk to try them. Be sure to bring two books to your desk, in case you don't like the first one. The most important thing to remember is that you need to read during this time, not look for books. It is always a good idea to have two books with you so you always have something to read.

If you need help, and I am working with other children, try to solve the problem by quietly asking someone near you. If that doesn't work, you may come near me and stand quietly until I speak to you. If you have an emergency, and that means that you are sick or hurt, you may interrupt me. Otherwise, I expect you to be considerate of the time I spend with your classmates.

After this explanation, spend the next few minutes having the children practice independent reading while you offer specific praise with regard to appropriate behaviors. If desired, you can then call all the children together to record what they saw and heard during independent reading time. This chart can serve as a reminder of appropriate behavior. Children in Pre-K, kindergarten, and beginning first grade can participate in independent reading time even though they may not be reading in a conventional way. You can teach them proper book handling technique as well as ways to interact with text without reading every word.

SAMPLE CHART FOR INDEPENDENT READING

WHAT IT LOOKS LIKE	WHAT IT SOUNDS LIKE
Children are seated, or quietly looking for books.	The room is very quiet.
Children are reading books that are not too hard.	Books that are not too hard are fun to read, so children may whisper some words or laugh quietly at the funny parts.
The teacher is working with one child or a small group of children.	The teacher is teaching, and children in the group are discussing books.
Children are working on their own while the teacher works with groups.	Children quietly ask a neighbor if they have a question.

Time spent modeling and practicing appropriate behaviors will pay dividends in increased instructional time throughout the school year. For every desired behavior in your classroom, consider modeling and practicing. For example, if children spend time at a listening station, model everything from how to put on the headphones to adjusting the volume on the recorder. Always show children how to put the materials in the proper place so that the next group can find them.

Differentiation During the Literacy Block

In many schools, time is set aside for literacy activities in what is sometimes called the literacy block. Very often, this time begins with a mini-lesson, a short lesson given to the whole group. Comprehension strategy lessons are a great fit for mini-lessons, because all children, regardless of reading level, can benefit from instruction in comprehension. The Pause-Think-Retell strategy lesson in section 7.2 is an example of a whole-group lesson. After the mini-lesson, the teacher explains to the group any work that needs to be completed independently during the literacy block. If possible, a sample should be available for children who may need help to complete this task. Even Pre-K and kindergarten children can learn to complete one or two simple tasks independently. As soon as the children have begun their work, you can begin to call small groups for instruction, or the children can begin their work at learning stations.

It is within these small groups that focused instruction takes place at children's instructional level, as determined by your assessment. Children should know about 95% of the words they encounter in instructional level text (Johns, 2005). This blend of a few unknowns among known words in text offers children the support they need with enough challenge to learn new skills and strategies. This time is often called guided reading, because the children will be learning new strategies and continuing to practice strategies as you coach them. You may have also heard the term "scaffolding," which refers to the variety of supports you offer to children as they learn to use strategies on their own. The idea that children can learn at a level above their current functioning as long as they have coaching from a capable adult or peer is supported by research (Vygotsky, 1978).

Sometimes teachers struggle to determine how many instructional level groups they will need. You may be familiar with the traditional, three reading group plan where one group works above grade level, one group works at grade level, and one group works below grade level. While this may work for you, it is likely that it will not. You may have one or two children who are functioning at a much lower level than the rest. These children deserve instruction at their current level, with the goal of helping them read grade level texts. You may also have a small group of children whose reading level is more than one grade level above average. These children also deserve instruction at their level, and they need to learn something new each day. The number of reading groups you need will depend on the makeup of your class, and this number may change over the course of the school year.

Designing the Daily Schedule

A literacy block model is an effective way to include guided reading and independent reading into your daily schedule. As you can see in the illustration on the next page, Mrs. Hansen has divided her second-grade class into five reading groups. Every day, she expects her children to read independently. Since she has modeled this activity, all the children are actively reading during part of the morning. In a mini-lesson, Mrs. Hansen reads a story aloud, teaches a reading skill, or models a comprehension strategy. In another part of the literacy block, the children write a response to the story, or they practice the strategy or skill taught in the mini-lesson. Mrs. Hansen selects three groups to receive a guided reading lesson each day. The other two groups complete independent work or use an activity bucket on days they do not have guided reading. The activity bucket could contain an audio tape and copies of a book for a listening station. It could also contain a Scrambled Text activity (section 2.3), a Making Words activity (section 3.3), or a Reader's Theater script for the group to practice together (section 4.2). Notice that the "red" group on the Literacy Schedule receives guided reading on Tuesday, Wednesday, and Thursday. Knowing that most days off are Mondays and Fridays, Mrs. Hansen plans to work with children who struggle in the middle part of the week. In addition to this schedule, Mrs. Hansen puts another schedule on the board. Each child's name is listed along with his or her group members. The expectations for the literacy block are clear.

Differentiation for Children Who Struggle

It is almost certain that some children in your class will find reading difficult. Whatever the reason, you can offer children what they need most: time. Allington (2001) found that children who struggle need to spend more time reading than others. Stanovich (1986) described what he called the "Matthew Effect," a phenomenon where the best readers tended to read more and got better at reading as a result. The struggling readers, on the other hand, spent less time reading and had less chance to improve. While children who struggle in reading may benefit from some skill work, such as word sorts and sight word practice, remember that what they need most is to read words in real books (Allington, 2001).

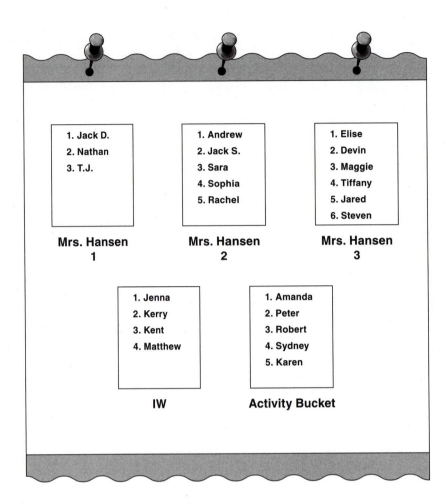

1. Jack D. 2. Nathan 3. T.J.	1. Andrew 2. Jack S. 3. Sara 4. Sophia 5. Rachel	1. Elise 2. Devin 3. Maggie 4. Tiffany 5. Jared 6. Steven
Mrs. Hansen **1**	**Mrs. Hansen** **2**	**Mrs. Hansen** **3**

1. Jenna 2. Kerry 3. Kent 4. Matthew	1. Amanda 2. Peter 3. Robert 4. Sydney 5. Karen
IW	**Activity Bucket**

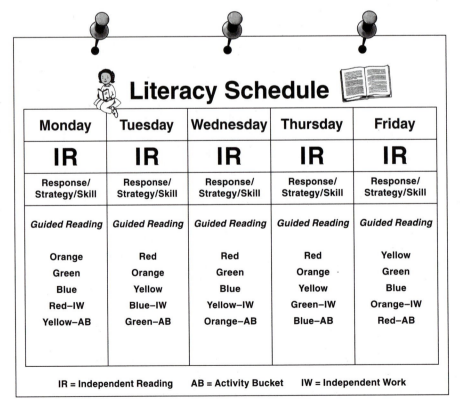

Literacy Schedule

Monday	Tuesday	Wednesday	Thursday	Friday
IR	**IR**	**IR**	**IR**	**IR**
Response/ Strategy/Skill	Response/ Strategy/Skill	Response/ Strategy/Skill	Response/ Strategy/Skill	Response/ Strategy/Skill
Guided Reading	*Guided Reading*	*Guided Reading*	*Guided Reading*	*Guided Reading*
Orange Green Blue Red–IW Yellow–AB	Red Orange Yellow Blue–IW Green–AB	Red Green Blue Yellow–IW Orange–AB	Red Orange Yellow Green–IW Blue–AB	Yellow Green Blue Orange–IW Red–AB

IR = Independent Reading   AB = Activity Bucket   IW = Independent Work

To gain extra reading time for readers who struggle, look for resources within your school. Some of your children may work with a reading specialist, Reading Recovery teacher, or Title I teacher. These programs should not be a replacement for high-quality reading instruction in your classroom. If need be, reduce some of the independent work required of your neediest children so that they can have two reading groups a day instead of one. Enlist parent volunteers if possible to give additional practice opportunities to these children. If you do find willing volunteers, don't expect them to instruct your children. Provide easy practice materials for the volunteer to read with them.

Many parents will ask how they can help at home. Home is a great place for children to practice reading books they have already read at school. Again, don't ask parents to instruct, and don't send home difficult books. Home reading should be supportive and help develop a daily reading habit. If a child needs practice with basic sight words, some parents have found it convenient to keep a set of words on a ring, and keep the set in the car. Many families are on the go after school, and a readily available set of cards is great for practice during down times. See Chapter 4 for examples of sight words that could be put on cards.

When it comes to struggling readers, it is tempting to want to slow down the pace of instruction. Slowing down is the worst thing you could do. Children who begin the school year behind the others can't afford to slow down, as the other children will not wait for them to catch up. What children who struggle with reading need is *more* instruction, not instruction at a slower pace. Creative thinking on your part can help provide extra reading opportunities for the children who need your help the most. Find extra minutes wherever you can. If you take your whole class on a bathroom break, for example, have them bring books along and encourage your neediest children to read to you. If your morning routine of attendance, note collection, and announcements takes more than five minutes, look for ways to reduce that time. In some classrooms, children move a popsicle stick with their name on it from a pocket chart to a pencil can when they arrive. To take attendance, the teacher looks to see which popsicle sticks are still in the pocket chart. If you find five minutes of instructional time each day, you have found 25 minutes each week, 100 minutes each month, and 900 minutes each year. That five minutes a day could add up to 15 hours of instructional time over the course of a school year!

Differentiating for High-Ability Children

Meeting the needs of high-ability children can be just as challenging as meeting the needs of struggling readers (Davis & Rimm, 1994). High-ability children often read above grade level, so you will need to make sure you have materials at those levels in your classroom. If above-level material is not included in your curriculum, you may need to ask teachers in grade levels above yours to share some resources.

When you teach high-ability children, be aware that some readers recognize words beyond their level of comprehension. Spend plenty of time discussing books in order to encourage comprehension. The DR-TA strategy (section 7.3) can work well in a small group. Instead of reading the book to the small group, instruct the children to stop at certain places in the book to make predictions. If your whole group mini-lessons have included instruction on comprehension, practice those skills in materials at the instructional level of your high-ability children.

Creating independent work for high-ability children can be a challenge. Some of the independent work you assign to the class may be appropriate for all children, but high-ability children will usually finish it more quickly. Although your struggling readers may have extra reading instruction with a specialist, many schools do not include enrichment services for the pre-K through third grades. Creating and differentiating independent work for high-ability children is essential. What follows are some possibilities:

- **Dialogue Journals:** Require some independent reading every day. This reading could be from a chapter book you are reading as a group or a book of the child's choosing. After reading each day, the child should write a short response in the journal. As you read this journal entry, jot down some thoughts or questions to the child. The next day, in addition to a new response, the child responds to your thoughts, thus creating a dialogue with you. Because they are so personal, dialogue journals lend themselves well to differentiation.

- **Contracts:** Some teachers meet with high-ability children to negotiate possible alternative projects that could be completed independently. For example, two children who are interested in snakes could prepare a report and art project to present to the class. Contracts should include time limits and behavioral expectations as well. A possible contract for you to use is found on page 432.

- **Menus:** Sometimes it is wise to encourage high-ability children to complete a variety of independent activities so that they can develop intellectually in a multitude of areas. These menus can be put together with input from the children. The other advantage to the menu approach is that they last for several days or longer so children know what is expected of them over a period of time. A "Bingo" card can work as a menu. The children choose preferred activities and color in the boxes as they are completed. The object is to complete boxes in order to get "Bingo." For more examples, see *Teaching Gifted Kids in the Regular Classroom* by Susan Winebrenner (1992). See an example Bingo Activity for an Insect Unit on p. 433.

Differentiating in Pre-K and Kindergarten

Differentiating in Pre-K and kindergarten presents some unique challenges because young children are less likely to be able to work independently. Children who read well may not be able to write well enough to complete menus or dialogue journals. The use of learning stations or centers as a method to help differentiate learning opportunities can work at any grade level, but they work especially well at the pre-K and kindergarten level.

Before Pre-K and kindergarten children are ready to work at learning stations, they must have ample practice working independently and with groups. Your modeling of expected behavior is important. Not only should children practice what they are to do at each learning station, they should also practice clean-up routines. For example, if you set up a learning station where children will put pictures in order to tell a story, model how they are to set up the materials and where and how those materials should be returned.

Using other adults in the classroom can help make learning stations work. In some schools, parents are invited to help in classrooms. Having parents in the room to keep children working at their stations will free you to work with small groups. In other schools, parent volunteers may work in the Learning Center. Check to see if you could send small groups there to work. You would plan the activity and leave directions for the parent helpers.

Should guided reading groups be included in Pre-K and kindergarten? A few Pre-K and some kindergarten children know how to read when they come to school. As soon as you are able to meet with small groups, and the other children can work at some level of independence, you need to use small group time to teach children at their instructional level. Children who can read should be given many opportunities for reading. Children who are unfamiliar with the alphabet should spend time learning and practicing their letters. Children who know their letters, but are not reading, can learn about print and gain exposure to print through simple books. All children will benefit from shared reading and read-aloud activities, and these are whole-group activities. Remember, the time you spend teaching, modeling, and having children practice independent work habits will allow you time to work with them at their level.

Differentiating for English Language Learners (ELLs)

Children acquiring English as they learn to read present another challenge for teachers. In some schools, children are taught in a bilingual classroom. In this type of classroom, children learn to read in their first language and then transfer those skills to English. In other schools, children are placed in English-only classrooms and receive support in order to learn English. These programs are sometimes called English as a Second Language (ESL) (Miramontes, Nadeau, & Commins, 1997). For these children, thematic units are especially useful (Freeman & Freeman, 2000). Teaching around thematic units helps ELLs learn vocabulary as they learn to read. Read-alouds are also important for English Language Learners. Keep plenty of visual cues available, and place children who speak the same language near each other in your classroom. Some teachers ask ELLs to speak only English in the classroom or on the playground, but remember that it is important that children use their first language, even as they are learning English (Miramontes, Nadeau, & Commins, 1997). If you are lucky enough to have bilingual children in your classroom, enlist their help as language brokers for the newcomers.

It is important to communicate with the parents of your English Language Learners. If you can find simple books in children's first language, send those home for parents to read aloud with their children. It is also important that you are patient. Children will not learn English overnight. It takes several years for ELLs to perform at an academic level similar to that of native speakers of English (Freeman & Freeman, 2000). More tips for teaching English Language Learners are found throughout this book. You will also find parent letters written in English in the book. The letters were also translated into Spanish and can be found on the CD-ROM.

The Path Ahead

Finding ways to differentiate instruction for diverse learners in a Pre-K through grade 3 classroom can seem like a daunting task. Just as you are patient with the children in your class, be patient with yourself. Spend the first few weeks of school setting the climate in your classroom, modeling, and having children practice the skills they will need in order to work independently. Get to know your children. Use the assessment strategies in this book along with your observation to make instructional level groups that will work well together. Remember that your groups will change, just as children change.

When you differentiate instruction in your classroom, you will find a sense of satisfaction at the end of the school year, knowing that you met all of the children right where they were, and that you helped all of them grow toward their potential as learners. All of the chapters of this text offer suggestions that can be used with children with differing levels of literacy skills. Get to know your children through assessment and observation—then use this book as a resource when planning your instruction. Soon you will be on your way to a differentiated classroom where instruction is responsive to children's needs.

Independent Work Contract

For the next _____ days, I will complete an

independent project about _____ . For this project,

I will read _____ . Next, I will complete a project

about this book. I will _____

_____ .

I understand that I must complete this work on my own (or

with a partner). I must not interrupt the teacher or the class,

and I must not draw attention to myself.

Date: _____ Child's signature: _____

Date: _____ Teacher's signature: _____

Bingo Activity for Insect Unit

B	I	N	G	O
Build an insect model	**I**dentify the body parts of an insect.	Read a **n**onfiction book about insects.	Make a **g**raph that shows how many legs, wings, and eyes an insect has.	Put insect names in alphabetical **o**rder.
Blend two insects together. Draw what the new insect looks like.	Write a story about an insect and draw an **i**llustration.	Free choice	Make a **g**ame about insects. Include facts in your game.	**O**pen a bug store. Write what you would sell.
Do insects like **b**right light? Find out.	**I**nvestigate what an insect does. Watch one for 5 minutes.	Take **n**otes about what an insect does.	**G**et a jar and make a bug house.	**O**bserve two insects together. Do they notice each other?

References

Adams, M. J. (1990). *Beginning to read: Thinking and learning about print.* Cambridge, MA: MIT Press.

Adams, M. J. (2001). Alphabetic anxiety and explicit, systematic phonics instruction: A cognitive science perspective. In S. B. Neuman & D. K. Dickinson (Eds.), *Handbook of early literacy research* (pp. 66–80). New York: Guilford.

Adams, M. J., Foorman, B. R., Lundberg, I., & Beeler, T. (1998). *Phonemic awareness in young children: A classroom curriculum.* Baltimore: Brookes.

Allington, R. L. (2001). *What really matters for struggling readers: Designing research-based programs.* New York: Longman.

Almaṣi, J. F. (2003). *Teaching strategic reading processes.* New York: Guilford.

Anderson, R. C. (1994). Role of reader's schema in comprehension, learning, and memory. In R. B. Ruddell, M. R. Ruddell, & H. Singer (Eds.), *Theoretical models and processes of reading* (4th ed.) (pp. 469–482). Newark, DE: International Reading Association.

Anderson, R. C., Hiebert, E. H., Scott, J. A., & Wilkinson, I. A. G. (1985). *Becoming a nation of readers: The report of the Commission on Reading.* Champaign, IL: The National Academy of Education.

Arbogast, J. M. (2004). *Buildings in disguise: Architecture that looks like animals, food, and other things.* Honesdale, PA: Boyds Mills Press.

Armbruster, B. B. (1986, December). *Using frames to organize expository text.* Paper presented at the National Reading Conference, Austin, TX.

Armbruster, B. B., Lehr, F., & Osborn, J. (2001). *Put reading first: The research building blocks for teaching children to read.* Washington DC: National Institute for Literacy.

Au, K. H. (1998). Constructivist approaches, phonics, and the literacy learning of students of diverse backgrounds. In T. Shanahan & F. V. Rodriguez-Brown (Eds.), *47th Yearbook of the National Reading Conference* (pp. 1–21). Chicago: National Reading Conference.

Au, K. H. (2000). Literacy instruction for young children of diverse backgrounds. In D. S. Strickland & L. M. Morrow (Eds.), *Beginning reading and writing* (pp. 35–45). Newark, DE/New York: International Reading Association/Teachers College Press.

Baker, L. (1991). Metacognition, reading, and science education. In C. M. Santa & D. E. Alvermann (Eds.), *Science learning: Processes and applications* (pp. 2–13). Newark, DE: International Reading Association.

Bannon, E., Fisher, P. J., Pozzi, L., & Wessel, D. (1990). Effective definitions for word learning. *Journal of Reading, 34,* 301–302.

Battle, J. (1995). Collaborative story talk in a bilingual kindergarten. In N. L. Roser & M. G. Martinez (Eds.), *Book talk and beyond: Children and teachers respond to literature* (pp. 157–167). Newark, DE: International Reading Association.

Bean, K. (2001). Using a content area word wall. *Illinois Reading Council Journal, 28*(1)*,* 62–64.

Bear, D. R., Invernizzi, M., Templeton, S., & Johnston, F. (2004). *Words their way: Word study for phonics, vocabulary, and spelling instruction* (3rd ed.). Upper Saddle River, NJ: Pearson.

Beck, I., & McKeown, M. (1991). Conditions of vocabulary acquisition. In R. Barr, M. L. Kamil, P. Mosenthal, & P. D. Pearson (Eds.), *Handbook of reading research* (Vol. II) (pp. 789–814). White Plains, NY: Longman.

Beck, I., Perfetti, C., & McKeown, M. (1982). The effects of long-term vocabulary instruction on lexical access and reading comprehension. *Journal of Educational Psychology, 74,* 506–521.

Beck, I. L., & McKeown, M. G. (2001). Text talk: Capturing the benefits of reading-aloud experiences for young children. *The Reading Teacher, 55,* 10–20.

Beck, I. L., McKeown, M. G., & Kucan, L. (2002). *Bringing words to life: Robust vocabulary instruction.* New York: Guilford.

Biemiller, A. (2004). Teaching vocabulary in the primary grades: Vocabulary instruction needed. In J. F. Baumann & E. J. Kame'eniu (Eds.), *Vocabulary instruction: Research to practice* (pp. 28–40). New York: Guilford.

Blachowicz, C. (1998). Remember the FUN in fundamentals: Word play in the classroom. *Illinois Reading Council Journal, 26*(3), 8–15.

Blachowicz, C., & Fisher, P. (2000). Vocabulary instruction. In M. L. Kamil, P. B. Mosenthal, P. D. Pearson, & R. Barr (Eds.), *Handbook of reading research* (Vol. III) (pp. 503–523). Mahwah, NJ: Erlbaum.

Blachowicz, C., & Fisher, P. J. (2006). *Teaching vocabulary in all classrooms* (3rd ed.). Columbus, OH: Merrill.

Blair-Larsen, S. M., & Williams, K. A. (Eds.). (1999). *The balanced reading program: Helping all students achieve success.* Newark, DE: International Reading Association.

Blevins, W. (1998). *Phonics from A to Z: A practical guide.* New York: Scholastic Professional Books.

Branley, F. M. (1990). *Earthquakes.* New York: Trumpet.

Brett, J. (1992). *Trouble with trolls.* New York: Scholastic.

Bromley, K. (2000). Teaching young children to be writers. In D. S. Strickland & L. M. Morrow (Eds.), *Beginning reading and writing* (pp. 111–120). Newark, DE/New York: International Reading Association/Teachers College Press.

Buehl, D. (2001). *Classroom strategies for interactive learning* (2nd ed.). Newark, DE: International Reading Association.

Buis, K. (2004). *Making words stick: Strategies that build vocabulary and reading comprehension in the elementary grades.* Markham, Ontario: Pembroke.

Burns, B. (2001). *Guided reading: A how-to for all grades.* Arlington Heights, IL: Skylight.

Calkins, L. (1986). *The art of teaching writing.* Portsmouth, NH: Heinemann.

Carle, E. (1969). *The very hungry caterpillar.* Cleveland, OH: Collins-World.

Carle, E. (1996). *Little Cloud.* New York: Scholastic.

Chomsky, N. (1968). *Language and mind.* New York: Harcourt Brace Jovanovich.

Clay, M. M. (1975). *What did I write? Beginning writing behavior.* Exeter, NH: Heinemann.

Clay, M. M. (1985). *The early detection of reading difficulties* (3rd ed.). Portsmouth, NH: Heinemann.

Clay, M. M. (1993). *Reading Recovery: A guidebook for teachers in training.* Portsmouth, NH: Heinemann.

Clay, M. M. (1998). *By different paths to common outcomes.* York, ME: Stenhouse.

Cochrane, D., Cochrane, D., Scalena, D., & Buchanan, E. (1988). *Reading, writing, and caring.* Katonah, NY: Richard C. Owen.

Cohen, M. (1979). *Lost in the museum.* New York: Bantam Doubleday Dell.

Collins, J. L. (1998). *Strategies for struggling readers.* New York: Guilford.

Connor, L. (2004). *Miss Bridie chose a shovel.* Boston: Houghton Mifflin.

Cromer, W. (1970). The difference model: A new explanation for some reading difficulties. *Journal of Educational Psychology, 61,* 471–483.

Cunningham, P. M. (1990). The Names Test: A quick assessment of decoding ability. *The Reading Teacher, 44,* 124–129.

Cunningham, P. M. (2005). *Phonics they use: Words for reading and writing* (4th ed.). New York: Longman.

Cunningham, P. M., & Allington, R. L. (1998). *Classrooms that work: They can all read and write* (2nd ed.). New York: HarperCollins.

Cunningham, P. M., & Hall, D. P. (1998). *Making words: Multilevel, hands-on, developmentally appropriate spelling and phonics activities* (2nd ed.). Parsippany, NJ: Good Apple.

Dale, E. (1965). Vocabulary measurement: Techniques and major findings. *Elementary English, 42,* 82–88.

Darling, K. (1996). *Rain forest babies.* New York: Scholastic.

Davis, G. A., & Rimm, S. B. (1994). *Education of the gifted and talented.* Needham Heights, MA: Simon and Schuster.

Duffelmeyer, F. A., Kruse, A. E., Merkley, D. J., & Fyfe, S. A. (1994). Further validation and enhancement of the Names Test. *The Reading Teacher, 48,* 118–129.

Duffy, G. G., & Roehler, L. R. (1989). *Improving classroom reading instruction* (2nd ed.). New York: Random House.

Duke, N. D. (2000). 3.6 minutes per day: The scarcity of informational texts in first grade. *Reading Research Quarterly, 35,* 202–224.

Duke, N. K., Bennett-Armistead, V. S., & Roberts, E. M. (2002). Incorporating informational text in the primary grades. In C. Roller (Ed.), *Comprehensive reading instruction across the grade levels* (pp. 40–54). Newark, DE: International Reading Association.

Duke, N. K., & Purcell-Gates, V. (2003). Genres at home and at school: Bridging the known to the new. *The Reading Teacher, 57,* 30–37.

Dyson, A. H. (2001). Writing and children's symbolic repertoires: Development unhinged. In S. B. Neuman & D. K. Dickinson (Eds.), *Handbook of early literacy research* (pp. 126–141). New York: Guilford.

Edwards, E. C., Font, G., Baumann, J. F., & Boland, E. (2004). Unlocking word meaning: Strategies and guidelines for teaching morphemic and contextual analysis. In J. F. Baumann & E. J. Kame'eniu (Eds.), *Vocabulary instruction: Research to practice* (pp. 159–176). New York: Guilford.

Edwards, P. A. (1986). *Parents as partners in reading.* Chicago: Children's Press.

Ehlert, L. (1989). *Eating the alphabet: Fruits and vegetables from A to Z.* San Diego: Voyager.

Ehri, L. C. (1987). Learning to read and spell words. *Journal of Reading Behavior, 19,* 5–31.

Ehri, L. C., & Nunes, S. R. (2002). The role of phonemic awareness in learning to read. In A. E. Farstrup & S. J. Samuels (Eds.), *What research has to say about reading instruction* (3rd ed.) (pp. 110–139). Newark, DE: International Reading Association.

Elkonin, D. B. (1973). USSR. In J. Downing (Ed.), *Comparative reading: Cross-national studies of behavior and processes in reading and writing* (pp. 551–579). New York: Macmillan.

Ellery, V. (2005). *Creating strategic readers: Techniques for developing competency in phonemic awareness, phonics, fluency, vocabulary, and comprehension.* Newark, DE: International Reading Association.

Ericson, L., & Juliebo, M. F. (1998). *The phonological awareness handbook for kindergarten and primary teachers.* Newark, DE: International Reading Association.

Fisher, P. J. (1998). Teaching vocabulary in linguistically diverse classrooms. *Illinois Reading Council Journal, 26*(3), 16–21.

Flavell, J. H. (1977). *Cognitive development.* Englewood Cliffs, NJ: Prentice-Hall.

Flood, J., & Lapp, D. (1990). Reading comprehension for at-risk readers: Research-based practices that can make a difference. *Journal of Reading, 33,* 490–496.

Flood, J., Lapp, D., & Fisher, D. (2005). Neurological Impress Method Plus. *Reading Psychology, 26,* 147–160.

Forman, J., & Sanders, M. E. (1998). *Project Leap first grade norming study: 1993–1998.* Unpublished Manuscript.

Fowler, G. L. (1982). Developing comprehension skills in primary students through the use of story frames. *The Reading Teacher, 36,* 176–179.

Freeman, D. E., & Freeman, Y. S. (2000) *Teaching reading in multilingual classrooms.* Portsmouth, NH: Heinemann.

French, J. (2002). *Diary of a wombat.* Boston: Houghton Mifflin.

Fry, E. B., Fountoukidis, D. L., & Polk, J. K. (2000). *The reading teacher's book of lists* (4th ed.). Upper Saddle River, NJ: Merrill.

Galda, L., & Cullinan, B. E. (2000). Reading aloud from culturally diverse literature. In D. S. Strickland & L. M. Morrow (Eds.), *Beginning reading and writing* (pp. 134–142). Newark, DE/New York: International Reading Association/Teachers College Press.

Gambrell, L. B., & Dromsky, A. (2000). Fostering reading comprehension. In D. S. Strickland & L. M. Morrow (Eds.), *Beginning reading and writing* (pp. 143–153). New York: Teachers College Press.

Ganske, K. (2000). *Word journeys: Assessment-guided phonics, spelling, and vocabulary instruction.* New York: Guilford.

Gaskins, I. W., Ehri, L. C., Cress, C., O'Hara, C., & Donnelly, K. (1997). Analyzing words. *Language Arts, 74,* 172–192.

Gentry, J. R. (1981). Learning to spell developmentally. *The Reading Teacher, 34,* 378–381.

Gentry, J. R. (1998). Spelling strategies. *Instructor, 107,* 40.

Gentry, J. R. (2000). A retrospective on invented spelling and a look forward. *The Reading Teacher, 54,* 318–332.

Gentry, J. R., & Gillet, J. W. (1993). *Teaching kids to spell.* Portsmouth, NH: Heinemann.

Gillam, R. B., & van Kleeck, A. (1996). Phonological awareness training and short-term working memory: Clinical implications. *Language Disorders, 17,* 72–81.

Gillet, J. W., & Temple, C., & Crawford, A. N. (2004). *Understanding reading problems: Assessment and instruction* (6th ed.). Boston: Allyn and Bacon.

Goodman, K. S. (1965). A linguistic study of cues and miscues in reading. *Elementary English, 42,* 639–643.

Goodman, K. S. (1996). *On reading.* Portsmouth, NH: Heinemann.

Goodman, Y. M. (1982). Kidwatching: Evaluating written language development. *Australian Journal of Reading, 5,* 120–128.

Graves, D. (1983). *Writing: Teachers and children at work.* Exeter, NH: Heinemann.

Graves, M. F. (2004). Teaching prefixes: As good as it gets? In J. F. Baumann, & E. J. Kame'eniu (Eds.), *Vocabulary instruction: Research to practice* (pp. 81–99). New York: Guilford.

Graves, M. F., Juel, C., & Graves, B. B. (2001). *Teaching reading in the 21st century* (2nd ed.). Boston: Allyn and Bacon.

Greene, F. (1979). Radio reading. In C. Pennock (Ed.), *Reading comprehension at four linguistic levels* (pp. 104–107). Newark, DE: International Reading Association.

Gunning, T. G. (1998). *Best books for beginning reading.* Boston: Allyn and Bacon.

Gunning, T. G. (2000). *Phonological awareness and primary phonics.* Boston: Allyn and Bacon.

Gunning, T. G. (2004). *Creating literacy instruction for all children in grades Pre-K to 4.* Boston: Allyn and Bacon.

Gunning, T. G. (2005). *Creating literacy instruction for all students* (5th ed.). Boston: Allyn and Bacon.

Guthrie, J. T., & Wigfield, A. (2000). Engagement and motivation in reading. In M. L. Kamil, P. B. Mosenthal, P. D. Pearson, & R. Barr (Eds.), *Handbook of reading research* (Vol. III) (pp. 403–422). White Plains, NY: Longman.

Hague, K. (1984). *Alphabears.* New York: Holt.

Harp, B. (2000). *The handbook of literacy assessment and evaluation* (2nd ed.). Norwood, MA: Christopher-Gordon.

Harris, T. L., & Hodges, R. E. (1995). *The literacy dictionary: The vocabulary of reading and writing.* Newark, DE: International Reading Association.

Harris-Wright, K. (2005). Building blocks for literacy development: Oral language. In B. Hammond, M. E. R. Hoover, & I. P. McPhail (Eds.), *Teaching African American learners to read* (pp. 173–188). Newark, DE: International Reading Association.

Hasbrouck, J. E., & Tindal, G. (1992). Curriculum-based oral reading fluency norms for students in grades 2 through 5. *Teaching Exceptional Children, 24,* 41–44.

Heckleman, R. G. (1966). Using the neurological impress method of remedial reading instruction. *Academic Therapy Quarterly, 1,* 235–239.

Heilman, A. W. (2005). *Phonics in proper perspective* (10th ed.). Upper Saddle River, NJ: Merrill Prentice Hall.

Henkes, K. (1991). *Chrysanthemum.* New York: Greenwillow.

Henkes, K. (1996). *Lily's purple plastic purse.* New York: Greenwillow.

Hiebert, E. H., & Martin, L. A. (2001). The texts of beginning reading instruction. In S. B. Neuman & D. K. Dickinson (Eds.), *Handbook of early literacy research* (pp. 361–375). New York: Guilford.

Hoffman, M. (1986). *Elephant.* Austin, TX: Steck-Vaughn.

Hudson, R. F., Lane, H. B., & Pullen, P. C. (2005). Reading fluency assessment and instruction: What, why, and how? *The Reading Teacher, 58,* 702–714.

International Reading Association (2005). *Literacy development in the preschool years.* Position statement. Newark, DE: Author.

International Reading Association and National Association for the Education of Young Children (1998). *Learning to read and write: Developmentally appropriate practices for young children.* Newark, DE: Author.

Jeunesse, G., Delafosse, C., Fuhr, U., & Sautai, R. (1991). *Whales: A first discovery book.* New York: Scholastic.

Johns, J. L. (1975). The Dolch list of common nouns—A comparison. *The Reading Teacher, 28,* 338–340.

Johns, J. L. (1980). First graders' concepts about print. *Reading Research Quarterly, 15,* 529–549.

Johns, J. L. (1981). The development of the Revised Dolch List. *Illinois School Research and Development, 17,* 15–24.

Johns, J. L. (2005). *Basic reading inventory* (9th ed.). Dubuque, IA: Kendall/Hunt.

Johns, J. L., & Berglund, R. L. (2006). *Fluency: Strategies & assessments* (3rd ed.). Dubuque, IA: Kendall/Hunt.

Johns, J. L., & Lenski, S. D. (2005). *Improving reading: Strategies and resources* (4th ed.). Dubuque, IA: Kendall/Hunt.

Johns, J. L., Lenski, S. D., & Berglund, R. (2006). *Comprehension and vocabulary strategies for the elementary grades* (2nd ed.). Dubuque, IA: Kendall/Hunt.

Joubert, D., & Joubert, B. (2001). *The Africa diaries.* Washington, DC: National Geographic.

Klenk, L., & Kibby, M. L. (2000). Re-mediating reading difficulties: Appraising the past, reconciling the present, constructing the future. In M. L. Kamil, P. B. Mosenthal, P. D. Pearson, & R. Barr (Eds.), *Handbook of reading research* (Vol. III) (pp. 667–690). Mahwah, NJ: Erlbaum.

Kletzien, S. B., & Dreher, M. J. (2004). *Informational text in K-3 classrooms: Helping children read and write.* Newark: DE: International Reading Association.

Koeze, S. (1990). The dictionary game. *The Reading Teacher, 43,* 613.

Lane, H. B., & Pullen, P. C. (2004). *Phonological assessment and instruction: A sound beginning.* Boston: Allyn and Bacon.

Lenski, S. D., & Ehlers-Zavala, F. (2004). *Reading strategies for Spanish speakers.* Dubuque, IA: Kendall/Hunt.

Lenski, S. D., & Johns, J. L. (2004). *Improving writing: Resources, strategies, and assessments* (2nd ed.). Dubuque, IA: Kendall/Hunt.

Lukens, R. J. (1995). *A critical handbook of children's literature* (5th ed.). Glenview, IL: Scott, Foresman.

Macon, J., & Macon, J. (1991). Knowledge chart. In J. M. Macon, D. Bewell, & M. E. Vogt (Eds.), *Responses to literature: Grades K-8* (pp. 13–14). Newark, DE: International Reading Association.

Martinez, M. G., & Roser, N. L. (1995). The books make a difference in story talk. In N. L. Roser & M. G. Martinez (Eds.), *Book talk and beyond: Children and teachers respond to literature* (pp. 32–41). Newark, DE: International Reading Association.

Mastropieri, M. A. (1988). Using the keyword method. *Teaching exceptional children, 20,* 4–8.

May, F. (2006). *Teaching reading creatively: Reading and writing as communication* (7th ed.), Columbus, OH: Merrill.

May, F. B., & Rizzardi, L. (2002). *Reading as communication* (6th ed.). Upper Saddle River, NJ: Merrill.

McGee, L. M., & Richgels, D. J. (2003). *Designing early literacy programs: Strategies for at-risk preschool and kindergarten children.* New York: Guilford.

McGee, L. M., & Richgels, D. J. (2005). *Literacy's beginnings: Supporting young readers and writers* (4th ed.). Needham Heights, MA: Allyn and Bacon.

McKenna, M. C., & Kear, D. J. (1990). Measuring attitude toward reading: A new tool for teachers. *The Reading Teacher, 43,* 626–639.

McKeown, M. G., & Beck, I. L. (2004). Direct and rich vocabulary instruction. In J. F. Baumann & E. J. Kame'eniu (Eds.), *Vocabulary instruction: Research to practice* (pp. 13–27). New York: Guilford.

Miramontes, O. B., Nadeau, A., & Commins, N. L. (1997). *Restructuring schools for linguistic diversity: Linking diversity to effective programs.* New York: Teachers College Press.

Mooney, M. E. (1990). *Reading to, with, and by children.* Katonah, NY: Richard C. Owen.

Morrow, L. M. (2001). *Literacy development in the early years: Helping children read and write* (4th ed.). Boston: Allyn and Bacon.

Morrow, L. M., & Gambrell, L. B. (2001). Literature-based instruction in the early years. In S. B. Neuman & D. K. Dickinson (Eds.), *Handbook of early literacy research* (pp. 348–360). New York: Guilford.

Moss, B. (2003). An exploration of eight sixth graders' engagement with nonfiction trade books. In C. M. Fairbanks, J. Worthy, B. Maloch, J. V. Hoffman, & D. L. Schallert (Eds.), *52nd Yearbook of the National Reading Conference* (pp. 321–331). Oak Creek, WI: National Reading Conference.

Moss, J. F. (1995). Preparing focus units with literature: Crafty foxes and authors' craft. In N. L. Roser & M. G. Martinez (Eds.), *Book talk and beyond: Children and teachers respond to literature* (pp. 53–65). Newark, DE: International Reading Association.

Nagy, W. E., & Anderson, R. C. (1984). How many words are there in printed school English? *Reading Research Quarterly, 19,* 303–330.

National Council of Teachers of English/International Reading Association (1996). *Standards for the English language arts.* Urbana, IL/Newark, DE: Author.

National Reading Panel. (2000). *Teaching children to read: An evidence-based assessment of the scientific research literature on reading and its implications for reading instruction.* Washington, DC: National Institute of Child Health & Human Development.

Neuman, S. B., & Dickinson, D. K. (Eds.). (2001). *Handbook of early literacy research.* New York: Guilford.

Neuman, S. B., Celano, D. C., Greco, A. N., & Shue, P. (2001). *Access for all: Closing the book gap for children in early childhood.* Newark, DE: International Reading Association.

Ogle, D. (1986). K-W-L: A teaching model that develops active reading of expository text. *The Reading Teacher, 38,* 564–570.

Orellana, M. F., & Hernandez, A. (2003). Talking the walk: Children reading urban environmental print. In P. A. Mason & J. S. Schumm (Eds.), *Promising practices for urban reading instruction* (pp. 25–36). Newark, DE: International Reading Association.

O'Shea, L. J., & Sindelar, P. T. (1983). The effects of segmenting written discourse on the reading comprehension of low- and high-performance readers. *Reading Research Quarterly, 18,* 458–465.

O'Shea, L. J., Sindelar, P. T., & O'Shea, D. J. (1985). The effects of repeated readings and attentional cues on reading fluency and comprehension. *Journal of Reading Behavior, 17,* 129–142.

Palazzo, J. (1988). *Rainy day fun.* Mahwah, NJ: Troll.

Palmer, R. G., & Stewart, R. A. (2003). Nonfiction trade book use in primary grades. *The Reading Teacher, 57,* 38–48.

Paris, S., Lipson, M., & Wixson, K. (1983). Becoming a strategic reader. *Contemporary Educational Psychology, 8,* 293–316.

Paris, S. G., Lipson, M. Y., & Wixon, K. G. (1994). Becoming a strategic reader. In R. B. Ruddell, M. R. Ruddell, & H. Singer (Eds.), *Theoretical models and processes of reading* (4th ed.) (pp. 788–810). Newark, DE: International Reading Association.

Parr, T. (2001). *It's okay to be different.* Boston: Little, Brown and Company.

Paynter, D. E., Bodrova, E., & Doty, J. K. (2005). *For the love of words: Vocabulary instruction that works, grades K-6.* San Francisco: Jossey-Bass.

Pelham, D. (1990). *Sam's sandwich.* New York: Dutton.

Peregoy, S. F., & Boyle, O. F. (2001). *Reading, writing, & learning in ESL* (3rd ed.). New York: Longman.

Pérez, A. I. (2002). *My diary from here to there: Mi diario de aquí hasta allá.* San Francisco: Children's Book Press.

Pikulski, J. J., & Chard, D. J. (2005). Fluency: Bridge between decoding and reading comprehension. *The Reading Teacher, 58,* 510–519.

Poe, V. L. (1986). Using multipared simultaneous oral reading. *The Reading Teacher, 40,* 239–240.

Polacco, P. (2001). *Mr. Lincoln's way.* New York: Penguin Putman Books.

Pressley, M. (1995). More about the development of self-regulation: Complex, long-term, and thoroughly social. *Educational Psychologist, 30,* 207–212.

Pressley, M., & Afflerbach, P. (1995). *Verbal protocols of reading: The nature of constructively responsive reading.* Hillsdale, NJ: Erlbaum.

Pressley, M., Allington, R. L., Wharton-McDonald, R., Block, C. C., & Morrow, L. M. (2001). *Learning to read: Lessons from exemplary first-grade classrooms.* New York: Guilford.

Pressley, M., Levin, J. R., & Delaney, H. D. (1983). The mnemonic keyword method. *Review of Educational Research, 52,* 6–91.

Prior, J., & Gerard, M. R. (2004). *Environmental print in the classroom: Meaningful connections for learning to read.* Newark, DE: International Reading Association.

Pulver, R. (2003). *Punctuation takes a vacation.* New York: Holiday House.

Purves, A. C., Rogers, T., & Soter, A. O. (1990). *How porcupines make love II: Teaching a response-centered literature curriculum.* White Plains, NY: Longman.

Rasinski, T. V. (1989). Fluency for everyone: Incorporating fluency instruction in the classroom. *The Reading Teacher, 42,* 690–693.

Rasinski, T. V. (1990). Effects of repeated reading and listening-while-reading on reading fluency. *Journal of Educational Research, 83,* 147–150.

Rasinski, T., & Padak, N. (2004). *Effective reading strategies: Teaching children who find reading difficult* (3rd ed.). Columbus, OH: Merrill.

Rathmann, P. (1997). *Ruby the Copycat.* New York: Scholastic.

Read, C. C. (1986). *Children's creative spelling.* London: Routledge & Kegan Paul.

Readence, J. E., Bean, T. W., & Baldwin, R. S. (2004). *Content area literacy: An integrated approach* (8th ed.). Dubuque, IA: Kendall/Hunt.

Readence, J. E., & Searfoss, L. W. (1980). Teaching strategies for vocabulary development. *English Journal, 67,* 43–46.

Rennick, L. W., & Williams, K. M. (1995). Flashlight reading: Making the reading process concrete. *The Reading Teacher, 49,* 174.

Reutzel, D. R., & Cooter, R. B. Jr. (2004). *Teaching children to read: Putting the pieces together* (4th ed.). Upper Saddle River, NJ: Pearson.

Richgels, D. J. (2001). Invented spelling, phonemic awareness, and reading and writing instruction. In S. B. Neuman & D. K. Dickinson (Eds.), *Handbook of early literacy research* (pp. 142–155). New York: Guilford.

Richgels, D. J., Poremba, K. J., & McGee, L. M. (1996). Kindergartners talk about print: Phonemic awareness in meaningful contexts. *The Reading Teacher, 49,* 632–642.

Robb, L. (1996). *Reading strategies that work: Teaching your students to become better readers.* New York: Scholastic.

Rockwell, A. (1999). *Bumblebee, bumblebee, do you know me?* New York: Scholastic.

Rosenblatt, L. (1978). *The reader, the text, the poem: The transactional theory of the literary work.* Carbondale, IL: Southern Illinois University Press.

Rosencrans, G. (1998). *The spelling book: Teaching children how to spell, not what to spell.* Newark, DE: International Reading Association.

Roser, N. L., & Hoffman, J. V. (1995). Language charts: A record of story time talk. In N. L. Roser & M. G. Martinez (Eds.), *Book talk and beyond: Children and teachers respond to literature* (pp. 80–89). Newark, DE: International Reading Association.

Roser, N. L., & Martinez, M. G. (Eds.) (2005). *What a character! Character study as a guide to literacy meaning making in grades K-8.* Newark, DE: International Reading Association.

Roskos, K. A., Tabors, P. O., & Lenhart, L. A. (2004). *Oral language and early literacy in preschool: Talking, reading, and writing.* Newark, DE: International Reading Association.

Roush, B. E. (2005). Drama rhymes: An instructional strategy. *The Reading Teacher, 58,* 584–587.

Routman, R. (1994). *Invitations: Changing as teachers and learners K-12.* Portsmouth, NH: Heinemann.

Rumelhart, D. E. (1985). Toward an interactive model of reading. In H. Singer & R. B. Ruddell (Eds.), *Theoretical models and processes of reading* (3rd ed.) (pp. 722–750). Newark, DE: International Reading Association.

Rupley, W. H. (2005). Introduction. *Reading Psychology, 26,* 103–105.

Salinger, T. S. (1999). *Literacy for young children* (3rd ed.). Columbus, OH: Merrill.

Salvia, J., & Ysseldyke, J. E. (2001). *Assessment* (8th ed.). Boston: Houghton Mifflin.

Samuels, S. J. (1979). The method of repeated readings. *The Reading Teacher, 32,* 403–408.

Samuels, S. J. (2002). Reading fluency: Its development and assessment. In A. E. Farstrup & S. J. Samuels (Eds.), *What research has to say about reading instruction* (3rd ed.) (pp. 166–183). Newark, DE: International Reading Association.

Schatschneider, C., Francis, D., Foorman, B., Fletcher, J., & Mehta, P. (1999). The dimensionality of phonological awareness: An application of item response theory. *Journal of Educational Psychology, 91,* 439–449.

Schmidt, B., & Buckley, M. (1991). Plot relationships chart. In J. M. Macon, D. Bewell, & M. Vogt (Eds.), *Responses to literature: Grades K-8* (pp. 7–8). Newark, DE: International Reading Association.

Schwartz, R., & Raphael, T. (1985). Concept of definition: A key to improving students' vocabulary. *The Reading Teacher, 39,* 198–205.

Scott, J. A., & Nagy, W. E. (2004). Developing word consciousness. In J. F. Baumann & E. J. Kame'enui (Eds.), *Vocabulary instruction: Research to practice* (pp. 201–217). New York: Guilford.

Sendak, M. (1963). *Where the wild things are.* New York: Harper and Row.

Snow, C. E., Burns, S. M, & Griffin, P. (Eds.). (1998). *Preventing reading difficulties in young children.* Washington, DC: National Academy Press.

Snowball, D. (1997). Use sentences with word blanks to pump spelling strategies. *Instructor, 101,* 22–23.

St. George, J. (2000). *So you want to be president.* New York: Philomel.

Staal, L. A. (2000). The Story Face: An adaptation of story mapping that incorporates visualization and discovery learning to enhance reading and writing. *The Reading Teacher, 54,* 26–31.

Stahl, S. A. (1997). What's in a word: Issues in learning word meanings (part I). *Illinois Reading Council Journal, 25*(2), 52–58.

Stahl, S. A. (2001). Teaching phonics and phonological awareness. In S. B. Neuman & D. K. Dickinson (Eds.), *Handbook of early literacy research* (pp. 333–347). New York: Guilford.

Stahl, S., & Vancil, S. (1986). Discussion is what makes semantic maps work in vocabulary instruction. *The Reading Teacher, 40,* 62–69.

Stanovich, K. E. (1986). Matthew effects in reading: Some consequences of individual differences in the acquisition of literacy. *Reading Research Quarterly, 21,* 360–397.

Stanovich, K. E. (2000). *Progress in understanding reading: Scientific foundations and new frontiers.* New York: Guilford.

Stauffer, R. G. (1969). *Teaching reading as a thinking process.* New York: Harper & Row.

Stauffer, R. G. (1970). *The language experience approach to the teaching of reading.* New York: Harper & Row.

Stein, N. L., & Glenn, C. G. (1979). An analysis of story comprehension in elementary school children. In R. O. Freedle (Ed.), *New directions in discourse processing* (pp. 53–120). Norwood, NJ: Ablex.

Stonehouse, B., & Bertram, E. (2003). *The truth about animal builders.* New York: Firecrest Books.

Strickland, D. S. (1998). *Teaching phonics today: A primer for educators.* Newark, DE: International Reading Association.

Strickland, D. S. (2001). Early intervention for African American children considered to be at risk. In S. B. Neuman & D. K. Dickinson (Eds.), *Handbook of early literacy research* (pp. 322–332). New York: Guilford.

Strickland, D. S., & Schickedanz, J. A. (2004). *Learning about print in preschool: Working with letters, words, and beginning links with phonemic awareness.* Newark, DE: International Reading Association.

Sulzby, E., & Teale, W. (1991). Emergent literacy. In R. Barr, M. L. Kamil, P. Mosenthal, & P. D. Pearson (Eds.), *Handbook of reading research* (Vol. II) (pp. 727–757). New York: Longman.

Sweeney, J. (1996). *Me on the map.* New York: Dragonfly Books.

Taberski, S. (2000). *On solid ground: Strategies for teaching reading K-3.* Portsmouth, NH: Heinemann.

Taylor, D. (1983). *Family literacy: Young children learning to read and write.* Exeter, NH: Heinemann.

Teale, W. H., & Sulzby, E. (1989). Emerging literacy: New perspectives. In D. S. Strickland & L. M. Morrow (Eds.), *Emerging literacy: Young children learn to read and write* (pp. 1–15). Newark, DE: International Reading Association.

Teale, W. H., & Yokota, J. (2000). Beginning reading and writing: Perspectives on instruction. In D. S. Strickland & L. M. Morrow (Eds.), *Beginning reading and writing* (pp. 3–21). Newark, DE/New York: International Reading Association/Teachers College Press.

Thaler, M. (1988). Reading, writing, and riddling. *Learning, 17,* 58–59.

Tomlinson, C. A. (2003). *Fulfilling the promise of the differentiated classroom.* Alexandria, VA: Association for Supervision and Curriculum Development.

Tompkins, G. (2002). *Literacy for the 21st century: A balanced approach* (2nd ed.). Columbus, OH: Prentice Hall.

Tower, C. (2002). "It's a snake, you guys!" The power of text characteristics on children's responses to information books. *Research in the Teaching of English, 37,* 55–88.

Tracey, D. H. (2000). Enhancing literacy growth through home-school connections. In D. S. Strickland & L. M. Morrow (Eds.), *Beginning reading and writing* (pp. 46–57). Newark, DE/New York: International Reading Association/Teachers College Press.

Trousdale, A., & Harris, V. (1993). Interactive storytelling: Scaffolding children's early narratives. *Language Arts, 67,* 164–173.

Turbill, J., Butler, A., Cambourne, B., & Langton, G. (1991). *Frameworks course notebook.* Stanley, NY: Wayne Finger Lakes Board of Cooperative Educational Services.

Vygotsky, L. S. (1978). *Mind in society: The development of higher psychological processes.* Cambridge: Harvard University Press.

Watson, R. (2001). Literacy and oral language: Implications for early literacy acquisition. In S. B. Neuman & D. K. Dickinson (Eds.), *Handbook of early literacy research* (pp. 43–53). New York: Guilford.

Weaver, C. A. (1994). *Reading process and practice.* Portsmouth, NH: Heinemann.

Wells, R. (2001). *Letters and sounds.* New York: Puffin.

Wilde, S. (2000). *Miscue analysis made easy: Building on student strengths.* Portsmouth, NH: Heinemann.

Williams, S. (1989). *I went walking.* New York: Trumpet.

Wilson, P. T. (1988). *Let's think about reading and reading instruction: A primer for tutors and teachers.* Dubuque, IA: Kendall/Hunt.

Winebrenner, S. (1992). *Teaching gifted kids in the regular classroom.* Minneapolis: Free Spirit Publishing.

Winters, R. (2001). Vocabulary anchors: Building conceptual connections with young readers. *The Reading Teacher, 54,* 659–662.

Wolfram, W., Adger, C. T., & Christian, D. (1999). *Dialects in schools and communities.* Mahwah, NJ: Erlbaum.

Wood, K. D., & Taylor, D. B. (2006). *Literacy strategies across the subject areas: Process-oriented blackline masters for the K-12 classroom* (2nd ed.). Boston: Allyn and Bacon.

Wylie, R., & Durrell, D. D. (1970). Teaching vowels through phonograms. *Elementary English, 47,* 787–791.

Yopp, H. K. (1992). Developing phonemic awareness in young children. *The Reading Teacher,* 49, 20–29.

Yopp, H. K. (1995). A test for assessing phonemic awareness in young children. *The Reading Teacher, 45,* 696–703.

Yopp, R. H., & Yopp, H. K. (2000). Sharing informational text with young children. *The Reading Teacher, 53,* 410–419.

Zeigler, L., & Johns, J. L. (2005). *Visualization: Using mental images to strengthen comprehension.* Dubuque, IA: Kendall/Hunt.

Zeno, S. M., Ivens, S. H., Millard, R. T., & Duvvuri, R. (1995). *The educator's word frequency guide.* Brewster, NY: Touchstone Applied Science.

Zutell, J. (1996). The directed spelling thinking activity (DSTA): Providing an effective balance in word study instruction. *The Reading Teacher, 50,* 98–108.

WS (Writing and Spelling Chapter—only on CD-ROM)

Kamberelis, G. (1999). Genre development and learning: Children writing stories, science reports, and poems. *Research in the Teaching of English, 33,* 403–468.

Lenski, S. D. & Johns, J. L. (2004). *Improving writing: resources, strategies and assessments.* Dubuque, IA: Kendall/Hunt.

Index

Italicized entries refer to Strategies and titles of books.